Cisco Firepower 6.x
with Firepower Threat Defense

Cisco's Threat-Focused Next Generation Firewall

Todd Lammle

Alex Tatistcheff

Table of Contents

About the Authors

Todd Lammle is the authority on Cisco certification and internetworking and is Cisco certified in most Cisco certification categories. He is a world-renowned author, speaker, trainer, and consultant. Todd has over three decades of experience working with LANs, WANs, and large enterprise licensed and unlicensed wireless networks, and lately he's been implementing both large Cisco data centers world-wide, including Cisco Firepower/FTD technologies.

His years of real world experience is evident in his writing; he is not just an author but an experienced networking engineer with very practical experience working on the largest networks in the world at such companies as Xerox, Hughes Aircraft, Texaco, AAA, Cisco, and Toshiba, among many others. Todd has published over 70 books, including the very popular *CCNA: Cisco Certified Network Associate Study Guide, CCNA Wireless Study Guide, CCNA Data Center Study Guide, SSFIPS Firepower Study Guide*, as well as coauthored this study guide. He runs an international consulting and training company based in Colorado.

You can reach Todd through his web site and find his Firepower 6.x/FTD classes at www.lammle.com/firepower

Alex Tatistcheff has over 17 years of information security experience. He first began using the Sourcefire 3D System as an Information Security Consultant for Idaho Power Company in 2005.

He was hired in 2008 by Sourcefire, where he worked as a Sr. Security Instructor and Professional Services Consultant until the Cisco acquisition in October, 2013. He is currently a Solution Architect for Cisco's Security Services organization.

Alex is also a co-author of the book "*SSFIPS Securing Cisco Networks with Sourcefire Intrusion Prevention System Study Guide: Exam 500-285*" by Sybex.

To find Firepower videos, practice questions and hands-on classes with Todd Lammle, please see www.lammle.com/firepower

Our New Cisco Firepower 6.x/FTD Book

The Greek philosopher Heraclitus said the only constant in this life is change. If he were alive today to see the rate of change in our world he would probably be dumbfounded. Nowhere is this more evident than in information technology. Going further, information security (or to succumb to popular terminology – cyber security) is one of the most dynamic areas within I.T. It's been called a cat-and-mouse game. I don't know about you but sometimes I wonder if I'm the cat or the mouse. With the volume of malware and attacks we constantly experience it feels more like we're the prey than the predator.

All pontificating aside, the purpose of this book is to help cyber security personnel understand, deploy and use the Cisco Firepower solution. Since Cisco's acquisition of Sourcefire was completed in October of 2013 development of what was formerly the Sourcefire 3D System has not slowed. If anything, access to Cisco's vast research and development resources has accelerated the rate of change in this product. Cisco has fully embraced Firepower technology based on open source Snort and cloud based malware protection across much of their security product line. In fact, one could say that Cisco is arguably one of the top players in network security due largely to this one product.

In our previous book, *SSFIPS Securing Cisco Networks with Sourcefire System Study Guide,* we focused on the information necessary to pass the SSFIPS exam. There was also a fair amount of practical information in that book but the scope was somewhat limited by the exam objectives. In this book, we are not writing to address any such objectives.

This book will focus on the features of Firepower 6.x and how to use the product in the real world. We will cover most features in the system but the main purpose is to help users understand what's important so you can deploy an effective security solution on your network.

To find Firepower videos, practice questions and hands-on classes with Todd Lammle, please see www.lammle.com/firepower.

What does This Book Cover?

You will learn the following information in this book:

Chapter 1: The Firepower Family

What is Firepower? What *was* FireSIGHT? What *was* Sourcefire? Understand Firepower by building a solid foundation in defining key, industry-wide and Cisco specific terms that we'll be using throughout this book. Various Firepower appliance models will be discussed as well as licensing and policies, and Firepower Threat Defense (FTD).

Chapter 2: Management Configuration

This chapter will cover the steps to configure the management network interface on your device and register it to the FMC. Once the device is registered, there is virtually no reason to return to its graphical or command-line interface under normal operations. From that point, you perform all day-to-day operations from the Firepower Management Center (FMC).

Chapter 3: System (FMC) Configuration

This chapter will cover how to login and configure your Firepower Management Center (FMC), and how to apply settings on the systems to control user preferences, NTP, time zones and other key factors.

Chapter 4: Device Management

In this chapter, we'll discuss and demonstrate registering the device with the FMC as well as touring each of the device's properties. For the FTD devices and 7000/8000 appliances, you'll discover the different settings for the interfaces and switch and router configurations, plus, we'll survey the different DHCP, VPN and NAT types available to managed devices as well. This chapter will help you understand how to configure your devices, and again we'll cover some best practices from the real world!

Chapter 5: Platform Settings and Health

In this chapter, we will discuss platform settings and the Health policy. If you have used previous versions of Firepower, you may be familiar with the System policy. Well, in version 6 the System policy is no more. We now have Platform Settings. There are two different types of policies you can create here, one for Firepower and one for Threat Defense (FTD). We will also briefly cover the Health settings, which have remained largely unchanged for over a decade.

Chapter 6: Object Management

This chapter will provide you with the understanding of object types that are used by the Firepower system. Firepower uses reusable configuration components—objects—to provide an easier way to use values across policies, searches, reports, dashboards, and so on.

Chapter 7: Firepower Network Discovery

Firepower Network Discovery (Formerly FireSIGHT) is the name given to a technology built into the Cisco Firepower NGIPS to provide us with contextual awareness regarding events, IP addresses, users on the network and even background about the hosts in the system. Once you've been acquainted with this awesome technology, we'll move on to explore discovery components like the discovery policy, type of data collected, connection events, and host attributes associated with it.

Chapter 8: Intrusion Policy

This chapter provides you with the background necessary for success in the real world with a thorough presentation of IPS Policy Management. This in-depth chapter covers IPS policies, which precisely describe the suspicious and/or malicious traffic that the system must watch out for and they also control how evil traffic is dealt with when it's discovered.

Chapter 9: Network Analysis Policy (NAP)

This chapter is the perfect time to introduce you to some essential advanced IPS policy settings and we'll also survey important application layer preprocessor settings, network and transport layer preprocessors and specific threat detection preprocessors. We'll also talk about the significant advantages gained via detection enhancements and performance settings.

Chapter 10: DNS and SSL Policies

In this chapter, we will look at two of the newer features in Firepower—the DNS and SSL policies. Both of these provide visibility beyond typical packet sniffing detection by providing additional insight into potentially compromised hosts or encrypted data.

Chapter 11: Identity Policy

This chapter covers identity—this translates to the ability for Firepower to take different actions depending on the user associated with a connection. The concept of using Firepower to block or allow traffic based on users or groups is one that appeals to many organizations. It sounds like a great way to keep employees more productive and allow or block access to websites or services based on job function.

Chapter 12: Malware & File Policy

A nickname derived from the term malicious software, malware comes in a variety of vile flavors from coded weapons fashioned to damage, control or disable a computer system, to reconnaissance and stealing data or identity theft. Firepower's Advanced Malware Protection (AMP) is designed to tackle one of the worst and arguably most prevalent threat vectors today—malware!

Chapter 13: Prefilter Policy

While it's not actually part of the Access Control policy, the Prefilter policy actually processes traffic first. It should be noted that this policy only applies to

Firepower Threat Defense (FTD) devices.

Chapter 14: Access Control Policy
Chapter 14 covers the heart of the Firepower system. An AC policy acts kind of like a central traffic cop for Firepower because all traffic passing through a device is processed through it. And you'll find plenty of help in this chapter along with real world examples on how to configure and implement this at work!

Chapter 15: Event Analysis
In this chapter, we'll review using the Firepower System to analyze intrusion event data. We'll explore some of the Workflows available when analyzing events and show you examples of how to drill into relevant event data. We'll also cover how to use the Dashboard and Context Explorer.

Chapter 16: User Management
In this chapter, we're going to cover a variety of administrative functions for user account management. We'll discuss creating and managing both internal and external users.

Chapter 17: Correlation Policy
Correlation Policy is an often overlooked but useful feature of the Firepower System. The features available in this area concentrate on detection of unusual activity rather than specific intrusion or malware events. By using Correlation Rules, White Lists and Traffic Profiles we can detect network or host behaviors that may be an indication of malicious activity.

Chapter 18: Cisco Firepower eXtensble Operating System (FXOS)
The Firepower eXtensible Operating System provides a web interface that makes it easy to configure platform settings and interfaces, provision devices, and monitor system status. This chassis manager is used on the Cisco 4100 and 9300 devices (but not the 2100!), and this chapter will help you login and configure the FXOS and get your 4100/9300 up and running, as well as configure high availability and discuss the inherit bugs in the FTD product

Chapter 1: The Firepower Family

In this first chapter, we'll cover some terminology and the history of Firepower. We'll also cover the Firepower product line, including the management center, Firepower appliances, various ASA models with FirePOWER, and the new appliances running Firepower Threat Defense.

We'll discuss some of their capabilities and interoperability, including what hardware supports the various flavors of Firepower.

To find Firepower videos, practice questions and hands-on classes with Todd Lammle, please see www.lammle.com/firepower.

Terminology

Because of all the product names involved, we would be remiss if we didn't take a brief detour to discuss terminology. The road to the current Firepower branding has been less than smooth. There was the original name of the system, Sourcefire, which was also the name of the company that developed the product before it was acquired by Cisco, so naturally this name had to be expunged.

First, a global search and replace was performed replacing Sourcefire with FireSIGHT. This wasn't good enough, so the name of the management console, Defense Center, was also replaced, with FireSIGHT Management Center (FMC), and a new product was introduced named FirePOWER Services for ASA.

Then, after a few years, the term *FireSIGHT* was similarly discarded and the global search and replace engine kicked in, this time changing that term universally to *Firepower*. Fortunately, in changing from FireSIGHT Management Center to Firepower Management Center, we got to preserve the acronym—FMC. At least there was one bright spot to the mess!

Rather than run through all the history and changes, Table 1.1 shows the changes in terminology. You will be forgiven if you slip now and then and use one of the older terms—we do it all the time!

Table 1.1: Terminology History

Refers to the company	Sourcefire	Cisco	Cisco
Management software	Defense Center (DC)	FireSIGHT Management Center (FMC) FireSIGHT Defense Center Defense Center	Firepower Management Center (FMC) Management Center (MC)
Sensing device (NGIPS)	Sensor	Device	Device
Product line	Sourcefire 3D System	FireSIGHT System	Firepower System
Firepower software running on ASA	N/A	Cisco ASA with FirePOWER Services ASA FirePOWER module	Cisco ASA with FirePOWER Services ASA FirePOWER module
Firepower Threat Defense on an ASA	N/A	N/A	Firepower Threat Defense (FTD)

The Product Line

There are three main product lines we will cover in this book:

- Firepower
- ASA with FirePOWER Services
- Firepower Threat Defense

It's important to note that these products run on what Cisco calls the "device." This is the technology that sits on the network, inspects traffic, and can alert or block unwanted or malicious activity. Nicely, a single management console—called the Firepower Management Center, or FMC—manages all of these devices. This book will primarily focus on the use of the FMC to manage the various Firepower flavors.

Firepower Management Center

The FMC is the heart of the Firepower System. While it doesn't do any detection itself, it provides the central management and event collection for all the devices (previously known as sensors) deployed on your network. The model of FMC selected depends on the number of devices and events you will be managing. Table 1.2 shows some of the capabilities of the various FMC models.

Table 1.2: FMC Models

	MC750	MC2000	MC4000	Virtual FMC
Max devices managed	10	70	300	25 10 2
Max IPS events	20 million	60 million	300 million	10 million
Event Storage	100 GB	1.8 TB	3.2 TB	250 GB
Max flows per second	2,000 fps	12,000 fps	20,000 fps	Varies*
High Availability	No	HA pairing, RAID 5	HA pairing, RAID 5	No

* Virtual FMC performance is highly dependent on factors in the virtual environment.

One noteworthy FMC feature is High Availability (HA). This involves two FMCs, which mirror configurations and event data. In case the primary fails, the secondary can be brought online to seamlessly maintain management and event reporting.

This feature had been available in the Sourcefire product since version 4.x; however, when version 6.0 was released in early 2016, this feature was removed. This was because due to a complete rebuild of the HA feature from the ground up, it was not ready in time for the initial 6.0 release date, and thus, adoption of Firepower version 6 has been much slower than prior versions.

Most large organizations depend on the HA feature and can't afford to lose management as well as alerting in the case of a FMC failure, so this feature has been re-introduced in version 6.1 of the Firepower System, and as a result, organizations are now adopting this version at a much greater rate.

High Availability is only supported on the MC1500, MC3500, MC2000, and MC4000 hardware platforms.

Firepower

While the term *Firepower* has been expanded to mean just about anything having to do with Cisco's NGIPS/NGFW, in this context it means traditional discrete appliances deployed within a network. This includes appliance models with numbers in the 7000 and 8000 range as well as the virtual appliance running on systems like VMware and Amazon AWS. These are still widely deployed and represent the bulk of the Firepower inspection performed on networks worldwide.

There is a Firepower device model to fit almost any network. The main difference between them is their bandwidth capacity. IPS throughput ratings range from 50 Mbps for the lowly FP7010 up to a whopping 60 Gbps for an FP8390 stack!

As is typical when you're faced with picking out networking equipment, appliance selection is narrowed down by the size of your budget and the amount of bandwidth you need. The good news is that Firepower is actually a really great value in terms of cost per megabit protected. Still, quality rarely comes cheap, and all that protection isn't inexpensive. Fortunately, the wide range of appliance choices helps out tremendously by offering enough options to ensure that you only pay for what you really need.

An important fact to remember is that the bandwidth numbers published for each appliance are guidelines based on IPS protection. Adding additional features such as Application Visibility and Control (AVC), URL Filtering, Malware file analysis, or SSL decryption will reduce this number. To arrive at the right appliance model for your network, work with your Cisco sales engineer (SE). This is not a "one size fits all" solution, and your SE has the tools to help understand your specific needs related to detection and traffic composition. Because there are so many factors affecting performance, Cisco does not publish detailed throughput numbers for various analysis scenarios.

The base IPS throughput numbers for each appliance are shown in Table 1.3.

Table 1.3: Firepower Device Models

Model	IPS Throughput
Virtual	150–200 Mbps/core
7010	50 Mbps
7020	100 Mbps
7030	250 Mbps
7110	500 Mbps
7115	750 Mbps
7120	1 Gbps
7125	1.25 Gbps
8120	2 Gbps
8130	4 Gbps
8140	6 Gbps
8350	15 Gbps
8360*	30 Gbps
8370*	45 Gbps
8390*	60 Gbps

* These models are stacked 8350 appliances.

The following features also differentiate hardware devices:

- Dual redundant power supplies

- Bypass/non-bypass interfaces

- Modular (SFP) interfaces
- Stacking capability

The devices above run the Firepower System software. This is the product line that can trace its roots directly back to Sourcefire before the Cisco acquisition, and these devices can operate in several modes:

- Passive
- Inline
- Routed
- Switchcd

The majority of these devices are deployed in inline mode, giving them the capability to inspect and block malicious traffic. The second most popular way to deploy devices is passive mode. In this design, the IPS receives a copy of network traffic via a tap or span port. The IPS can alert on malicious traffic but cannot block it. Firepower hardware devices also have routing and switching capabilities, but these are deployed less often. Routing and switching are not core strengths of the product and have received only minor enhancements since their introduction several years ago.

A major consideration if deploying in routed or switched mode is that the fail-open, or bypass, functionality, which allows traffic to pass in case of certain failures, is only available in inline mode. We'll cover the various detection modes in more detail later in the Chapter 4: Device Management.

ASA with FirePOWER Services

The Adaptive Security Appliance (ASA) has been Cisco's traditional core firewall product for many years. It is deployed in thousands of networks at the edge or internally to provide typical stateful firewall features based on IP address and port. The FirePOWER Services product adds Next Generation Firewall (NGFW) capability to the existing ASA software. This is accomplished by the ASA forwarding traffic for inspection to Firepower processes running on the appliance. Depending on the ASA model, this may be a virtual machine running Firepower or—in the case of the 5585-X—on a separate Security Services Processor (SSP).

The key thing to keep in mind about this solution is that it runs traditional ASA software in addition to Firepower. Managing an ASA with FirePOWER Services requires two separate management tools/techniques. The Firepower services are managed via the FMC and the ASA services are managed through some other method. This could be via the command-line interface (CLI), Adaptive Security Device Manager (ASDM), or Cisco Security Manager (CSM).

As with Firepower devices, there are numerous ASA models to choose from (Table 1.4). Throughput numbers are the primary differentiator as you move through the model numbers. Cisco provides several throughput numbers for these devices, depending on the traffic analysis features enabled.

Table 1.4: ASA Models

Model	Stateful Inspection Throughput	Application Visibility (AVC) and Control Throughput	AVC and IPS Throughput
5506	750 Mbps	250 Mbps	125 Mbps
5508	1 Gbps	450 Mbps	250 Mbps
5516	1.8 Gbps	850 Mbps	450 Mbps
5512	1 Gbps	300 Mbps	150 Mbps
5515	1.2 Gbps	500 Mbps	250 Mbps
5525	2 Gbps	1,100 Mbps*	650 Mbps
5545	3 Gbps	1,500 Mbps*	1,000 Mbps*
5555	4 Gbps	1,750 Mbps*	1,250 Mbps*
5585-X SSP-10	4 Gbps	4.5 Gbps**	2 Gbps
5585-X SSP-20	10 Gbps	7 Gbps	3.5 Gbps
5585-X SSP-40	20 Gbps	10 Gbps	6 Gbps
5585-X SSP-60	40 Gbps	15 Gbps	10 Gbps

* For some reason, Cisco spec sheets show some numbers in thousands of megabits instead of gigabits.

** Based on available Cisco ASA data sheets, the SSP-10 performs better with AVC than it does as a traditional firewall (no this doesn't make sense to us either).

As mentioned previously, the numbers in Table 1-4 should be considered best case and may not reflect your traffic composition. Your best source of design guidance on which device is right for you is your Cisco sales engineer.

Firepower Threat Defense

The new kid on the block is called Firepower Threat Defense (FTD). FTD is the "converged" software image, which runs on ASA and new Firepower hardware. This does away with the two-system approach that is ASA with

FirePOWER Services. Instead, the ASA device is reimaged with the FTD operating system and now runs the Cisco Fire Linux OS.

All of a sudden, the device looks a lot more like Firepower than ASA. The ASA functions have been ported over to FTD and everything operates under a single operating system with a single detection path. The big win for this design is that now there is a single management console—you guessed it, the FMC! At the time of this writing, FTD is still in its toddler stage, as some of the ASA features have not been ported yet to the FMC. But this is the future folks. FTD will eventually be *the* operating system on all ASAs. FTD and FMC will rule the world!

One important caveat to FTD is that it does not work on one particular type of ASA hardware. The ASA 5585-X will not (ever) run FTD because of the separate SSP architecture of the device. It will always have separate ASA and Firepower processes and currently requires separate management tools for the Firepower and ASA functions. Cisco may address this with future FMC enhancements, allowing the 5585 to benefit from the single management console. At this point we don't know if such plans exist, but it seems like a good strategy to protect customer investments in these expensive 5585 devices.

While FTD will run on all the existing 55*xx* models (except the 5585-X), there is also a new breed of hardware appliance designed specifically with FTD in mind. Oh, and just to avoid confusion, Cisco has called these Firepower appliances too.

The new Firepower devices are capable of running FTD or ASA software but not Firepower software. Confused yet? Don't worry; we will put it all together in a minute.

Cisco started at the top of the performance scale with the 9300 Firepower device and is moving down the curve with subsequent models. We're not prophets, but the writing on the wall says that eventually, the new Firepower devices will replace the existing Firepower 7000/8000 and ASA 55*xx* product lines.

One look at the performance numbers in Table 1.5 and you can see that the 9300 is the big kid on the block. With ASA Firewall throughput topping out at 225 Gbps, it is one beefy piece of hardware. With a retail price of $1 million when fully loaded (hardware only), you can tell Cisco is proud of this one.

The table 1.5 shows the new Firepower device model breakdown.

Table 1.5: New Firepower Models

Model	Firewall Throughput (ASA)	FW + AVC (FTD)	FW + AVC + IPS (FTD)
4110	20 Gbps	12 Gbps	10 Gbps
4120	40 Gbps	20 Gbps	15 Gbps
4140	60 Gbps	25 Gbps	20 Gbps
4150	TBD	TBD	TBD

9300 1xSM-24	75 Gbps	25 Gbps	20 Gbps
9300 1xSM-36	80 Gbps	35 Gbps	30 Gbps
9300 3xSM-36	225 Gbps	100 Gbps	90 Gbps

As mentioned earlier, not all the Firepower flavors will run on all the Cisco hardware. In fact, no one device will run all the Firepower versions available.

The compatibility matrix in Table 1.6 shows which Cisco security product will operate on the various device models.

Table 1.6: Product Matrix

	Firepower 7000/8000	All ASA except 5585-X	ASA 5585-X	Firepower 4000/9300
ASA		X	X	X
Firepower	X			
FirePOWER Services on ASA		X	X	
Firepower Threat Defense		X		X

Chapter 2: Management Configuration

This chapter will cover the steps to configure the management network interface on your device and register it to the FMC. Once the device is registered, there is virtually no reason to return to its graphical or command-line interface under normal operations. From that point, you perform all day-to-day operations from the FMC.

Lastly, we will also cover Classic and Smart Licensing, which enable the various detection features available.

Management Network Interfaces

In this section, we will discuss the process of initially configuring your devices. This procedure will get you to the point from which you can then move to the FMC to register the device. The main goals are to get an IP address assigned to the management interface and prepare for registration with the FMC. Once connected to the FMC, we will proceed with configuring the detection interfaces and device settings.

The FMC will have only management interfaces; remember, it does not do any detection itself but gets events from the devices. Each device will have at least two types of network interfaces—management and detection (actually the 9300 and 4100 have three types of interfaces) as some device types can be configured with multiple management interfaces for redundancy or additional bandwidth. In practice, most devices are configured with a single 1 Gb port for management traffic.

Your first task after getting the appliance racked and powered will be to connect and configure the management network interface. This procedure will vary depending on the device type.

Firepower Management Center

This section technically covers devices. While the FMC is not actually a device, it is an appliance. We will slip it in here since it also requires some initial management configuration. The procedure to configure the management IP is the same for all FMC types. It involves logging in from the console and setting the management IP address from the command line. To access the console, there are three options: (1) connect a USB keyboard and VGA monitor, (2) connect to the serial console port, or (3) connect via SSH to the default IP address. For virtual FMCs, you will access the console through your virtualization app.

For the first option the procedure is fairly simple: find a keyboard and monitor and plug it into the appropriate ports on the rear of the appliance. This is the simplest method if you have a keyboard and monitor handy.

For the second option, you may connect a computer to the serial console port on the appliance using a rollover serial cable.

If you don't have a keyboard and monitor, you can also connect from a laptop computer via SSH. The FMC ships with the default IP address of 192.168.45.45, which is assigned to its management port. Simply configure your computer with an IP address in the same subnet—such as 192.168.45.2—and use an SSH client to connect. You can even use a normal Ethernet cable to connect directly between your computer and the FMC - the Ethernet port will automatically crossover if needed.

Once you connect to the console, you will be greeted with a login prompt.

Log in with the default credentials:

Username: **admin**
Password: **Admin123**

Run the configure network script with the following command:

`sudo /usr/local/sf/bin/configure-network`

You will be led through the steps to assign the management interface IP address, netmask, and gateway. You can also configure DNS servers if desired, and this is highly recommended. Does changing the IP drop the currently active SSH session

After this is complete, you can connect the management interface to your network and navigate to your FMC's IP address using a web browser. Note that you must use the **https://** prefix in your browser URL bar because the FMC does not listen on port 80 (http).

Firepower 7000/8000 Devices

Initial IP Address Configuration

For Firepower devices, there are several methods to set the initial IP address.

1. The device ships with the default IP of 192.168.45.45.

2. You can use the keyboard/monitor ports on the back of the appliance to log in and perform the initial configuration.

3. You can use the serial port on the back of the appliance along with a serial terminal application (or actual serial terminal if you can find one).

4. You can use the LCD panel on the front of the appliance.

The first three methods are fairly self-explanatory. Each one will land you at the login prompt where you can perform the steps under Initial Login below. These steps include assigning an intial IP address and performing the initial setup.

Let's discuss the LCD technique a bit further. Firepower devices allow configuring the mangement IP address via the LCD screen and four buttons on the front (Figure 2.1). By following the instructions on the LCD, you can set the network information with just your finger!

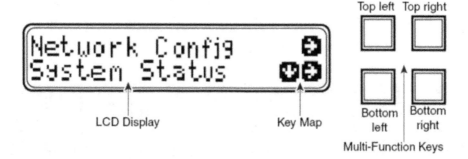

Figure 2.1: LCD panel

Basically, you follow the prompts on the screen using the four buttons on the right to set the IP, netmask, and gateway information. Once you are finished, you can SSH to the device and continue either at the command line or connect with a web browser. We will discuss the command line method next.

Initial Login

One you have access to the device console command-line interface, log in as **admin** with the password **Admin123**. After logging in, you will be led through the setup process. You will be prompted to accept the EULA and change your password.

Next you will be led through the configuration of the management IP address settings and the detection mode. If you already set the IP address, you can change it here or just accept the existing settings. When you get to detection mode, you can choose inline or passive. This setting is easily changed, so if you're not sure you can accept the default (inline). This takes the first two interfaces in the device (s1p1 and s1p2) and creates a default inline set. Traffic will then be allowed to pass between these two interfaces

Configuring FMC Management

When you are finished with the configuration wizard, you will see the **>** prompt; this is the Firepower CLI. From the CLI prompt, you will use the `configure manager` command. The command has several advanced options you will find in the Cisco installation guide. Here we will stick with the syntax that is used the majority of the time. You will need to know your FMC's management IP address and an arbitrary registration key. This key is a one-time secret used in the initial device registration. You only need to remember it long enough to type it into your FMC when you register this device. Most people go with something simple like Cisco123. Make it easy on yourself and don't overthink this one!

The syntax is **configure manager add <FMC IP address> <registration key>** (See Figure 2.2 for an example of this command.)

```
************* WARNING *************
This is a private system.  All access is logged.
Unauthorized access is prohibited.
firepower login: admin
Password:
Last login: Sun Jul 17 17:19:57 UTC 2016 on tty1

Copyright 2004-2015, Cisco and/or its affiliates. All rights reserved.
Cisco is a registered trademark of Cisco Systems, Inc.
All other trademarks are property of their respective owners.

Cisco Fire Linux OS v6.0.0 (build 258)
Cisco NGIPSv for VMware v6.0.1.1 (build 24)

> configure manager add 10.0.0.9 cisco456
Manager successfully configured.
Please make note of reg_key as this will be required while adding Device in FMC.

> _
```

Figure 2.2: The configure manager add **command**

This prepares the device to receive the registration from the FMC. Later you will use the FMC UI to complete this process.

FirePOWER on ASA Devices

Configuration of FirePOWER on ASA devices follows a similar process as the process for Firepower devices described earlier. In fact, they run the same Firepower Linux operating system within the SFR module.

The *Cisco ASA FirePOWER Module Quick Start Guide* does a very good job of explaining the specific steps to install and configure the software. In this case, your best bet is to follow the Cisco quick start guide for your ASA model, which will lead you through the steps to log in and configure the management interface.

There are two scenarios when configuring FirePOWER on an ASA. The first is if you are adding the FirePOWER module to an *existing* ASA. In this case, you will have to upload a new boot image ASA boot I assume - then a reload of the ASA? and then upload and configure the FirePOWER System software. The second scenario is if you purchased a new ASA with FirePOWER Services already installed. For each of these, the quick start guide is your friend.

Let's start with scenario 1, installing on an existing ASA. Rather than repeat the guide here, let's go over the process from a high level

To accomplish these steps, you will need the following items:

- The ASA FirePOWER boot image for your device. The filename is similar to `asasfr-5500x-boot-6.2.0-2.img` and you will load this into Flash memory on your ASA

- An HTTP, HTTPS, TFTP, or FTP server where you can host this file.

- The FirePOWER System software image for your device. This filename will be similar to `asasfr-sys-6.2.0-362.pkg` and this file needs to be put on your FTP server.

- An HTTP, HTTPS, or FTP server where you can host this file.

Once you have these items, you can proceed to install the module on your ASA.

1. First you will need to shut down and uninstall any existing software module such as the Cisco IPS or CX module. If you aren't currently running a software module, you can skip this step.

2. Next you will use the ASA Device Manager (ASDM) or the ASA CLI to copy the boot image file to flash memory. To do this, you will need the boot image from the Cisco support site and a TFTP, HTTP, HTTPS, or FTP server on your network.

3. You will then set the image to boot and then load it, for example:

```
ASA#sw-module module sfr recover configure image disk0:/asasfr-
5500x-boot-6.2.0-2.img

ASA#sw-module module sfr recover boot
```

4. Next, log in to the running image and configure a temporary IP address. You can use the same IP address you plan to assign to perform Firepower management on your ASA. The purpose of this image is simply to download the Firepower installation package.

5. Upload the ASA FirePOWER package file. To do this, you will need the file for your particular ASA model and an HTTP, HTTPS, or FTP server on your network. For example:

```
boot>system install FTP://10.11.11.250/asasfr-sys-6.2.0-362.pkg
```

6. Once this is completed, the module will reboot and load the FirePOWER on ASA module. From this point, you will use the

session sfr command from the ASA CLI to connect to the FirePOWER module. Log in as **admin** with the password **Admin123** and follow the same procedure as on a Firepower 7000/8000 device to accept the EULA, change the default password, and configure the management IP information.

7. Finally, you will use the **configure manager add** command to identify the FMC that will manage this device. For example:

```
>configure manager add 1.2.3.4 cisco
```

For scenario 2 (if you bought a new ASA with FirePOWER Services), you simply start at step 6 above.

> **Note:** One important difference between the FirePOWER on ASA module and a Firepower device is the lack of a Web UI. On an ASA with FirePOWER, you must use the CLI to perform the FMC registration steps. The ASA SFR module does not have a web-based interface.

ASA Devices Running FTD

The procedure to set up an ASA with FTD is similar to the procedure for setting up the ASA with FirePOWER Services. Again, there are two scenarios, the first being an existing ASA you want to convert to FTD. The second is a new ASA purchased with FTD preinstalled.

Again, we will start with scenario 1, the more difficult of the two. This time, instead of just loading a software module, you will be completely reimaging your ASA so that FTD is the only operating system. Scary stuff, but if you are ready to take the plunge, then read on!

Remember, we're not going to try to repeat the installation or quick start guide here. The idea is to give you a high-level view of the process so you can better understand it. Note that to do this on an ASA, you must connect to the serial console port. This process cannot initially be performed via SSH or from ASDM. Once you have the management IP address assigned, you can complete the rest of the setup for SSH if desired. However, by that time you will be 90 percent through, so most folks just perform the entire process via the serial console.

As with the ASA FirePOWER module, you must have the following items to upgrade an existing ASA to FTD:

- The Firepower Threat Defense OS image for your device. For an ASA-5506, 5508, or 5516, the filename will have a `.lfbff` extension. For an ASA-5512, 5515, 5525, 5545, and 5555, the filename will have a `.cdisk` extension.

- A TFTP server where you can host this file. Note that the OS image must be uploaded via TFTP; you can't host this on your web or FTP server.

- The Firepower Threat Defense system package for your device. This filename will have a `.pkg` extension.

- An HTTP, HTTPS or FTP server where you can host this file. Note that this file cannot be hosted via TFTP.

Here are the high-level steps to reimage an existing ASA and run Firepower Threat Defense:

1. Verify and upgrade the ROMMON. You may be able to skip this step if your ROMMON is already at a new enough version.

2. Upload and install the FTD OS image from your TFTP server. This process involves setting a temporary IP address on the ASA management interface and uploading the OS image. When the upload is finished, the system will automatically boot and stop at the boot CLI prompt.

3. From the boot CLI, you will once again assign a temporary IP address, then upload and install the FTD System package from your HTTP, HTTPS, or FTP server.

4. Next you will configure the device for management from the Firepower Management Center (FMC). This procedure is almost identical to the procedure on other Firepower devices. You will accept the EULA, change the password, and for the third time, configure the management IP.

Note: You will be given the choice to configure the ASA in routed or transparent mode. This is an important decision! You may have seen a similar question for Firepower devices, but in that case it only determines the initial interface configuration and is easily changed later by configuring the interfaces as passive, inline, switched, etc. In the case of FTD, you cannot simply switch an ASA from routed to transparent mode. To do so, you must first unregister the ASA from the FMC, which erases the configuration. Then you can change the mode. After this, you re-register the device. Best to get this right the first time.

5. Use the **`configure manager add`** command to identify the FMC that will manage this device.

For scenario 2 (if you bought a new ASA with FTD or x100/4100/9300), you simply start at step 4 above. You can use the serial console or SSH to the default IP address of 192.168.45.45 (sound familiar?).

Log in as **admin** with **Admin123** for the password, and then proceed through the wizard to set the IP information and configure the FMC management connection.

FTD on Firepower 4100/9300 Devices

The Firepower 4100/9300 devices are the first of a new breed of network security appliances from Cisco. These devices can run the legacy ASA operating system or Firepower Threat Defense. Since this is a Firepower book, we will only discuss the FTD option here. Again, this will be a high-level discussion; you should use the appropriate guide(s) from Cisco to get the detailed and up-to-date information for your platform.

These devices are different than any of the previous hardware we've discussed. It's not just that they are newer; they run a new operating system called the Firepower eXtensble Operating System, or FXOS. This operating system forms the foundation on which the ASA or FTD code will run. FXOS runs the Firepower Chassis Manager, which provides GUI-based management of the device. A component called the supervisor is responsible for the physical interfaces and for managing the images (ASA or FTD) that will run on the device.

The 4100 devices can load a single image, while the 9300 can have up to three modules, each one running the FTD or ASA software image. However, the 9300 cannot currently mix software images; all the modules must run either FTD or ASA.

Initial Configuration

As with the other ASA hardware, your initial configuration will be via the console port.

1. Log in with username **admin** and password **cisco123** (notice this is different than we've seen on the previous devices).

2. You will be prompted by the setup wizard to complete the configuration information. Here's an example:

```
Enter the setup mode; setup newly or restore from backup.
(setup/restore) ? setup
You have chosen to setup a new Security Appliance. Continue?
(y/n): y
Enforce strong password? (y/n): n
Enter the password for "admin": <new password>
Confirm the password for "admin": <repeat password>
Enter the system name: FTD-SSP-3RU
Physical Switch Mgmt0 IP address : 10.127.56.61
Physical Switch Mgmt0 IPv4 netmask : 255.255.255.0
IPv4 address of default gateway : 10.127.56.1
Configure the DNS Server IP address? (yes/no) [n]: n
Configure the default domain name? (yes/no) [n]: n

Following configurations will be applied:
Switch Fabic=A
System Name=FTD-SSP-3RU
Enforced Strong Password=no
Physical Switch Mgmt0 IP Address=10.127.56.61
Physical Switch Mgmt0 IP Netmask=255.255.255.0
Default Gateway=10.127.56.1
Ipv6 value=0

Apply and save the configuration (select 'n' if you want to re-
enter)? (yes/no): yes
Applying configuration. Please wait.
```

3. After this, you will use a supported browser (Chrome or Firefox) to log in to the Firepower Chassis Manager as so: `https://<chassis-mgmt-IP-address>`.

Use the username **admin** and the new password you set up in step 2. The Firepower Chassis Manager screen is shown in Figure 2.3.

Figure 2.3: Firepower Chassis Manager login

Download Software Images (Firepower 9300 Only)

In this step, you will download the appropriate software images from Cisco.com for your device. Note that you must have a Cisco.com account and Internet access.

1. From the Chassis Manager UI, go to System → Updates. You will see a list of the Firepower 9300 platform bundle images and application images available.

2. Click the "Download latest updates from CCO" link at the bottom of the page. The software download page will open in a new browser tab. Note: In our testing, this link only takes you to www.cisco.com so you'll have to navigate to the software download yourself.

3. Download the appropriate software images to your local computer. The FXOS platform bundle will be similar to `fxos-k9.x.x.x.SPA`. The FTD application image will be similar to `cisco-ftd-6.x.x.x.csp`.

4. Return to `System` → `Updates`, click Upload Image, and select the images you downloaded in step 3. Follow any system prompts and accept the EULA if needed.

Deploy Firepower Threat Defense

The next steps in setting up your 4100/9300 device involve NTP and interface configuration and then deploying the FTD logical device. Because these steps will vary greatly depending on your specific installation, we will not try to go into all the steps or scenarios in this chapter, but will cover them in the new **Chapter 18: Cisco Firepower eXtensble Operating System.**

The quick start guide for each platform is your best up-to-date reference for the specific steps to finish your initial configuration. At the end, you will have a device that is ready to be registered and managed with the Firepower Management Center.

FMC Registration

Once your devices are prepared, your next task is to register each one with the FMC. The steps for each device type are very similar.

1. Log in to your FMC and navigate to `Devices → Device Management`.

2. Click the Add button in the upper-right corner and select Add Device.

3. Enter the information in the various fields (see Figure 2.4):

   a. Host: This is the hostname or IP address of your device. Using an IP address is the most common technique.

   b. Display Name: This is the display name you want for your device on the FMC.

   c. Registration Key: The one-time key you used when you configured the device.

   d. Group: This is optional if you want to group your devices for ease of management.

   e. Access Control Policy: You must pick an initial policy here or you can create one. If you want something simple and quick, you can use Discovery Only.

   f. Smart Licensing: If you have Smart Licenses configured, you can apply them here. If not, or if you are using Classic Licensing, then skip this and we will do it later.

g. Advanced – Unique NAT ID: This is only needed if you are performing NAT translation between your FMC and device.

h. Advanced – Transfer Packets: This should normally be checked. Un-checking means IPS alerts will not have packet data stored on the FMC. This makes analysis more difficult and is only required in specific data privacy scenarios.

Figure 2.4: Add Device dialog

4. When you are ready, click the Register button and the FMC will reach out and register the device. Note that this can take several minutes, so be patient. Navigating away during the device registration process will not interfere with this step.

When registration is completed, you will see your newly registered device in the Devices list (Figure 2.5).

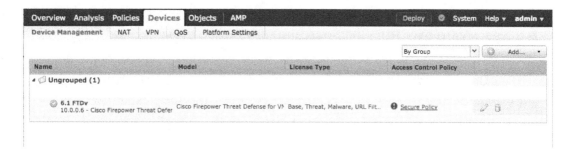

Figure 2.5: The Devices list

Licensing

Classic Licensing

Classic Licensing is unchanged from version 5 of Firepower. (If you are keeping up with names, Firepower was actually called FireSIGHT in version 5.) The process for licensing devices and features remains the same in version 6. If you are deploying Firepower 7000/8000, FirePOWER on ASA, or virtual Firepower devices, you will use Classic Licensing.

First, you purchase the features you want for your devices. These are as follows:

- Protect: This is your basic, entry-level license for a device that you have ear marked to become an NGIPS. It enables intrusion detection/prevention, file control, and Security Intelligence filtering.

- Control: The Control license enables NGFW features like user and application control as well as switched and routed interfaces. This license is also required for clustering or stacking supported devices.

- URL Filtering: URL Filtering enables allowing/blocking websites based on their category or reputation. Information such as category and business relevance is updated on the FMC via a cloud connection.

- Malware: Advanced Malware Protection (AMP) provides cloud-based malware lookup and sandbox analysis, including file trajectory and tracking across the network.

- VPN: The VPN license enables site-to-site VPN capabilities between devices and it's what you'll need to create a secure tunnel to a remote office location without having to install separate VPN hardware.

Note that the Protect and Control licenses are always bundled together. This is a legacy carryover from the Sourcefire days when these licenses were sold separately.

The process of adding a Classic License starts with the product authorization key (PAK). This is an 11-digit code provided usually via hard copy and mailed along with your devices. You take this PAK and register it at the Cisco licensing portal at **https://www.cisco.com/go/license**. In exchange, you will receive a license key, which is a fairly lengthy block of characters that looks somewhat like a cryptographic key. Armed with this code, proceed with the following steps:

1. Navigate to System → Licenses → Classic Licenses and select Add New License. You will see the Add Feature License page.

2. Paste your license code into the License field (Figure 2.6). You'll want to paste everything between the BEGIN and END lines. You can include them or leave them out but you have to do the same for both. That is, you can't leave in the BEGIN line and leave out the END line.

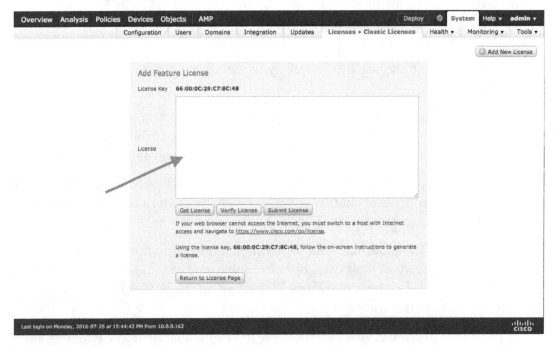

Figure 2-6: License page

3. Click the Submit License button. After a few seconds you will be greeted with a success dialog. This screen also contains license

details confirming the feature you just enabled and the device model it applies to.

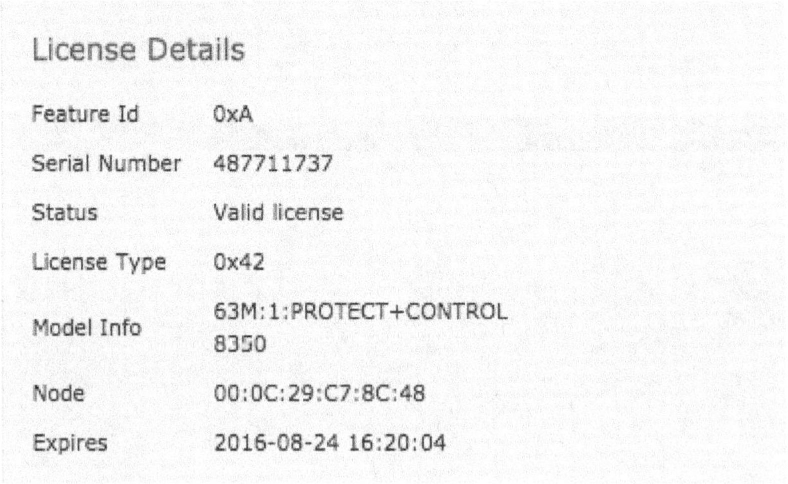

License Details

Feature Id	0xA
Serial Number	487711737
Status	Valid license
License Type	0x42
Model Info	63M:1:PROTECT+CONTROL 8350
Node	00:0C:29:C7:8C:48
Expires	2016-08-24 16:20:04

Figure 2-7: License Details

4. To add more licenses, just click the Add New License button in the upper right and paste your next key.

Smart Licensing

With FTD, Cisco has introduced a new licensing model—Smart Licensing. Smart Licensing centrally manages a pool of licenses. Unlike the older method of using a product authorization key (PAK), Smart Licenses are not tied to a specific serial number or license key. Each customer account receives a token code, which is used to register your FMC with the Cisco central licensing manager. After this, any licenses you purchase are automatically available on your FMC. Firepower Threat Defense devices use Smart Licensing, while classic devices (Firepower 7000/8000, FirePOWER on ASA, NGIPSv) use Classic Licensing.

One very nice thing about the FMC and Smart Licensing is that you get a 90-day grace/evaluation period when you first install your FMC. During this period, you can try out any of the features. Figure 2.8 shows our FMC currently in this evaluation period.

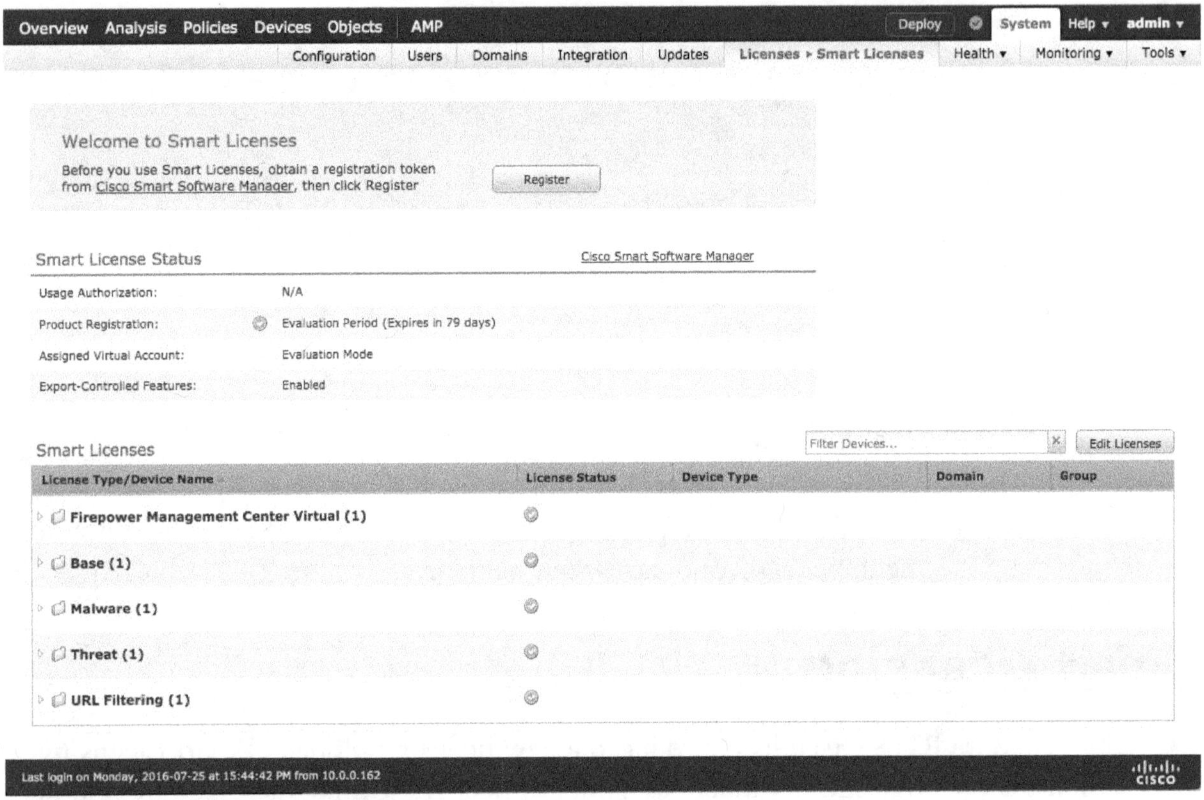
Overview Analysis Policies Devices Objects AMP
Deploy System Help admin
Configuration Users Domains Integration Updates Licenses ▸ Smart Licenses Health Monitoring Tools
Welcome to Smart Licenses
Before you use Smart Licenses, obtain a registration token from Cisco Smart Software Manager, then click Register
Register
Smart License Status
Cisco Smart Software Manager
Usage Authorization: N/A
Product Registration: Evaluation Period (Expires in 79 days)
Assigned Virtual Account: Evaluation Mode
Export-Controlled Features: Enabled
Smart Licenses
Filter Devices...
Edit Licenses
License Type/Device Name
License Status
Device Type
Domain
Group
Firepower Management Center Virtual (1)
Base (1)
Malware (1)
Threat (1)
URL Filtering (1)
Last login on Monday, 2016-07-25 at 15:44:42 PM from 10.0.0.162
cisco

Figure 2.8: Smart Licenses screen

The process of registering your FMC is pretty straightforward. It will require a visit to the online Cisco Smart Software Manager. There you will log in and generate a new token. To find the manager URL, you can navigate to `System` → `Licenses` → `Smart Licenses` on your FMC. There you will find a link to the Smart Software Manager.

Then simply click the Register button and paste the token into the field (Figure 2.9).

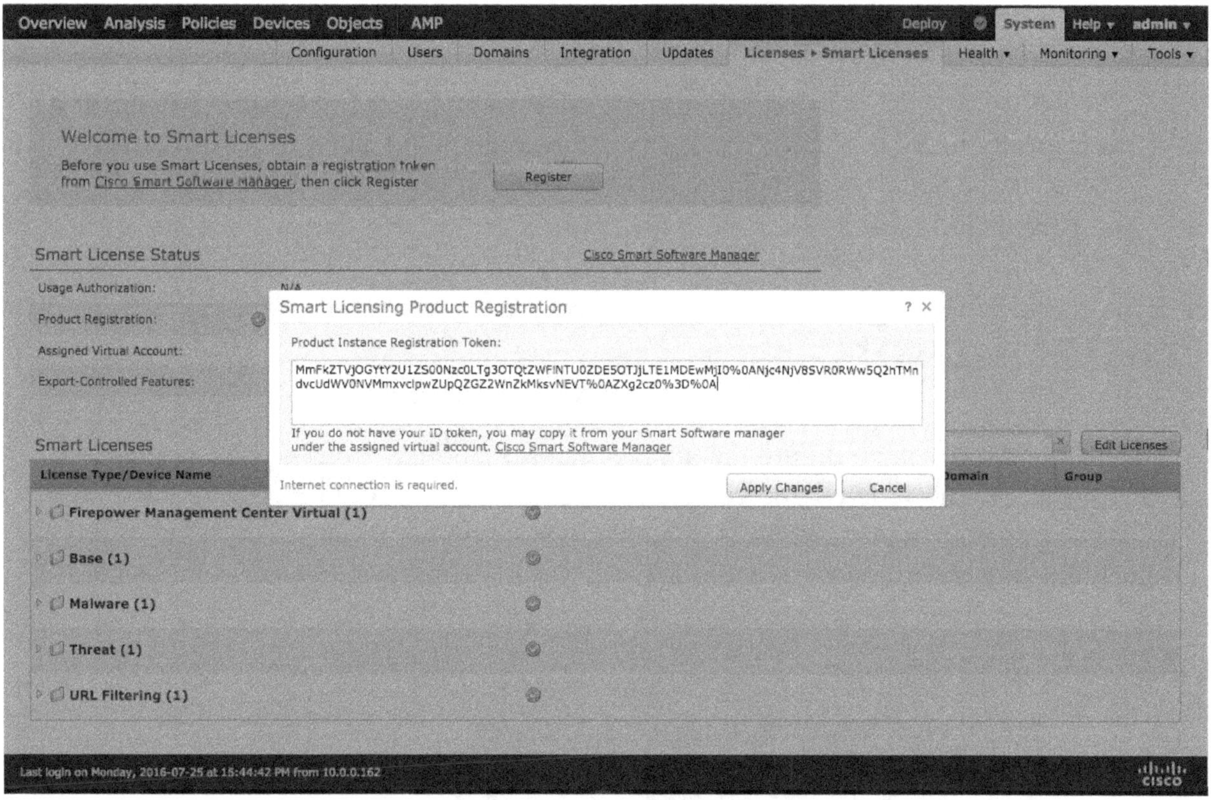

Figure 2. 9: Smart License token

After this, any licenses you have will automatically be downloaded and synchronized with your FMC. The FMC must have an active Internet connection to maintain your Smart Licenses. If this connection is interrupted or you have been connected for too long (over 90 days), your licenses could be deactivated.

Chapter 3: System (FMC) Configuration

In this chapter, we will begin working with the Firepower Management Center, or FMC. The title may seem fairly broad, but it comes from the Firepower menu item with the same name.

When we say, "system configuration," what we really mean is the configuration of Firepower using the FMC. Since we will be using the FMC to perform virtually all the management tasks, it makes sense to spend a little time up front on its configuration.

Initial Login

After you configure the management IP address, your next step will be to connect to the Web UI and complete the initial setup. To do this, you will connect to **https://<your-FMC-IP>**, where you will be presented with the initial login screen as shown in Figure 3.1.

Figure 3.1: FMC Login page

Enter **admin** for the username and **Admin123** for the password. Once logged in, you will see the initial settings page where you can configure some basic FMC settings. This is the only time you will see this page. Upon subsequent logins, you will be taken to the main FMC landing page (the Dashboard by default).

Figure 3.2, shows the top of the initial page, Figure 3.3 shows the middle, and Figure 3.4 shows the bottom.

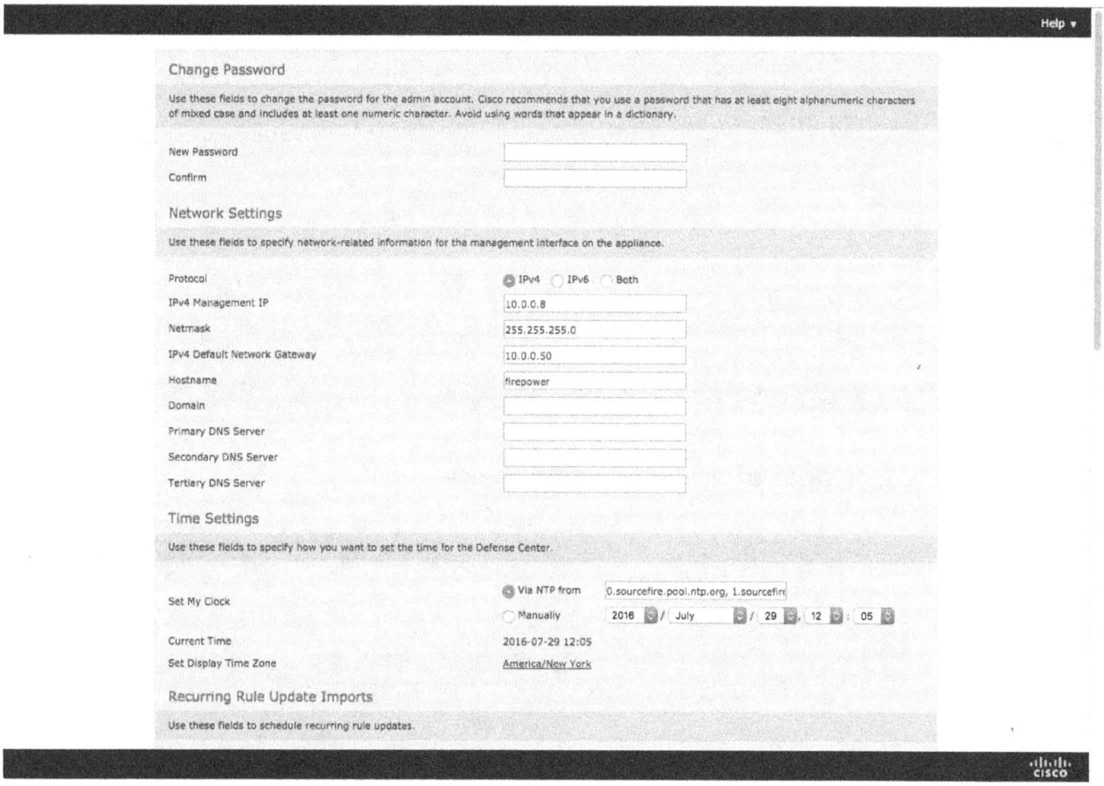

Figure 3.2: Top of the FMC initial page

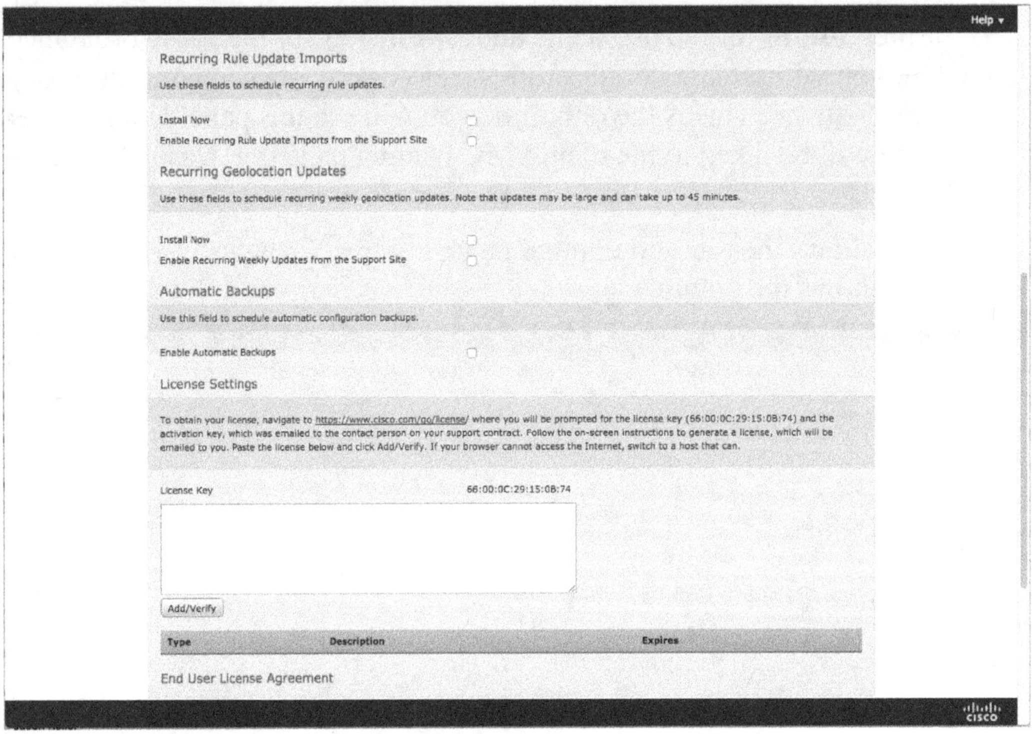

Figure 3.3: Middle of the FMC initial page

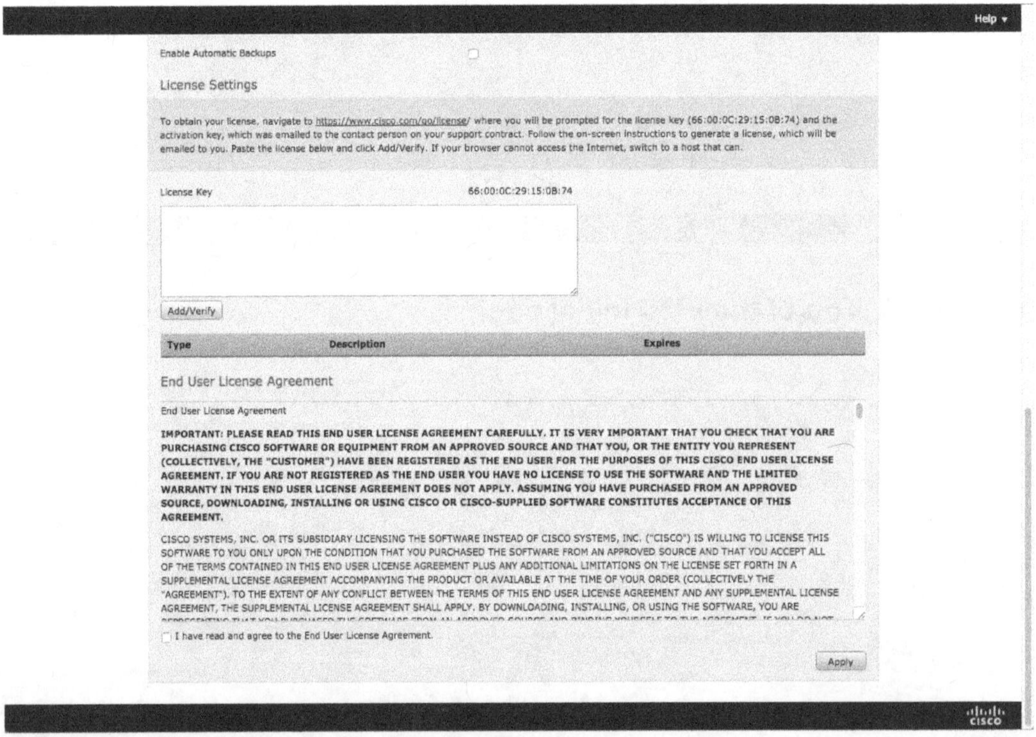

Figure 3.4: Bottom of the FMC initial page

There are a number of settings that can be configured here, such as the following:

- Admin Password*
- Network Settings
- Time Settings
- Recurring Rule Updates
- Recurring Geolocation Updates
- Automatic Backups
- License Settings
- End User License Agreement*

Of all of these, note that two of them are shown above with an asterisk. These are the only two you are required to change. The rest can be left alone and changed later. In fact, that's what we are going to recommend that you do. Rather than spend a lot of time here figuring out what NTP server you are using or when you should update various rules, let's get on with the actual FMC interface. All of these other items can be set later.

Of course, as with most things in life there are a couple of notes/caveats. First, the default time settings use NTP servers like 0.sourcefire.pool.ntp.org and 1.sourcefire.pool.ntp.org, which you should change, however, please note that if you do not have a DNS server configured in Network Settings, you will receive an error when you try to save them. The moral of the story: add DNS servers to your network settings!

Another note is that changing the password here will change both the Web UI and the console/SSH passwords. This is the last time you will have the opportunity to change them together. From here on out, you change the admin Web password in the Web UI and the admin console password from the console.

So for now, change the password, configure DNS server(s), and check the box saying you have read the EULA (you really did, right?). When you're finished, click the Apply button and read on.

Navigation Overview

The Firepower menu system is fairly intuitive—especially once you've been using it for several years! There is a top menu bar with sub-menu items. There are also various tabbed windows for access to different types of settings. One thing you will get used to quickly is hovering. Most of the time, you will want to navigate down to a sub-menu item by hovering over the menus as they appear rather than starting out by clicking on the top-level items.

Top-level menu items are divided into two groups on the right and left. The items on the right—Deploy, System, Help, and <user-name>—are focused on "operational" tasks (Figure 3.5). Here you'll find items such as health, licensing, user management, backups, task monitoring, etc.

Figure 3.5: Operational menu items

The items on the left—Overview, Analysis, Policies, Devices, Objects, and AMP—are where you will go to configure the actual detection and prevention settings as well as analyze events (Figure 3.6). Generally speaking, you will spend more of your time on the left side of the menu bar after the first few days of system setup.

Figure 3.6: Policy/analysis menu items

Firepower Management Configuration

Let's start by looking at the FMC configuration settings. You can find these by navigating to System → Configuration. This is where you will find all of the items that apply to the FMC itself. One change from version 5 is the removal of the System Policy. In v5 you would configure some of the settings in the System Policy and some in the local configuration. In version 6, all of these have been rolled into the System Configuration with a few more added for good measure. When you arrive at this screen, you will find a list of the configuration items running down the left side of the screen. Selecting an item will display the screen to modify these settings.

There is one very important note to remember if you are accustomed to editing these settings in version 5 and prior. Unlike with System Policy in version 5.x or earlier, the settings here go into effect right away.

Instead of several changes being made and then applied, every setting you change is applied to the FMC as soon as you click the Save button. Something else to keep in mind is that navigating between links on the left does not automatically save your work. For some of the settings, you will receive a warning pop-up if you click away without saving, but for some you will find that the information you modified will be silently discarded.

Key tip—use the Save button! Anytime you change a parameter, you must click Save before navigating away from the page.

Information

When you first navigate to the System Configuration page, you will find FMC information. This includes the name, model, serial number, etc. This is shown in Figure 3.7.

Figure 3.7: System Configuration start page

All you can really change here is the FMC name. You can use whatever name you want, and your name can even have spaces, if desired. If you need quick access to other information, like version or serial number, this is a good page to remember.

Access List

This setting configures the local host (iptables) firewall on the FMC. By default, any source IP address is allowed to connect on port 443 or 22 for management (Figure 3.8).

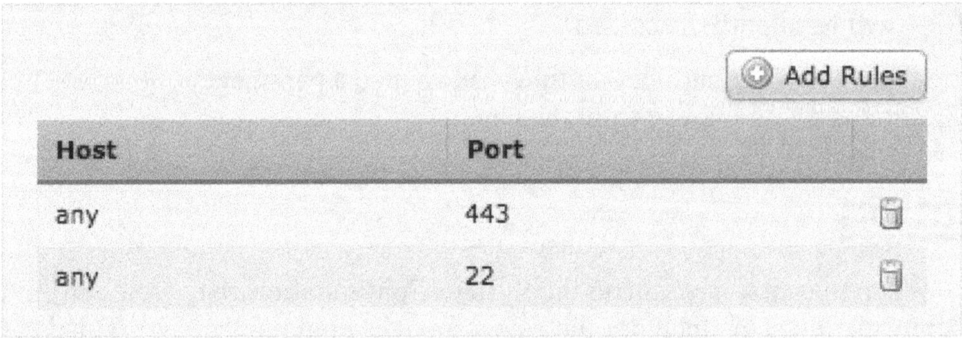

Host	Port	
any	443	🗑
any	22	🗑

Add Rules

Figure 3.8: Default access list

To restrict access, simply click the Add Rules button and enter the IP/CIDR address to you want to allow. Then check one, two, or all of the three ports—SSH, HTTPS, or SNMP. You will do this as many times as needed to add each source IP or CIDR block. In Figure 3.9 below, we are adding the 10.0.0.0/24 network and allowing SSH and HTTPS access.

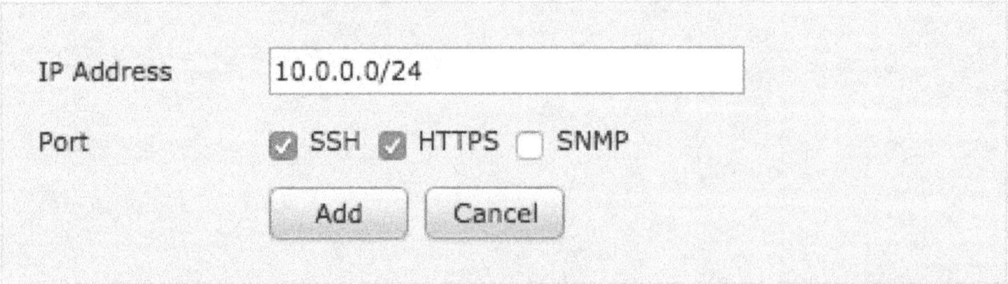

IP Address	10.0.0.0/24
Port	☑ SSH ☑ HTTPS ☐ SNMP
	Add Cancel

Figure 3.9: Adding the access list entry

When you are finished, you will have your allowed IP ranges as well as the "any" rules, as shown in Figure 3.10.

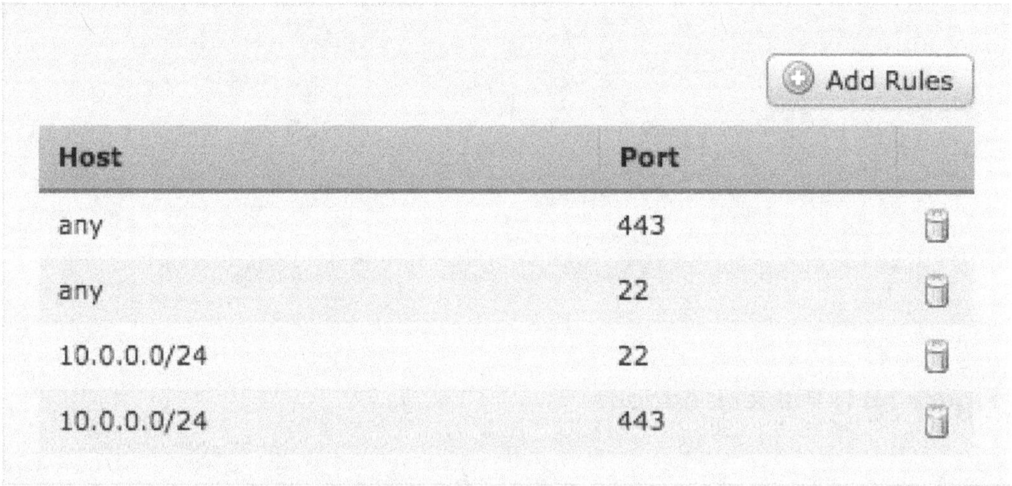

Host	Port	
any	443	🗑
any	22	🗑
10.0.0.0/24	22	🗑
10.0.0.0/24	443	🗑

⊕ Add Rules

Figure 3.10: Modified access list

Now, we haven't actually restricted access yet since the "any" rules are still there. The last step is to delete these rules, which will then restrict access to just the remaining entries (**Note that you can shoot yourself in the proverbial foot here).** If you remove the "any" rules and have not added the IP address you are currently logged in from, you will immediately lose access to the FMC! Once you click the Save button over on the right side of the screen. these iptables entries will go into effect immediately. You have been warned! If you're sure your entries are correct, then click Save and move on to the next setting.

Also, be advised that you MUST put in your NMS station IP address set as SNMP here if you want to send traps from the FMC to the NMS station! Most people miss this setting.

Process

The Process section is not actually a configuration page. It is a way to shut down or restart the FMC or the web services. These would only be used for maintenance or if directed by Cisco TAC. Clicking the green arrow will run the command selected. Note that if you select Shutdown, you will need some way to start the FMC back up! You will have to either use the lights-out functionality or have someone actually press the power button to start the appliance again. The Process screen is shown in Figure 3.11.

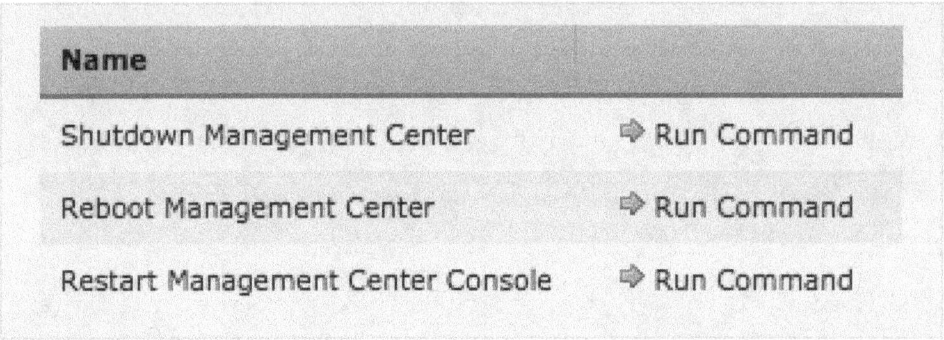

Name	
Shutdown Management Center	➡ Run Command
Reboot Management Center	➡ Run Command
Restart Management Center Console	➡ Run Command

Figure 3.11: Process options

Audit Log Certificate and Audit Log

These two groups of settings are related, so we'll talk about them together. The Audit Log settings allow you to stream the FMC audit log to an external system. The audit log is updated as users log in and use the FMC Web UI to administer the system. User activity of various types is recorded in the audit log, including each page visited, policy changes, and user account activity. All of these entries are saved in the FMC database automatically. This setting allows you to send these to an external system as well.

Send Audit Log to Syslog	Disabled
Host	
Facility	USER
Severity	INFO
Tag (optional)	
Send Audit Log to HTTP Server	Disabled
URL to Post Audit	

Figure 3.12: Audit log settings

You can send your audit entries via syslog (UDP/514) or HTTP (Figure 3.12). If using syslog, you can also add an optional tag, which will accompany each event. You can also log via plain HTTP or HTTP with SSL. The Audit Log Certificate settings are where you would generate a Certificate Signing Request (CSR) to be signed by your certificate authority (Figure 3.13). Once signed, you would return to this page and import the signed client certificate. You can also optionally specify a certificate revocation list (CRL) URL.

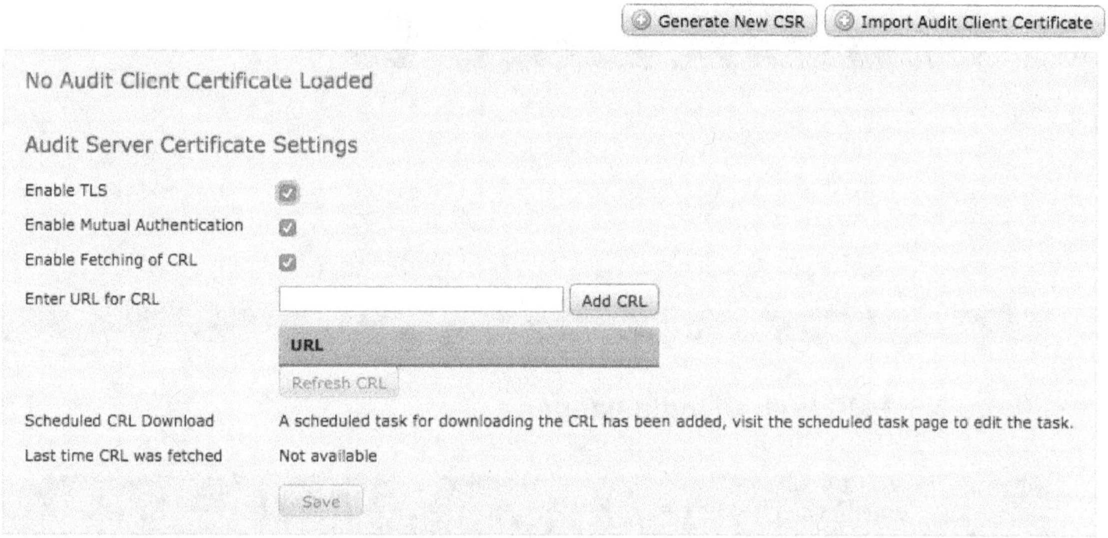

Figure 3.13: Audit Log Certificate settings

Login Banner

The login banner is a simple concept. This is text that will display on the Web UI and the console prior to users logging in. Generally, this is some verbiage provided by your legal department and is standardized across the organization. Figure 3.14 and Figure 3.15 show what the login banner looks like once configured.

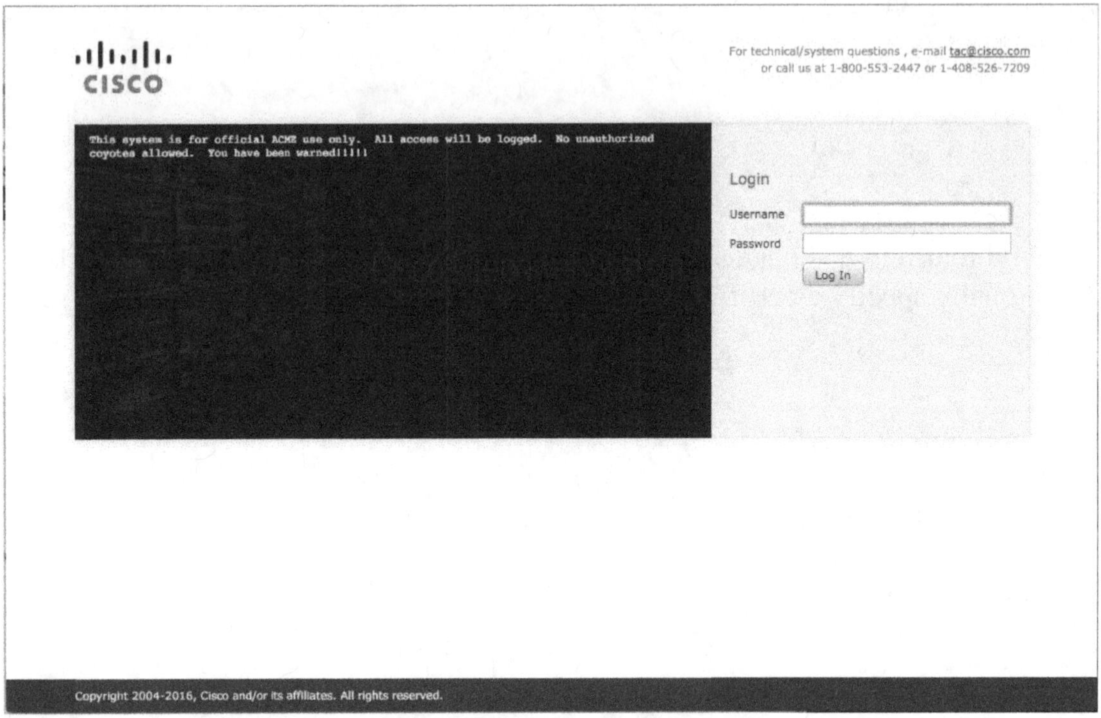

Figure 3.5: FMC Web UI login banner

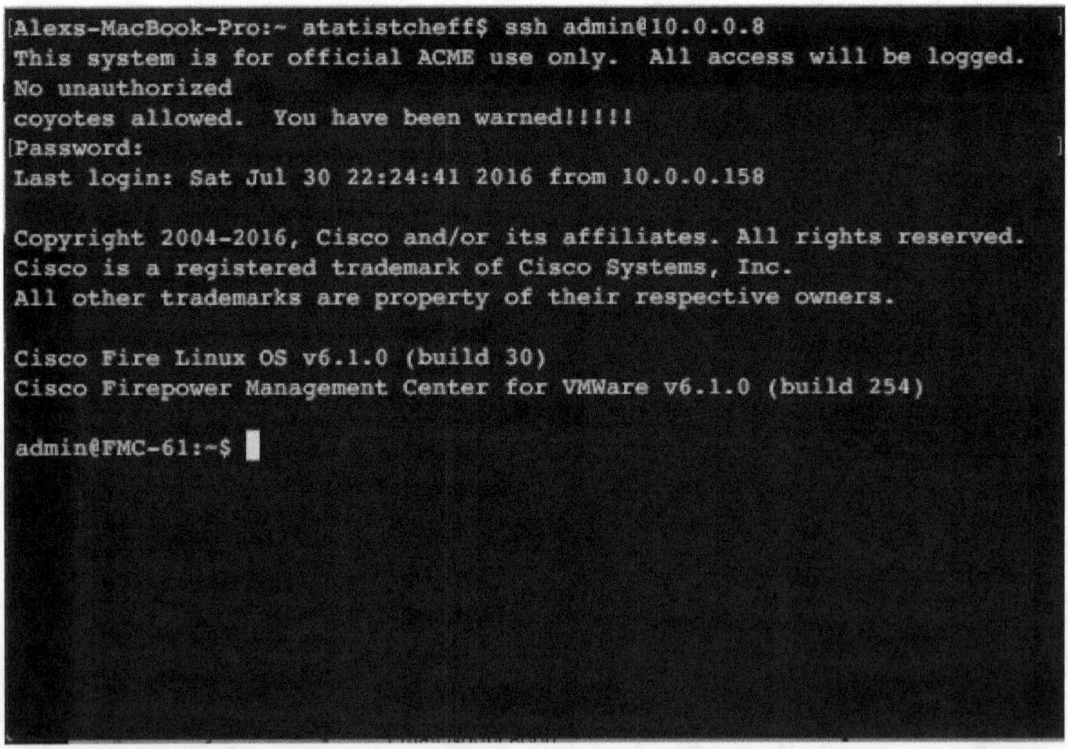

Figure 3.6: SSH login banner

Change Reconciliation

This group of settings allows you to send a daily Change Reconciliation report with any configuration changes to the FMC in the previous 24 hours (Figure 3.16). Note that to use this, you must first configure a mail relay, which we will see in a moment. Once you do so, you can enter the email address you want the report sent to. Once you have sent at least one report, you will also see a Resend Last Report button on this page that allows you to do pretty much what it says—resend the last report.

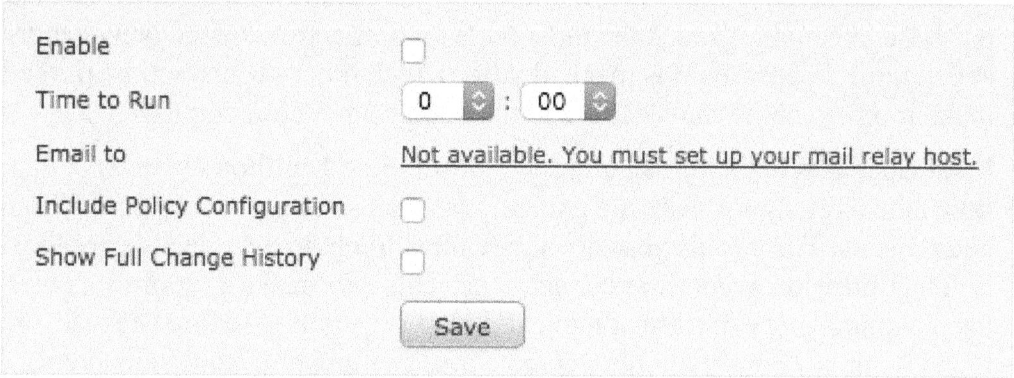

Enable	☐
Time to Run	0 ⬍ : 00 ⬍
Email to	Not available. You must set up your mail relay host.
Include Policy Configuration	☐
Show Full Change History	☐
	Save

Figure 3.7: Change Reconciliation settings

DNS Cache

The DNS Cache setting controls the length of time hostnames will be cached within the UI for the various event types (Figure 3.17). This prevents the FMC from constantly performing DNS lookups every time you load an event view page. Shorten this default if you have a more dynamic environment; otherwise, the default of 300 minutes (5 hours) is generally just fine.

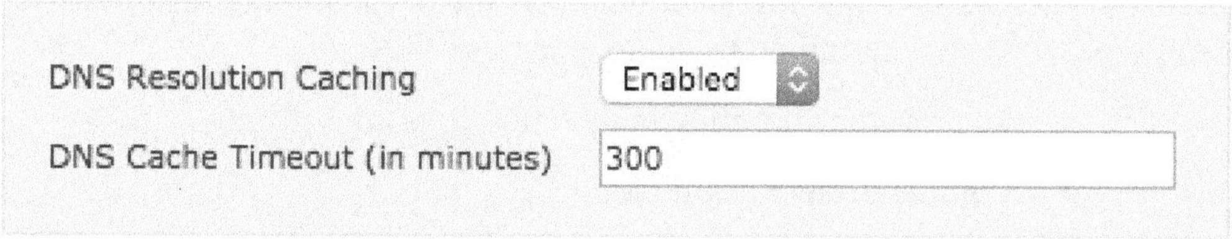

| DNS Resolution Caching | Enabled ⬍ |
| DNS Cache Timeout (in minutes) | 300 |

Figure 3.8: DNS Cache settings

Dashboard

This contains one setting, which honestly is a throwback to a time when some low-powered appliances could not handle displaying all the Dashboard widget types. This defaults to being enabled—you should leave it that way.

Database

The Database page is where you will configure the maximum size of the various databases within the FMC. Each of the databases listed is a "circular" database, meaning it keeps the most recent n number of events. New events will be added until the threshold is reached, after which older events will be purged to make room, keeping the database at the maximum record count.

Most databases default to keeping the most recent 1 million events. A quick look down the page shows there are exceptions, such as connection summaries and audit events. The two databases you are most likely to ever change are those holding intrusion events and connections. This is because a lot of folks want to keep a long history of intrusion events. That is usually possible because, once tuned, your system should not generate a large number of intrusion events. When it comes to connection events, even though a long history may not be needed, the default number may only represent a few hours or even a few minutes on a busy network. Because of this, the default number is often increased.

We can spend a lot of time discussing the factors influencing these settings, but suffice it to say, a larger number means more history. That is, you can look back further in time for events. In the end, the amount of history is related to the event rate and the database capacity.

You will have to experiment with these settings and balance the need for historical event storage with the performance of your FMC. The more events you store, the further back in history you can look but the slower your FMC will perform these searches. There is no "right" answer here; the history available for the various event types will be determined by factors such as these:

- Access control policy connection logging settings
- Volume of network traffic
- IPS policy
- IPS rule tuning
- FMC model
- External logging capability (maybe you can store the events externally rather than on the FMC)

For now, let's look at how the FMC model impacts these settings. Each FMC provides a specified amount of event storage and processing power. A large appliance such as the MC4000 can store and process many times more events than an MC750. How much more you say? Well, fortunately the built-in help system has an answer for that. It shows the various upper limits for the different event types by FMC model. Figure 3.18 shows some of the information from this help topic. Note that for each model, the maximum number of events is shown.

Database Event Limits

The following table lists the minimum and maximum number of records for each event type that you can store on a Firepower Management Center.

Database Event Limits

Event Type	Upper Event Limit	Lower Event Limit
intrusion events	10 million (Management Center Virtual) 20 million (MC750) 30 million (MC1500) 60 million (MC2000) 150 million (MC3500) 300 million (MC4000)	10,000
discovery events	10 million 20 million (MC2000 and MC4000)	zero (disables storage)
connection events Security Intelligence Events	10 million (Management Center Virtual) 50 million (MC750) 100 million (MC1500) 300 million (MC2000) 500 million (MC3500) 1 billion (MC4000) Upper event limit is shared between connection events and Security Intelligence events; the sum of configured maximums for the two events cannot exceed the upper event limit.	zero (disables storage)
connection summaries (aggregated connection events)	10 million (Management Center Virtual) 50 million (MC750) 100 million (MC1500)	zero (disables storage)

Figure 3.9: Sample of FMC database limits

Before you read on there, is a very big caveat here. Just because an MC4000 can store 1 billion (yes, that's a *b*) connection events doesn't mean you should automatically pick that! Although you can store that many events, even a beefy MC4000 will *never* return a query of that many rows. It will timeout before the query finishes. Cisco recommends—as do we—that you use care in increasing the defaults for any of your databases. Don't be greedy; just as with the buffet, take only what you can eat (use). Your FMC will thank you and your admins will not be frustrated with slow query performance.

If you are performing an initial configuration of your FMC, you should probably leave these numbers as is for now. Once you start collecting events, you will have a better idea if you need to come back here and change anything.

External Database Access

This group of settings controls access to the FMC database for a custom reporting tool. Most people will not need this, as the built-in report generator is quite capable. However, if you want to use an external tool such as Crystal Reports or iReport Designer, then read on.

To enable external access, you will enter the hostname or IP of your report server (the host that will be connecting to the FMC to query the database). You also must add the IP address to the access list. You will also need to download the client JDBC driver, which is provided as the file `client.zip`. This archive contains a Java query app and client certificate installation tool. You will install these on your reporting host to provide the ability to query the database.

Rather than us spend multiple pages covering this, your best source of information is the *Firepower System Database Access Guide*, which is available on the Cisco.com site. The FMC configuration page is shown in Figure 3.19.

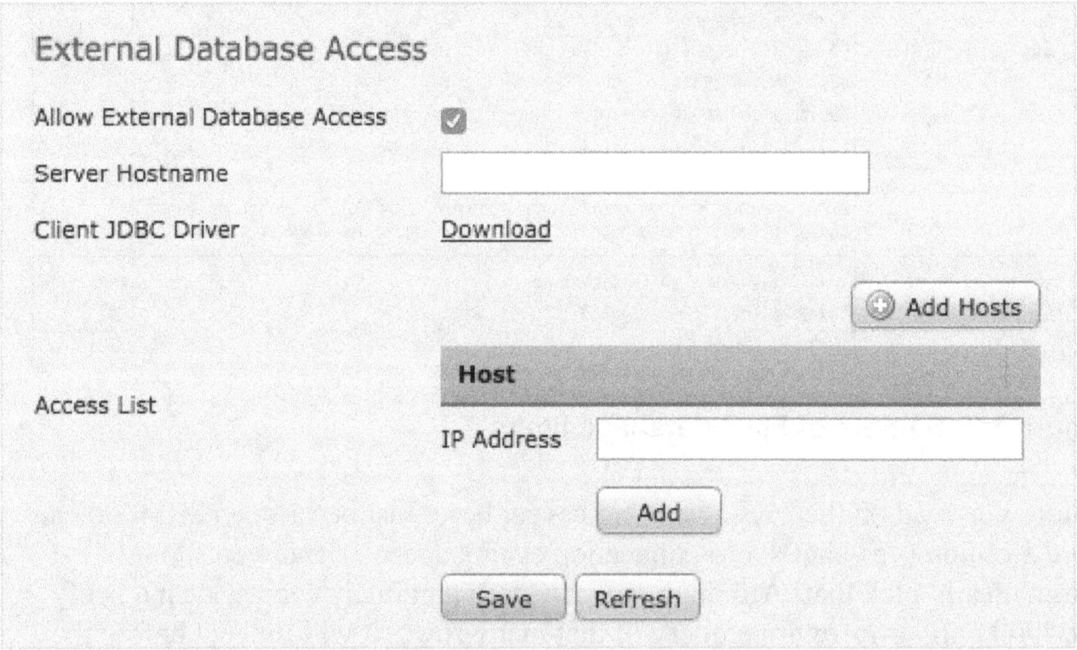

Figure 3.10: External DB Access page

Email Notification

This is another group of fairly simple settings. If you want your FMC to send email notifications (and everyone does), then you have to configure an SMTP mail relay. Once you configure the settings here, you can use the Test Mail Server Settings button to send yourself a test email. The settings page is shown in Figure 3.20.

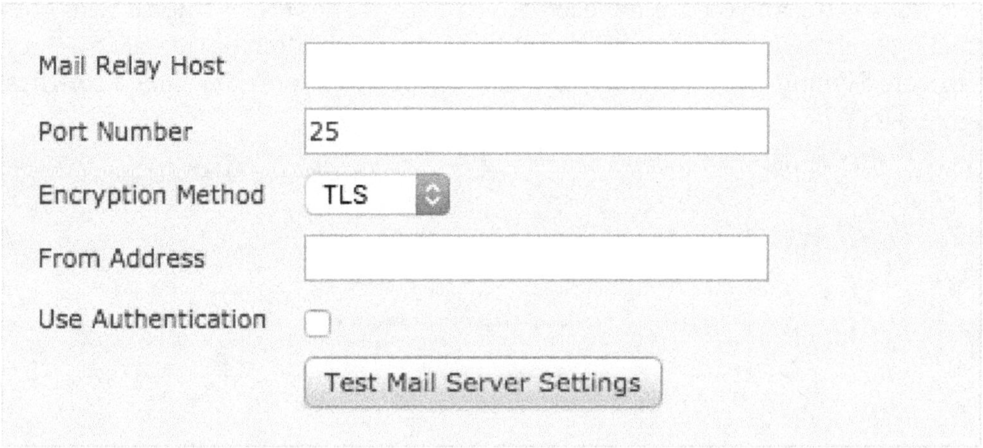

Mail Relay Host	
Port Number	25
Encryption Method	TLS
From Address	
Use Authentication	☐
	Test Mail Server Settings

Figure 3.11: Email Notification settings

If you are just setting up a test FMC and don't have an enterprise email server, you can use gmail, however, you may get an email from google if you don't have a business gmail account. The settings for testing would be smtp.gmail.com, port: 587 or 465, TLS and use your username and password for authentication.

Access Control Preferences

These are simple settings that control rule comments. There are three settings: Disabled, Optional, and Required.

- Disabled (default): When you edit an access control rule, nothing happens upon saving the rule.

- Optional: When you save an access control rule, the comment dialog appears and you can either add a comment or use the Cancel button to decline.

- Required: When you save an access control rule, the comment dialog appears and you must enter a comment.

Comments inserted this way are saved with the rule in the Access Control policy.

There is also a check box for writing changes to the audit log, which is checked by default. This increases the level of detail when an Access Control policy is updated. If you don't need this level of detail, you can uncheck this.

HTTPS Certificate

This is where you can replace the self-signed HTTPS certificate with one signed by your own certificate authority. It includes a button to generate a Certificate Signing Request (CSR) and another one to import the signed certificate (Figure 3.21).

Figure 3.12: HTTPS Certificate settings

Note that the Enable Client Certificates check box is used to require clients (like you) to use a known certificate, which is stored on the server. People have lost access to their FMC by unknowingly checking this box. Don't do it unless you have uploaded your client certificate(s) to the FMC and know what you are doing!

Intrusion Policy Preferences

This group of settings controls comment and logging behavior for Intrusion policies. The Comments on Policy Change setting has three options: Disabled, Optional, and Required. When you edit an Intrusion policy, this setting controls what happens when you commit the changes.

- Disabled: Nothing happens; your policy is committed.

- Optional (default): A comment dialog appears where you can enter comments or click the Cancel button.

- Required: A comment dialog appears and you must enter some text before committing the policy.

Admins sometimes think this is a good idea at first to require comments. Later, they tired of constantly being required to insert comments upon changing the Intrusion policy and reverted to Optional or Disabled. Any comment entered here is inserted into the audit log.

There is also a check box for writing changes to the audit log, which is checked by default. This increases the level of detail and can mean hundreds of audit log entries when an Intrusion policy is updated. If you don't need this level of detail, you can uncheck this.

Language

English, Japanese, Chinese, Korean—not much more to say about that.

Management Interfaces

This is where you will set the network connection details for the management interface(s). Let's start with the items you are most likely to look at first. Since you are connected with the Web UI, we know you already have at least some of the network information configured. Your screen may look similar to the one in Figure 3.22.

Figure 3.13: Management Interfaces settings

This is really all you need for a fully functional FMC in many environments. You may want to enter domains or a tertiary DNS server. However, as long as traffic can reach the FMC and the FMC can communicate with the managed devices and Cisco's Internet-based update servers, you can move on.

Some environments will require configuration of the Proxy settings to allow the FMC to download the various security feeds and updates. Firepower supports unauthenticated or authenticated proxies, as shown in Figure 3.23.

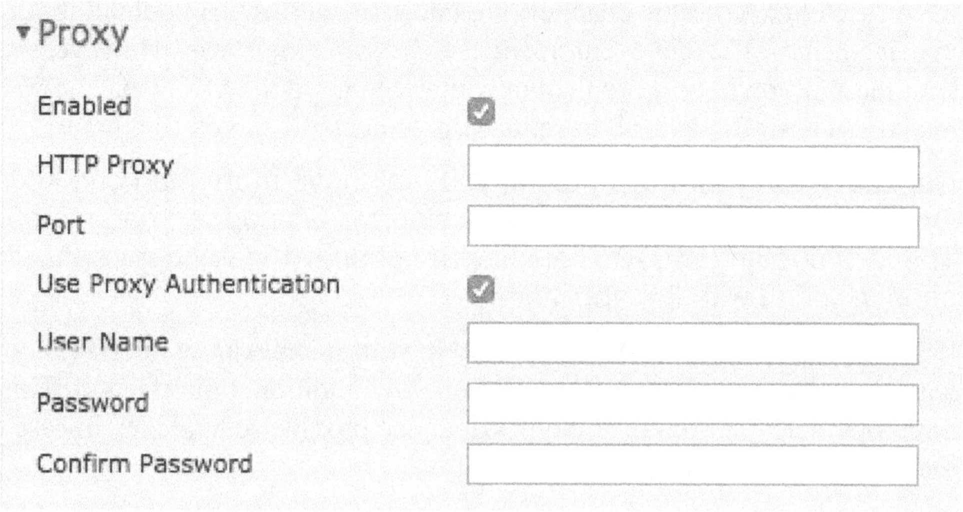

Proxy

Enabled	☑
HTTP Proxy	
Port	
Use Proxy Authentication	☑
User Name	
Password	
Confirm Password	

Figure 3.14: Management Proxy settings

To Split or Not to Split

If your FMC has more than one management interface, you also have the option to use multiple ports and decide what type of traffic to use each one for. Clicking on the pencil icon by one of the interfaces will bring up the dialog in Figure 3.24.

Edit Interface   ? ✕

Enabled:	☑
Channels:	☑ Management Traffic ☑ Event Traffic
Mode:	Autonegotiation ▾
MDI/MDIX:	Auto-MDIX ▾
MTU:	1500
IPv4 Configuration:	Static ▾
IPv4 Management IP:	10.0.0.8
IPv4 Netmask:	255.255.255.0
IPv6 Configuration:	Disabled ▾

OK   Cancel

Figure 3.15: Management Interfaces details

Here you can set some of the properties of the physical interface, but you also have check boxes for the channels the interface will use. By default, both management traffic and event traffic use the same interfaces. However, you can split these if you have more than one interface in your FMC. This allows event and management traffic to each have its own dedicated 1 Gb or 10 Gb port.

Depending on your FMC model, you may have more than one interface available. All FMCs will default to a single 1 Gb copper management port. The MC4000 and MC2000 also have optional 10 Gb fiber ports, which are often included with the appliances.

If you are just interested in redundancy in your management interfaces, you can leave both Channels settings checked on your additional interface(s). This will use both interfaces for both traffic types and also provide redundancy in case one of the network paths goes down.

On a practical note, even on a busy MC4000, a single 1 Gb management interface will not normally represent a bottleneck even at the appliance's maximum event rate (20,000 events/sec). Writing to the disk is still the choke point that limits the rate at which the device can process event data.

Network Analysis Policy Preferences

These settings apply to the Network Analysis policy and are identical to the setting for comments in the Intrusion policy.

Remote Storage Device

Remote storage can be configured to store backups and reports. This is a fairly common configuration and allows backups to be written off-box as soon as they occur. This saves the step of copying the backup files off of the FMC and ensures that you are not storing the backups on the appliance you are backing up. For reports, it allows automatically generated reports to be stored on a remote file share where they can be made accessible to a wider audience without worrying about granting access to the FMC. There are three types of remote storage supported:

- NFS – Network File System

- SSH – Secure Shell (SCP)

- SMB – Server Message Block (Windows) file systems

Note that this is *not* for event storage, it is only for backups and reports. There is (currently) no way to store the FMC event databases anywhere but on the FMC.

Depending on which one you select, you will see the appropriate dialog to collect the connection information. The SMB dialog is shown in Figure 3.25.

Storage Type	SMB ⬍	
Connection		
Host		IP or hostname
Share		
Domain		MSHOME
Username		
Password		
Advanced		
Use Advanced Options	☐	
System Usage		
Use for Backups	☐	
Use for Reports	☐	
Disk Space Threshold	90 %	
	Save Test	

Figure 3.16: Management Interfaces details

The process is fairly simple: you complete the Connection information and use the Test button to test it. When you do, the FMC creates a directory structure on the share where the reports/backups can be stored. Check the appropriate System Usage check boxes and note the Disk Space Threshold setting. It's important to note that the FMC will not store data to the share if the utilization exceeds the percentage shown. This prevents the FMC from filling up your storage.

When this feature is enabled, reports and backups will now automatically be saved to the remote storage location.

REST API Preferences

This is a new feature in version 6.1 allowing a lightweight interface for third-party applications to view and manage configurations using a REST (representational state transfer) client. By default, the FMC rejects REST clients; to enable this feature, check the Enable REST API check box. For more information on using REST, see the *Firepower REST API Quick Start Guide.*

SNMP

An SNMP manager can be used to query the FMC for appliance health status. The FMC uses a fairly standard Linux MIB (Management Information Base) to define what types of information can be queried. Remember, this is simply operating system/hardware data; we're not talking about event data here.

To enable, first select the SNMP version and then enter the appropriate community string or user information.

UCAPL/CC Compliance

These settings apply configurations to the FMC to make it compliant with the US Department of Defense Unified Capabilities Approved Products List (UCACL) or the ISO/IEC Common Criteria (CC). These are new settings for version 6. Changing these will first bring up a warning dialog that they are non-reversible. If you continue, the changes will be made and the FMC rebooted.

Note that you should *not* make these changes unless you are *sure* you need to. Oftentimes these introduce limitations in functionality or performance in the system, which could ruin your whole day!

Shell Timeout

These settings have to do with the browser session and SSH shell timeouts. The defaults are shown in Figure 3.26. If you need to modify these based on your organization's policies, you can do so here.

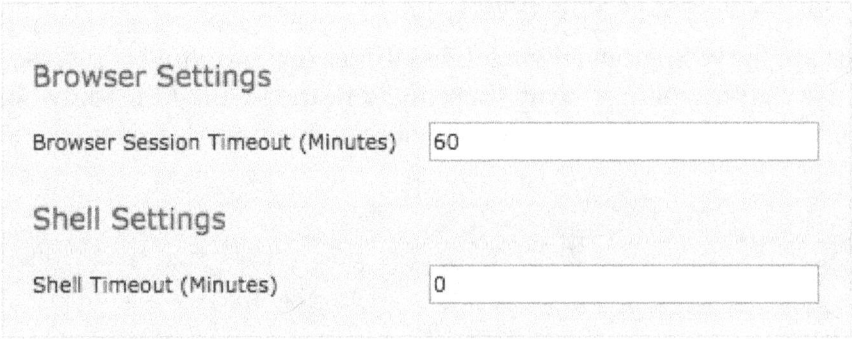

Browser Settings

Browser Session Timeout (Minutes)   60

Shell Settings

Shell Timeout (Minutes)   0

Figure 3.17: Browse/Shell timeouts

Time

The Time settings are not so much configuration items. They control the display of the current time and a history of the last few NTP server connections. Clicking on the Time Synchronization link takes you to our next item, where you can actually configure the time settings (Figure 3.27).

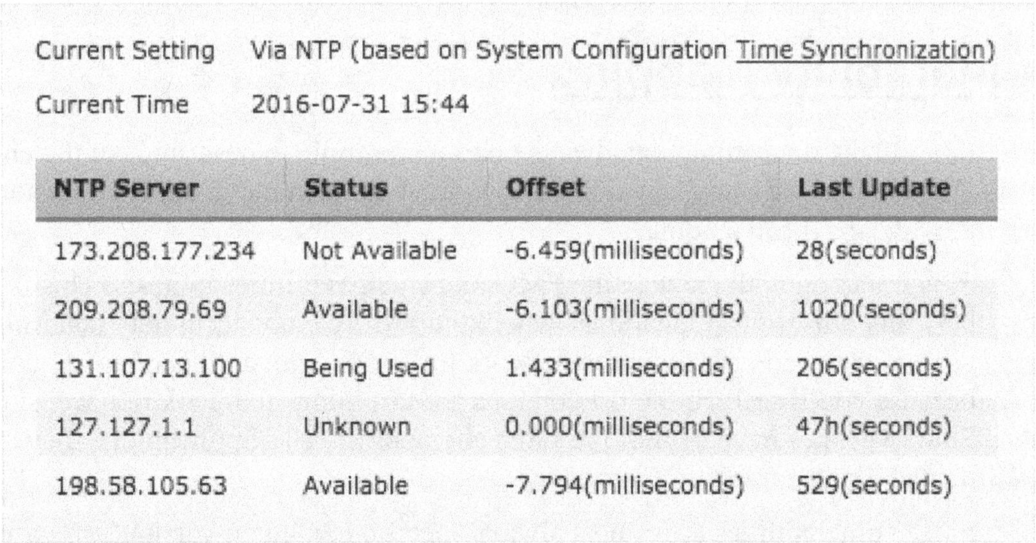

Current Setting   Via NTP (based on System Configuration Time Synchronization)

Current Time   2016-07-31 15:44

NTP Server	Status	Offset	Last Update
173.208.177.234	Not Available	-6.459(milliseconds)	28(seconds)
209.208.79.69	Available	-6.103(milliseconds)	1020(seconds)
131.107.13.100	Being Used	1.433(milliseconds)	206(seconds)
127.127.1.1	Unknown	0.000(milliseconds)	47h(seconds)
198.58.105.63	Available	-7.794(milliseconds)	529(seconds)

Figure 3.18: Time status

Time Synchronization

Time is very important in Firepower. It's important that the FMC and managed devices are in sync with each other. Time synchronization is also important for Smart Licensing to function correctly. Because of this, you should always use an accurate NTP time source.

The options are fairly Spartan (Figure 3.28). Enter one or more NTP servers the FMC will use as time sources. Any "serving" of time by the FMC only occurs over the management connection to the devices and is tunneled over port 8305/tcp.

Figure 3.19: Time Settings

VMware Tools

This is a simple check box to enable/disable VMware Tools. If you install the virtual FMC on VMware, it will automatically enable this. If you use the virtual FMC, you should probably leave it enabled.

Vulnerability Mapping

This is a setting that always takes a long time to describe, but the end is always the same—leave it alone. If you trust us, then move on. If you want the gory details, keep reading.

This has to do with the way the FMC maps vulnerabilities to hosts. This is basically a list of "applications" where the FMC cannot accurately determine the vendor or version based on the network traffic. We put applications in quotes because you'll see that the list contains a lot of things that look like websites. Since websites have a lot of the same characteristics as applications, they are often treated like them within Firepower.

Since vulnerabilities are almost always specific to a given version/vendor of an application, just because Firepower detects a given application doesn't mean it's the vulnerable one. We always use DNS—the Domain Name System—as our example. Firepower can detect the DNS protocol on a server and deduce that the server is offering DNS services; however, DNS is a pretty lightweight protocol, so there is nothing in the DNS traffic that indicates who the vendor is. Is this a BIND server? Is it Microsoft? In addition, there's no way to tell which version of the vendor's application we're seeing: BINDv7, BINDv9, etc.

You can be sure that the vulnerabilities in Microsoft's DNS services are different than the ones in BIND. Again, between BIND versions these vulnerabilities will be different. So if we're going to map vulnerabilities to a DNS server, we really need to know which vendor and version of DNS it's running. But, since we can't learn that from the network traffic, we have two options:

1. Map all the possible DNS vulnerabilities to any host offering DNS services.

2. Don't map any DNS vulnerabilities to DNS servers

The default behavior for all applications in this list is #1 above. Mapping all of those extra vulnerabilities will probably just cause more false positive, high-impact intrusion events to be generated. Rather than do that, Cisco has opted not to map these vulnerabilities.

To be clear, this has nothing to do with the number if intrusion events generated. If the particular DNS rules are enabled, you will still get intrusion events for a BINDv7 attack on a Microsoft DNS server. However, instead of that being a red (high) impact event, it will have a lower impact assigned.

If your brain hurts now, just take our word for it and leave these all disabled. You'll sleep better and you won't be chasing down as many high-impact false positive events.

Chapter 4: Device Management

In this chapter, we will cover getting your managed devices (which can be an ASA, ISRG2 or Meraki Firewall with Firepower, or even a 4100 in native FTD!) connected to the FMC and getting them set up. For the FTD devices and 7000/8000 appliances, this involves configuring the interfaces, routing, NAT, etc.

We are going to assume that you already have a network design and are armed with the details you will need. This includes whether your interfaces will be passive, inline, transparent, switched, or routed, also whether you will need to configure NAT translation or DHCP services.

This chapter will help you understand how to configure your devices, and again we will cover some best practices from the real world!

Device Settings

So far you have registered your device with the FMC. The next step is to configure it to work with your network. We will start with the basic device settings. Navigate to Devices → Device Management. Then select the device to configure by clicking the pencil icon to the right.

The next screen will have different tabs depending on whether this is a Firepower device, an ASA with FirePOWER Services, or running Firepower Threat Defense (FTD). Whatever the device, you will start at the Interfaces tab, as shown in Figure 4.1.

Figure 4.1: Device interfaces page

From here, click on the Device tab to view the device properties. You will see a page similar to the one in Figure 4.2.

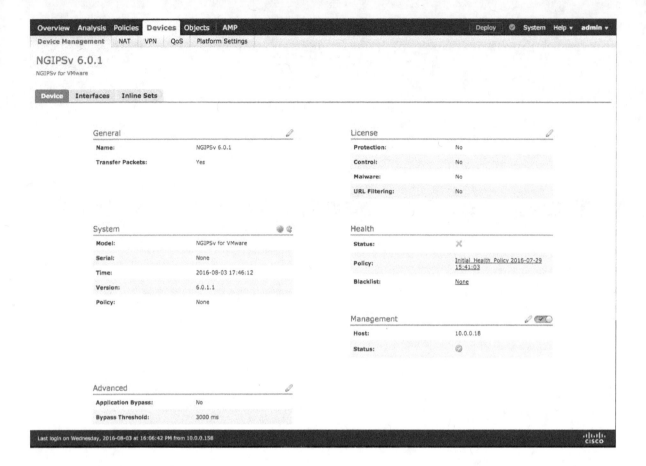

Figure 4.2: Device tab

The example in the figure is from a Firepower NGIPSv virtual device. Let's run through the sections of this screen and discuss their functions.

The General Section

In the upper left is the General section. It contains several items:

- Name: This is the "friendly" name you want to call this device within the FMC. You don't have to use a hostname, and you can even use spaces here. Generally, administrators will use the hostname to identify devices here, but use whatever makes the most sense.

- Transfer Packets: This setting controls whether or not the device will send packet data to the FMC for intrusion events. By default, this is enabled, meaning that when an Intrusion Prevention System (IPS) Snort rule matches a packet, that packet will be sent to the FMC and stored in the database. This helps tremendously when you are analyzing an event and trying to determine if it was false or true. If you uncheck this box, packet data will not be sent. This may be necessary because of the sensitive nature of the network traffic seen by a certain device. However, keep in mind that this makes analysis much more difficult.

- Mode (FTD Firepower Threat Defense only): This is a read-only display of the current mode of the FTD device—routed or transparent.

- Force Deploy: This little gem is hidden until you actually click the pencil to edit this section. Force Deploy will force all policies to be applied to the device whether they are out-of-date or not. It's unlikely you will ever need to do this, probably only on the advice of Cisco Technical Assistance Center (TAC).

The General section is shown in Figure 4.3.

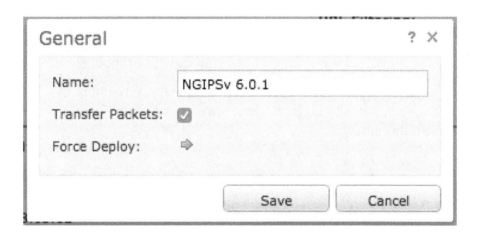

Figure 4.3: Editing the device general properties

License

The License section is where you will assign various feature licenses to your device (Figure 4.4). Regardless of how the device feature is licensed (Smart or Classic) the procedure to assign a license is the same. Clicking the edit pencil will display the license dialog. Then check the appropriate box.

License

Capabilities
Protection: ☑

Control: ☑

Malware: ☐

URL Filtering: ☐

Save   Cancel

Figure 4.4: License properties

System

The System section shows information about the device (Figure 4.5). There isn't anything to edit here. However, you can shut down or reboot the device by using the ⬤ and ↻ symbols, respectively. As always, remember that if you shut down the device, you should have some way to start it up again. It might be a long hike to the data center!

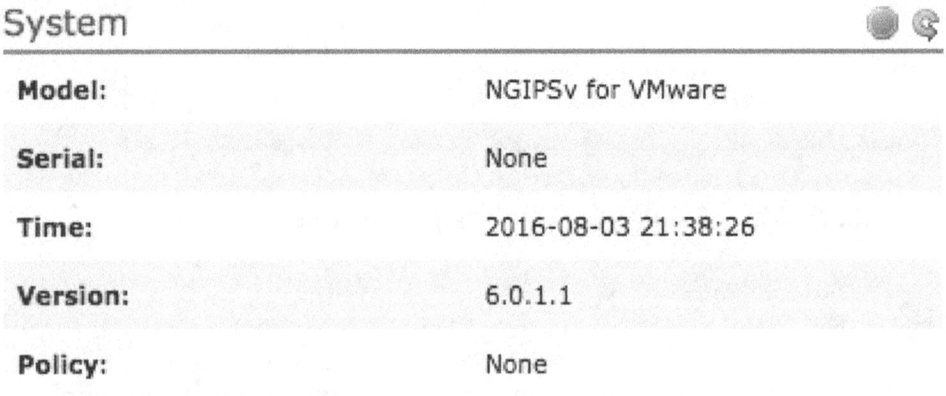

System

Model:	NGIPSv for VMware
Serial:	None
Time:	2016-08-03 21:38:26
Version:	6.0.1.1
Policy:	None

Figure 4.5: System properties

Health and Management

Like the System section, the Health section has no settings per se. Here you can see the current health status, the health policy applied, and whether the device has a health blacklist enabled. In our example in Figure 4.6, the device health status is red because we do not have any traffic on the detection interfaces yet.

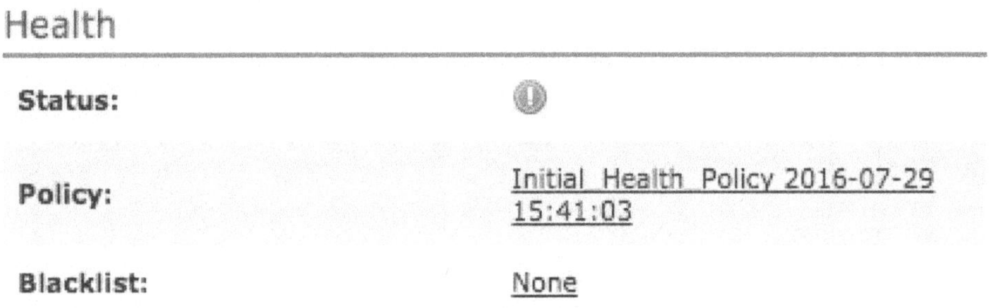

Health

Status:	ⓘ
Policy:	Initial_Health_Policy 2016-07-29 15:41:03
Blacklist:	None

Figure 4.6: Health properties

In the Management section, we see the IP address of the device and the management status, which should always be a green check mark, showing that the device is registered to the FMC (Figure 4.7). You can disable communications with the FMC here by clicking the switch icon. Also, if you find that you need to change the IP address of the device, you can change that by clicking the pencil icon. Note that this just changes the FMC's information. You still need to go to the device itself and change to the new management IP address.

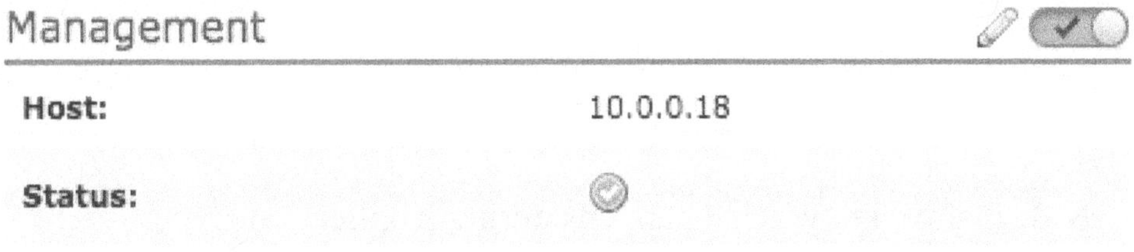

Management

Host:	10.0.0.18
Status:	⊘

Figure 4.7: Management properties

Advanced

The Advanced section contains the settings for Application Bypass (Figure 4.8). You will notice that FTD devices do not have an advanced setting, as they do not use Application Bypass.

Application Bypass is a feature designed to prevent the device from impacting latency-sensitive applications. Normally, the packet latency introduced by the inspection process is on the order of just a few milliseconds or even microseconds.

However, in some cases due to high traffic load or poor performing rules, this latency number can climb. Application Bypass is like a safety valve that will kick in if latency grows so high that it may cause applications to fail.

The default setting is disabled with a 3,000 millisecond bypass threshold. Three seconds is a long time for a packet to pass through a device!

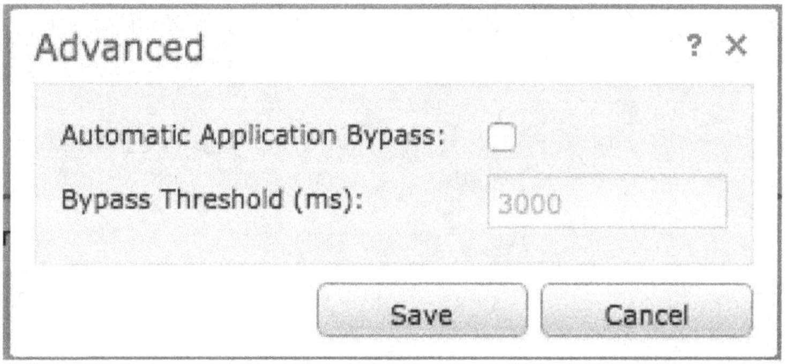

Figure 4.8: Automatic Application Bypass settings

If this setting is enabled, the effect of exceeding this threshold is that the Snort processes on the device will be shut down and the traffic will go into software bypass. This means no Snort inspection at all. Of course, it also takes care of the latency problem!

When this occurs, a health event is generated and a core memory dump is written to disk. The reason for this is so the dump can be analyzed by Cisco TAC to determine what caused the latency to spike. The Snort processes will automatically restart within 10 minutes once the process monitor detects that they are not running.

Now that we know what happens during Application Bypass, here are some considerations for its use.

- If you decide to enable this setting, pick a latency number based on the applications on your network. The default of 3,000 milliseconds (ms) is a good round number but you may want to set it higher or lower depending on your needs.

- Configure a health monitor alert to send you an email, syslog, or SNMP message in case the system goes into bypass. Otherwise, if you don't happen to be monitoring the health at the time, this condition could go unnoticed.

- Remember the core dump? This represents several gigabytes of disk storage used each time this kicks in. These will build up over time, and if you aren't monitoring this health alert, you may end up filling up your device's disk.

Interfaces

The Interfaces tab is going to be a bit different depending on the type of device you are managing. We will cover several of the device types in the following sections.

Security Zones

Before we dive into the various device types, there is one common concept we should discuss—security zones. During your configuration, each port on a device should be assigned to a security zone. Configuring a security zone is actually optional, but as a best practice you should assign one to each port for more flexibility in your policies.

The security zone is just a name for a physical (or logical) port on the device. Each port does not have to have a unique zone name; you can assign the same zone name to multiple ports. You can even use the same zone name across multiple devices. For example, say you have several devices located at the network edge in different locations. You could use a zone naming convention such as "Outside" for all inline interfaces that connect to the external firewall. For the other interface in these inline sets, you use the zone name "Inside." If you do this consistently across your environment, what advantage is there?

First of all, in your Access Control policy, one of the criteria you can use for a rule is the security zone. You can configure a source and destination zone for each rule. By doing this you could have a rule in your policy that specifies a certain type of inspection for all traffic where (for example) the source is Outside and the destination is Inside. Now, if you apply that policy across all your devices, any device containing these zones will process the traffic according to this rule. No need for IP addresses or other criteria; if the traffic comes from Outside, we know it came from the firewall, and if it was initiated from Inside, we know it came from our network.

Another place where zones come in handy is in event analysis. Any event detected—like connection, intrusion, security intelligence, file, malware, etc.—will each have the ingress and egress zones noted in the event. This gives the analyst a quick way to characterize the traffic and understand right away if they are dealing with an inbound or outbound connection.

One caveat you should keep in mind: To use common zones across multiple devices/interfaces, the interface must be the same type (passive, inline, switched, routed, ASA). A zone cannot contain different interface types. Version 6.1 also introduces a new concept called interface groups. This adds another layer of flexibility because you can now group security zones with different names together and use the group name in your Access Control rules. For example, if you create security zones like Outside-NY and Outside-Denver, you can create an interface group named Outside and add each of these zones to the group. Then your Access Control rule can specify the Outside interface group as the source or destination zone. Note that all security zones added to an interface group must still be the same type.

We will discuss security zones and interface groups a bit more in the Objects chapter.

Firepower 7000/8000 Device

For 7000/8000 hardware, your Interfaces tab is going to show a graphical representation of the front of the device with each of the available hardware ports listed below. Figure 4.9 shows a Firepower 7030 device with 8x1Gb copper ports.

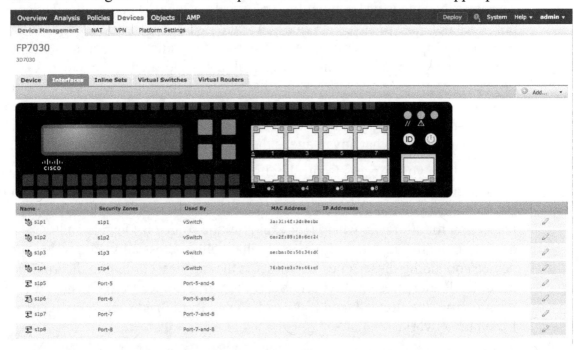

Figure 4.9: 7030 device Interfaces tab

The graphic showing the device even includes the various LEDs that are visible on the actual device. Are these showing the actual color status?

To configure one of the interfaces, just click the pencil on the right. If the interface is not configured, you will see the dialog in Figure 4.10.

Figure 4.10: 7000/8000 interface dialog

This device type offers several ways to configure an interface:

- Passive: This port will be connected to a tap or span interface. Traffic will pass into the device but not out.

- Inline: This port is part of an inline set. You must configure at least two ports this way so traffic can pass from one to another through the device.

- Switched: The port is part of a virtual switch.

- Routed: The port is part of a virtual router.

- HA Link: The port is used as the HA link for two devices in an HA pair.

If you select Passive, the configuration is fairly simple (Figure 4.11). Just select the security zone and adjust the port properties if needed.

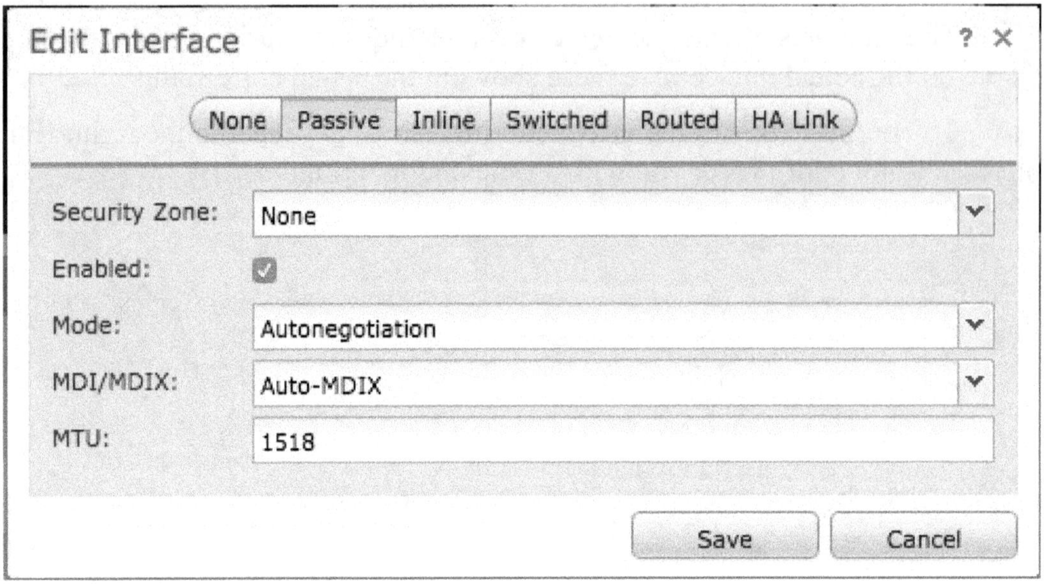

Figure 4.11: 7000/8000 Passive dialog

For an inline set, is "inline set" correct terminology? in addition to the security zone, you must also either select an existing inline set or create a new one (Figure 4.12).

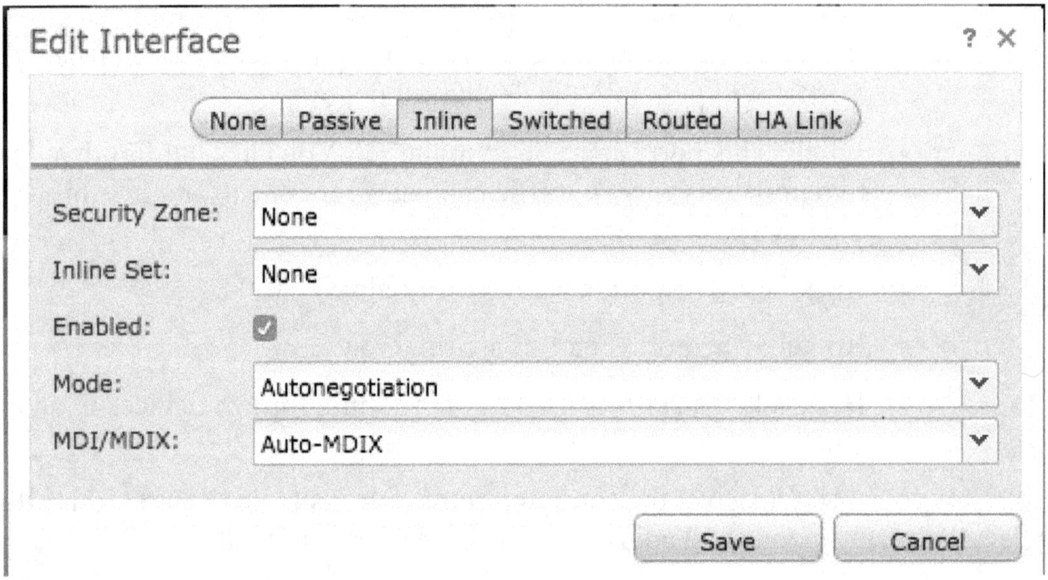

Figure 4.12: 7000/8000 Inline dialog

For a switched interface, you select the security zone and the virtual switch this interface will be a member of. You can create a new virtual switch from this dialog as well (Figure 4.13).

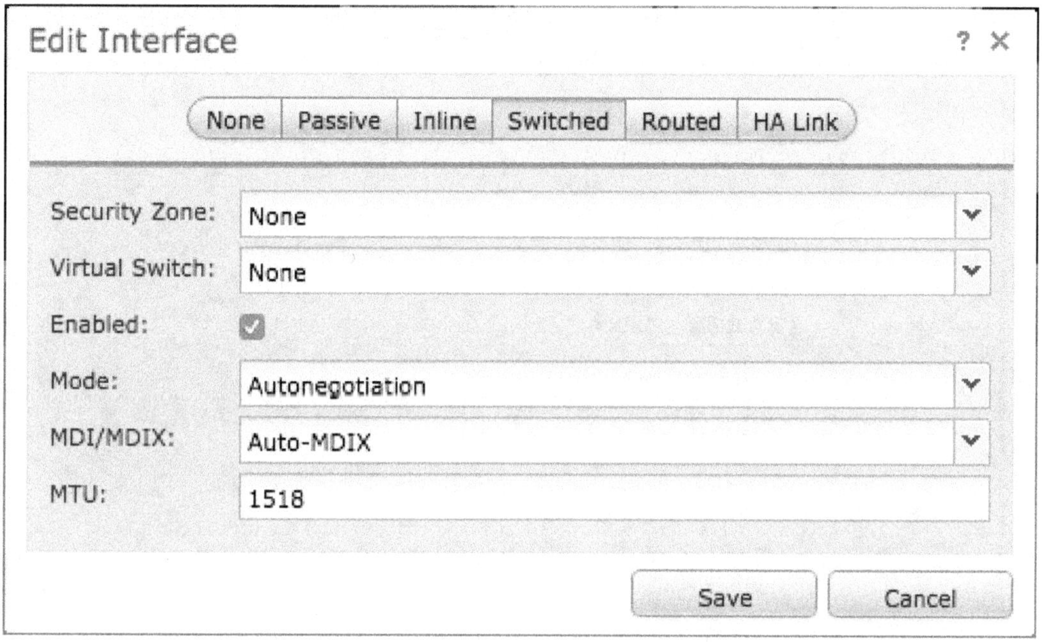

Figure 4.13: 7000/8000 Switched dialog

To configure an interface as routed, you will need the security zone, virtual router (select existing or create a new one), and interface IP address(es). You can also decide whether to allow ICMP responses and add static ARP entries here (Figure 4.14).

Figure 4.14: 7000/8000 Routed dialog

For HA Link, there is no configuration apart from the physical interface settings (Figure 4.15).

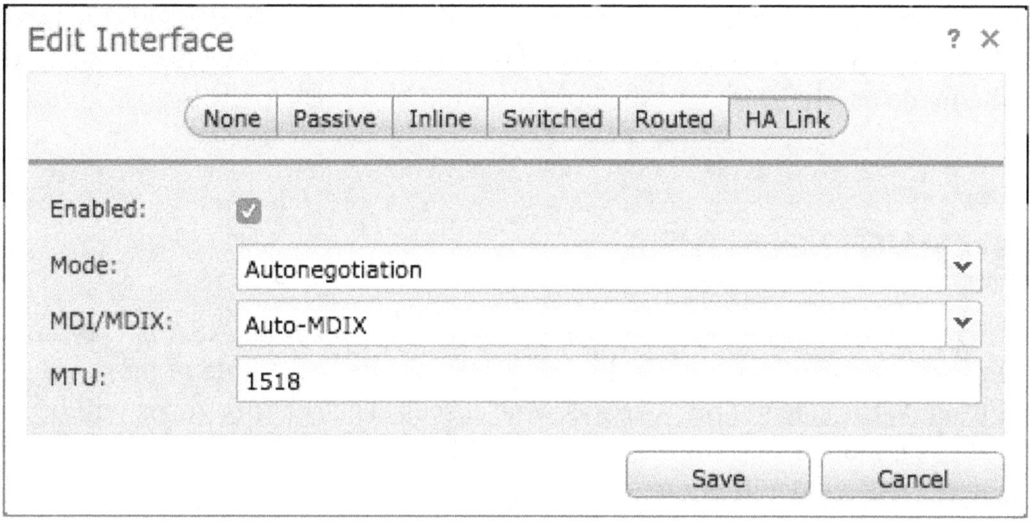

Figure 4.15: 7000/8000 HA Link dialog

Virtual Firepower Device

If you have a virtual Firepower device, you will not see all the interface types. Virtual devices only support passive and inline interface types. The settings for these are the same as for the Firepower devices just discussed. When you click on an interface, you will see the "reduced fat" version of the interface dialog, shown in Figure 4.16.

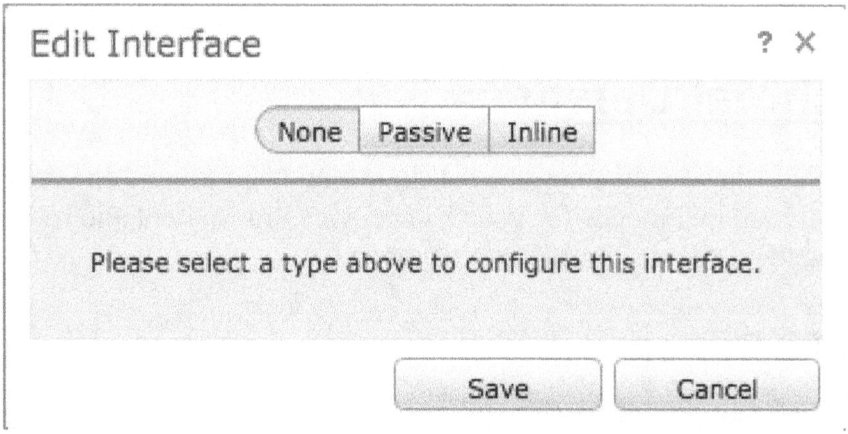

Figure 4.16: Virtual Firepower interface dialog

As we mentioned, the settings are similar to those for the physical Firepower interfaces with the exception that you do not have the option to change the mode or MDI/MDX of the port since the VM host controls this.

FirePOWER on ASA

The interface configuration for the FirePOWER on ASA is very minimal. In fact, the interfaces are wholly configured on the ASA side of the device. The FirePOWER side simply displays what it sees. The security zones will be assigned based on the ASA configuration and will be of type ASA. An example of an ASA interface is shown in Figure 4.17.

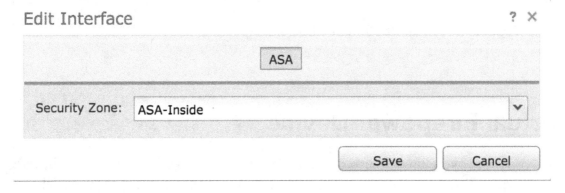

Figure 4.17: ASA interface

Firepower Threat Defense

For an FTD device, the interface configuration is quite a bit different. Remember, there are two modes for your FTD device, transparent and routed. We will start with an FTD device in transparent mode.

Transparent FTD Device

When you start at your Interfaces tab, you will see that all the physical interfaces on the ASA are listed. Figure 4.18 shows a virtual FTD device, which supports three detection interfaces by default.

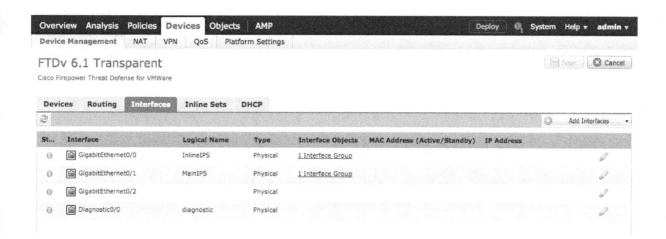

Figure 4.18: Virtual FTD interfaces

Clicking on one of the unconfigured interfaces displays the dialog shown in Figure 4.19.

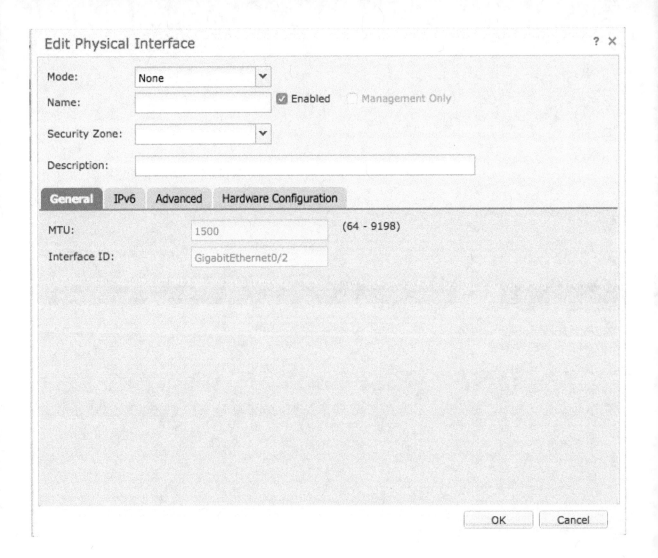

Figure 4.19: Virtual FTD interface dialog

The options are as follows:

- **Mode**: you can select from Passive, None, or ERSPAN* (routed only). Curiously, you select None if you want this port to be part of an inline set. Select passive if this port will be connected to a tap or switch span port.

- **Name:** The logical name of the interface.

- **Security Zone:** Select a zone or create a new one here.

- **Description:** Optional description of the interface.

- **General tab:** The MTU and interface ID; these are read-only on a virtual device.
- **IPv6 tab:** Complete these if applicable to your environment.
- **Advanced tab:** Here you can configure MAC addresses if this port will be part of an active/standby pair.
- **Hardware Configuration tab:** This allows you to configure the speed and duplex of the port.

What will you actually configure for these ports? Probably just the mode, name, and security zone. Since this is a transparent FTD device, your choice is really whether this device will be passive or inline.

* What is ERSPAN? It stands for encapsulated remote switched port analyzer. Basically it allows you to send monitor traffic from switch ports through a GRE tunnel to a remote analyzer (FTD). Pretty cool! You connect your FTD sensing interface to an ERSPAN-capable switch and then you can forward traffic from other switches to it. If your FTD device is in routed mode, you will see this as one of the interface types.

Routed FTD Device

For an FTD device in routed mode, there are a few more options when setting up the interfaces. Strangely enough, they all have to do with assigning IP addresses. In the interest of not repeating everything in the preceding section, we will just discuss the additional options here.

IPv4 tab: On this tab, you will configure the type and IP address for the interface. If you pick Use Static IP, it is a pretty simple matter of entering the IP address with the subnet bits in CIDR notation.

If you are using DHCP or PPPoE, then there are a load of additional options to fill in. We're going to assume if you are using these other methods to assign an IP address, you already know what these items should be. You don't need us to tell you to put the VPDN group name in the field named "VPDN Group Name."

IPv6 tab: If you're using IPv6, you have no shortage of configuration options on this tab and it's sub-tabs. We could spend a lot of pages talking about IPv6, but again, the field names are self-explanatory and if you are using IPv6 in your environment, you should know what options you need to set here.

Routing

Both the Firepower 7000/8000 and FTD devices can perform routing functions. In fact, the only device that cannot be used as a router is the virtual

Firepower IPS, also known as NGIPSv. Since FTD is the future of the Adaptive Security Appliance (ASA), the routing features there are more robust and will continue to be fleshed out to eventually achieve parity with the legacy ASA operating system.

The routing feature set on Firepower devices is almost identical to what we saw when version 5.0 first shipped. They support static routes and the RIP and OSPF dynamic routing protocols. They do not support BGP. Honestly, these devices were designed first and foremost as a Next Generation IPS (NGIPS), and while they can and are configured with routed interfaces, these installations are definitely not as common.

We're going to discuss the routing features available here but don't expect this to be the authoritative guide on how to configure routing. Our assumption is that if you need to set up your devices as routed, this isn't your first rodeo. Of course, if you need training on how to configure a router, Todd Lammle has a few books found at www.lammle.com/ccna

Firepower 7000/8000 Routing

To configure routed interfaces, first you configure one or more interfaces as routed, as we described in the section above. When you do this, you will assign the interface(s) an IP address. Then you will need one or more virtual routers. You will find the virtual router (VR) configuration on the aptly named Virtual Routers tab. When you edit an existing virtual router or create a new one, you will see the dialog in Figure 4.20.

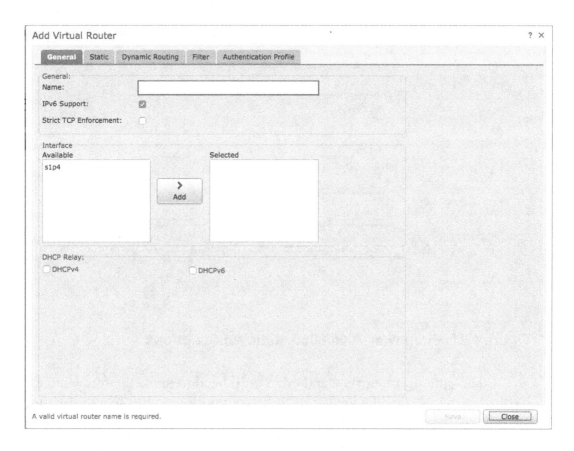

Figure 4.20: Firepower 7000/8000 virtual router dialog

Your virtual router will need a name. Then, in the Interface box, you will see a list of all the routed interfaces that are not already part of another VR. Use the Add button to add them to this VR.

Next you will configure the routing options. Most of the time these devices are deployed in routed mode they are configured with static routes. Generally speaking, VRs we've seen typically have just two interfaces, so the device is really used like an inline IPS with IP addresses on the interfaces. If that is the case, then you can use the Static tab to add the necessary routes with their associated information. This dialog is shown in Figure 4.21.

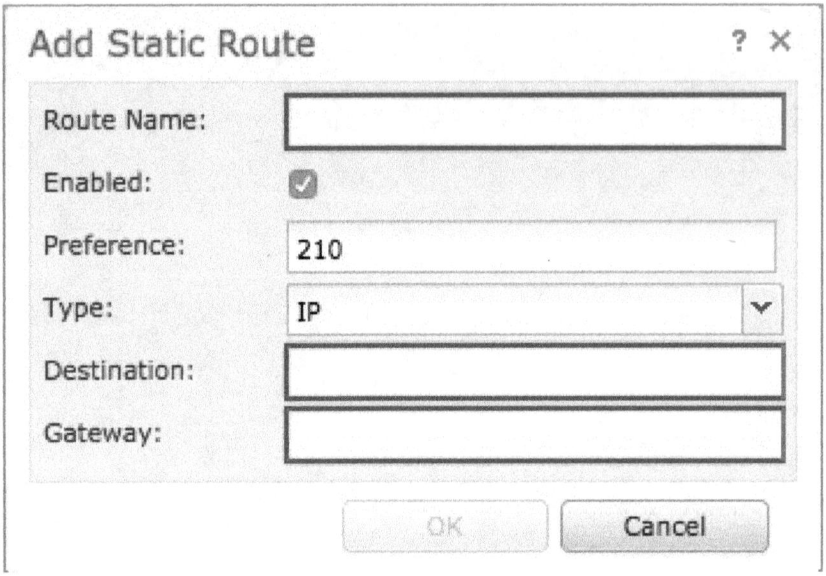

Figure 4.21: Firepower 7000/8000 static route options

The options are fairly standard. You'll need to name the route and enter the destination network and gateway. If there are multiple routes to a destination, the system will select the route with the highest preference lowest administrative distance = highest preference right? That can be confusing . If all you have are static routes, then you are finished; the other tabs will not apply.

If you do need to configure one of the dynamic protocols, then proceed to the Dynamic Routing tab. Here you will select one of the supported protocols, RIP or OSPF, by clicking the appropriate button. Clicking RIP or OSPF will change the dialog to collect the various options available for each protocol. Note that if you need to share routes and authenticate with other routers, you'll also need to configure an authentication profile using the tab with the same name.

After this you may want to move to the Filter tab. Here you set up filters for sharing routes with other routers.

That's it for VR configuration on a Firepower 7000/8000 device. You will find a more detailed description of the various options using the online help. In case you don't know, the online help with Firepower is quite good. Clicking either the Help item in the main menu or the question mark (**?**) icon in the upper right of many of the dialogs will take you to a context-sensitive help topic. If that doesn't show you what you need, there's also the Search field in the upper right of each help page. For example, the help page in Figure 4.22 appears when you click either of the two options mentioned above while configuring a virtual router.

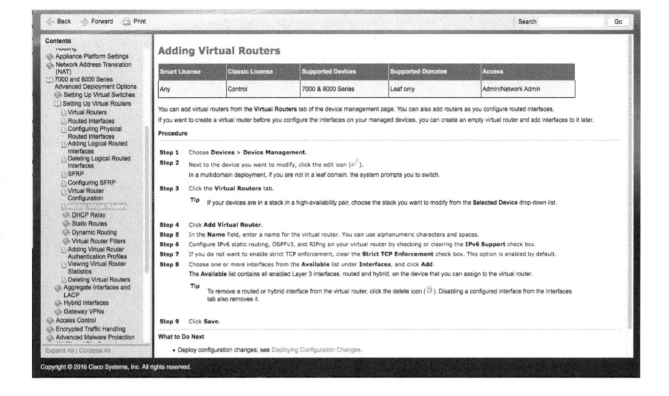

Figure 4.22: Virtual router help screen

The navigation tree on the left also gives you quick access to any help topic available in the area of the product you are currently viewing.

FTD Routing

The routing options for FTD are quite a bit more robust than those on the Firepower 7000/8000 devices. This speaks of the lineage of an FTD device, which leverages a combination of features from both the Firepower and ASA code base. Also, as we mentioned earlier, FTD is the future for Cisco's enterprise network security NGFW/NGIPS portfolio. As such, you can expect to see a significant level of development effort go into the FTD line.

You can find this configuration on the Routing tab under Device Management. Here you will see there are more options available for dynamic routing protocols. You'll see OSPF, OSPFv3, and RIP as well as BGP for both IPv4 and IPv6 and the venerable Static Route option. Note that to have all of these options, your FTD device must be set up in routed mode. In transparent mode, you can still configure static routes but dynamic routing is not available. These static routes are used for traffic originating from the FTD device.

As we mentioned previously, we could spend a significant number of pages explaining these various options, but the online help is your best friend here. Just keep in mind that the settings you saw in the section on Firepower device routing may not apply here. One example is the static route configuration dialog in Figure 4.23. Notice here instead of a Preference setting, each route entry has a Metric setting. The metric in this case is the number of router hops to the network on which a specific host resides. Here, the lower-cost route will be used, which is the opposite of what Firepower does with the Preference field.

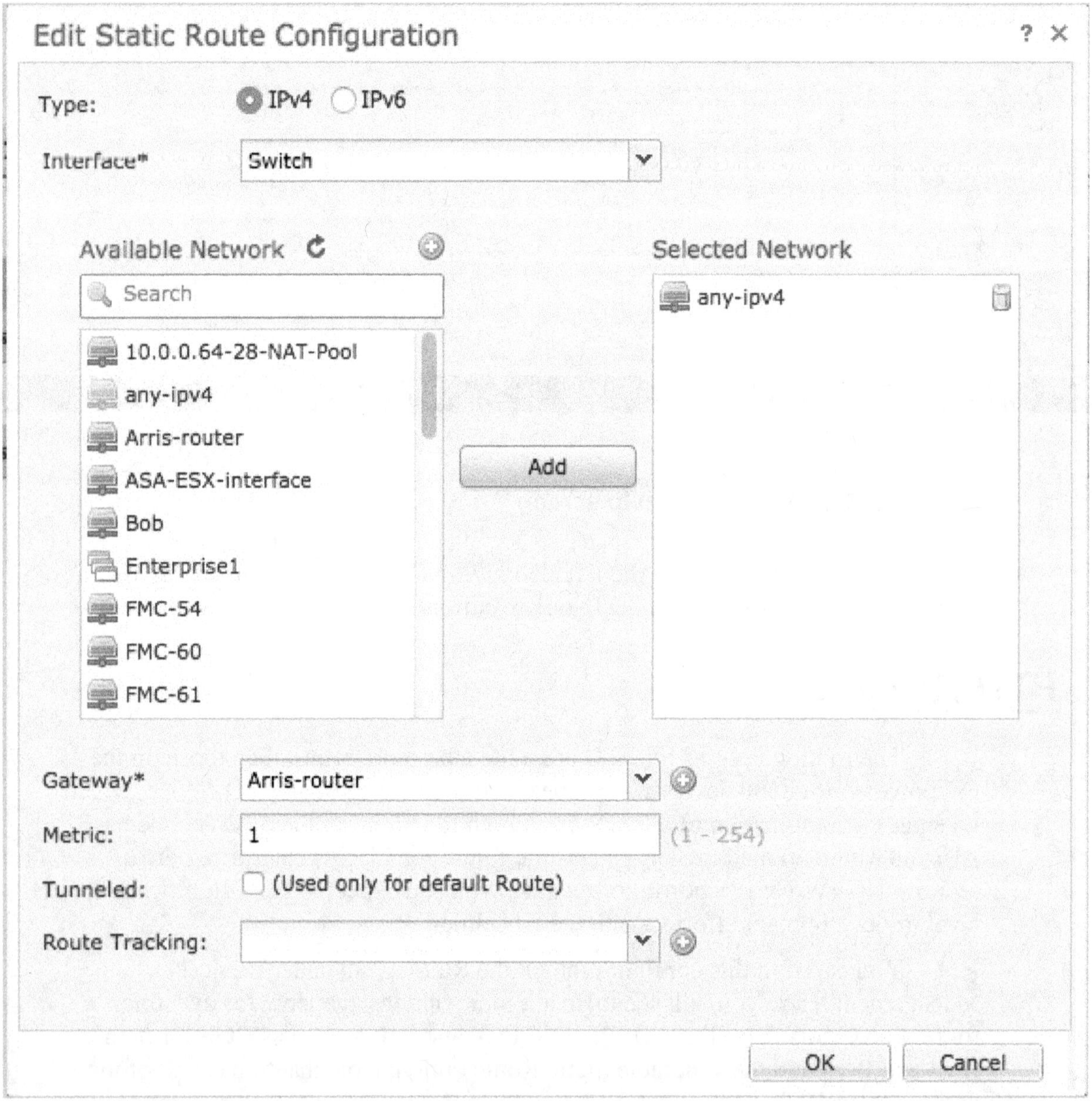

Figure 4.23: FTD static route dialog

Inline Sets

Not sure what to comment here but I found this to be very confusing!

An inline set is one or more pairs of interfaces that pass traffic through the device. These interfaces do not have IP addresses, and they do not even operate like switched ports. They are completely invisible to the other network devices. Traffic comes in one port, is inspected according to the policies deployed, and then—if it isn't blocked—exits the other interface.

An inline set can consist of a single pair or multiple pairs of interfaces. The diagram in Figure 4.24 shows what a multi-pair interface set would look like.

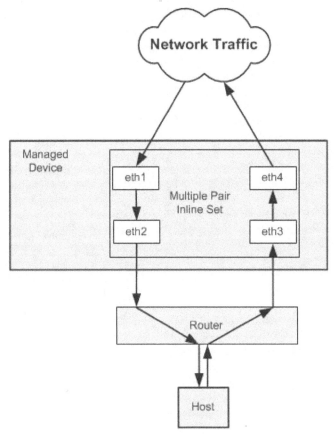

Figure 4.24: Multiple-pair inline set

Why create a multi-pair set? You could just create two single-pair inline sets, right? In the example shown in the figure, the reason for the two pairs is because the router is sending traffic asynchronously. Notice that outbound traffic takes the path to the right and return traffic comes down the left side. For the device to perform proper reassembly and detection, it must see both sides of the conversation. This is accomplished by putting both of the pairs into a single inline set.

There are some minor differences in the way inline sets are configured in Firepower and FTD. First of all, navigate to Devices, edit a device, then select Inline Sets. To create a new one, click the Add Inline Set button. The options are almost identical.

Firepower Inline Sets

For a Firepower 7000/8000 device you will see a dialog like the one in Figure 4.25.

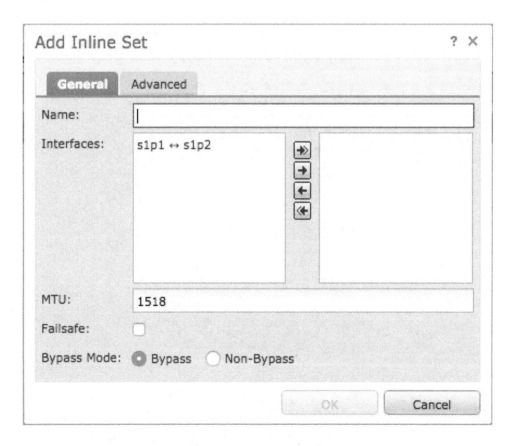

Figure 4.25: Firepower device inline configuration

Here you can give your inline set a name and then select the interface pairs to add to it. Any interfaces configured as inline but not already part of an inline set will be listed.

You will notice the Bypass Mode setting on this screen. This is an important setting and determines whether the interface pair will continue to pass traffic in case of a power failure on the device. You will only see this option if your device netmod hardware is bypass capable. Just because the hardware is capable of bypass doesn't mean you have to use it. This will be enabled by default, but you can disable it here if desired.

The Advanced tab, shown in Figure 4.26, gives you a few more options.

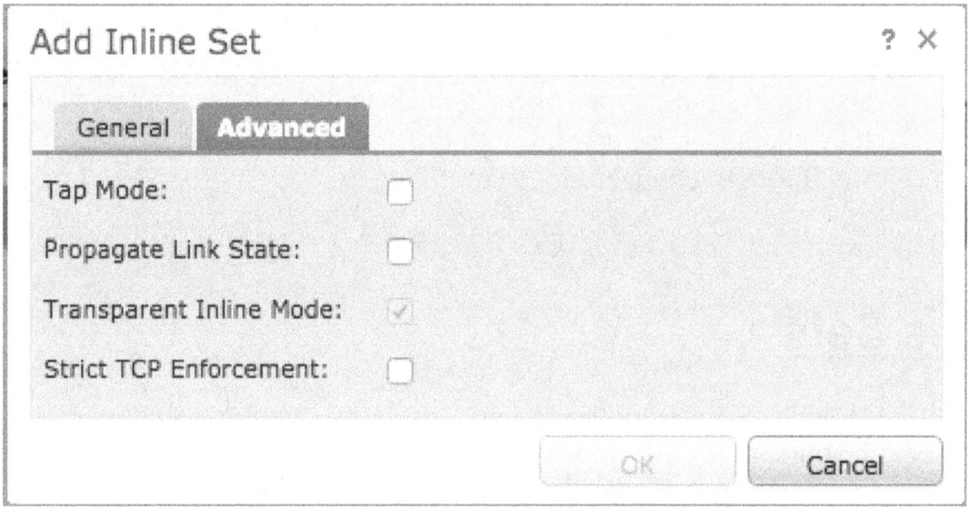

Figure 4.26: Firepower device inline advanced configuration

Advanced options are as follows:

- **Tap Mode:** When this is enabled, the device passes traffic through the inline set and sends a copy of the traffic for inspection. Tap mode is really designed for an initial deployment where you want to ensure that the device won't impact traffic flow. Once you know how the device will perform, you can then return and uncheck this box. Drop or block rules in policies will not drop traffic while the device is in tap mode.

- **Propagate Link State:** This setting propagates a link state failure from one side of the inline set to the other. This prevents the situation in which a failure on one side of the IPS cannot be seen by a network device on the other side. The idea is to propagate the failed link state across both interfaces and let the network respond accordingly—possibly by failing over to a redundant link.

- **Transparent Inline Mode:** Notice that this is grayed out. The reason is that this option is only available on a virtual Firepower device. It causes the inline pair to function like a two-port switch instead of a bump in the wire. You cannot disable this for 7000/8000 devices.

You will see this available if you are using a virtual Firepower device. The reason is that if you wanted a two-port switch on a 7000/8000, you can configure a virtual switch and use switched ports. However, on a virtual device, switched ports are not supported, so this checkbox is enabled.

- **Strict TCP Enforcement:** This enables strict enforcement blocking connections where the three-way handshake has not completed. It also blocks other types of SYN packets that occur at times when they shouldn't. Be careful with this one; it can cause hard-to-troubleshoot connectivity issues.

FTD Inline Sets

For FTD devices, the options are very similar to the options we just discussed, with some minor differences. Depending on the hardware, you may not have the Bypass Mode option and you will not see the Transparent Inline Mode check box. Otherwise, the configuration options are the same.

NAT

Network Address Translation (NAT) is another example of a feature that exists in both Firepower and FTD devices but where there are some differences between platforms.

First, let's start with the caveats (there are always caveats). Since NAT is a function of a router, you cannot apply a NAT policy to a virtual Firepower device. This should be fairly obvious, but we just want to make sure. NAT is similar to routing in that it only works on Firepower 7000/8000 or FTD (hardware or virtual) devices.

To configure NAT, you start with a NAT policy. Of course, there are two flavors of NAT policy: Firepower and Threat Defense. Navigate to Devices → NAT to get started. Click the New Policy button in the upper right and pick your policy type. Let's start with Firepower NAT.

Firepower NAT

When you create a Firepower NAT policy, you will notice that you can only target Firepower devices with it—makes sense, right? You do not have to target a device however; you can create the policy and select the device(s) later if desired. Your new policy has no rules and the screen looks like Figure 4.27.

Figure 4.27: Blank Firepower NAT policy

Notice you have two types of NAT translations listed: Static and Dynamic. Clicking the Add Rule button takes you to the Add Rule dialog shown in Figure 4.28.

Figure 4.28: Add Firepower NAT rule

The Add Rule dialog has the following options:

- **Name**: Your rule name; maximum of 30 characters.

- **Type:** The choices are Static, Dynamic IP Only, and Dynamic IP + Port.

- **Zones**: Optional source/destination security zones for this NAT rule.

- **Source Network:** This tab is blank if you're configuring a static NAT rule; otherwise, enter the original and translated source network or pick one of the available network objects.

- **Destination Network:** For a static NAT, you can enter both the original destination and the translated destination. For a dynamic NAT, the Translated Destination Network option is grayed out.

- **Destination Port:** For a static NAT, you can enter both the original and translated port. For a dynamic NAT, the Translated Port option is grayed out.

Using the various rule types and options, you can create various types of NAT translations. Note that you can either enter IP addresses/CIDR blocks manually or use network objects.

Firepower NAT Examples

Let's go over a few NAT rule examples. These are not exhaustive but should give you some idea of how to create different types of NAT rules.

Static NAT for a Single Host

To create a static rule, on the Destination Network tab, specify the original destination IP and the translated IP. This will translate all traffic for the original host to the translated IP address.

Single NAT for a Single Host on Port 80

Say you have an internal host with a private IP address. You want to run a web server on port 80. You don't want to expose the entire host to the big bad Internet, just the HTTP port.

Create a static rule as described above. On the Destination Port tab, specify HTTP for the original and translated port. This will cause only traffic destined for port 80 on the original destination IP to be sent to your internal host.

Dynamic NAT Pool

What if you want to hide/change the original IP address for a block of IP address space? Sounds like a job for a dynamic NAT pool. To create this rule, you would pick the rule type of Dynamic IP Only. Then on the Source Network tab, specify your original source network and translated source network. These would both be CIDR blocks. In Figure 4.29, we are translating the 10.0.0.0/24 address space to 172.17.0.0/25.

Figure 4.29: Dynamic NAT rule example

This rule will work fine as long as no more than 126 hosts from the 10.0.0.0 network need to be translated. However, since the netmask on the 10.0.0.0 network is /24, that means there could be up to 254 hosts on that network! Firepower will allow you to create this rule, but if you click the Show Warnings button (right next to the Add Rule button), you will see that the rule has a warning triangle next to it. Hovering over that triangle will display the following message:

```
Warning: There are not enough IP addresses specified
for source network translation.  Consider using
"Dynamic IP + Port"
```

Firepower is warning you that you could run out of IP addresses to translate to in your 172.17.0.0/25 network.

Dynamic IP + Port

       This rule type is typically used to allow internal hosts with private IP addresses to access the Internet. Since their addresses are not routable outside the private network, they must be translated to a public address. Now, nobody but a few large corporations (you know who you are) has enough public IP addresses to provide one for every computer, thus the dynamic IP and port translation. This is also sometimes called a "Hide NAT" because it "hides" the internal IP addresses behind the external NAT address. We are going to translate a number of internal IP addresses to a single external IP. In addition to translating the source IP, we will also dynamically translate the source port. This way, even if clients are using the same source port to connect externally, the device can map the connection to the right host based on the dynamic source port assigned on the external network.

       This rule will be a Dynamic IP + Port rule. The Original Source Network field will be your internal address space – say 10.0.0.0/24. The Translated Source Network field will be your single public IP address (this could also be a CIDR block or even multiple external IP addresses). You could also use zones to specify the source and destination of your traffic. Your source zone would be where your internal hosts reside and the destination zone would be Internet facing.

       When created, your rule may look something like the one in Figure 4.30.

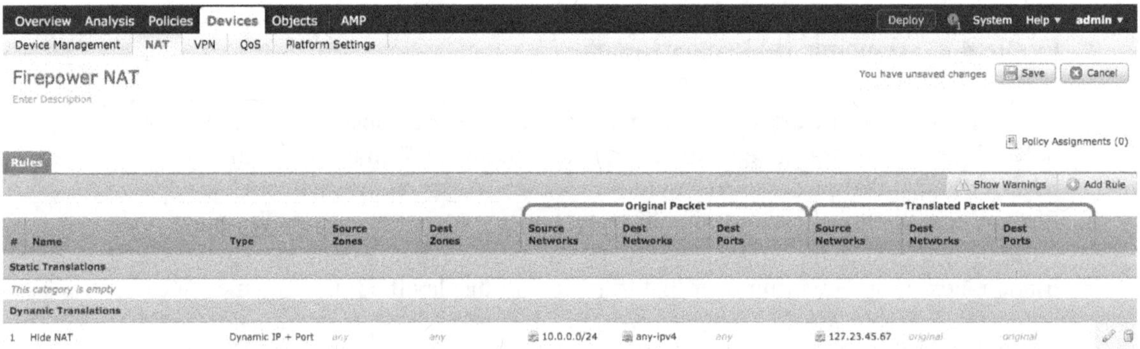

Figure 4.30: Dynamic IP + Port rule example

Threat Defense NAT

FTD includes the basic NAT features available in Firepower devices but also adds more options. You can use NAT on a device in either routed or transparent firewall mode. There are a few limitations for transparent firewalls, so refer to the online help or user guide for specifics. You cannot configure NAT for interfaces operating in inline, inline tap, or passive modes.

To create a new policy, navigate to Devices → NAT, click the New Policy button, and select Threat Defense NAT for the policy type. Give your policy a name and optionally select one or more FTD device targets. Your new policy will look similar to the one in Figure 4.31.

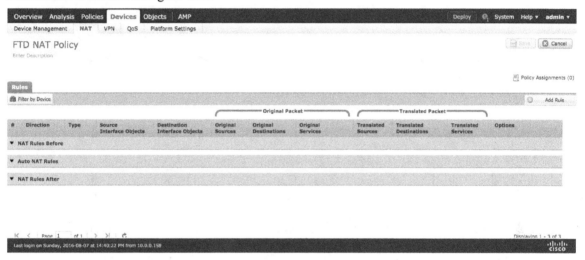

Figure 4.31: Blank FTD NAT policy

You can see that this policy is similar but not quite the same as the Firepower NAT policy. One difference is in the rule order. In both Firepower and FTD, static NAT rules are evaluated first, but in Firepower, these go into their own rule section in the policy. In the Firepower policy, static NAT rules are listed above dynamic rules. In FTD however, manual static and dynamic rules are mixed together. However, this rule order does not matter; static NAT rules will still be evaluated before dynamic rules. In the example in Figure 4.32, the order of evaluation of the rules is not 1, 2, 3. Instead, since rules 1 and 3 are static, the order would be 1, 3, 2.

Another interesting difference is that NAT rules don't have names. You can add a rule description but not a name. The Description is only visible when editing the rule.

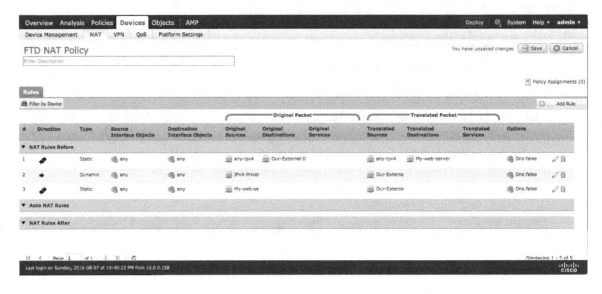

Figure 4.32: FTD static-dynamic rule example

Auto NAT or Manual NAT?

Another difference between Firepower and FTD is Auto NAT and manual NAT rules. Auto NAT has some limitations but is intended to be an easy way to create a NAT rule. When creating an Auto NAT rule, your original source must be a network object; you cannot use network object groups. This object can be a single IP or CIDR block. In addition, you can't configure a translated destination; it works only by translating the source address. Under the hood, the Auto NAT is actually a parameter for the network object, similar to the Network Object NAT on an ASA. The difference is that you can't actually see the NAT in the object itself, but it's there!

You can use an Auto NAT rule to translate a single source to another source either statically or dynamically or to perform Port Address Translation (PAT). Remember, if all you need to do is translate source IP addresses, then an Auto NAT is easier to use. However, if you need to use multiple CIDR blocks in your rule or specify destination addresses, then you will need to do a manual NAT rule.

FTD NAT Examples

Of course, you can perform the same NAT translations in FTD as you can on Firepower devices. We're not going to repeat all the various NAT types here.

The only one that is significantly different is the Dynamic IP and Port or "Hide NAT" rule. Now, this is not NAT; it's actually PAT (Port Address Translation). FTD gets this right by calling the rule what it really is. To create a Hide NAT rule you can follow these steps:

1. Select Dynamic for the rule type.

2. On the Translation tab, enter your internal address space as the original source. Leave the Translated Source field blank.

3. On the PAT Pool tab, check the Enable PAT Pool box.

4. In the Address field, enter your external (public) IP address. You have more options here for the port selection, such as Round Robin, Extended PAT Table, and Flat Port Range.

DHCP

Dynamic Host Configuration Protocol (DHCP) is available only on FTD devices. The device can be in routed or transparent mode to provide DHCP services. The device must be in routed mode to be a DHCP relay or provide DDNS services.

Configuring these services is an intuitive process. Just fill in the relevant information in the user interface and off you go. Figure 4.33 shows a simple DHCP configuration.

Figure 4.33: FTD DHCP example

Deploying Policies

You may have noticed that your settings do not take effect when you click the Save button WOW, That's a really critical piece of information.. can you stress this point?. There is another step needed to push the configuration changes out to the device. Deploying policies and settings has moved from a fairly disjointed process in version 5 to a one-stop shop in version 6. Now there is a single Deploy button to push all policies and configuration changes out to your devices. "One button to rule them all!" When you click the Deploy button, you will see a list of the devices that have settings or policies pending deployment (Figure 4.34).

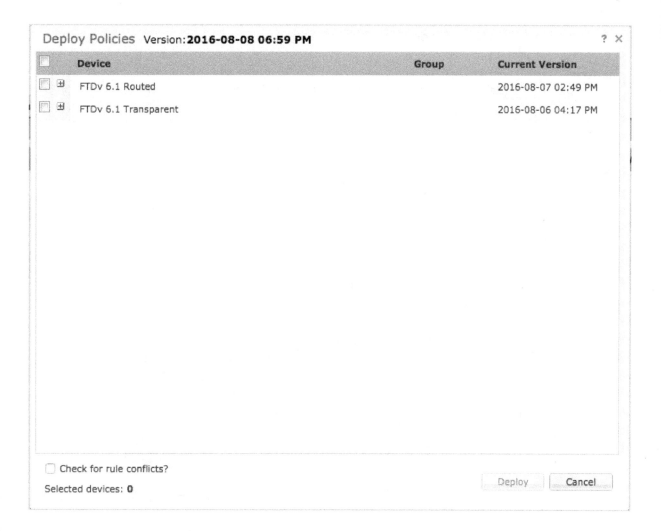

Figure 4.34: Deploy dialog

If you want to know what types of settings will be deployed, you can click the + icon next to the device. In Figure 4.35, we have expanded the items by our routed FTDv device.

Deploy Policies Version:**2016-08-08 06:59 PM**		? ×
Device	**Group**	**Current Version**
⊟ FTDv 6.1 Routed		2016-08-07 02:49 PM

- Access Control Policy: Discovery Only
  - Intrusion Policy: Balanced Security and Connectivity
  - Intrusion Policy: No Rules Active
  - DNS Policy: Default DNS Policy
  - Prefilter Policy: Default Prefilter Policy
- Network Discovery
- ↺ Device Configuration (Details)

Figure 4.35: Deployment pending changes

The green check icons (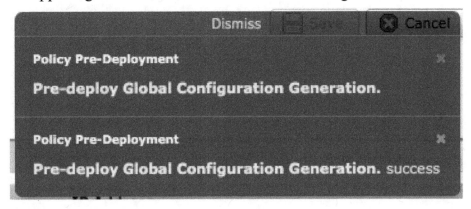) are up-to-date policies. The circle-clock icon (⟳) shows changed policies that need to be deployed. In this case, you can even hover over the "Details" link and get more details on just what will be updated on the device.

To deploy policies for a device, check the box and then click the Deploy button at the bottom. You can then track the progress of the deployment with the notification center by clicking the icon between the Deploy and System items on the menu, the System Status icon. This icon will also show if you have any health or other device issues by changing from green to yellow to red.

You will see various status messages appear and automatically disappear in the upper-right corner of the screen as shown in Figure 4.36.

Dismiss	🖫 Save	⊗ Cancel

Policy Pre-Deployment ✕

Pre-deploy Global Configuration Generation.

Policy Pre-Deployment ✕

Pre-deploy Global Configuration Generation. success

Figure 4.36: Deployment messages

These messages are nice, but after a while they can get annoying. If you find yourself wishing they would go away, you can turn this behavior off by clicking the gear icon in the notification center as shown in Figure 4.37.

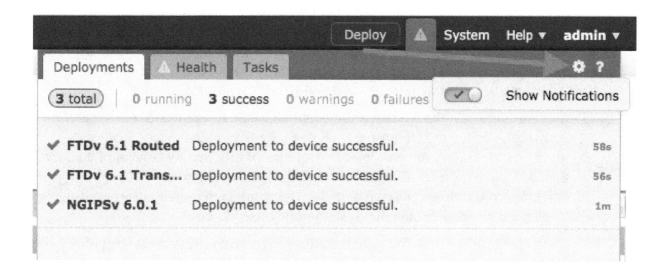

Figure 4.37: Disable annoying notifications

You can then click the Show Notifications switch to disable these pop-ups. You can still follow the progress of your deployment on the Deployments tab or get the blow-by-blow by clicking the Tasks tab. All of your device settings and policies will be applied using the Deploy button.

Add the "Summary H1" here

In this chapter, we covered a lot of information on device management. The goal was to help you understand the major moving parts and help you get your devices up and running. The *Firepower System User Guide* and online help will always have the latest details on even the minutest features. If there are any concepts that are still a little fuzzy, you will probably find your answers there.

Chapter 5: Platform Settings and Health

In this chapter, we will discuss platform settings and the Health policy. If you have used previous versions of Firepower, you may be familiar with the System policy. Well, in version 6 the System policy is no more. We now have Platform Settings. There are two different types of policies you can create here, one for Firepower and one for Threat Defense (FTD). You could say that these policies replace the System policy and you would be partially correct.

In previous versions, the System policy applied to the Firepower Management Center (FMC, called the Defense Center back then) and the devices. Today, Platform settings apply only to devices. Because of this, settings that applied only to the FMC have been removed. These settings are found under System → Configuration, which we covered already. The result is that the Platform settings policies are a bit smaller than the System policy used to be.

We will also briefly cover the Health settings, which have remained largely unchanged for over a decade.

Firepower Platform Settings

To begin, from the FMC, navigate to Devices → Platform Settings. By default there are no platform policies created. Click the New Policy button in the upper right and select Firepower Settings.

The default device settings will allow a managed device to function indefinitely with no changes. As long as you don't care about things like the access list, external audit logging, the login banner, and so on, you really don't need to create this policy. However, most organizations will modify at least a few of the default settings to comply with security or audit standards. Let's take a look at the settings in the Firepower Platform policy.

When you first create a policy, you will be prompted for the name and the device targets. This is where the policy will be applied when you use the Deploy button in the main menu. After this you will be presented with the list of settings, as shown in Figure 5.1.

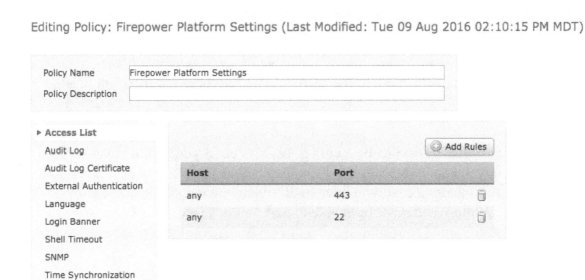

Figure 5.1: Firepower Platform Settings

Access List

This is the same as the Access List setting in the FMC System Configuration. It controls what IP addresses can access the management ports on the device. Note that although port 443 is listed, if this policy is applied to a virtual device without a Web UI, it will have no effect.

Audit Log

Complete this section to send audit events to an external syslog or HTTP server. Audit events are generated for any logins/page views in the Web UI as well as any commands typed into the Cisco CLI via SSH or the console. Note that one of these CLI commands is **expert**, which gives the user a Linux bash shell. Once the user is at this Linux shell, commands are no longer audited.

Note that in order to use the **expert** command, your users must have configuration access to the CLI. If you set up users with just basic CLI access, they will not be able to run configuration commands on the system or exit the CLI to a bash shell. The type of CLI access for a user can be configured via the device's web interface or through the LDAP/RADIUS object if you're using external authentication.

If this is still a concern, you can disable expert mode on a managed device, preventing any and all access to the bash command processor. You can disable expert mode from the device CLI with the command **system lockdown-sensor**.

Wait – what? Disable all access to bash? Yes, if you disable expert mode on a device, you cannot re-enable it. The idea is that you want to be able to audit all activity on the device, so you have to eliminate the use of the non-auditable bash shell. While you cannot re-enable expert mode, Cisco TAC can assist you if this becomes required to troubleshoot a device issue. Another option is to reimage the device and revert to the original settings.

Audit Log Certificate

If your audit logging server supports Transport Layer Security (TLS), you can enable it here.

External Authentication

Use these settings to enable authentication of users on the device from an external authentication source (LDAP, RADIUS, etc.). To enable this feature, you must first set up an external authentication source under System → Users → External Authentication. After this, you can return here and enable the external authentication method on your device(s).

Language

This is where you set the language. The choices are English, Japanese, Chinese, and Korean.

Login Banner

We've already discussed the login banner under the FMC settings. It's the same thing here. This is text that will display on the Web UI and the console prior to users logging in. Generally, this is some verbiage provided by your legal department and is standardized across the organization.

Shell Timeout

This setting has to do with the browser session and SSH shell timeouts. The defaults are shown in Figure 5.2. If you need to modify these based on your organization's policies, you can do so here.

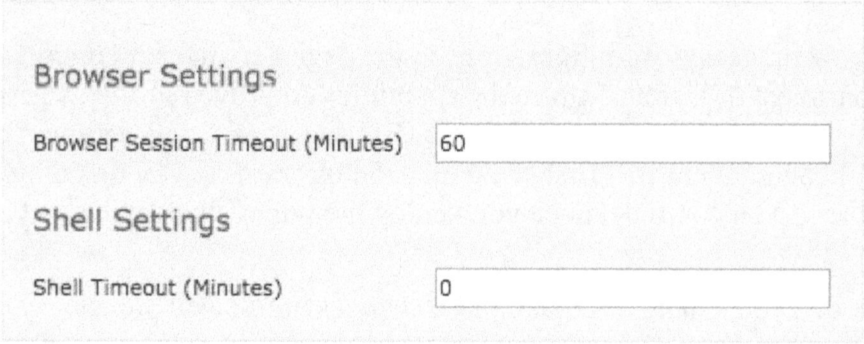

Browser Settings

Browser Session Timeout (Minutes)   60

Shell Settings

Shell Timeout (Minutes)   0

Figure 5.2: Browser/Shell timeouts

SNMP

An SNMP manager can be used to query the device for health status. Devices use a fairly standard Linux MIB (management information base) to define what types of information can be queried. Remember, this is simply operating system/hardware data; we're not talking about event data here.

To enable, first select the SNMP version and then enter the appropriate community string or user information.

Time Synchronization

Keeping the time in sync across the devices and FMC is a pretty big deal. If the time is allowed to drift, events will not appear in the proper order on the FMC. This is because the event timestamp comes from the device time where it was detected.

You have two options here; the device can get its time from the FMC or from an external NTP time source (Figure 5.3). The FMC is the default, but pick the one that works best in your environment.

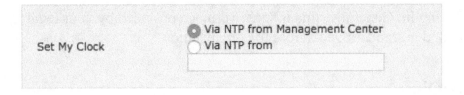

Figure 5.3: Time Synchronization settings

UCAPL/CC Compliance

These settings apply configurations to the device to make it compliant with the US Department of Defense Unified Capabilities Approved Products List (UCACL) or the ISO/IEC Common Criteria (CC). These are new settings for version 6. Changing them will first bring up a dialog warning you that they are nonreversible. If you continue, once you deploy the policy, the device will be rebooted.

Note that you should *not* make these changes unless you are *sure* you need to. Oftentimes these settings introduce limitations in functionality or performance in the system that could ruin your whole day!

Threat Defense Platform Settings

If you are using FTD devices, there is a separate platform policy. Because the devices' ancestry includes the Cisco ASA, the settings are quite dissimilar to the settings for Firepower devices.

To get started, navigate to System → Devices → Platform Settings. By default there are no platform policies created. Click the New Policy button in the upper right and select Threat Defense Settings. You will see the initial settings screen, shown in Figure 5.4.

Figure 5.4: Threat Defense Platform Settings screen

ARP Inspection

This setting only applies to transparent mode FTD devices.

The default setting for transparent mode devices is to allow Address Resolution Protocol (ARP) packets to pass through. This setting allows you to control the flow of these packets. ARP Inspection is useful for preventing malicious use of the ARP protocol known as ARP spoofing.

To enable ARP Inspection, click the Add button in the upper right. This will bring up the dialog in Figure 5.5.

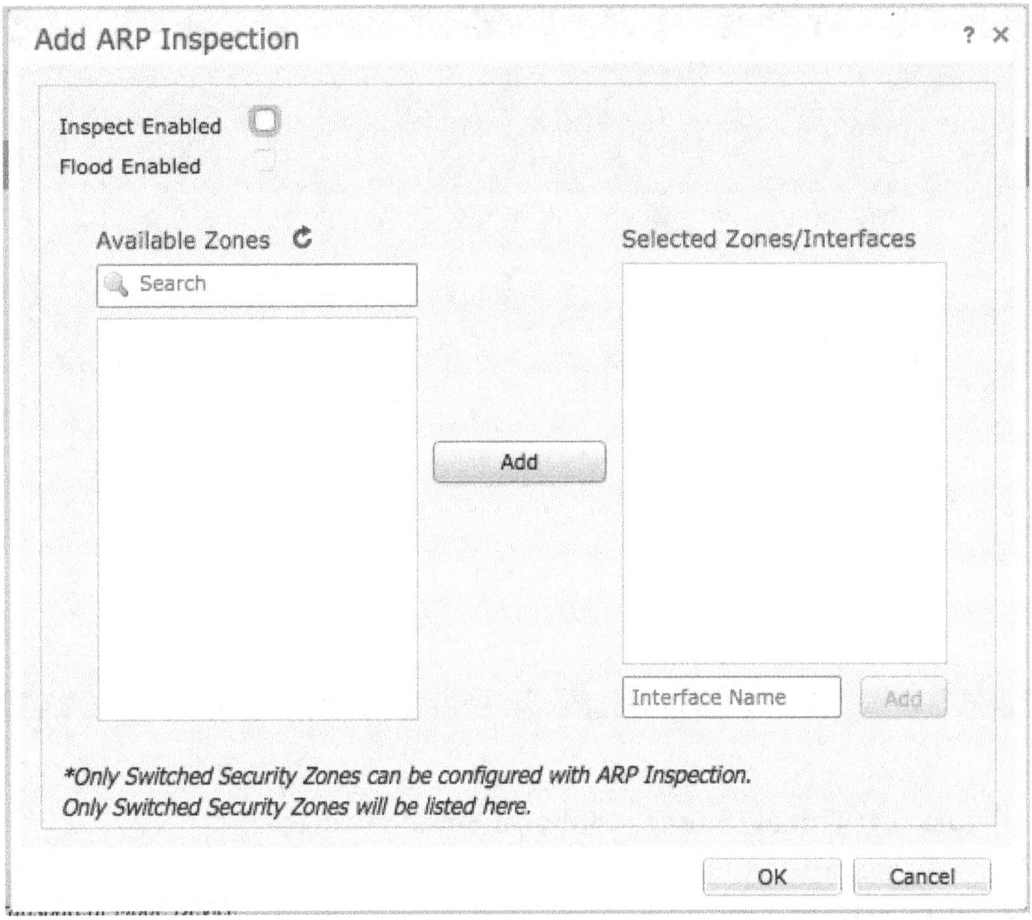

Add ARP Inspection   ? ✕

Inspect Enabled ▢
Flood Enabled   ▢

Available Zones ↻   **Selected Zones/Interfaces**

🔍 Search

[Add]

Interface Name   [Add]

Only Switched Security Zones can be configured with ARP Inspection.
Only Switched Security Zones will be listed here.

[OK]   [Cancel]

Figure 5.5: ARP Inspection settings

Note that for this to work you must have switched security zones on your device. When you check the Inspect Enabled box and select the available switched zones, the device will filter ARP packets according to the following criteria.

- If the IP address, MAC address, and source interface match an ARP entry, the packet is passed through. The entry is the ARP cache in the FTD right?

- If there is a mismatch between the MAC address, the IP address, or the interface, then the Firepower Threat Defense device drops the packet.

- If the ARP packet does not match any entries in the static ARP table, then you can set the Firepower Threat Defense device to either forward the packet out all interfaces (flood) or drop the packet.

Banner

This is similar to the Login Banner setting on Firepower devices and the FMC. However, it only applies to the CLI as there is no Web UI on an FTD device. Also, you can use the variables **$(hostname)** or **$(domain)** to dynamically add the appropriate text to your device banner.

Fragment Settings

This setting controls how fragmented IP packets are handled. The default settings for Size, Chain and Timeout are shown in Figure 5.6.

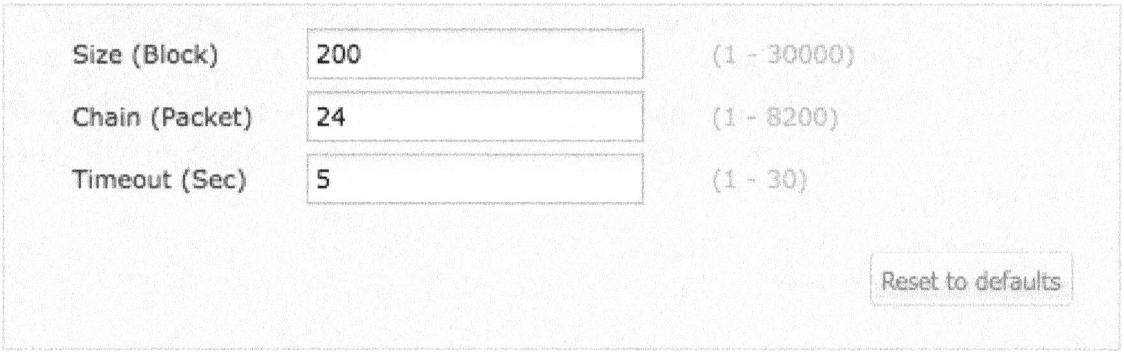

Size (Block)	200	(1 - 30000)
Chain (Packet)	24	(1 - 8200)
Timeout (Sec)	5	(1 - 30)

Reset to defaults

Figure 5.6: Packet fragmentation defaults

Here are brief descriptions of the settings

- **Size (Block):** The maximum number of fragments from all connections that can be waiting for reassembly.
- **Chain (Fragment):** The maximum number of packets into which a full IP packet can be fragmented. Set to 1 to disallow fragments.
- **Timeout (Sec):** The maximum number of seconds to wait for an entire fragmented datagram to arrive. If they are not received in this time, all fragments are discarded.

The idea is that FTD will not just allow any and all IP fragmentation to occur. The reason is that, while there are some legitimate reasons for packets to be fragmented, much of the time it is part of a denial of service (DoS) or an attempt to evade detection.

Note that the settings here become the defaults for the device but can be overridden in the interface configuration.

HTTP

The HTTP setting controls HTTPS access to interfaces on the FTD device. This doesn't mean the device actually has a web-based user interface. This connection is only for downloading PCAP files you have created by capturing traffic on the device.

The process to do this is an involved one that we will not cover here, but the basic procedure is to (1) connect to the device CLI via SSH or some other means, (2) create a packet capture, and (3) connect using HTTPS to download the PCAP file.

Now, you don't have to do it this way. If you have an available TFTP, SCP, or another supported server type, you can simply copy the pcap file from the device while you are still at the CLI. Downloading via HTTPS is just another way to do this and doesn't require any other servers. You simply browse to the device interface and grab the PCAP file.

The configuration here is minimal: first check the box to enable the HTTP server, confirm or change the port, then click the Add button. You will then see the dialog in Figure 5.7.

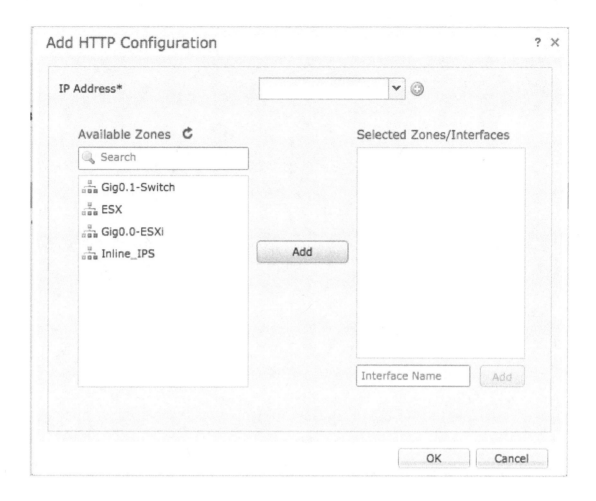

Figure 5.7: HTTP access configuration

In the IP Address field, select an existing network object to allow connections from that address. Then add the interfaces where you would like to allow access by selecting them from the Available Zones list.

ICMP

This setting controls how the FTD device responds to Internet Control Message Protocol (ICMP) packets. By configuring rules here, you can limit ICMP to certain hosts, networks, or ICMP types. The interface is fairly straightforward; you will begin at the screen shown in Figure 5.8.

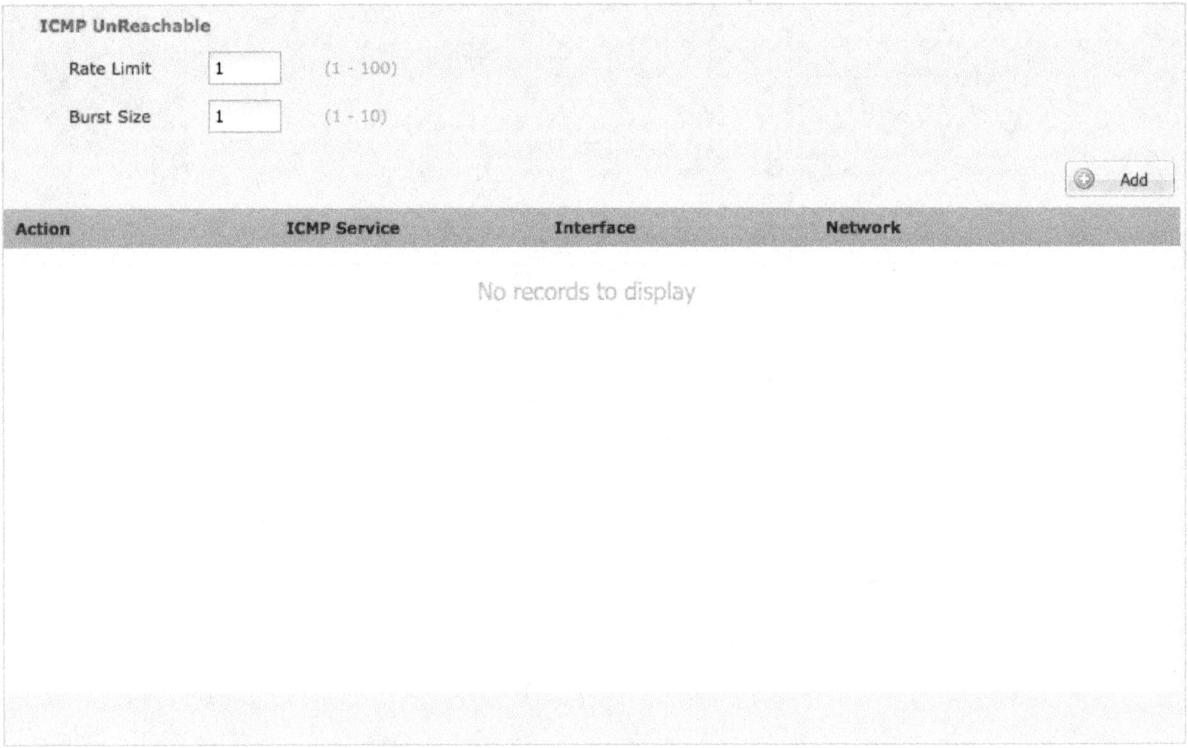

ICMP UnReachable

Rate Limit	1	(1 - 100)
Burst Size	1	(1 - 10)

Add

Action	ICMP Service	Interface	Network

No records to display

Figure 5.8: ICMP settings

The main ICMP page allows setting the rate limit for ICMPv4 unreachable messages. This can be set from 1 to 100 per second; the default is 1 message per second. Burst size is currently not used by the system.

By clicking the Add button, you can add ICMP rules. These are used to permit or deny specific ICMP services based on network, zone, ICMP type, and code. The way the rule set works is similar to how any other access control list (ACL) works in that rules are evaluated from top to bottom. For example, if you wanted to allow the ICMP TTL Exceeded message but deny all other ICMP, your list would look like the one in Figure 5.9.

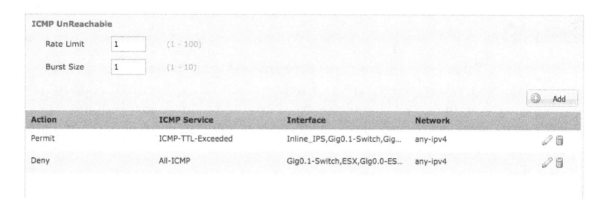

Figure 5.9: ICMP rules example

Secure Shell

To configure Secure Shell (SSH) access to one of the device's detection interfaces, simply create one or more entries here. Specify the source IP address and zone(s) to allow SSH communications. This is the same management CLI you have on the management interface already.

SMTP Server

This is a Simple Mail Transport Protocol (SMTP) server through which you can relay email messages configured later in the Syslog section.

SNMP

Simple Network Management Protocol (SNMP) is provided to monitor the health and status of many of the components of the FTD device. To configure access, simply add the community string or user/password depending on the SNMP version.

Note that unlike Firepower, which provides read-only access, you can configure SNMP traps here for conditions such as SNMP authentication errors, link up/down, system restarts, and so on.

Syslog

FTD offers a much greater depth of syslog alerting than previously available with Firepower. In fact, Firepower has no GUI configuration for remote syslog from the underlying operating system and requires hand editing the `/etc/syslog.conf` file. The Syslog configuration page is shown in Figure 5.10.

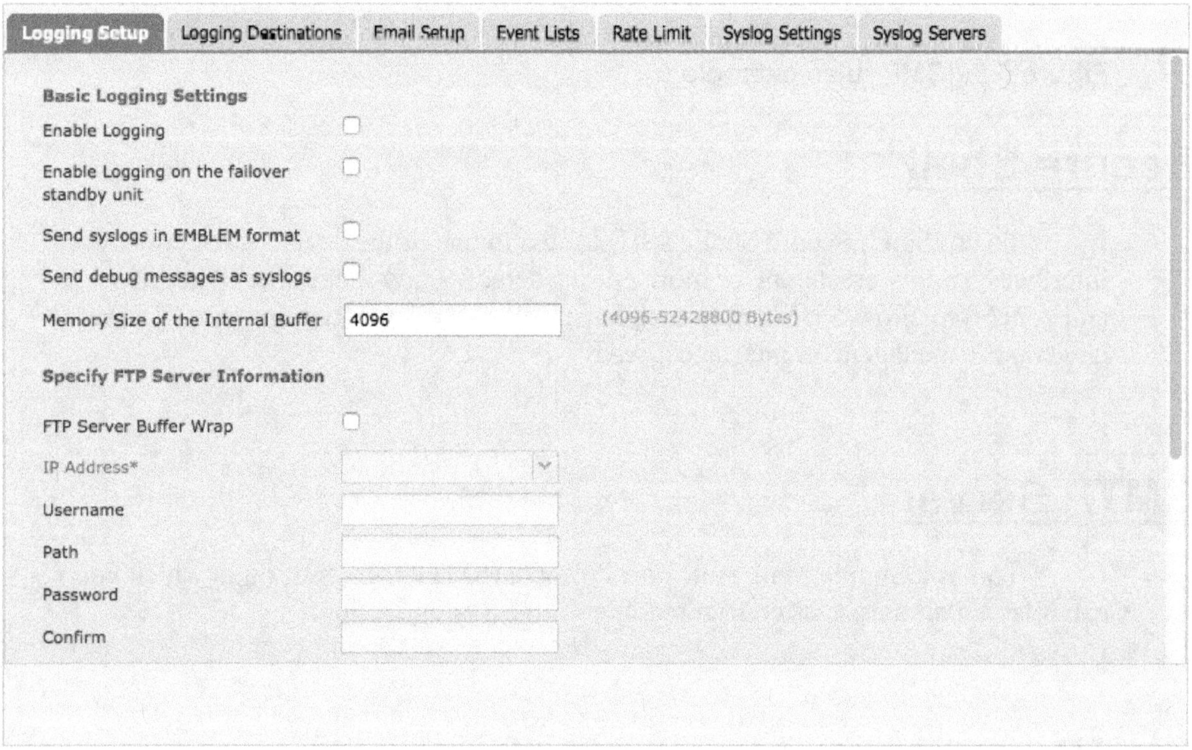

| Logging Setup | Logging Destinations | Email Setup | Event Lists | Rate Limit | Syslog Settings | Syslog Servers |

Basic Logging Settings

Enable Logging ☐

Enable Logging on the failover standby unit ☐

Send syslogs in EMBLEM format ☐

Send debug messages as syslogs ☐

Memory Size of the Internal Buffer `4096` (4096-52428800 Bytes)

Specify FTP Server Information

FTP Server Buffer Wrap ☐

IP Address*

Username

Path

Password

Confirm

Figure 5.10: FTD syslog configuration

Here you can configure options such as the type of logging, destinations, email messages based on severity, custom event lists, rate limits, and more. Rather than go into all of these gory details, we will leave it up to you to dig into this feature set and see what it may offer.

Timeouts

This section allows for customization of timeout values for a list of common network conditions. The defaults should be reasonable and are listed to the right of each setting. A partial list of the items available is shown in Figure 5.11.

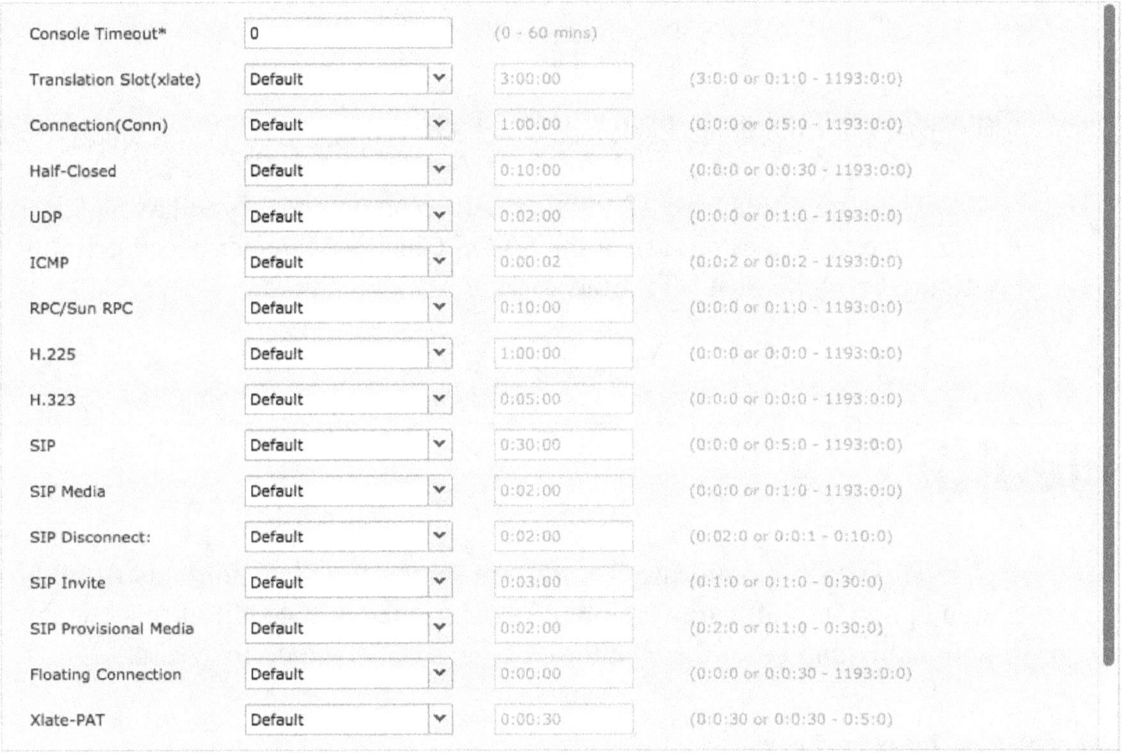

Console Timeout*	0	(0 - 60 mins)	
Translation Slot(xlate)	Default ⌄	3:00:00	(3:0:0 or 0:1:0 - 1193:0:0)
Connection(Conn)	Default ⌄	1:00:00	(0:0:0 or 0:5:0 - 1193:0:0)
Half-Closed	Default ⌄	0:10:00	(0:0:0 or 0:0:30 - 1193:0:0)
UDP	Default ⌄	0:02:00	(0:0:0 or 0:1:0 - 1193:0:0)
ICMP	Default ⌄	0:00:02	(0:0:2 or 0:0:2 - 1193:0:0)
RPC/Sun RPC	Default ⌄	0:10:00	(0:0:0 or 0:1:0 - 1193:0:0)
H.225	Default ⌄	1:00:00	(0:0:0 or 0:0:0 - 1193:0:0)
H.323	Default ⌄	0:05:00	(0:0:0 or 0:0:0 - 1193:0:0)
SIP	Default ⌄	0:30:00	(0:0:0 or 0:5:0 - 1193:0:0)
SIP Media	Default ⌄	0:02:00	(0:0:0 or 0:1:0 - 1193:0:0)
SIP Disconnect:	Default ⌄	0:02:00	(0:02:0 or 0:0:1 - 0:10:0)
SIP Invite	Default ⌄	0:03:00	(0:1:0 or 0:1:0 - 0:30:0)
SIP Provisional Media	Default ⌄	0:02:00	(0:2:0 or 0:1:0 - 0:30:0)
Floating Connection	Default ⌄	0:00:00	(0:0:0 or 0:0:30 - 1193:0:0)
Xlate-PAT	Default ⌄	0:00:30	(0:0:30 or 0:0:30 - 0:5:0)

Figure 5.8: Protocol timeouts

Time Synchronization

This is the same setting we discussed earlier for Firepower devices. Keeping the time in sync across the devices and FMC is a pretty big deal. If the time is allowed to drift, events will not appear in the proper order on the FMC. This is because the event timestamp comes from the device time where it was detected.

You have two options here: the device can get its time from the FMC or from an external NTP time source. The FMC is the default, but pick the one that works best in your environment.

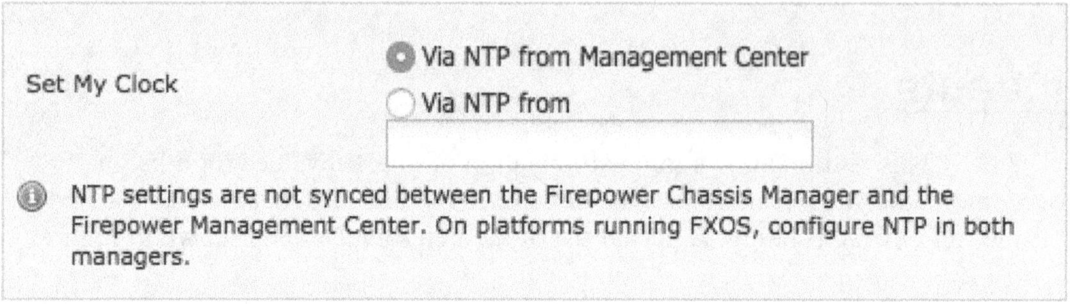

Figure 5.9: FTD Time Synchronization settings

The note in Figure 5.12 is fairly self-explanatory. If you have a 9300 or 4100 device, this does not affect the FXOS Chassis Manager because it must be configured with its own NTP time source.

Health

The health monitoring features are some of the last holdouts from the old 5.x and previous software versions. As mentioned at the start of this chapter, the functionality and UI of the Health policy has not changed for years.

Health Monitor

The first item under System → Health is the *Health Monitor*, which reveals details about the health of your system. There are several different status messages that can be displayed, with Normal being optimal. Critical indicates just what you would think—that there are issues that probably require immediate attention, and Warning indicates something worth keeping an eye on as well. A status of Recovered indicates that a health check previously reported a problem condition (Critical or Warning) but is now okay. Disabled indicates that there's no health policy loaded, and Error tells you that there's an issue with the health system itself.

The Count column next to a particular status shows the number of appliances in that specific state. Notice in Figure 5.13 that there's a small triangle to the right of the number for the Normal status. Clicking it will expose details of the appliances.

Timeouts

This section allows for customization of timeout values for a list of common network conditions. The defaults should be reasonable and are listed to the right of each setting. A partial list of the items available is shown in Figure 5.11.

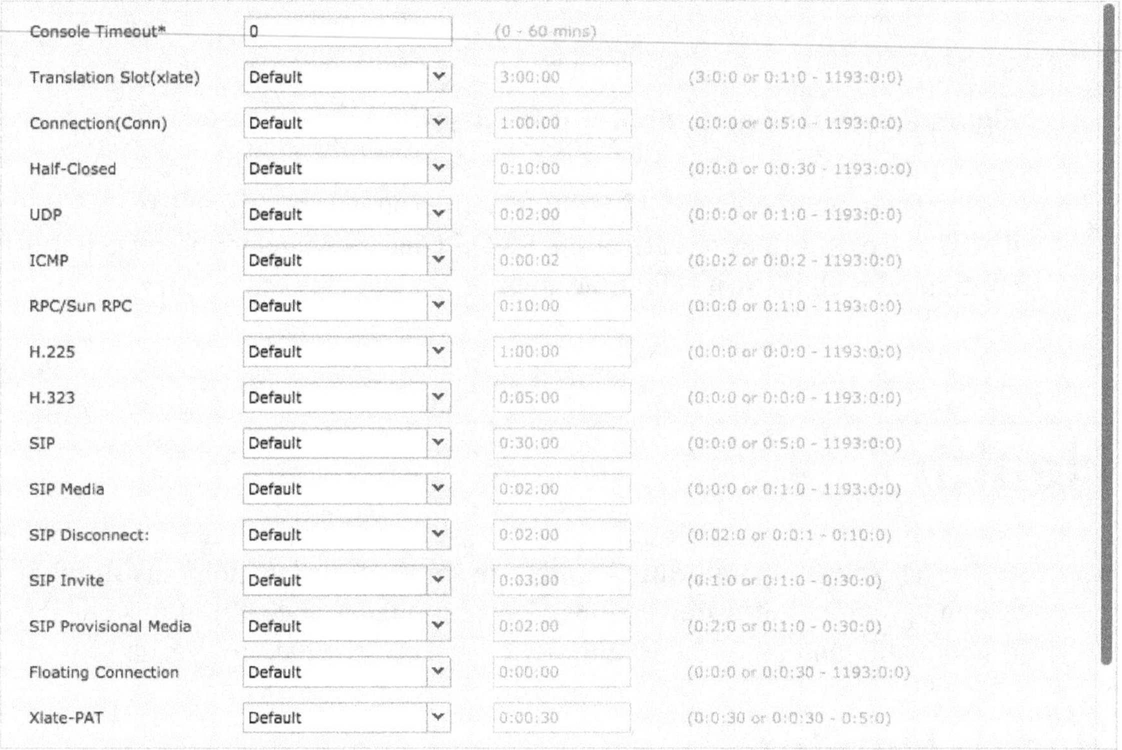

Console Timeout*	0		(0 - 60 mins)
Translation Slot(xlate)	Default ⌄	3:00:00	(3:0:0 or 0:1:0 - 1193:0:0)
Connection(Conn)	Default ⌄	1:00:00	(0:0:0 or 0:5:0 - 1193:0:0)
Half-Closed	Default ⌄	0:10:00	(0:0:0 or 0:0:30 - 1193:0:0)
UDP	Default ⌄	0:02:00	(0:0:0 or 0:1:0 - 1193:0:0)
ICMP	Default ⌄	0:00:02	(0:0:2 or 0:0:2 - 1193:0:0)
RPC/Sun RPC	Default ⌄	0:10:00	(0:0:0 or 0:1:0 - 1193:0:0)
H.225	Default ⌄	1:00:00	(0:0:0 or 0:0:0 - 1193:0:0)
H.323	Default ⌄	0:05:00	(0:0:0 or 0:0:0 - 1193:0:0)
SIP	Default ⌄	0:30:00	(0:0:0 or 0:5:0 - 1193:0:0)
SIP Media	Default ⌄	0:02:00	(0:0:0 or 0:1:0 - 1193:0:0)
SIP Disconnect:	Default ⌄	0:02:00	(0:02:0 or 0:0:1 - 0:10:0)
SIP Invite	Default ⌄	0:03:00	(0:1:0 or 0:1:0 - 0:30:0)
SIP Provisional Media	Default ⌄	0:02:00	(0:2:0 or 0:1:0 - 0:30:0)
Floating Connection	Default ⌄	0:00:00	(0:0:0 or 0:0:30 - 1193:0:0)
Xlate-PAT	Default ⌄	0:00:30	(0:0:30 or 0:0:30 - 0:5:0)

Figure 5.8: Protocol timeouts

Time Synchronization

This is the same setting we discussed earlier for Firepower devices. Keeping the time in sync across the devices and FMC is a pretty big deal. If the time is allowed to drift, events will not appear in the proper order on the FMC. This is because the event timestamp comes from the device time where it was detected.

You have two options here: the device can get its time from the FMC or from an external NTP time source. The FMC is the default, but pick the one that works best in your environment.

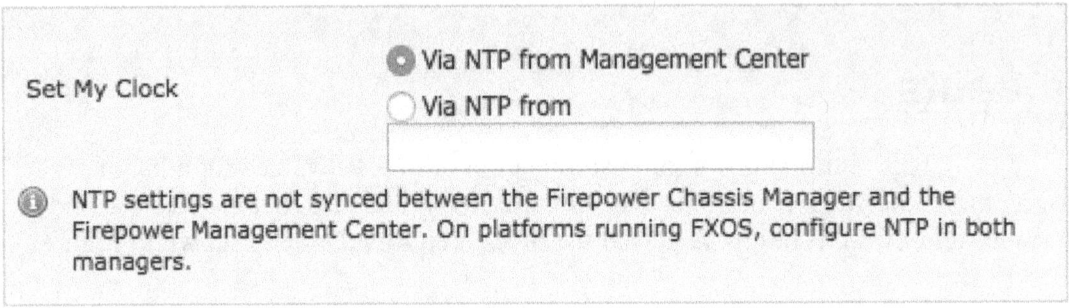

Figure 5.9: FTD Time Synchronization settings

The note in Figure 5.12 is fairly self-explanatory. If you have a 9300 or 4100 device, this does not affect the FXOS Chassis Manager because it must be configured with its own NTP time source.

Health

The health monitoring features are some of the last holdouts from the old 5.x and previous software versions. As mentioned at the start of this chapter, the functionality and UI of the Health policy has not changed for years.

Health Monitor

The first item under System → Health is the *Health Monitor*, which reveals details about the health of your system. There are several different status messages that can be displayed, with Normal being optimal. Critical indicates just what you would think—that there are issues that probably require immediate attention, and Warning indicates something worth keeping an eye on as well. A status of Recovered indicates that a health check previously reported a problem condition (Critical or Warning) but is now okay. Disabled indicates that there's no health policy loaded, and Error tells you that there's an issue with the health system itself.

The Count column next to a particular status shows the number of appliances in that specific state. Notice in Figure 5.13 that there's a small triangle to the right of the number for the Normal status. Clicking it will expose details of the appliances.

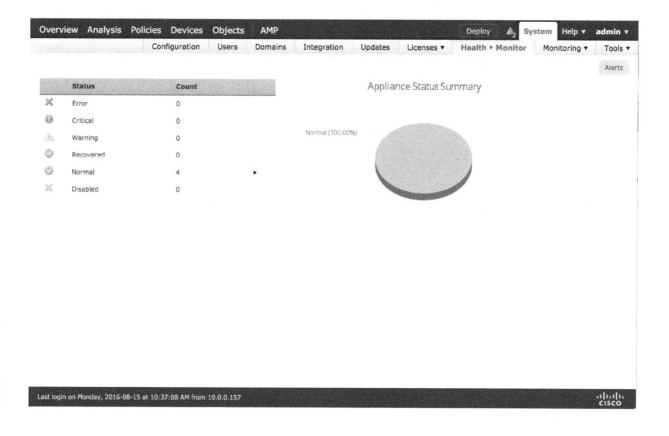

Figure 5.10: Health Monitor

Health Policy

Data for the Health Monitor comes from the *health policy*, which is a collection of checks that are executed every 5 minutes by default. You can modify the health policies to meet the needs of each environment. Health checks can also be disabled. To edit or create a new health policy, navigate to System → Health → Policy and either click the edit icon or click Create Policy. When creating a new policy, you get the option to copy an existing health policy.

There are many different checks in a list to the left of the policy. Each setting can be enabled or disabled, and some allow you to specify thresholds for warnings or critical alerts (Figure 5.14). Most of the default settings work just fine, but if you make any changes, be sure to use the Save Policy And Exit button on the bottom and then reapply the policy.

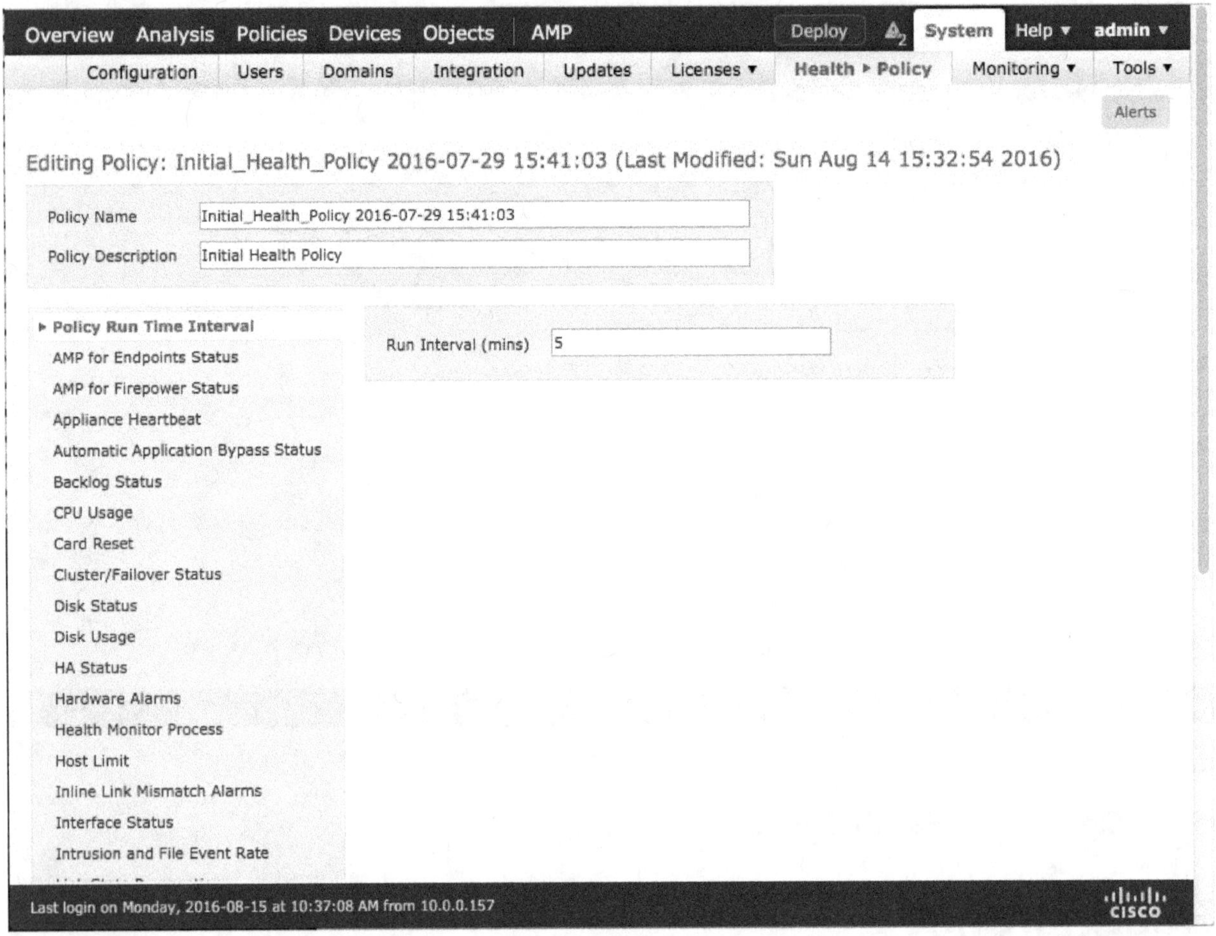
Overview
Analysis
Policies
Devices
Objects
AMP
Deploy
System
Help ▾
admin ▾
Configuration
Users
Domains
Integration
Updates
Licenses ▾
Health ▸ Policy
Monitoring ▾
Tools ▾
Alerts
Editing Policy: Initial_Health_Policy 2016-07-29 15:41:03 (Last Modified: Sun Aug 14 15:32:54 2016)
Policy Name
Initial_Health_Policy 2016-07-29 15:41:03
Policy Description
Initial Health Policy
▸ Policy Run Time Interval
AMP for Endpoints Status
AMP for Firepower Status
Appliance Heartbeat
Automatic Application Bypass Status
Backlog Status
CPU Usage
Card Reset
Cluster/Failover Status
Disk Status
Disk Usage
HA Status
Hardware Alarms
Health Monitor Process
Host Limit
Inline Link Mismatch Alarms
Interface Status
Intrusion and File Event Rate
Run Interval (mins)
5
Last login on Monday, 2016-08-15 at 10:37:08 AM from 10.0.0.157
cisco

Figure 5.11: Health Policy

It is worth noting here that this is the one policy that is not deployed with the Deploy button. As we mentioned, this policy is a dinosaur and still follows the old ways! To deploy the health policy, you click on the icon in the health policy list. This will present a list of all the appliances, including the FMC itself, as shown in Figure 5.15. Select the appropriate appliances and then click the Apply button at the bottom of the screen.

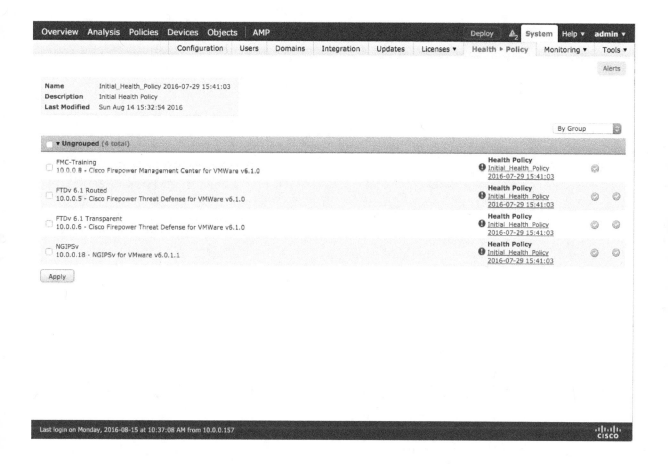

Figure 5.12: Applying a Health Policy

Health Events

To view current and past health events, select System → Health → Events. The health events will be displayed from all your devices, as shown in Figure 5.16. If you're looking for a specific health event, use the Search feature and specify your search criteria. You can also adjust the time window to a specific range.

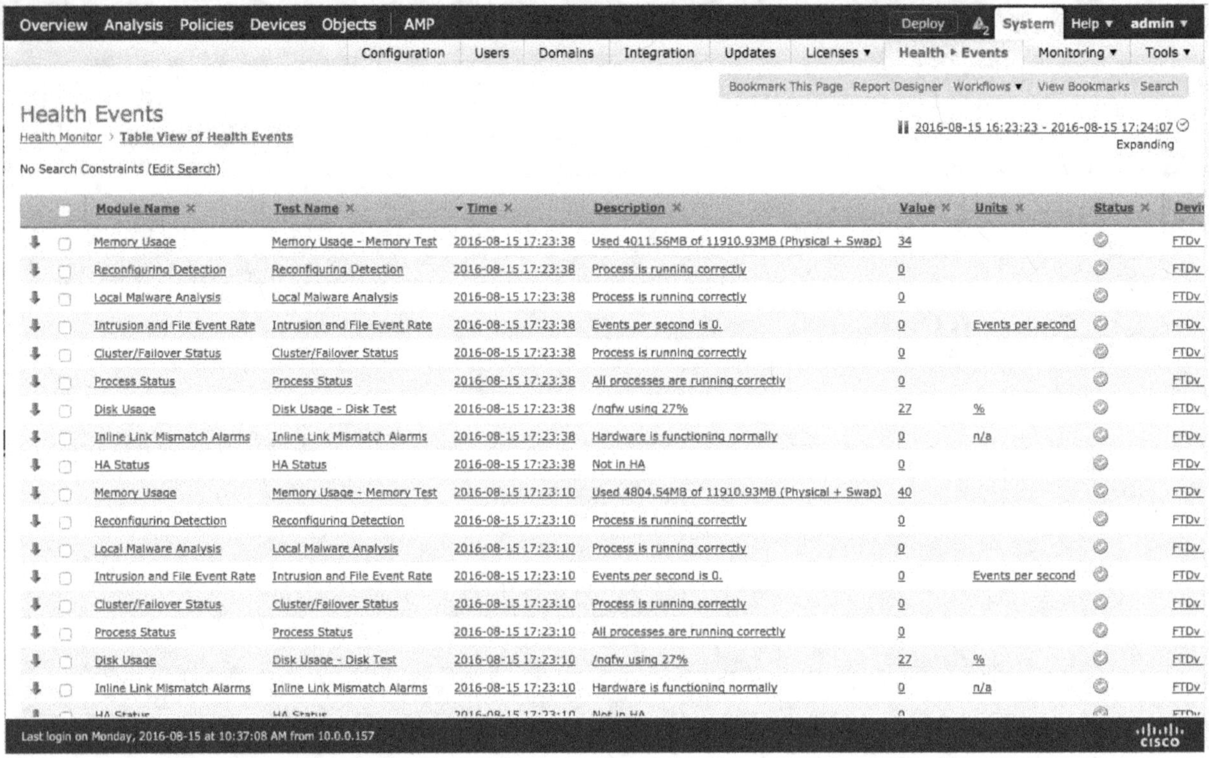

Figure 5.13: Health events

Blacklist

The health blacklist (System → Health → Blacklist) allows you to set up exclusions to health checks. You can blacklist an entire device or just individual checks. This can be helpful when there's a known issue but you don't need alerts nagging you about it every 5 minutes. A good example is when you've had a power supply fail but you've contacted Cisco for a replacement. Here, you would just blacklist the power supply health check for the appliance until you get the replacement. Figure 5.17 shows some of the elements available for a blacklist.

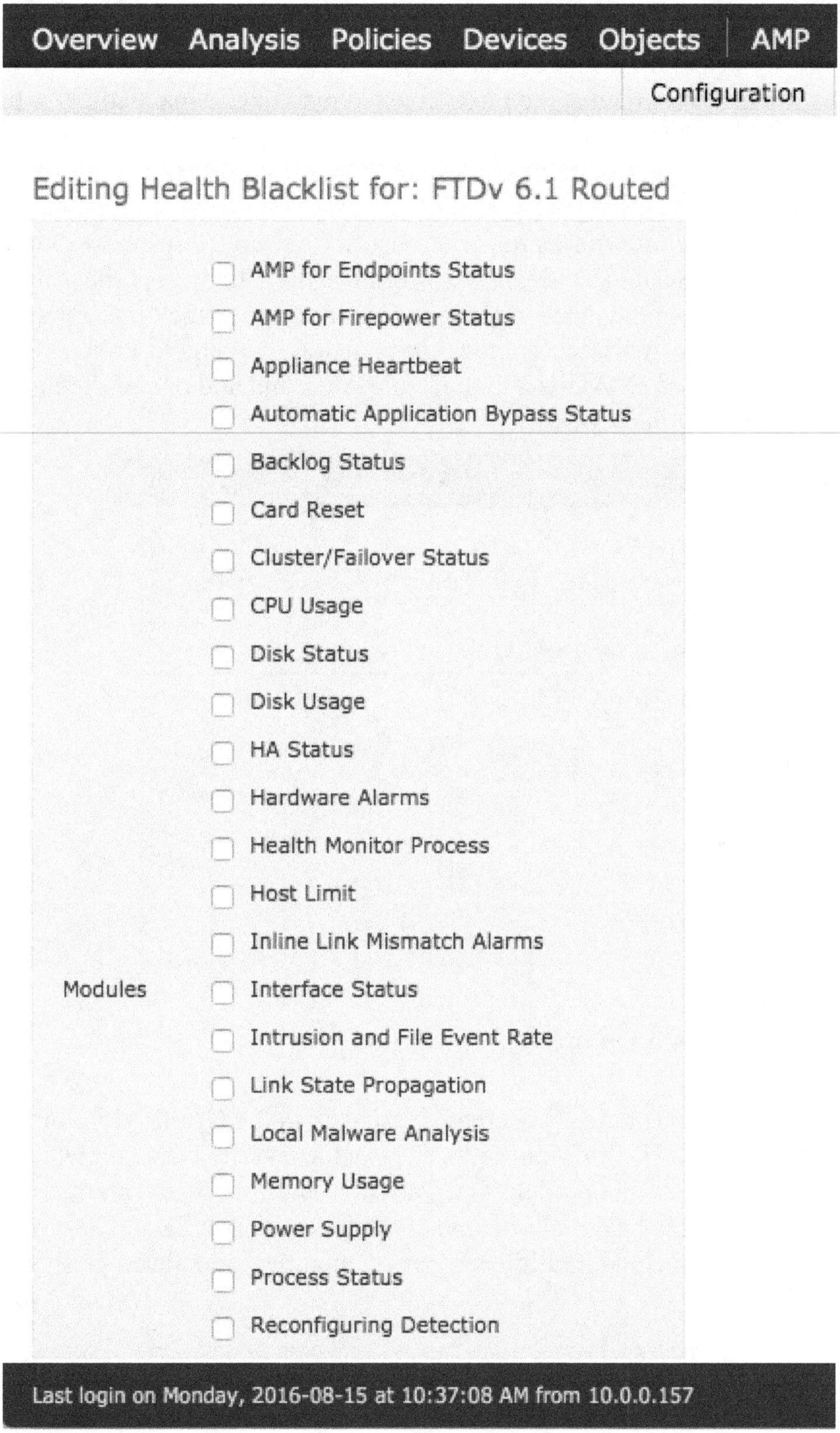
Overview Analysis Policies Devices Objects AMP
Configuration
Editing Health Blacklist for: FTDv 6.1 Routed
Modules
AMP for Endpoints Status
AMP for Firepower Status
Appliance Heartbeat
Automatic Application Bypass Status
Backlog Status
Card Reset
Cluster/Failover Status
CPU Usage
Disk Status
Disk Usage
HA Status
Hardware Alarms
Health Monitor Process
Host Limit
Inline Link Mismatch Alarms
Interface Status
Intrusion and File Event Rate
Link State Propagation
Local Malware Analysis
Memory Usage
Power Supply
Process Status
Reconfiguring Detection
Last login on Monday, 2016-08-15 at 10:37:08 AM from 10.0.0.157

Figure 5.14: Health blacklist

Health Monitor Alerts

In some environments, the FMC console may not be manned 24/7. In these situations, it's a good idea to have external alerts set up to notify people immediately to any health conditions that crop up. This is where Health Monitor alerts come in—with them, you can send emails, SNMP traps, or syslog messages. To configure Health Monitor alerts, you must first set up the responses known as alerts. Navigate to System → Health → Monitor Alerts to display the configuration page. In the upper-right corner is the Alerts quick link for setting up the responses. You can also access the Alerts dialog by going to Policies → Actions → Responses → Alerts. Click Create Alert and add one of the three alert types, as shown in Figure 5.18.

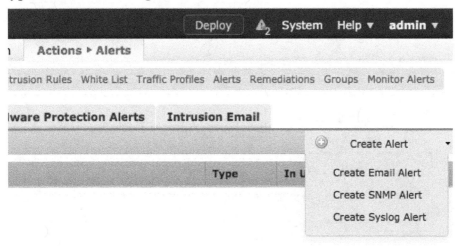

Figure 5.15: Create an alert

Once the alert (or alerts) is created, go back to the Health Monitor Alerts screen. To create the Health Monitor alert, select a severity based on when you want the alert to occur, the module(s) to monitor, and finally, the alert you want generated. Specify the health alert name at the top and click Save. Keep in mind that you can opt to include multiple severities, modules, and alerts, as shown in Figure 5.19.

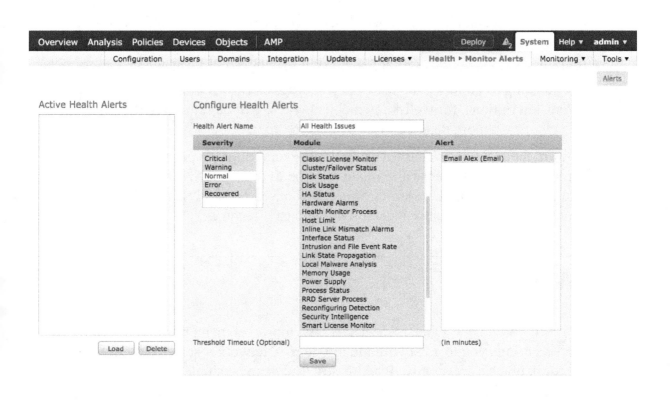

Figure 5.16: Health Monitor alert

Chapter 6: Objects

Welcome to objects! We are finally getting into the meat of the Firepower system. Firepower uses reusable configuration components—objects—to provide an easier way to use values across policies, searches, reports, dashboards, and so on. You may think a chapter describing these components would be boring; however, understanding the objects themselves will require an understanding of how they are used within the rest of the system. Because of this, we will wind up digging into several interesting areas in our discussion of this subject.

We're going to go down the list of object types as shown in the user interface. Some descriptions, for well-known object types, will be rather brief, but for other object types, a more detailed discussion is in order.

Toward the end of this chapter we will hit several object types that apply only to Firepower Threat Defense and relate to some of the legacy ASA routing and VPN features. Once again, because this book is focused primarily on the NGFW/NGIPS functionality, we will only touch on these legacy features.

Network

In Firepower, Objects merits its own top-level menu position. Clicking on Objects brings you to a list with the top item—Network—selected by default. Network objects are simply IP addresses. They can be single IPs, CIDR blocks, and even ranges. There are quite a number of default Network objects already present. These will be useful in many deployments to identify ranges such as RFC 1918 private addresses or multicast addresses.

To create your own Network object, click the Add Network button. You can then select Add Object or Add Group. A group is simply a number of objects bundled together. The New Network Objects dialog is shown in Figure 6.1.

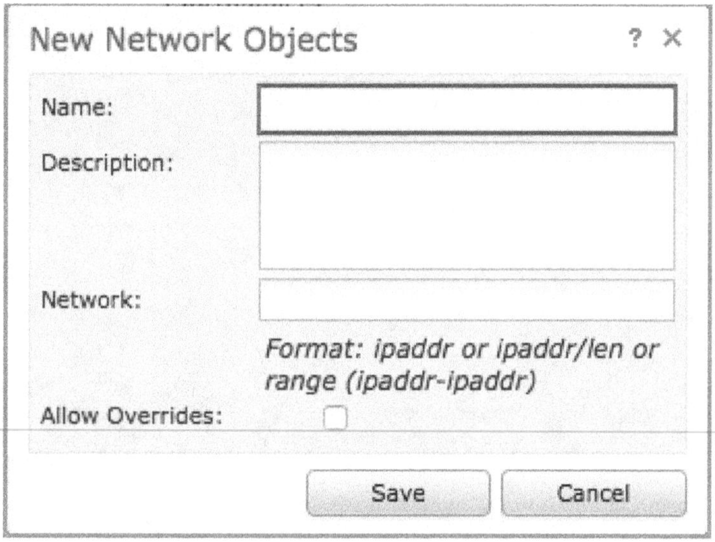

Figure 6.1: New Network Objects dialog

We're not going to say a whole lot about this dialog, it's fairly easy to understand. However, one feature does warrant highlighting. From the inception of the Sourcefire 3D System through its many updates and name changes to FireSIGHT and now Firepower, one oft asked-for feature has never been available. That is, the ability to enter a range of IP addresses. You could always enter a single IP or a CIDR block, but there was no way to enter an arbitrary range such as 10.0.0.5–10.0.0.12. Version 6.1 of Firepower will go down in history as the first version that allows this flexibility.

I know it may not sound like a big deal - unless you've had students asking you that question in nearly every class for five years!

The Allow Overrides box also warrants some explanation. Checking this allows overriding this object's value at the device level if desired. When you check the Allow Overrides box, another section of the screen appears. You can then select Devices or Domains, add one or more, and select a different value for this object when used in the selected context. For example, in Figure 6.2 the object bob has the value of 10.0.0.1 except when it's used on the device named FTDv 6.1 Routed, where the value is 10.0.0.2.

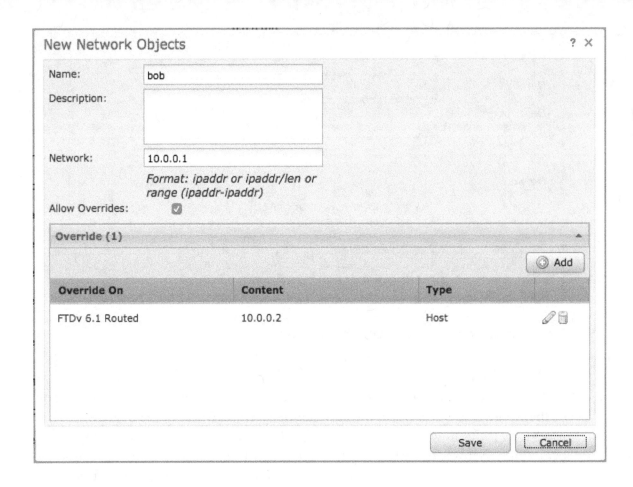

Figure 6.2: Network object override

Lastly, we said that a group is a collection of one or more objects. You can also nest object groups within object groups—up to 10 levels!

Port

Like Network objects, Port objects are a pretty basic concept. These are most commonly the TCP/UDP port numbers that live at the Transport layer of the OSI model. Port objects can also be ICMP or IPv6-ICMP Type/Code combinations or any other IP protocol number.

Clicking on the Port link in the upper left of the screen brings you to the list of default Port objects. All the common TCP/UDP ports are here. These default objects cannot be edited or deleted. To create a new Port object, click the Add Port button and select Add Object. Figure 6.3 shows the New Port Objects dialog.

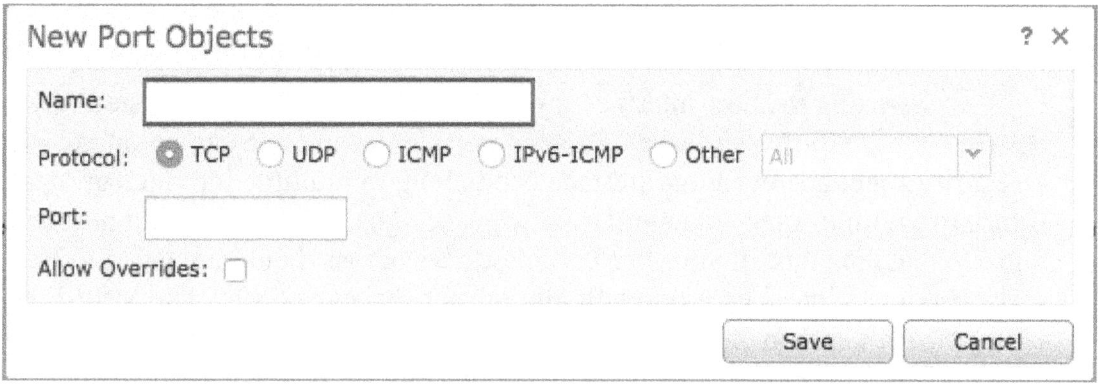

New Port Objects

Name:	[ ]
Protocol:	⦿ TCP ○ UDP ○ ICMP ○ IPv6-ICMP ○ Other [All ▾]
Port:	[ ]
Allow Overrides:	☐

[Save] [Cancel]

Figure 6.3: New Port Objects dialog

Again, rather than discuss the mundane steps to create a Port object, we will just note one bit of flexibility offered in Firepower. In the Port field, you can enter a single port in the range 1 to 65535, or you can enter an arbitrary range such as 25–35. You can also create Port Group objects, which are a combination of one or more Port objects.

Interface

If you've been using Firepower since the 5.x version, you will be familiar with zones. In version 6.1, these are now under the broad heading of Interface objects. There are two types of Interface objects – zones and interface groups. A zone—or more accurately a security zone—is a descriptive name for an interface. There is a slight difference between FTD and a Firepower device here. In FTD, your interface has a logical name, which is assigned through the Device Management → Interfaces page. With a Firepower device, you do not have this capability so the zone becomes your only friendly name for the interface. Therefore, one benefit of using zones is you get a friendly, or descriptive, name for the interface. So, if you are connecting a firewall and a switch through an inline interface pair, you can name the zone on the one side Firewall and the zone on the other side Switch.

This works fine for a simple network, but what if we have a similar network design in several sites? We can use the same zone name of "Firewall" for all of our firewall facing interfaces, but that could get confusing for an analyst looking at an event. The source zone of "Firewall" could be anywhere in the world. It would be better to name them something more appropriate, like NY-

Firewall, MSP-Firewall, etc. Now when reviewing events, the ingress and egress zones will provide the analyst with more context surrounding the event.

By using the new interface group feature, we can even go a step further in providing flexibility and ease of management. An interface can belong to just one security zone; however, an interface can belong to multiple interface groups. In the case of multiple sites with similar network designs, you can have an interface group that contains all your firewall interfaces across the organization. You can also create an interface group will all your interfaces in a site. The MSP-Firewall interface could then be a member of both of these groups. Note that the interface group feature is only available on FTD devices.

Let's walk through an example. First, we will navigate to Objects →
Interface, click the Add button, and select Security Zone. The resulting dialog is shown in Figure 6.4.

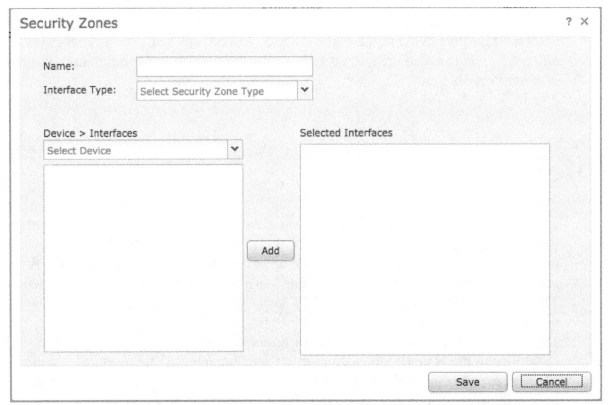

Figure 6.4: Adding a security zone

When adding a security zone, you must select the zone type, and all interfaces in this zone must be of the same type. Your choices are Passive, Inline, Switched, Routed, and ASA. Once you have the type selected, choose your device from the Device > Interfaces drop-down. At this point, any interfaces not already members of another zone will appear. In the example in Figure 6.5, we are creating an inline zone named MSP-Firewall. We've selected the FTDv Transparent 2 device and there are two interfaces we can choose from: MSP-Firewall and MSP-Switch. We have added the MSP-Firewall interface to this zone.

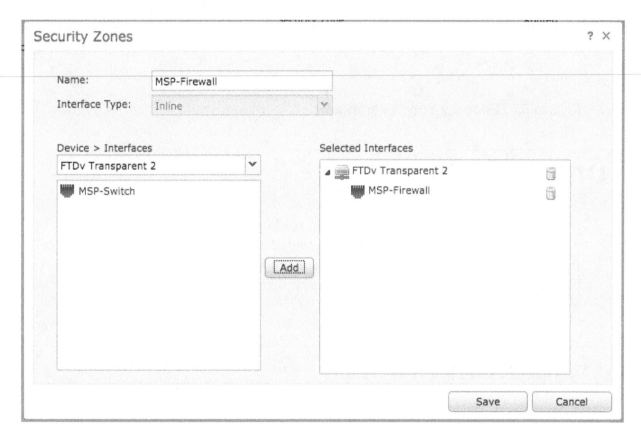

Figure 6.5: Adding Interfaces to a security zone

Now, if you have other inline firewall-facing interfaces in the MSP location, you can add them to this same zone. They can even be on different devices. In the example in Figure 6.6, we have created the MSP-Firewall and MSP-Switch zones and added inline interfaces from an FTD and a NGIPSv device. Notice the logical names for the FTD device and the system-assigned name for the Firepower NGIPSv. Remember, this is because you can name the actual interface on FTD, but on a Firepower device you will use the slot/port notation such as s1p1, s1p2, etc.

Figure 6.6: Security zone examples

Tunnel Zone

The Tunnel Zone object is used in conjunction with the new Prefilter policy. Tunnel zones can be assigned to tunneled traffic and then referred to later in Access Control rules. This will be discussed in more detail in the Prefilter policy section. Tunnel Zone objects are simply arbitrary names you create to assign to tunneled traffic.

Application Filters

One of the benefits of a next-generation firewall is application awareness. At the time of this writing, Firepower can identify over 3,200 applications. These are further categorized according to risk, business relevance, and type. In addition, applications are assigned tags such as evasive, blog, webmail, etc. The purpose of an Application Filter object is to allow you to define your own criteria to allow or block applications in your environment. This can be done in an Access Control rule without using a pre-created Application Filter object, but if you need to reuse these filters across multiple policies, then creating an object is the way to go.

When you click the Add Application Filter button, you are presented with the dialog shown below in Figure 6.7.

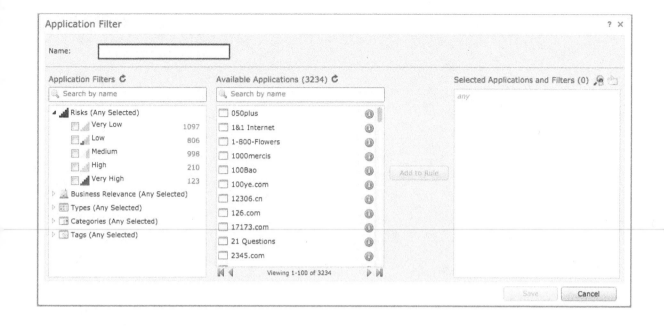

Figure 6.7: Application Filter dialog

By checking the appropriate boxes under Risks, Business Relevance, Types, etc., you narrow down the list of available applications in the center column. You can also use the Search by Name field in either the left or center columns to zero in on the apps you want. Once you have what you're looking for, click the Add to Rule button to add them.

The mechanics of the user interface are easy enough to figure out; however, there are some important points you should keep in mind as you're setting up these filters.

First, the blue information icon (ⓘ) is your friend. In Figure 6.8, we have clicked on the icon next to LinkedIn Job Search. Here you can see how this application is classified according to risk, business relevance, type, and so on. Notice this is also tagged as "not work related."

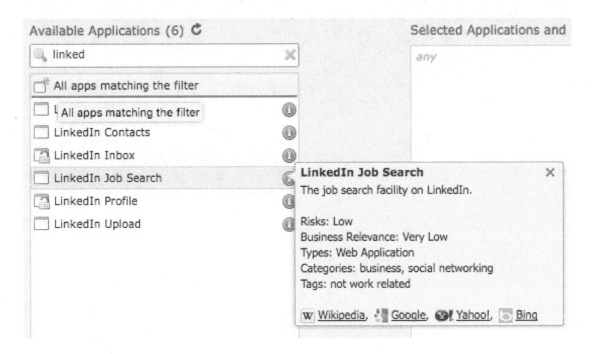

Figure 6.8: Application information

Also, notice the lock icon ( ). This indicates applications that the system can detect only if the traffic is decrypted. Keep in mind that this is not all-inclusive. You will find applications that do not have this icon but may still be encrypted. With more and more applications and websites defaulting to SSL, decryption is becoming an even more important tool for network traffic inspection.

Finally, if you have been living on a deserted island for the past 10 years, you can use one of the search engine links to find out what this LinkedIn application is all about. Actually, there may be some applications in the list that are not as well known, so these search links do come in handy from time to time.

When you are finished, you will have application filter(s) you can then use in your Access Control rules to allow or restrict access for your users.

VLAN Tag

The VLAN Tag object is simply a VLAN number or range. You can set these up ahead of time for use in your Access Control rules. See Figure 6.9 for an example of the VLAN Tag object dialog.

Figure 6.9: VLAN Tag object dialog

Security Group Tag

The Security Group Tag (SGT) object is used in conjunction with Cisco's Identity Services Engine (ISE). The SGT is a field added to network packets that is used by Firepower to identify the source machine or user. It is only available if you have *not* configured ISE as an identity source. If you have configured ISE, then the available SGTs are pulled from the ISE server rather than using custom SGT objects.

Yes, the identity subject is quite involved, and for now, we will limit the discussion to just the use of the Security Group Tag object. Creating an object is very simple: just give it a name, an optional description, and the tag. This is shown in Figure 6.10.

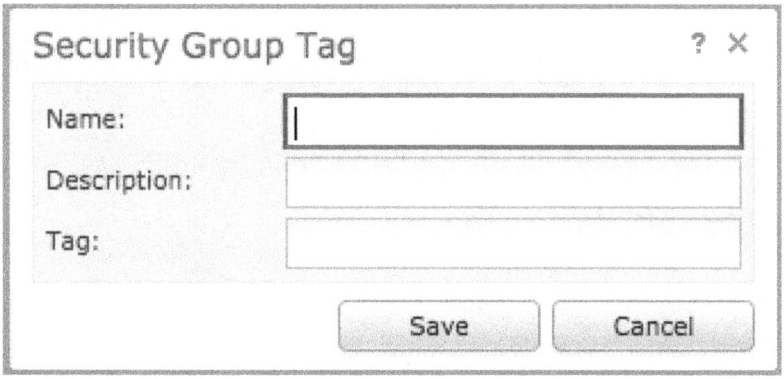

Figure 6.10: Security Group Tag object dialog

URL

The URL object is another pretty simple concept. You give a URL a friendly name that you can then reuse in various Access Control rules. The process for creating these objects is straightforward.

There are a couple of things you should remember when creating URL objects. First, if you plan to use the object to match HTTPS traffic, create the object based on the common name in the public key certificate used by the server. Also, the system disregards subdomains within the common name. For example, use badsite.com rather than www.badsite.com.

Second, the system performs a substring match on the URL. For example, if you create an object to match ign.com, it will match *any* URL that contains this text. This means you will also match verisign.com. This can yield unexpected results if you are not careful.

The fact that the system ignores subdomains for HTTPS, coupled with the substring matching behavior, can provide some challenges in filtering exactly the URLs you are looking for. Our advice is to be thoughtful and test extensively! The URL object dialog is shown in Figure 6.11.

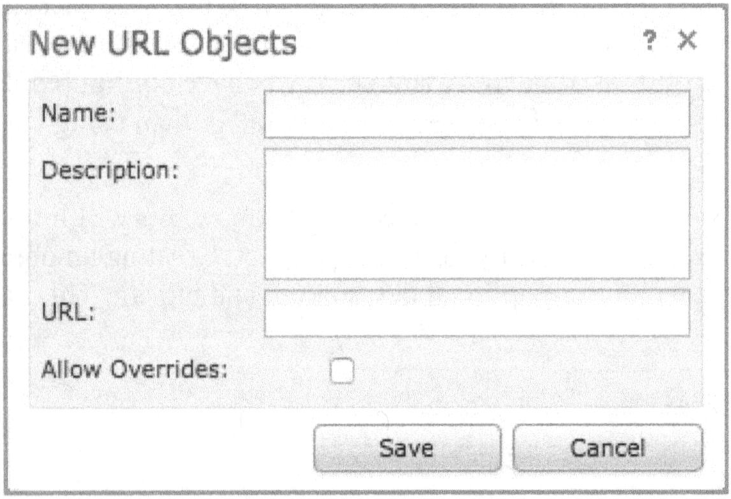

New URL Objects	? ✕
Name:	
Description:	
URL:	
Allow Overrides:	☐
	Save Cancel

Figure 6.11: URL object dialog

Geolocation

The Geolocation object allows for defining country and continent constraints for use in your Access Control rules. This is based on an IP address-to-geolocation mapping database that is updated periodically on your FMC.

Creating a new object is a simple process of clicking on the Add Geolocation button, giving your object a name, then checking the boxes by the continents or countries you want to include. This object will then be available for you to use as you wish in Access Control rules. The Geolocation Object dialog is shown in Figure 6.12.

Figure 6.12: Geolocation Object dialog

Variable Set

The Variable Set object relates directly to the use of Snort rules in the Intrusion policy. Each Snort rule contains two parts—the header and the body. The rule header determines things like the IP protocol, source/destination ports, and source/destination IP addresses to which the rule applies. The body is where the detection keywords are located. These do the magic of inspecting the packet contents looking for, well, whatever the rule writer wants to find. We will look at rules in more detail in the chapter in Chapter 8 "Intrusion Policy." For now, let's examine a simple rule header to get a basic understanding of what these variables are all about.

Consider the following Snort rule header:

```
alert tcp $EXTERNAL_NET any -> $HOME_NET $HTTP_PORTS
```

Let's break down the various keywords used in this rule header.

- **alert** – This is the rule action. In this case the rule will generate an event (alert) but will not drop the packet.

- **tcp** – The protocol; it can be ip, tcp or udp.

- **$EXTERNAL_NET** – the source IP address(es).

- **any** – The source port.

- **->** –The directional operator. This means the packet must be traveling from the source (on the left) to the destination (on the right).

- **$HOME_NET** – The destination IP address(es).

- **$HTTP_PORTS** – The destination port(s).

As you probably guessed, some of the items above are variables. See them? They are the ones that start with the dollar sign ($). These are defined by the Variable Set object.

If you only remember one thing about this section, remember this: Nearly every Snort rule you will find contains the variables $HOME_NET and $EXTERNAL_NET. This is because you are always looking at traffic either *to* or *from* your "trusted network." Sometimes Snort rules are designed to detect an attack in a packet traveling *to* your protected network. Sometimes they are designed to detect the evidence of an attack, data leakage, or maybe signs of a malware-infected host in a packet traveling *from* your protected network.

As you probably guessed by now, the variable $HOME_NET contains the IP address range(s) of your protected network. Oftentimes we include all the RFC-1918 private address space plus any public IP space owned by your organization.

Conversely, the $EXTERNAL_NET variable points to the unprotected network or maybe the "suspect" network if you would rather. This is commonly the Internet but it may also include your $HOME_NET as well. You do not have to exclude the $HOME_NET range from the $EXTERNAL_NET variable. In fact, in many cases, we recommend you leave $EXTERNAL_NET at the default value of *any*. By doing this you can protect yourself from any internal hosts that may misbehave and start spreading mischief.

One last thing to keep in mind. The default value of both $HOME_NET and $EXTERNAL_NET is *any*. In addition, nearly all of the other IP variables are based on the value of $HOME_NET. Some of these are variables like the following:

- DNS_SERVERS
- HTTP_SERVERS
- SIP_SERVERS
- SMTP_SERVERS
- SQL_SERVERS

All of these default to the value of $HOME_NET. They are provided to allow for further narrowing down of the IP range for a specific rule type, if desired. For example, you will find that rules written to protect web servers contain the variable $HTTP_SERVERS as their destination IP in the rule header. We find that in the vast majority of installations there is no need to refine these IP variables. Our advice—leave them alone. Define $HOME_NET with your internal IP address ranges, leave $EXTERNAL_NET at *any*, and go from there. You will be getting the best detection and also adding efficiency by inspecting traffic in the direction each Snort rule was designed to operate.

Another option is to leave both $HOME_NET and $EXTENAL_NET to *any*. The problem with this is now you're forcing Snort to inspect traffic without regard to its source or destination IP. Rules designed to inspect inbound traffic will also be forced to inspect outbound traffic as well. This will reduce the efficiency of the system and increase false positive intrusion events.

Now that you have an understanding of variables and their importance in Snort, let's look at the Variable Set object. First, you will notice that there is a default set (named Default-Set) already created. This is the system-provided variable set. If your deployment is small or you do not need to specify different variables for different devices in your network, then you can simply make any changes to this Default-Set. It will then be used automatically by any Access Control rules where you implement an Intrusion policy.

Your other option is to create your own Variable Set objects and customize them for use in various Access Control rules. These new Variable Set objects will start off using the values in the Default-Set, but you can override any or all of them to create your custom object.

Let's take a look at the Default-Set provided with the system in Figure 6.13.

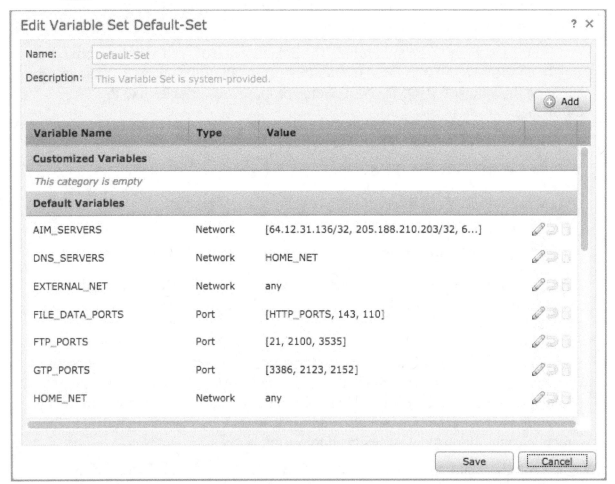

Figure 6.13: Default variable set

Notice our two rock stars $HOME_NET and $EXTERNAL_NET? They default to "any" as we mentioned previously. You can modify these by clicking the pencil icon and adding your own IP ranges. You can use an existing Network object (which is what we recommend) or type in your own IP address information on the fly. The Edit dialog is shown in Figure 6.14.

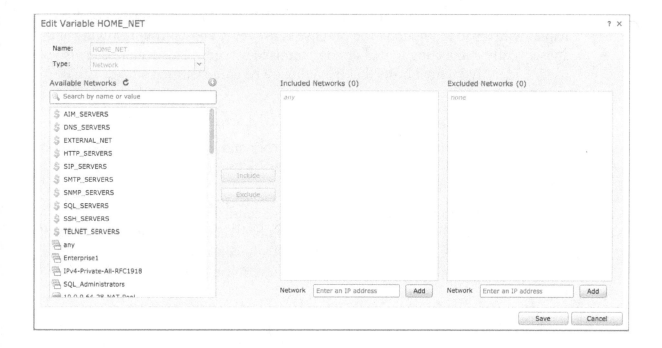

Figure 6.14: Editing HOME_NET

Once you change the values in the Default-Set, any new custom Variable Set objects will start out with these values. Also, keep in mind that once you override the default value for any of these variables, any subsequent updates from Cisco will not take effect. You will find that some of the variables—particularly the port variables—are updated by Cisco from time to time.

Security Intelligence Overview

Security Intelligence is an object category that contains three different categories of lists and feeds:

- Network

- DNS

- URL

Network Security Intelligence objects are simply IP addresses. These can be used to blacklist or whitelist traffic based on the source/destination IP address. The intent is to block malicious attackers or compromised hosts and also provide a safety net to prevent inadvertently blacklisting critical assets.

DNS Security Intelligence applies to DNS servers. This consists of domain names with a bad reputation. The purpose is to prevent hosts from resolving and subsequently connecting to evil or compromised servers. This feature can also be used to identify internal hosts that may already be compromised so they can be remediated.

URL Security Intelligence consists of URLs with a poor reputation.

Two of the three objects above—Network and URL—are implemented through the Access Control policy. DNS Security Intelligence is implemented through the DNS policy.

Each of these is capable of receiving a Security Intelligence feed from Cisco Talos. This feed is a dynamic collection of IP addresses, URLs, or domain names that the FMC downloads at an interval you configure. Changes to this feed are immediately applied to all devices without requiring a manual policy deployment.

Talos is the name of Cisco's threat intelligence organization. Among other things, they conduct security research, perform intelligence analysis, educate, and maintain a number of Cisco security tools, including Snort and Snort rules. For more information, visit http://www.talosintelligence.com.

You can also create your own custom feeds for any of these categories. Custom feeds are hosted on an HTTP or HTTPS server and—like the Cisco Talos feed—they can be automatically downloaded at a customizable interval. This method also applies the updated feed data to all devices immediately.

You can also create custom lists that you then upload as a Security Intelligence object. However, this is a rather inflexible method because any change requires re-uploading the entire list. In addition, if a custom list is added or changed, you must deploy policies for it to take effect. This method may be more appropriate for static information such as a whitelist containing your critical routers or gateways.

Network Security Intelligence

Network lists and feeds have been included with the Firepower product since version 5.x. They are simply lists of IP addresses. They are implemented on the Advanced tab in the Access Control policy where they can be used to blacklist or whitelist traffic. The system comes with three Network Security Intelligence objects by default:

- The Cisco-Intelligence-Feed
- The Global-Blacklist

- The Global-Whitelist

The Cisco-Intelligence-Feed is actually several lists of IP addresses in different categories. We will see this later when we look at the Access Control policy. This feed is updated by Cisco constantly, and you can download it as often as once every 30 minutes. Note, the default setting for this interval is 2 hours. However, because of the fast-paced nature of some malware campaigns, we recommend taking advantage of this update frequency and setting it to the minimum interval.

The Global-Blacklist and Global-Whitelist are empty by default. They are designed to be populated with your own custom IP addresses during the process of event analysis. By right-clicking on an IP address in any of the various event views or in the Context Explorer, you can add it to either of these lists on the fly.

The scenario goes something like this:

"Holy malware Batman. This intrusion event is really bad. We should block all communications to/from that host."

<right-clicks on IP address and selects Blacklist IP Now>

"Whew, that was close!"

Figure 6.15 shows what the right-click menu looks like for an intrusion event.

Figure 6.15: Right-click menu for an intrusion event

When you select this menu item, you receive an "Are you sure?" confirmation dialog. Selecting Blacklist Now adds the IP to the Global-Blacklist and updates this list on all your devices within seconds.

You can also use the Whitelist IP Now option to add the host to the Global-Whitelist and allow the IP to bypass any Network Security Intelligence blacklists.

When you click on Network Lists and Feeds under the Security Intelligence category, you will see the default lists and the Cisco-Intelligence-Feed. This is shown in Figure 6.16.

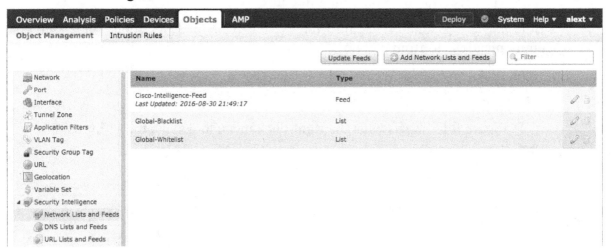

Figure 6.16: Default Network Security Intelligence objects

While it appears that you can edit the Global-Blacklist and Global-Whitelist here, you are actually limited to removing IP address entries only. They can only be added through the right-click method mentioned previously.

Note that according to the Firepower online help, adding an entry to either global list causes the devices to update immediately; however, removing an entry from either list requires a policy deployment. This is mostly true, but what really happens is when you add an entry to a global list, the entire list is pushed out immediately. So if you have also just removed an item from a list, that change will also be pushed out with the new list.

To add a custom list or feed, click the Add Network Lists and Feeds button. Next, enter the name and pick the type of object, either Feed or List (Figure 6.17).

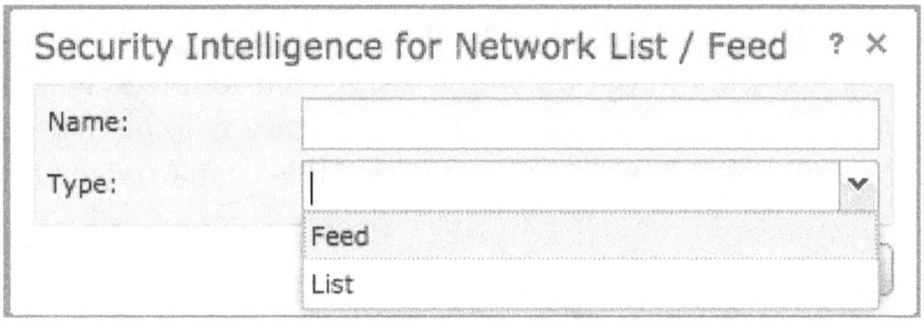

Figure 6.17: Security Intelligence for Network types

If you selected List, you will be presented with a dialog to browse to the list, which should be a text file (.txt) with one IP/CIDR entry per line. The file can be a maximum of 500 MB in size.

If you select Feed, you will see the dialog shown in Figure 6.18.

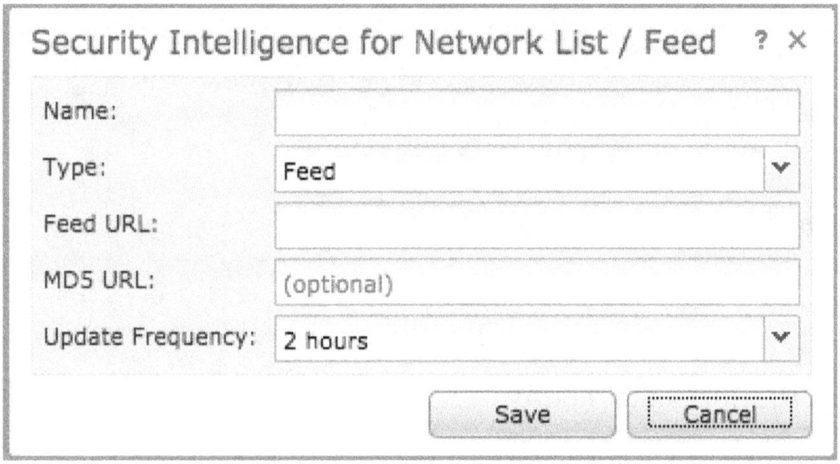

Figure 6.18: Network feed

Here you enter the URL where the feed file is located and an optional MD5 URL that can be used to determine if the file has been updated. If the MD5 hash has not changed since the previous update, the feed file will not be downloaded. The Update Frequency option will default to 2 hours, but you can set it as low as 30 minutes to update your feed more quickly.

DNS Security Intelligence

The DNS Security Intelligence feature was added in Firepower version 6. It works like its Network sibling by receiving a feed from Cisco. However, these are domain names with a poor reputation rather than IP addresses. Also similar to Network Security Intelligence, there is a global blacklist and a global whitelist.

You can add your own lists and feeds, which operate pretty much the same way, by either uploading a text file full of domains or using a custom feed that can be updated at an interval you select. DNS Security Intelligence is implemented via the DNS policy. We will cover how this works in detail later in Chapter 10 "DNS and SSL Policy."

The dialogs for adding/removing DNS lists and feeds are identical in nearly every way to those for network lists and feeds. The only difference is how you go about adding entries to the global whitelist and blacklist. Instead of right-clicking on an IP address, you do so on a URL. Figure 6.19 shows an example of the menu you will see if you right-click on a URL in a connection event.

URL	URL Category
https://www.alext.info	Uncategorized
https://www.al€	Open in New Window
https://www.al€	Blacklist HTTP/S Connections to URL Now
https://ssl.goo(	Whitelist HTTP/S Connections to URL Now
https://ssl.goo(	Blacklist HTTP/S Connections to Domain Now
	Whitelist HTTP/S Connections to Domain Now
	Exclude

Figure 6.19: URL right-click menu

By selecting Blacklist HTTP/S Connections to URL Now, you will add this entry to the URL global blacklist. By selecting Blacklist HTTP/S Connections to Domain Now, you will add this entry to the DNS global blacklist.

URL Security Intelligence

The last intelligence category is URL Security Intelligence. As you may have guessed, this is for URLs with a poor reputation. When you select URL Lists and Feeds from the Security Intelligence object list, you will see a page similar to the ones for Network and DNS. However, one thing is missing—there is no entry for the Cisco feed. This is because the DNS and URL entries are combined into a single feed, which is managed under DNS Lists and Feeds. If you return to the DNS Lists and Feeds page, you will notice that the built-in feed is called Cisco-DNS-and-URL-Intelligence-Feed. So, while there are three Security Intelligence categories (Network, DNS, and URL), there are only two Cisco-provided feeds.

As with URL objects, the URL Security Intelligence Lists and Feeds entries will match any URL that contains the entry. Thus a feed entry of www.alext.info will match any page on the site.

Security Intelligence Under the Hood

Since this is an advanced book, let's talk about some of the under-the-hood mechanics when it comes to security intelligence. A common question is, "Where can I find a list of the IP, URL, DNS entries in the Cisco feed?" There is no way within the graphical user interface to find this information. The best you can do is to see how many entries are in a given feed category. To find out how many entries are in a given category, navigate to Polices → Access Control → Access Control. Then edit one of your policies and click the Advanced tab. You can then use your mouse to hover over one of the Network, DNS, or URL categories. A pop-up will indicate how many entries are currently in this category. This is illustrated in Figure 6.20.

Figure 6.20: SI category entries

But what about the actual entries? To find these you must SSH to either a device or the FMC. You will find the three types of Security Intelligence entries in the following three locations:

Network – `/var/sf/iprep_download`

DNS – `/var/sf/sidns_download`

URL – `/var/sf/siurl_download`

Here you will find separate text files for each Security Intelligence category. You will find text files for any of your custom feeds as well. Figure 6.21 shows the contents of the **sidns_download** folder.

```
● ● ●                ⌂ atatistcheff — ssh admin@10.0.0.9 — 80×24
[root@FirepowerManagement:/var/sf/sidns_download# ls
032ba433-c295-11e4-a919-d4ae5275b77b   6ba968f4-7a25-4793-a2c8-7cc77f1f1074
1b117672-7453-478c-be31-b72e89ca2dde   A27C6AAE-8E52-4174-A81A-47C59FECd3a5
23f2a124-8278-4c03-8c9d-d28fe08b71ab   Cisco_DNS_Intelligence_Feed
2CCDA18E-DDFF-4F5C-AF9A-F00985219707   IPRVersion.dat
2b15cb6f-a3fc-4e0e-a342-ccc5e5804576   b1df3aa8-2841-4c88-8e64-bfaacec7111f
30f9e69c-d64c-479c-821d-0e4edab8348d   d7d996a6-6b92-4a56-8f10-e8506e432fb8
3e2af68e-5fc8-4b1c-b5bc-b4e7cab5abcd   health
5a0b6d6b-e2c3-436f-b4a1-48248b331d39   peers
5f8148f1-e5e4-427a-aa3b-ee1c2745d663   rep_dd.yaml
60f4e2ab-d96c-44a0-bd38-830252b65259   tmp
root@FirepowerManagement:/var/sf/sidns_download#
```

Figure 6.21: SIDNS files

The files have unrecognizable UUID (Universally Unique IDentifier) names, but if you use **cat**, **head**, or **tail** to look at their contents, you will see that they are simply text files. Each one contains the name of the list as a comment in the first line. Figure 6.22 shows the contents of one of these. Turns out it is the file for the Command and Control (CnC) DNS list.

```
● ● ●                ⌂ atatistcheff — ssh admin@10.0.0.9 — 80×24
[root@FirepowerManagement:/var/sf/sidns_download# head 60f4e2ab-d96c-44a0-bd38-83]
0252b65259
#Cisco DNS and URL intelligence feed: DNS CnC
www.weddingsonthefrenchriviera.com
www.gjscomputerservices.com.au
www.taoblu.com
www.feddoctor.com
www.plexipr.com
www.kadinweb.net
www.001edizioni.com
www.healthstafftravel.com.au
www.rippedknees.co.uk
root@FirepowerManagement:/var/sf/sidns_download#
```

Figure 6.22: DNS CnC file contents

Using this technique, you can find out the contents of any of the Security Intelligence download files for each of the three categories. One huge caveat however: These files are updated frequently. Depending on the update frequency you have selected, an entry that was here 30 minutes ago may be gone now. If you're trying to troubleshoot an issue or predict whether a given IP, domain, or

URL will be blocked, this may not be a viable technique. It's nice to know however, and now you can impress your friends with your in-depth knowledge of Firepower!

Sinkhole

The Sinkhole object is another one that is new in version 6. We will go into detail on how this works in the chapter on DNS and SSL policy. For now, we will whet your appetite with a brief description of the Sinkhole object and a bit of information on how to create one.

A sinkhole is a DNS server that is designed to return non-routable addresses in response to DNS queries. More accurately, these IP addresses—routable or not—do not resolve to an actual server. Since DNS resolution is the first step in virtually any TCP/IP connection, this is designed to prevent a user/host from successfully establishing a connection. By making it impossible to resolve a name to an IP address, the connection is stopped dead in its tracks.

You might ask, "Why not just block the DNS request? Why use a sinkhole?" That's a good question. One reason has to do with the placement of the IPS in relation to your internal DNS server. Oftentimes, the IPS sees a DNS request for an evil domain coming from your DNS server, which forwarded it on behalf of an infected client. The IPS can easily block this request using a Snort rule; however, what you really want to know is, Which of my hosts made that DNS query? Since the host is trying to resolve an "evil" hostname, it would be very helpful to know which host this is and maybe send in the incident response team. By using a sinkhole, we can return a bogus IP address to the DNS server, which relays that to the (infected) host. Now when the host tries to actually connect to this sinkhole IP, BAMO! We've got him! The IPS can see this request and generate an alert that somebody is trying to connect to our sinkhole IP. The only way a host would get the sinkhole IP address in the first place is if we gave it to him in response to an evil DNS request.

We said this would be a short description, so let's stop here while we're ahead. We will explain this further with fancy pictures and diagrams in the DNS and SSL policy chapter. For now let's talk about how you would go about setting up a Sinkhole object.

There are no Sinkhole objects created by default. To create, one click the Add Sinkhole button. This will display the dialog shown in Figure 6.23.

Figure 6.23: Creating a Sinkhole object

The options for your sinkhole are as follows:

- **Name:** Friendly name. You can use spaces if desired.

- **IPv4 Address:** The IPv4 address. Pick an address that resolves to something north of your IPS (outside your network) but that no host should ever try to connect to. One suggestion is to use the IPv4 space reserved for "documentation" according to RFC 5737. There are three ranges: TEST-NET-1 **192.0.2.0/24**, TEST-NET-2 **198.51.100.0/24**, and TEST-NET-3 **203.0.113.0/24**. While technically public space, some people also use **1.1.1.1** because it's so easy to pick out when scanning an event view page. Keep in mind that this should be a single IP address entry, not a range.

- **IPv6 Address**: IPv6 does not have a specifically reserved range for documentation; however, RFC 3849 suggests using **2001:DB8::/32** as a documentation-only prefix.

- **Log Connections to Sinkhole or Block and Log Connections to Sinkhole:** This is fairly straightforward. Do you want to allow this packet to continue or block it at the IPS? If you are using an actual server listening on port 53/UDP for your sinkhole IP address, you may want to allow the connection so you can log the request there. Either way, Firepower will log it as a Security Intelligence event.

- **Type:** The DNS Security Intelligence category breaks down into three types:

  - Command and Control (CnC)

- o Malware
- o Phishing

The purpose of this selection is to allow you to have different DNS sinkhole IPs for each type of DNS request. You may want to prioritize CnC events and remediate these more quickly. This way, you can set up special alerting for any hosts triggering your CnC sinkhole IP.

Once your Sinkhole objects are added, you can use them in your DNS policy to catch more evil on your network!

Sinkhole Reloaded

Now that you know how a sinkhole works let's think of ways we can (ab)use this feature. Since you can now make the DNS server return whatever IP you want, you control *everything*! Say, you have a list of sites that you'd rather nobody go to. Maybe you want everyone to use only your favorite dating site—farmersonly.com. To implement your evil plan using the DNS sinkhole feature, here are the steps to take:

1. Create a text file with all the domains of all those other sites like eharmony.com, match.com, okcupid.com, etc.

2. Upload this file as a custom DNS Security Intelligence object.

3. Create a Sinkhole object and use the actual farmersonly.com site for the IP address (see Figure 6.24). Make sure you don't block the connections to this sinkhole.

4. In your DNS policy, add a rule with an action of Sinkhole, and for the Sinkhole, select your Farmersonly-dot-com Sinkhole object. On the DNS tab, add only your custom DNS Security Intelligence object.

5. Deploy policies.

What you did is tell the device to sinkhole any request for one of those other dating sites and instead return the farmersonly.com IP address. The result will be that anyone trying to go to match.com, eharmony.com, and so on will find themselves looking at the farmersonly.com site. Then get ready for the help desk calls!

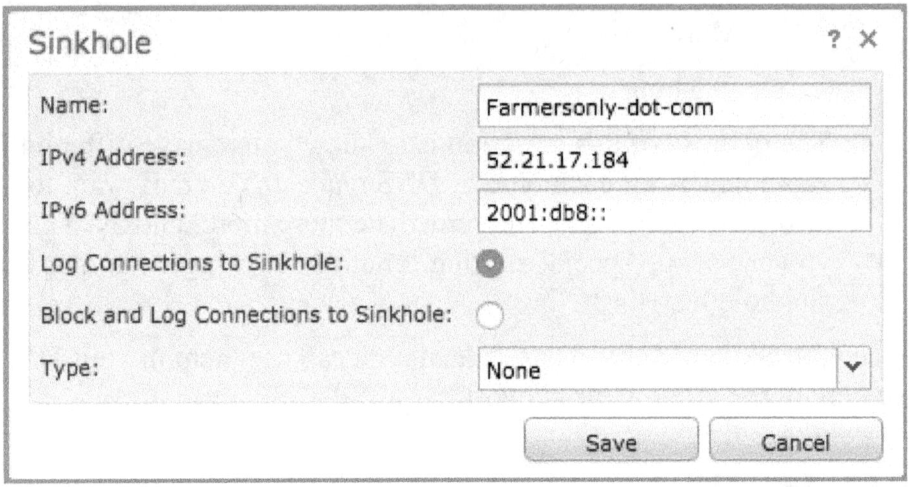

Figure 6.24: Farmers only sinkhole

File List

The File List object has not changed since version 5 of Firepower. It simply provides a way to customize file detection much like the blacklist or whitelist in Security Intelligence. There are two objects here, the Clean-List and the Custom-Detection-List. Both of these contain SHA-256 file hashes. They are designed to override the system's default behavior for a given SHA-256 hash.

The Clean-List contains SHA-256 hashes that should be considered clean regardless of their disposition in the Cisco cloud. Conversely, the Custom-Detection-List contains hashes considered to be malicious. Both of these lists are checked by the FMC prior to querying the Advanced Malware Protection (AMP) cloud when performing malicious file checks. The option to use this feature is controlled from the Malware & File policy.

If you click the pencil icon to the right of either of the two lists, you get a dialog like the one in Figure 6.25.

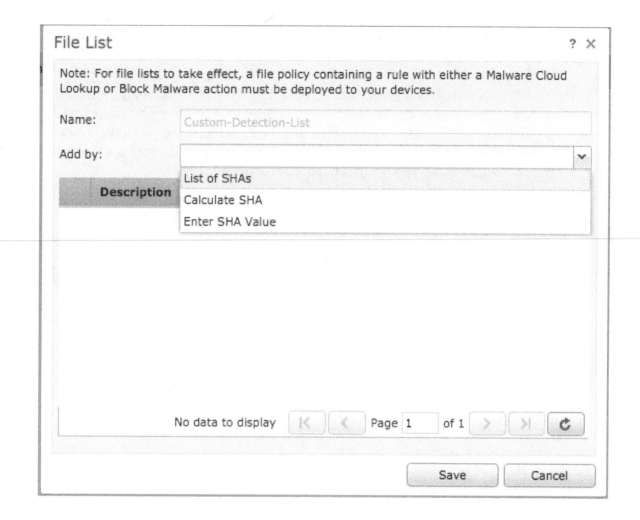

Figure 6.25: Custom detection list

There are three ways to add SHA-256 values to this object:

1. List of SHAs: This is a text file containing SHA-256 hash values, one per line. You can give this entry a description when you upload the file. You can upload multiple SHA lists in this manner.

2. Calculate SHA: If you have the file but do not know the SHA-256 hash, you can upload the file and let the FMC calculate the hash value. The file is not saved on the FMC; it's only used to calculate the hash for this entry.

3. Enter SHA Value: If you know the SHA-256 value, you can use this option and paste the value into the SHA256 field.

Cipher Suite List

The Cipher Suite List object can be used if you are performing SSL decryption on your device. The object comprises one or more cipher suites, each representing a method used to negotiate SSL or TLS encrypted sessions. You can use this list in your SSL rules to control which cipher suites the rule applies to. Figure 6.26 shows an example of a Cipher Suite object.

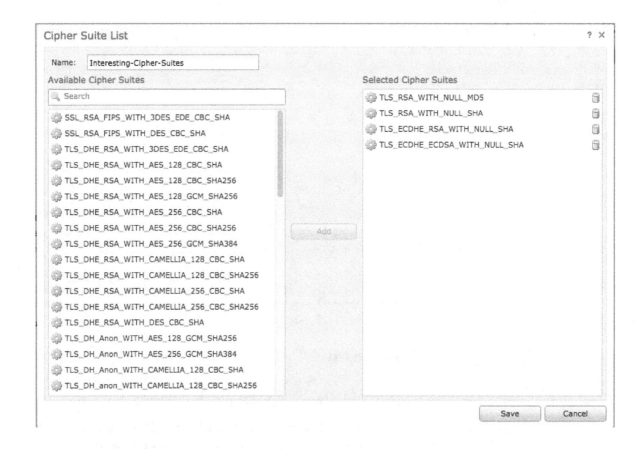

Figure 6.26: Cipher Suite object

Distinguished Name

Distinguished Name is another object related to SSL/TLS decryption. Each object represents the distinguished name for a public key certificate's subject or issuer. The idea is that you can use these objects in your SSL policy to control decryption based on server certificates with a certain subject or issuer. Oftentimes these are used to determine which SSL sites *not* to perform decryption for. This typically applies to outbound connections. This is illustrated by the names of the default objects that come with the system. Figure 6.27 shows the list of default Distinguished Name individual objects.

Figure 6.27: Default Distinguished Name objects

All of the default objects are sites where the use of SSL decryption will break the underlying application. This usually stems from the fact that some sites add extra or nonstandard functionality to their SSL communications. Because these deviate from "normal" SSL, any attempt to decrypt these communications will cause the underlying application or process to fail.

Other sites that may be good candidates to bypass decryption include online banking and health care sites—in other words, any site that you trust as legitimate and you do not want to decrypt for privacy reasons. Remember, we're talking mostly about outbound SSL, so one of your users would have initiated the connection. Cracking open someone's online banking transaction, even in the name of cyber security, is pretty much always a bad idea.

You can add your own objects and object groups. As you can see from the examples, wildcards are also supported.

PKI

Public Key Infrastructure (PKI) objects are used when you are performing SSL decryption on your device(s). Rather than going into detail on how PKI works, we will give a short description of each of the objects.

- Internal CAs: If you are performing outbound decryption, it means you will have to re-sign SSL communications. In this re-signing process, you will use a certificate that was either (a) generated by your FMC or (b) imported into your FMC from an external certificate authority (CA). The Internal CA object allows you to perform either operation.

- Trusted CAs: These objects represent the CA public certificate, which belongs to a trusted CA. You can import your own trusted CA objects. The system comes with over 200 preconfigured Trusted CAs.

- External Certs: These objects represent a server public key certificate that does not belong to your organization. They consist of the object name and the certificate. You can used these in SSL rules to control whether or not you decrypt traffic using the server certificate. An example would be a self-signed server certificate that you trust but cannot verify because it's not signed by a trusted CA.

- Internal Certs: These objects represent server public key certificates that belong to your organization. These consist of the object name, public key certificate, and the paired private key. These are used as follows:

  o Decrypting incoming traffic to one of your organization's servers using the known private key

  o Identity Services Engine (ISE) integration

  o Captive portal configuration to authenticate the identity of your captive portal device when users connect via a web browser

FTD-Only Settings

The following objects are only available when FTD devices are used. They are more commonly associated with some of the advanced routing or VPN features courtesy of the system's ASA lineage. We will touch on each one; for more information check out the online help or the user guide.

SLA Monitor

The SLA (Service Level Agreement) Monitor object is used to monitor connectivity to a monitored address through a given interface. It tracks the availability of the route to the address. This is accomplished by periodically sending ICMP echo request (ping) packets and waiting for a response. If the request times out, the route is removed from the routing table and replaced with a backup route. These objects are used in the Route Tracking field of an IPv4 Static Route policy. You'll find this configuration under Routing → Static Route on your FTD device. Clicking the Add SLA Monitor button displays the dialog shown in Figure 6.28.

Summary section for consistency

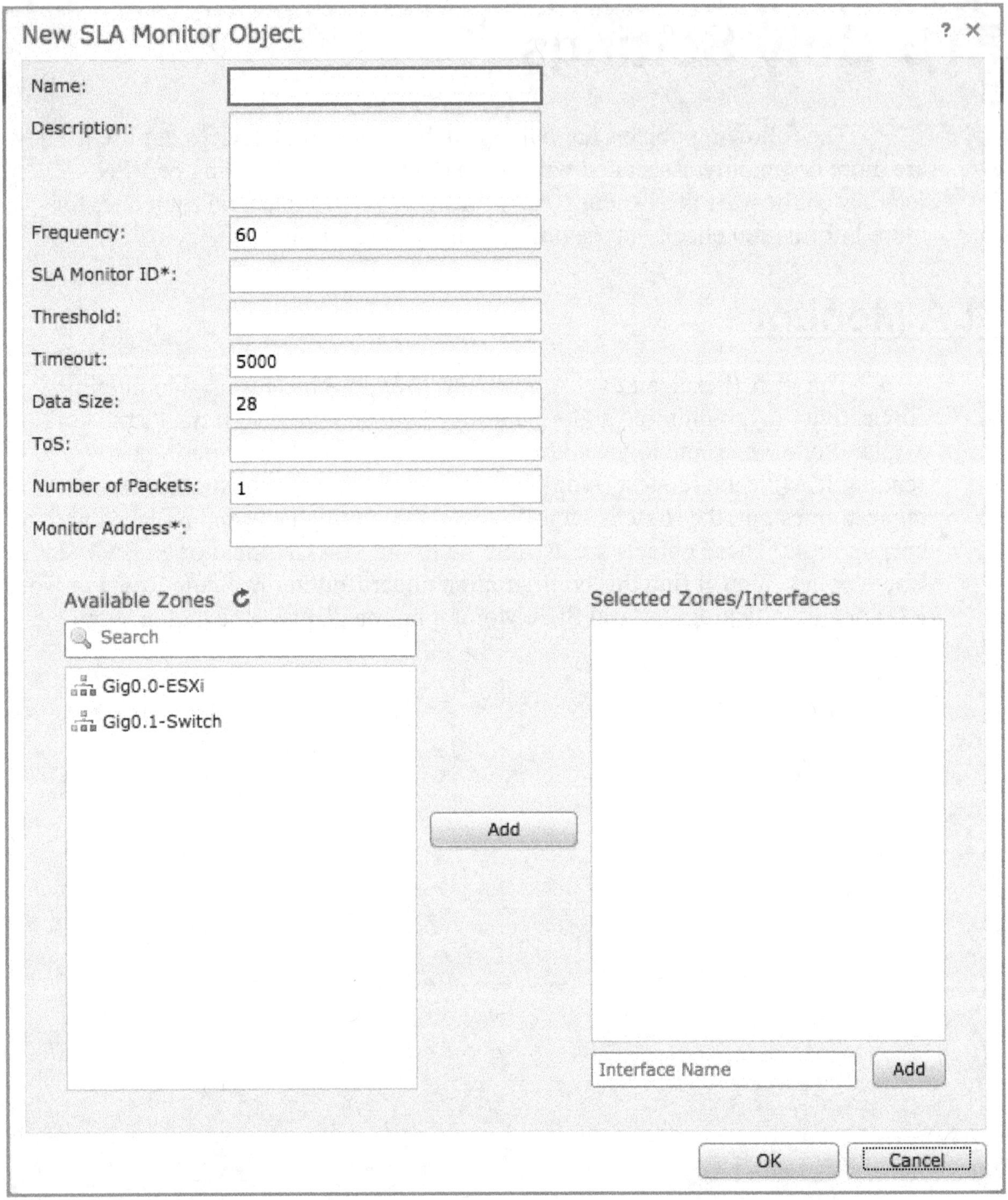

Figure 6.28: SLA Monitor object

Prefix Lists

The IPv4 and IPv6 Prefix List objects are used when configuring route maps, policy maps, OSPF filtering, and BGP neighbor filtering.

Route Map

The Route Map object is used when redistributing routes into any routing process. They are also used when generating a default route into a routing process. A route map defines which of the routes from the specified routing protocol are allowed to be redistributed into the target routing process.

Access List

Access lists (ACLs) come in two types: standard and extended. You can use them when configuring particular features, such as route maps. Traffic identified as allowed by the ACL is provided the service. Blocked traffic is excluded from the service. Excluding traffic from a service does not mean that it is blocked altogether.

A standard access list only uses a destination IPv4 address to define an entry. The action can be Allow or Block.

An extended access list allows matching traffic based on source and destination IP, protocol, and port and also supports IPv6 addresses.

AS Path

An AS Path is mandatory when setting up BGP routing. It consists of a sequence of AS numbers through which a network can be accessed. To learn more about AS Path, the online help is your friend!

Community List

A community is an optional attribute for configuring BGP. It is a group of destinations sharing a common attribute and is used for route tagging. Once again, check out the help for more information on this feature.

Policy List

The Policy List object is used when configuring route maps. When a policy list is referenced within a route map, all of the match statements in the list are evaluated and processed.

VPN

The objects under the VPN category are used in configuring the key exchange and encryption protocols used for VPN communications. There are several pre-created policies and proposals. You can also create your own.

Chapter 7: Firepower Network Discovery

Firepower Network Discovery, once just called simply FireSIGHT, and is still a better name for this technology, will be discussed in detail in this chapter.

Originally called Realtime Network Awareness (RNA) and Realtime User Awareness (RUA), this power technology provides us with the information we need to be able to analyze our data and fine tune our policies.

Once you've been acquainted with this awesome technology, we'll move on to explore discovery components like the discovery policy, type of data collected, connection events, and host attributes associated with it.

By the end of this chapter, you'll have gained sharp insight into exactly how Firepower Network Discovery is used to powerfully enhance event analysis.

To find Firepower videos, practice questions and Firepower hands-on classes with Todd Lammle, please see www.lammle.com/firepower.

Firepower Technologies

FireSIGHT was the name given to a technology built into the Cisco Firepower NGIPS to provide us with contextual awareness regarding events, IP addresses, users on the network, and even background about the hosts in the system.

This powerful technology will collect information about each IP address and build a host profile that includes the operating system, services, applications users, and network connections. Firepower will even include assumed vulnerabilities in profiles based upon those factors and additional data it has collected. This information is then used to automatically present an impact flag in the IPS analysis views to indicate whether or not the systems involved in the IPS events are susceptible to threats.

All of this vital intelligence is gained as a result of analyzing the packets on the wire and leveraging patented passive fingerprinting technology. For this to happen, either packets must traverse the managed device or the device must actually see the traffic itself during passive deployments.

A key benefit to this automated collection process is that it requires no additional software and doesn't probe the network. Furthermore, the more traffic that's seen moving to and from hosts, the more accurate the information entered into the database will be. And if that's not enough, you can even supplement the Firepower information with active techniques.

On the other hand, when there's a limited amount of traffic to collect, we can leverage the host input API—a strategy that allows us to import data from a separated values file, Nmap, or even third-party vulnerability scanners.

Network Discovery Policy

The Firepower network discovery policy is configured on the Firepower Management Center (FMC) and controls the Firepower technology. There's one discovery policy per FMC, and it should be specific to the environment it's being

| Networks | Users | Advanced | | | | |

Networks	Zones	Source Port Exclusions	Destination Port Exclusions	Action	
0.0.0.0/0 ::/0	any	none	none	Discover: Applications	

deployed in.

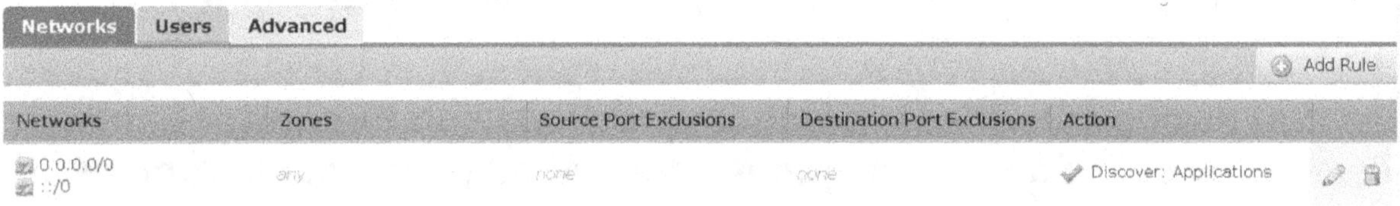

To configure the policy, navigate to **Policies ➤ Network Discovery**.

Figure 7.1: Network discovery policy

There are three main tabs across the top of the policy:

Network—Allows you to define the IP addresses on which you want to perform discovery.
User—Includes a list of protocols to discover users.
Advanced—Contains a variety of settings used to tweak the discovery settings.

Networks

The default discovery takes place on all IPv4 and IPv6 networks as noted with specified networks 0.0.0.0/0 and ::/0. So if we see a packet originating to and from anywhere, a host profile will start being generated for the IP addresses involved. The more paranoid among us will be tempted to track absolutely everything, but understand that the FMC is licensed based on model type to only handle a certain number of hosts.

For instance, the Firepower 750 is set to a maximum of 2,000 hosts, but the Firepower 4000 can handle 600,000 hosts. Considering that the clients on your internal network could easily be communicating to hundreds of web IP addresses each, your license could max out its limit pretty fast—choose wisely!

The good news here is that you can modify or delete the built-in rule and even add rules to create a specialized policy ideally suited to your particular environment's needs.

Looking at Figure 7.2 please notice that it is showing some of the options available for the rules. So, if licensing worries are keeping you up at night, just create rules limiting discovery to only the high-value networks in your organization. By adding rules like this, you're basically entering guidance to either

discover or exclude individual IP addresses, networks, or network objects. You can also configure discovery based on zones.

Figure 7.2: Network discovery rule

Notice in the rule I only configured the RFC 1918 addresses to be discovered, and enabled Hosts, Users, and Applications to be added to the database.

Another way to free up some resources is to exclude specific ports from discovery. You can also exclude protocols that probably aren't really that important to keep track of because they're unlikely to contain threat data.

While you can specify whether user or host information is collected, application inspection is automatically set to *on* because the FirePOWER system is designed to be application aware. So just because there's check box that makes it look like you can deselect it, you really can't. You also don't get to deselect host discovery unless user discovery is also deselected.

User Discovery

Figure 7.3 shows the User tab. This tab allows you to focus on the specific protocols on which you want to detect user logins, enabling or disabling them at will.

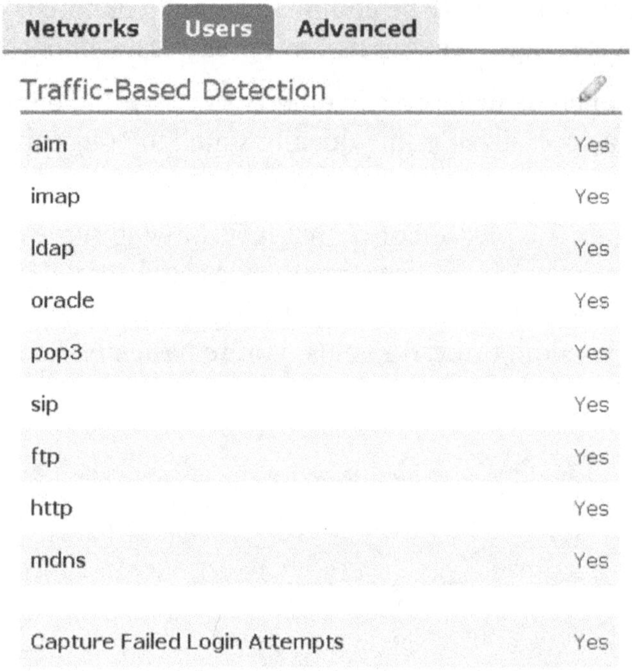

Networks	Users	Advanced	
Traffic-Based Detection			🖉
aim			Yes
imap			Yes
ldap			Yes
oracle			Yes
pop3			Yes
sip			Yes
ftp			Yes
http			Yes
mdns			Yes
Capture Failed Login Attempts			Yes

Figure 7.3: User tab

But here again, the number of users is restricted just as it was with IP addresses based upon the Defense Center model, and restricting the protocols up for detection here is helpful for managing your license count.

The following protocols are supported:

- AIM
- IMAP
- LDAP
- Oracle
- POP3
- SIP
- FTP
- http
- mdns

You can also pick up users from Active Directory, but that's handled through an agent and configured in System>Integration.

Advanced Discovery Settings

The Advanced tab, shown in Figure 7.4, contains settings key to tweaking the actual inspection being performed on the traffic. Here's a list of the sections into which these settings are sorted:

- General Settings
- Identity Conflict Settings
- Vulnerabilities to use for Impact Assessment
- Indications of Compromise Settings
- NetFlow Devices
- Network Discovery Data Storage Settings
- Event Logging Settings
- OS and Server Identity Sources

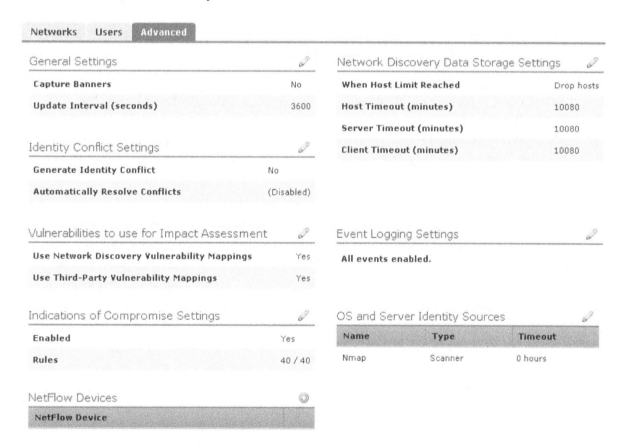

Figure 7.4: Discovery policy advanced tab

General Settings

In the General Settings section, you'll find the Capture Banners and Update Interval options. Capture Banners is off by default, but you can enable it to collect the protocol banners for an array of services. Update Interval is set to 3600 seconds by default and specifies how often to refresh data in the database, such as the last time an application was seen, the last time an IP address was seen, how many times a certain protocol was used, and so on. Setting Update Interval to a lower value would display more recent info on the FMC, but predictably, that can also result in more overhead.

Identity Conflict Settings

Identity conflicts can crop up if you're leveraging third-party data like Nmap, host input, and so on for information about the host OSs in your environment. When the data gathered conflicts with data from these third-party sources, you can generate an alert indicating that a conflict has occurred. Conflicts can be manually resolved in the host profiles or resolved automatically based on which options you select, such as Keep The Passive Information From Firepower or Use The Active Information From Other Sources.

Vulnerabilities to Use for Impact Assessment

One of Firepower's most beneficial features is its ability to automatically correlate vulnerability information with intrusion data. By leveraging this information, you can quickly eliminate false positives from analysis. You can choose to discontinue this feature or third-party vulnerability mappings, but we strongly recommend not doing that!

Indications of Compromise Settings

Indications of compromise (IOC) offer another way to make hosts stand out in analysis. Figure 7.5 shows some of the indications of compromise that are enabled by default. This set includes 31 different kinds of rules, which perform important correlations by analyzing data about IPS, vulnerability, file activity, security intelligence, or malware events to indicate a "compromised host."

Compromised hosts will show up in any analysis view with a red icon instead of a normal, blue one, making them easy to spot. You can disable these rules individually if you want to.

Edit Indications of Compromise Settings

Note: To detect Indications of Compromise, you must enable each IOC rule here and also enable the features, such as Security Intelligence logging and intrusion and malware protection, that the rules below depend on.

Enable IOC   40 out of 40 Rules Enabled

Category	Source	Event Type	Description	Enabl...
Adobe Reader Compromise	Malware Events	PDF Compromise Detected by AMP for Endpoints	Generic Adobe Reader Compromise	✓
Adobe Reader Compromise	Malware Events	Adobe Reader launched shell	A shell was launched on the host by Adobe Reader	✓
CnC Connected	Security Intelligence Events	Security Intelligence Event - CnC	The host may be under remote control	✓
CnC Connected	Intrusion Events	Intrusion Event - malware-cnc	The host may be under remote control	✓
CnC Connected	Intrusion Events	Intrusion Event - malware-backdoor	The host may be under remote control	✓
CnC Connected	Malware Events	Suspected Botnet Detected by AMP for Endpoints	The host may be under remote control	✓
CnC Connected	Security Intelligence Events	Security Intelligence Event - DNS CnC	The host may be under remote control	✓
CnC Connected	Security Intelligence Events	Security Intelligence Event - URL CnC	The host may be under remote control	✓

Figure 7.5: Indications of compromise rules

NetFlow Devices

If you have NetFlow devices in your environment, you can export information from them to your device to supplement connection information. This is an extremely rare configuration, in fact we've never seen anyone use it.

Network Discovery Data Storage Settings

These two settings deal primarily with the retention of data in the following two ways:

When Host Limit Reached—When you reach your host license limit, you can choose to either drop newly detected hosts or overwrite older ones. The default is to drop new hosts.

Host, Server, and Client Timeout—This time-out occurs in minutes, indicating when you would like to remove information from the database. If one of the items hasn't been seen for the length of the specified time-out value, the information will be removed. The default time is 10080 minutes, or seven days.

Event Logging Settings

There are 33 different types of data that can be logged with Firepower and 20 different settings that can be leveraged through the host input API. All of them are enabled by default, but these data types can be turned off or on as needed. Figure 7.6 displays these settings.

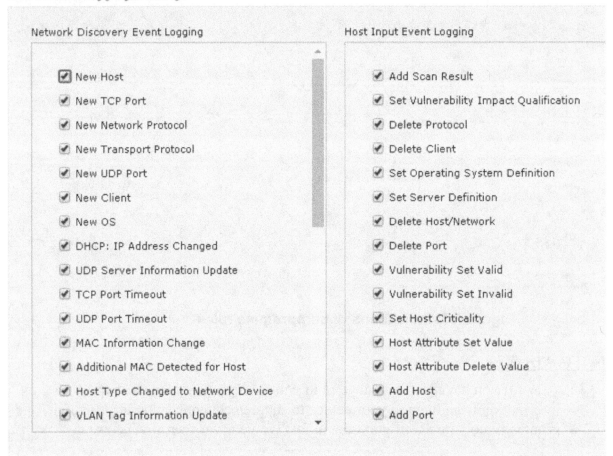

Edit Event Logging Settings

Network Discovery Event Logging	Host Input Event Logging
☑ New Host	☑ Add Scan Result
☑ New TCP Port	☑ Set Vulnerability Impact Qualification
☑ New Network Protocol	☑ Delete Protocol
☑ New Transport Protocol	☑ Delete Client
☑ New UDP Port	☑ Set Operating System Definition
☑ New Client	☑ Set Server Definition
☑ New OS	☑ Delete Host/Network
☑ DHCP: IP Address Changed	☑ Delete Port
☑ UDP Server Information Update	☑ Vulnerability Set Valid
☑ TCP Port Timeout	☑ Vulnerability Set Invalid
☑ UDP Port Timeout	☑ Set Host Criticality
☑ MAC Information Change	☑ Host Attribute Set Value
☑ Additional MAC Detected for Host	☑ Host Attribute Delete Value
☑ Host Type Changed to Network Device	☑ Add Host
☑ VLAN Tag Information Update	☑ Add Port

Figure 7.6: Event logging settings

OS and Server Identity Sources

This is where you can add additional sources of host identities like Nmap or other third-party applications. You can also specify a time period after which the data becomes stale and the other identity sources take priority over it.

Keep in mind that once you have made changes to the policy, you need to click the Apply button in the upper right portion of the interface to make them stick.

Firepower Discovery Information

Once the Firepower network discovery policy is created and applied, the managed devices begin sending information to the Firepower Management Center (FMC). This information can be viewed in many ways, but to get started, we're going to take a look at **Analysis ➤ Hosts**.

Figure 7.7: Host event views

The following views are available:

Network Map—A tree view of all IP hosts discovered on the network, broken out by subnet. You can also type in an IPv4 or IPv6 address/subnet at the top of the list to view information on specific hosts/networks.

Hosts—A listing of hosts organized by operating system.

Indications of Compromise—A listing of the IOC's that have been triggered by category.

Applications—A list of applications along with the number of hosts the applications have been detected on.

Application Details—An inventory of detected application client software and web applications.

Servers—An inventory of application server types along with the application vendors.

Host Attributes—An index of hosts by attribute, which are user-created definable fields. We'll describe these fields more a bit later.

Discovery Events—A list of items that were either seen for the first time (discovery events) or changed in the database (change events).

Discovery Events

Discovery events are a great way to find out exactly what's popped up on your network. You can create searches based on subnets and event types that will present you with a list of hosts based on their first appearance on the network or network segment, as seen in Figure 7.8.

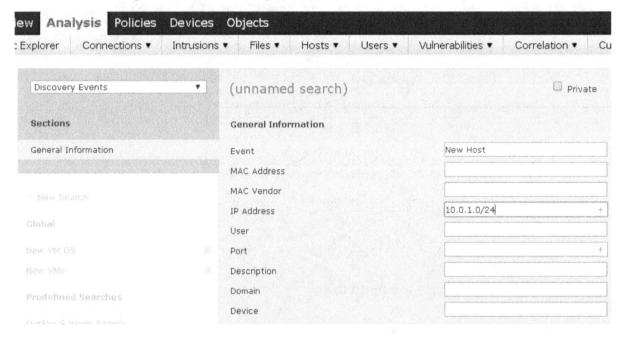

Figure 7.8: Creating an event search

Doing this would get you results like the list shown in Figure 7.9.

Figure 7.9: Newly discovered hosts

When you click on any of the items in this list, you're actually drilling down in a workflow. This is also restricting the view to the items you've selected. Ultimately you'll arrive at a host profile.

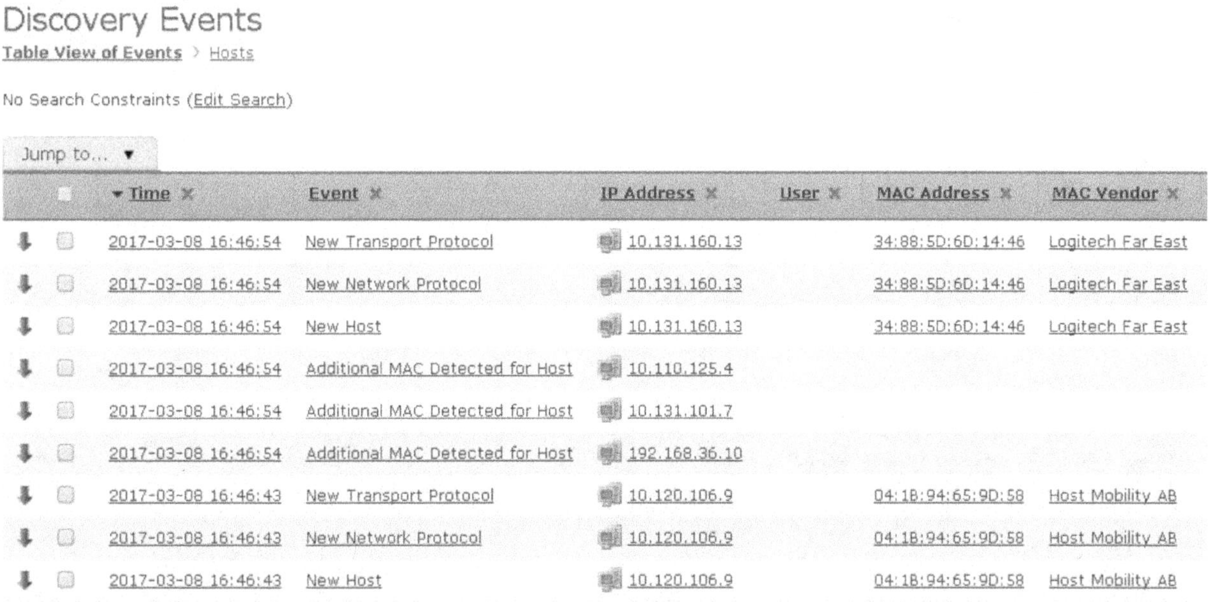

Discovery Events
Table View of Events > Hosts

No Search Constraints (Edit Search)

Jump to... ▼

		▼ Time ✕	Event ✕	IP Address ✕	User ✕	MAC Address ✕	MAC Vendor ✕
⬇	▢	2017-03-08 16:46:54	New Transport Protocol	10.131.160.13		34:88:5D:6D:14:46	Logitech Far East
⬇	▢	2017-03-08 16:46:54	New Network Protocol	10.131.160.13		34:88:5D:6D:14:46	Logitech Far East
⬇	▢	2017-03-08 16:46:54	New Host	10.131.160.13		34:88:5D:6D:14:46	Logitech Far East
⬇	▢	2017-03-08 16:46:54	Additional MAC Detected for Host	10.110.125.4			
⬇	▢	2017-03-08 16:46:54	Additional MAC Detected for Host	10.131.101.7			
⬇	▢	2017-03-08 16:46:54	Additional MAC Detected for Host	192.168.36.10			
⬇	▢	2017-03-08 16:46:43	New Transport Protocol	10.120.106.9		04:1B:94:65:9D:58	Host Mobility AB
⬇	▢	2017-03-08 16:46:43	New Network Protocol	10.120.106.9		04:1B:94:65:9D:58	Host Mobility AB
⬇	▢	2017-03-08 16:46:43	New Host	10.120.106.9		04:1B:94:65:9D:58	Host Mobility AB

Host Profile

The *host profile* contains the most detail about a system, and you can get to it from any of the analysis views. Take a look at Figure 7.10 and Figure 7.11. The host profile will serve up detailed information about the IP address, hostname, indications of compromise, applications, services, attributes and potential vulnerabilities that exist on the hosts.

Host Profile

		Scan Host	Generate White List Profile

Domain	Global \ Cisco_Backend \ Cisco_SOC
IP Addresses	10.120.10.254
NetBIOS Name	
Device (Hops)	vNGIPS.dcloud.cisco.com (0)
MAC Addresses (TTL)	00:15:F7:7D:89:F8 (Wintecronics Ltd.) (64)
	00:55:44:33:22:11 (64)
	28:6A:BA:17:9B:5C (Apple, Inc.) (64)
	... (show all)
Host Type	Host
Last Seen	2017-03-08 16:09:23
Current User	
View	Context Explorer | Connection Events | Intrusion Events | File Events | Malware Events

Indications of Compromise (1) ▾

	Edit Rule States	Mark All Resolved

Category	Event Type	Description	First Seen	Last Seen	
Malware Detected	Threat Detected in File Transfer	The host has encountered malware	2017-03-07 20:36:51	2017-03-08 12:38:57	🗑

Operating Systems (3) ▾

	Edit Operating System	View Operating Systems

Vendor	Product	Version	Source
Linux	Linux	2.6	Firepower
CentOS	Linux	5.5	Firepower
IBM	AIX	5.x, 5L 5.x	Firepower

Applications (1) ▾

	Application Protocol	Client	Version	Web Application		
❶	☐ HTTP	☐ Firefox	2.0.0.17	Web Browsing	📄	🗑

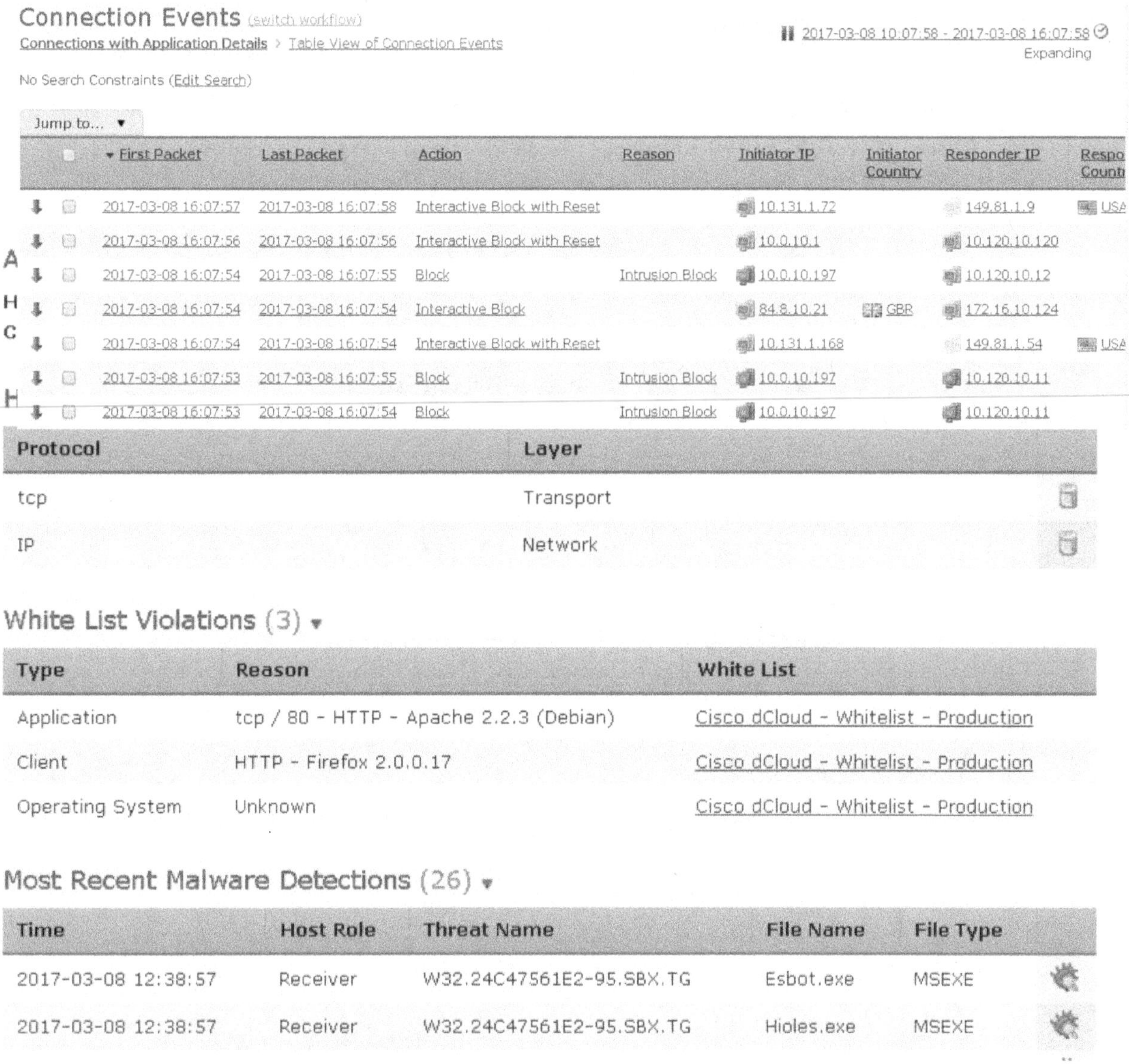

Connection Events (switch workflow)

Connections with Application Details > Table View of Connection Events

No Search Constraints (Edit Search)

Jump to... ▼

		▼ First Packet	Last Packet	Action	Reason	Initiator IP	Initiator Country	Responder IP	Respo Count
↓	☐	2017-03-08 16:07:57	2017-03-08 16:07:58	Interactive Block with Reset		10.131.1.72		149.81.1.9	USA
↓	☐	2017-03-08 16:07:56	2017-03-08 16:07:56	Interactive Block with Reset		10.0.10.1		10.120.10.120	
↓	☐	2017-03-08 16:07:54	2017-03-08 16:07:55	Block	Intrusion Block	10.0.10.197		10.120.10.12	
↓	☐	2017-03-08 16:07:54	2017-03-08 16:07:54	Interactive Block		84.8.10.21	GBR	172.16.10.124	
↓	☐	2017-03-08 16:07:54	2017-03-08 16:07:54	Interactive Block with Reset		10.131.1.168		149.81.1.54	USA
↓	☐	2017-03-08 16:07:53	2017-03-08 16:07:55	Block	Intrusion Block	10.0.10.197		10.120.10.11	
↓	☐	2017-03-08 16:07:53	2017-03-08 16:07:54	Block	Intrusion Block	10.0.10.197		10.120.10.11	

Protocol	Layer	
tcp	Transport	🗑
IP	Network	🗑

White List Violations (3) ▼

Type	Reason	White List
Application	tcp / 80 - HTTP - Apache 2.2.3 (Debian)	Cisco dCloud - Whitelist - Production
Client	HTTP - Firefox 2.0.0.17	Cisco dCloud - Whitelist - Production
Operating System	Unknown	Cisco dCloud - Whitelist - Production

Most Recent Malware Detections (26) ▼

Time	Host Role	Threat Name	File Name	File Type	
2017-03-08 12:38:57	Receiver	W32.24C47561E2-95.SBX.TG	Esbot.exe	MSEXE	👹
2017-03-08 12:38:57	Receiver	W32.24C47561E2-95.SBX.TG	Hioles.exe	MSEXE	👹

Figure 7.10: Host profile

Figure 7.11: Host profile

Connection Events

Devices can also collect connection data, and you can check out the events by going to Analysis ➢ Connection Events. By doing that, you'll get information about protocols, applications, bytes transferred, URLs, and more, as shown in Figure 7.12. But keep in mind that the data will be found here only if the appropriate logging is enabled in the Access Control policy.

Figure 7.12: Connection events

One of the very cool things you can do with this information is look at it in the context of different workflows. Choosing Switch Workflows next to Connection Events will get you the options shown in Figure 7.13.

Figure 7.13: Connection event workflows

Figure 7.14 shows an example of the Traffic Over Time workflow. The graphs are interactive, and you can drill down on individual elements by clicking them.

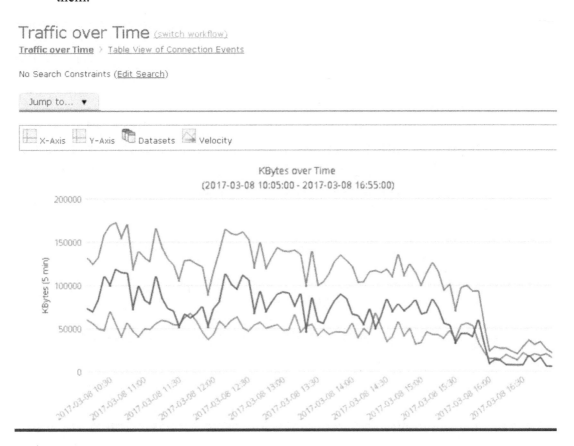

Figure 7.14: Traffic Over Time workflow

Connection Summaries

Another way to view connection information is via a dashboard. Choose Overview ➢ Dashboard ➢ Connection Summary to get the following three tabs in the summary (shown in Figure 7.15):

Figure 7.15: Connection event summary

Connections—Displays information on the number of connections by initiator, application, port, and responder and over time.

Traffic—Refers to traffic bytes by initiator, application, port, and responder and over time.

Geolocation—Displays information about the source and destination countries and continents.

SSL—Displays information about the SSL decryptions and certificates

URL—Displays information about the URL's allowed, connections, and traffic by URL

Each of these graphs is interactive, and you can use any or all of them to get even more detailed information.

User Information

User information is collected either passively, using the protocols in the discovery policy, via the Firepower Active Directory User Agent, and now even Integrated Services Engine (ISE). We'll concentrate on the User Agent for this chapter, but more information on the ISE integration can be found in the Firepower classes at www.lammle.com/firepower.

The Active Directory agent communicates with specified AD servers to collect login information based upon the audit logs. An AD agent can be installed on a Windows-based system inside your environment, but you must provide the name of an account with the capability to read the logs on the AD servers as well as a password. One AD agent can communicate with up to five AD servers.

In addition to reading the logs, you can connect with an AD server via LDAP to read other attributes on accounts. Information including the first and last name, email, department, and phone number would be included provided the data is populated in the AD server. You can also use this LDAP connection to pull user/group account information for use in AC policies.

It's also good to know that connections can be made to non-AD LDAP servers and user data can be pulled for the other discovered user types as long as there's corresponding information in LDAP.

User Analysis

Once user discovery is enabled, the users table and user activity in the database will populate. You can see their contents by navigating to `Analysis ➤ Users ➤ Users`; an example is shown in Figure 7.16. This will display all users that have been identified by the system.

Users
Table View of Users > Users

▶ Search Constraints (Edit Search)

Jump to... ▼

		▲ User ✕	Realm ✕	Username ✕	First Name ✕	Last Name ✕	E-Mail ✕	Department ✕
⬇	☐	zola mumford (DCLOUD-AD_1\ymumf, LDAP)	DCLOUD-AD_1	ymumf	zola	mumford	zola.y.mumford@dcloud.cisco.com	z (corporate directory)
⬇	☐	zola mumford (DCLOUD-SOC\ymumf, LDAP)	DCLOUD-SOC	ymumf	zola	mumford	mumford	z (corporate directory)
⬇	☐	zona atchley (DCLOUD-AD\zatch, LDAP)	DCLOUD-AD	zatch	zona	atchley	zona.z.atchley@dcloud.cisco.com	z (corporate directory)
⬇	☐	zona atchley (DCLOUD-AD_1\zatch, LDAP)	DCLOUD-AD_1	zatch	zona	atchley	zona.z.atchley@dcloud.cisco.com	z (corporate directory)
⬇	☐	zona atchley (DCLOUD-SOC\zatch, LDAP)	DCLOUD-SOC	zatch	zona	atchley	atchley	z (corporate directory)
⬇	☐	zonia bahena (DCLOUD-AD\sbahe, LDAP)	DCLOUD-AD	sbahe	zonia	bahena	zonia.s.bahena@dcloud.cisco.com	z (corporate directory)
⬇	☐	zonia bahena (DCLOUD-AD_1\sbahe, LDAP)	DCLOUD-AD_1	sbahe	zonia	bahena	zonia.s.bahena@dcloud.cisco.com	z (corporate directory)
⬇	☐	zonia bahena (DCLOUD-SOC\sbahe, LDAP)	DCLOUD-SOC	sbahe	zonia	bahena	bahena	z (corporate directory)
⬇	☐	zora gammon (DCLOUD-AD\bgamm, LDAP)	DCLOUD-AD	bgamm	zora	gammon	zora.b.gammon@dcloud.cisco.com	z (corporate directory)

Figure 7.16: Table view of users

Figure 7.17 shows the User Activity view, which is opened by going to `Analysis➤Users➤User Activity`. This view will reveal precisely when all those users were seen performing activities such as newly discovered, logging in, or logging out. Logouts, however, can only be seen if you are using the User Agent.

User Activity
Table View of Events > Users

No Search Constraints (Edit Search)

		▼ Time ✕	Event ✕	Username ✕	Realm ✕	Authentication Protocol ✕	Authentication Type ✕	IP Address ✕
⬇	☐	2017-03-08 18:52:12	User Login	marre	DCLOUD-AD_1	LDAP	Passive Authentication	10.112.196.11?
⬇	☐	2017-03-08 18:52:06	User Login	choar	DCLOUD-AD_1	LDAP	Passive Authentication	10.131.117.48
⬇	☐	2017-03-08 18:52:05	User Login	ddevo	DCLOUD-AD_1	LDAP	Passive Authentication	172.16.10.208
⬇	☐	2017-03-08 18:52:04	User Login	jsarm	DCLOUD-AD_1	LDAP	Passive Authentication	10.110.84.46
⬇	☐	2017-03-08 18:52:04	User Login	khend	DCLOUD-AD_1	LDAP	Passive Authentication	10.0.91.111
⬇	☐	2017-03-08 18:52:01	User Login	hmund	DCLOUD-AD_1	LDAP	Passive Authentication	10.0.83.146
⬇	☐	2017-03-08 18:52:00	User Login	yloom	DCLOUD-AD_1	LDAP	Passive Authentication	10.131.10.104
⬇	☐	2017-03-08 18:52:00	User Login	gdesm	DCLOUD-AD_1	LDAP	Passive Authentication	10.0.30.52

Host Attributes

There's one more data type available to you in the Firepower Manager. Host attributes are elements that you can create on your own and either automatically or manually assign to systems. These attributes can then be used as sorting and search criteria to make it easier to locate systems or tag machines that you want to flag as "special."

The attributes can be one of these four types:

Text—Creates a text box for a user to input information.

URL—Creates a field where a URL may be entered

List—Allows you to access a drop-down list with choices you create

Integer—Creates a field for a numeric value to be assigned.

To create attributes, navigate to Analysis ➢ Host Attributes and choose Host Attribute Management in the upper-right corner. You'll see a default attribute called White List there, and we'll tell you all about it later in the book. In the upper right, there will be a button labeled Create Attribute.

Clicking the Create Attribute button will open a screen presenting you with a selection of attributes you can create, as seen in Figure 7.18. Creating the URL, text, and integer attributes will cause those characteristics to appear in the host profiles of each host in your network. The list attribute also allows for the option to automatically assign the attribute based upon a network/subnet combination.

Hosts ▸ Host Attributes   Users ▾   Vulnerabilities ▾   Correlatic

Create Host Attribute

Name

Type   Text   ▾
        Text
        Integer   Save   Cancel
        List
        URL

Figure 7.18: Host attribute creation

First, create the list attributes and then specify which network the attributes belong to. If anything falls outside of those parameters, it would still show up in a category called Unassigned. A configured list attribute is shown in Figure 7.19.

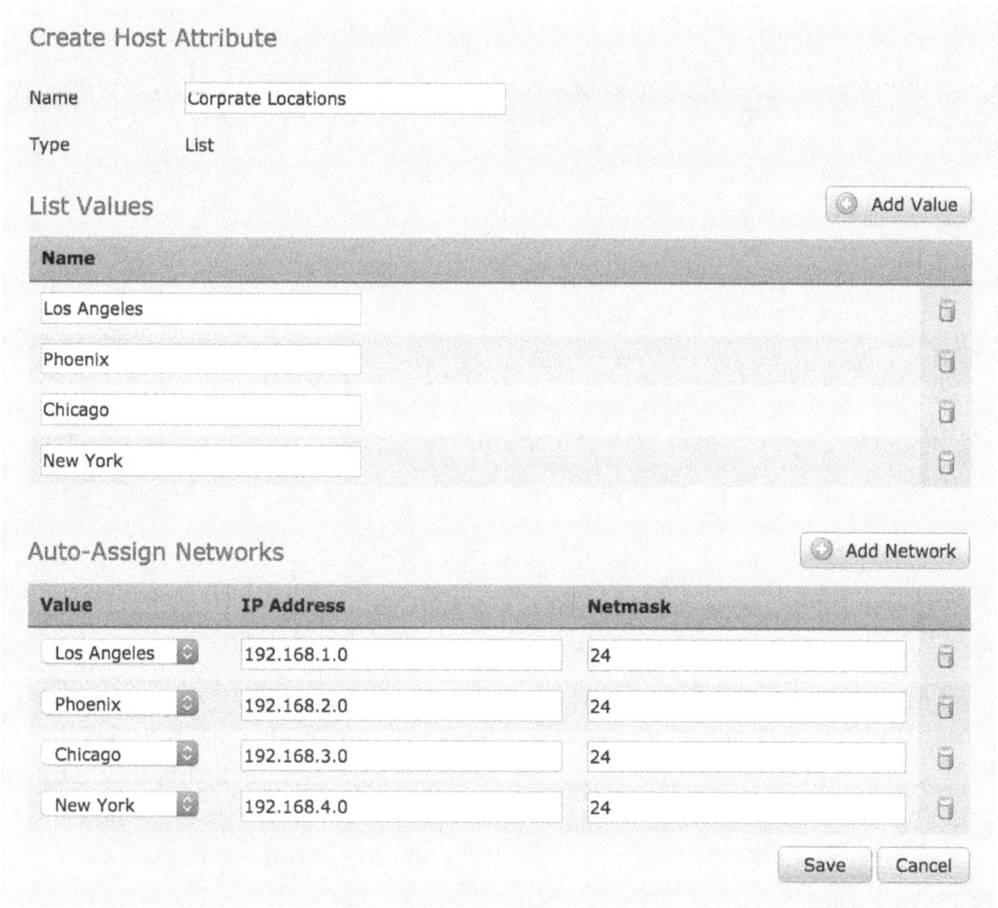

Create Host Attribute

Name	Corprate Locations
Type	List

List Values   Add Value

Name

Los Angeles

Phoenix

Chicago

New York

Auto-Assign Networks   Add Network

Value	IP Address	Netmask	
Los Angeles	192.168.1.0	24	
Phoenix	192.168.2.0	24	
Chicago	192.168.3.0	24	
New York	192.168.4.0	24	

Save   Cancel

Figure 7.19: List attribute creation

Once you've created your attributes, you can check up on them in several ways. You can use the host profile, but you can also check out the Network Map Host Attribute view.

There's even a link on the create attribute page. If that's not enough, you can access them by going to Analysis ➤ Hosts ➤ Network Map and clicking the Host Attributes tab.

Figure 5.20: Network Map Host Attribute view

This gets you to a drop-down list where you can select any of the host attributes you or someone else created. The three attributes associated with whitelists are compliant, non-compliant, and not assigned, options that can't be assigned by an administrator. These characteristics can only be assigned based on the actual whitelist values, which we'll cover in detail in the Chapter on Correlation Policies.

Chapter 8: Intrusion Policy

This chapter focuses on the Intrusion policy for the FMC. You can think of this policy as your Snort rule configuration because that's its primary purpose.

There are a few advanced settings included, but for the most part, it's all about Snort rules.

We are going to focus on the concepts and give some practical advice for creating and managing your policies. We will then demonstrate how to implement these using the FMC web user interface.

Policy Basics

The main purpose of the Intrusion policy is to select the Snort rules that will be enabled to perform packet inspection. An organization may create anywhere from one to dozens of Intrusion policies. This allows tailoring the Snort rule set to specific devices and/or portions of your network.

Now, one might ask, "Why not just enable all the rules? Wouldn't that be more secure?" Of course, it's not that simple. Snort rules run the gamut from detecting an iTunes login attempt to triggering on evidence of a CryptoLocker infected workstation. Enabling all the rules would result in a huge number of false positive alerts. These false positives would quickly overwhelm your intrusion analysts, making it extremely difficult to ferret out alerts with actual security implications. We will discuss the difference between a false positive and a true positive event later, in Chapter 14: Event Analysis.

Another reason we only enable a subset of the total rules is the sheer size of the rule set. At the time of this writing there are over 30,000 rules shipping with Firepower! Enabling all of these rules would put a tremendous load on the device and performance would be dismal. If the device is inline, you are virtually guaranteed that it will cause significant latency and even drop packets as it tries to evaluate such a huge rule set.

To address this, Cisco's Talos group has created three base policies you can use as a starting point for your environment. We like to call them small, medium and large.

- Connectivity over Security: This is the small rule set policy. In this policy, connectivity is king. Only a small subset of the total rules is enabled. The actual number fluctuates as rule sets are updated, but you can expect somewhere around 500 rules will be set to generate alerts or drop and generate alerts.

- Balanced Security and Connectivity: This is the medium rule set. As you might guess, here the needs of connectivity and security are balanced. This is hands down the most popular policy with Firepower customers. The rule set is designed to alert or block on the most important vulnerabilities or attacks while at the same time providing good performance. It is important to note that the throughput rating for Firepower devices is based on the use of this rule set. Expect roughly 8,000 rules in this set.

- Security over Connectivity: Another popular rule set is the "shoot first, ask questions later" security rule set. This will enable a few more rules than the balanced rule set. These additional rules will cover threats that may be slightly older, and it also adds a few additional rule categories to the mix. You can expect to see around 11,000 rules or so in this set. Note that this rule set is not typically recommended for inline devices due to the reduced throughput, but it may be desired in higher security environments. Your Firepower device is *not* guaranteed to perform at its rated speed if you use this rule set. If you have a passive device and you want to see what it can do, then this may be the policy for you.

Talos uses some objective criteria for selecting the enabled rules in each of the Cisco policies we just described.

Connectivity over Security Base Policy

The criteria for selecting the rules in the Connectivity over Security Base policy are as follows:

- Common Vulnerability Scoring System (CVSS) score of 10
- Date the vulnerability was discovered:
  - o Current year and two years prior
- Rule category
  - o Not used for this policy

Balanced Security and Connectivity Base Policy

Here are the criteria for the Balanced Security and Connectivity Base policy:

- CVSS score of 9 or greater
- Date the vulnerability was discovered:
  - Current year and two years prior
- Rule category (regardless of CVSS)
  - Malware-CnC
  - Blacklist
  - SQL
  - Exploit-kit

Security over Connectivity Base Policy

Here are the criteria for the Security over Connectivity policy:

- CVSS score of 8 or greater
- Date the vulnerability was discovered:
  - Current year and three years prior
- Rule category (regardless of CVSS)
  - Malware-CnC
  - Blacklist
  - SQL
  - Exploit-kit
  - App-detect

The criteria come with some caveats. First, Talos reserves the right to not follow these criteria for any rule. Threats and vulnerabilities are individual, and a long-running threat may mean the rule will be enabled longer or shorter than the time frame specified in the policy. Also, not all the rules in the categories listed will automatically be enabled. The idea is that the particular category will be considered and rules enabled if deemed necessary. These policies are constantly tuned ensuring the best protection is provided while staying within the performance constraints of the Firepower devices.

Note there is another policy called Maximum Detection that has even more rules enabled. The associated Network Analysis policy of the same name also includes some significant changes from the others. Talos does not recommend using this policy for production devices due to its processing overhead.

Of course, there is still another option. You can start with no rules enabled and go through the entire rule set yourself to decide which rules to turn on. If you have the time and the expertise equivalent to the entire Cisco Talos group, then this might be an option. Realistically, nobody has this much time or is as intimately familiar as Talos with their own Snort rules.

You may want to tweak one of the provided rule sets we just discussed, but starting from scratch is really not a viable option; however, to provide this functionality, there is a Talos provided policy called No Rules Active.

Rule States

Before we go on, let's talk about the options available for enabling rules in a policy. There are three states a Snort rule can have in Firepower:

1. Disabled: The rule will not be deployed to devices.

2. Generate Events: The rule will generate an alert if it encounters a packet matching the rule criteria.

3. Drop and Generate Events: The rule will generate an alert and drop a packet matching the rule criteria. By default, this is a "silent" drop; that is, no TCP reset or UDP port unreachable response is sent to the source or destination.

You may also hear the three states described as disabled, alert, and drop. This comes from the fact that the actual keyword in the rule itself for a Generate Event state is *alert*. Likewise, the keyword for a Drop and Generate rule state is *drop*.

Layers

To understand how you can use a rule set provided by Cisco yet still be able to modify it yourself, you must understand the concept of layers. In Firepower, an Intrusion policy consists of at least two layers, and more layers can also be added if desired. To help us as we explain this concept, keep the following principles in mind:

1. Settings in higher layers always override settings in lower layers.
2. Layers can be private or they can be shared across multiple policies.
3. Layers can be merged together.
4. The base layer in a policy is read-only and cannot be edited.
5. The base layer in a policy is actually another policy.

Okay, let's see if we can help make some sense of this. First of all, when you create a new policy, it will *always* be based on some other policy. This is your base layer. That other policy can be one you have previously created or it could be one of the Talos base policies. If you use a custom policy as your base, that custom policy also has a base layer. The bottom line is, if you trace any Intrusion policy back to its roots, it originally started with a Talos policy.

In addition to the base layer, each policy comes with a single private layer called My Changes. The My Changes layer sits atop the base policy or base layer. This is illustrated in Figure 8.1.

Intrusion Policy

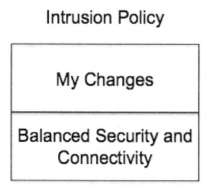

Figure 8.1: Balanced Intrusion policy

In this example, we selected the Cisco Balanced Security and Connectivity policy as our base layer. This means we are starting with the balanced rule set. Initially, the My Changes layer makes no modifications to the Cisco policy. In any policy, the resulting rule set will be the combination of settings in the layers. Since My Changes has no settings yet, the resultant rule set will have only the Cisco balanced rules enabled.

Keeping in mind principle #1 above, if we make any change to a rule state in the My Changes layer, it will override the rule state from the layer (or layers) below. This is how you can start with a Cisco provided policy and then modify rule states to customize the resultant rule set. Once you make your own decision on a rule state, you have overridden Cisco's default state for that rule. From that point forward, no rule state changes for that rule will be inherited from the base layer. Note that this will not prevent rule structure changes. If Talos decides to modify the rule to improve detection or maybe add documentation, these updates will still take effect. Only the rule state or alerting capability is affected in the My Changes layer.

Private and Shared Layers

Fasten your seat belts because it's about to get bumpy! Using a single private layer as in the preceding example is fairly straightforward. However, you can do more. In addition to using private layers, you can add shared layers. These layers can be added to a policy and then shared across other policies. By using shared layers, you can make a single change to a shared layer and change rule states across multiple policies. This eliminates the need to visit multiple policies to make the same change over and over. Figure 8.2 shows an example of three policies sharing a layer.

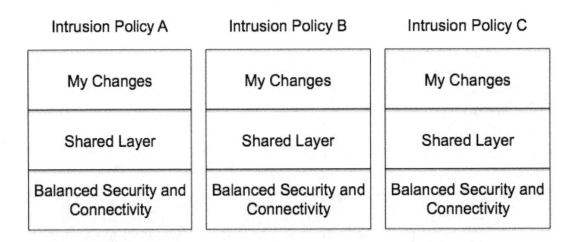

Figure 8.2: Shared layer

In the example in the figure, when a change is made to the shared layer, it affects all three policies. At the same time, if you need to make a change to just one of the policies, you still have that option. To do so, you make the change to the specific policy's My Changes layer.

In our example, we used a rather generic name for our shared layer. However, you can add multiple shared layers with descriptive names across a number of policies as part of your design.

Before we go much further, let's discuss some of the considerations for using shared layers. First, while the layer is shared across multiple policies, it can only be changed in the policy where it was first created. In our example, if the layer was created in policy A, it is read-only in the other policies. This means you have to remember the policy where you actually created the shared layer if you want to modify it. One way around that is to create an Intrusion policy that does nothing but house your shared layers. Name it something like "Shared Layers" and now you know where to go to edit them.

Another caveat is that the Firepower Management Center (FMC) does not have a good way of displaying the fact that a policy has a shared layer or which other policies are sharing layers. The policy list view is decidedly flat and contains only the policy name and description. Because of this, your external documentation is key to helping you and the other Firepower administrators remember where the shared layers are and what policies will be affected if you change one. If you edit a policy, you can see the layers more clearly, but continuously editing policies to understand what layers are present is a time-consuming process.

A Shared Layer Alternative

Let's discuss another way to achieve similar results but in a more user-friendly manner. Instead of using shared layers to house common rule settings, you can achieve similar functionality by creating your own base policies. This method has a couple of advantages over using shared layers.

First and foremost, it is easier to see within the Firepower user interface. While layers are not visible from the policy list, a separate base policy does show up as a distinct entry. Along with this, it's easy to tell which policy you need to edit to affect the other policies. You also don't need to worry about making the change in the right layer as each policy has only one editable layer by default—the private layer named My Changes. This technique is illustrated in Figure 8.3.

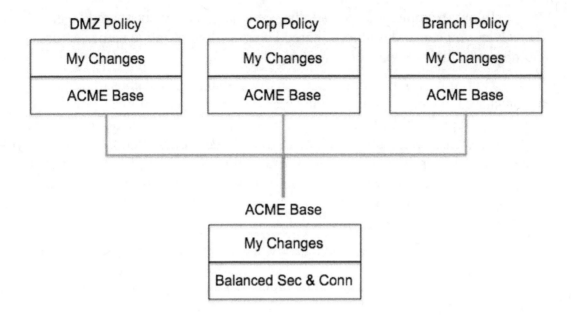

Figure 8.3: Base policy tree

As you can see, there are four Intrusion policies used in this example. The ACME Base is used as the base layer in the top three policies. By doing this, we can start with the Cisco Balanced Security and Connectivity rule set. Then any changes you want to take effect throughout your organization you make to the ACME Base policy. These settings will then be inherited by the policies above. If, for example, you need to make a change to just the DMZ policy, you edit that policy directly. Any change made to the top three policies will override the setting inherited from below.

It's important to note that in this design, the ACME Base policy will never be deployed to a device. It exists only as a base for the other policies. You may want to include this in the policy description just so everyone is clear. Something like "This policy is never deployed!" may be helpful.

By using this policy hierarchy, you get the best of all worlds:

- You leverage the expertise of the Talos team in determining which rules are most effective.

- You have the option to override any of the Talos default rule states across your organization by editing the ACME Base policy just once.

- You have the option to customize your specific policies if needed.

Of course, this can also be expanded with additional base policies if desired. If you have a large number of Intrusion policies deployed, creating an overall base and another set of intermediate base policies may work for you. However, keep in mind, the saying "Complexity is the enemy of security" is in full force here. Making your policy structure too complex can lead to unintended rule states, confusion among your Firepower administrators, cats and dogs living together—mass hysteria!

The Intrusion Policy Web Interface

Okay, we have discussed some basics of the Intrusion policy as well as some options for helping you manage rules across multiple policies. Next we will dive into the mechanics of what this looks like in the user interface.

Intrusion Policy Editing

To start, you'll find the Intrusion policy under Policies → Access Control → Intrusion. If your system is new, you will have an empty list. To create a new policy, click the Create Policy button. The initial policy creation dialog is shown in Figure 8.4.

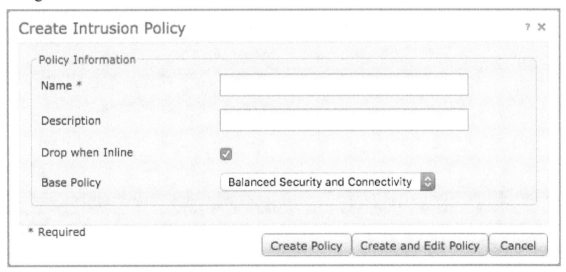

Figure 8.4: Create Intrusion Policy dialog

In the dialog you will see the following options:

- Name: The display name for your policy. Make it descriptive.

- Description: Optional description. This will appear in the policy list.

- Drop when Inline: Checking this box allows "Drop and Generate" rules to actually drop packets. Unchecking it means these rules will only generate alerts. This is handy for initial deployments before you have tuned your rules to ensure that you don't block legitimate traffic.

- Base Policy: The base policy or base layer for this policy. This must be another policy; it can be a system-provided (Talos) policy or a user-created policy.

The Create Policy button simply creates the policy and returns you to the policy list. Using the Create and Edit Policy button creates the policy and takes you into the policy management interface, which is shown in Figure 8.5.

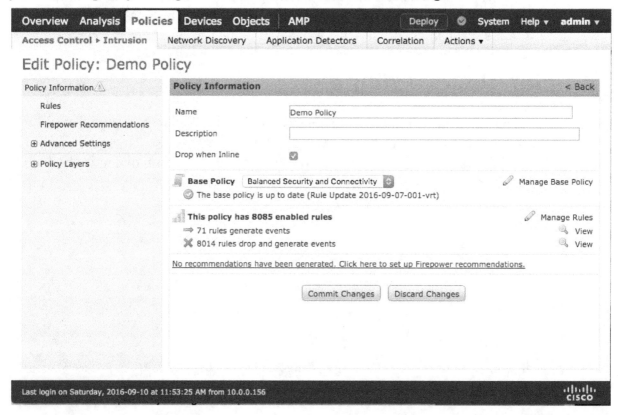

Figure 8.5: Edit Policy page

On the left is the navigation pane that includes the various policy sections:

- Policy Information: Displays a summary screen that lists the basic settings of the policy. This one is important because if you make any changes, you must return here to either commit the changes (save the policy) or discard them, otherwise you or other admins will be unable to edit other policies. Understand that choosing Commit

Changes here only saves the changes in the FMC database; it does not actually push the settings to the managed device!

- Rules: Displays all the rules available to the policy.

- Firepower Recommendations: Allows Firepower to recommend which rules to enable or disable based on host data collected from your network.

- Advanced Settings: Contains logging, global rule threshold, and sensitive data settings.

- Policy Layers: Allows you to expand and view the policy layers, including the base layer and any user-defined layers.

Rule Management

Clicking the Rules link brings you to the rule management interface. This is where you will spend most of your time when editing an Intrusion policy. The rule management interface is shown in Figure 8.6.

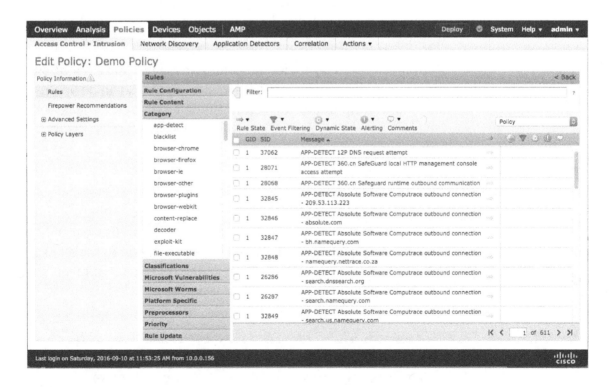

Figure 8.6: Rule management

Let's take a look at each section:

- Filter panel: This is the vertical column that lets you view rules associated with specific categories, classifications, priorities, or rule updates. Selecting an option from the filter panel will populate the filter bar at the top of the rules list. Clicking the sections will expand or contract other sections.

- Filter bar: This is in the top of the interface. Use this to manually input search criteria for rules. You also get the option to populate the filter bar by selecting items from the rules filter panel.

- Rules list: This makes up the main part of the display. It shows you all the rules based on the criteria specified on the filter bar.

- Policy drop-down: Located on the right below the filter bar and above the rules list. This allows you to examine a specific layer of your Intrusion policy. The default view, "Policy," shows the cumulative values of all layers.

- Show Details: If you have a specific rule selected in the rules list, you'll see a Show Details button appear at the bottom of the interface. Clicking it will bring up the details of that rule, including the text of the rule itself, documentation, overhead, and reference websites.

- Button bar: Directly under the filter bar, you'll find a set of buttons for settings that can be applied to rules. Settings can be applied to single or multiple rules by selecting their associated check boxes in the rules list.

The Rule Button Bar

The button bar is used to make various changes to rule settings within the policy. It's important to remember that whatever you select in this bar only applies to rules with their check boxes selected. If you attempt to make a selection from the button bar without first checking at least one rule you will receive an error. Figure 8.7 shows a close-up of the rule button bar.

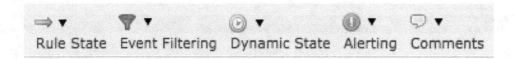

Figure 8.7: Rule button bar

Let's take a look at what each of these does:

Rule State

The first menu drop-down is Rule State, which lets you specify one of three conditions: Generate Events (alert only), Drop and Generate Events (alert and drop matching packets), or Disable (turn the rule off). Remember that if your device is inline, you gain the ability to drop traffic provided the rules are set to Drop and Generate and the Drop When Inline check box is selected in the policy.

Event Filtering

The Event Filtering settings allow you to specify whether you want to decrease the frequency of the alerts generated by the rule. When you click this button you have the option to adjust Suppression or Threshold settings.

Suppression

Suppression settings are straightforward and used when you don't want alerts generated for a specific rule. This can be based on the rule, source, or destination IP address. The Suppression dialog is shown in Figure 8.8.

Note that suppression only suppresses the alert generated by the rule; it has no effect on the ability of the rule to drop packets. That bears repeating, so let's put it another way: If you add a suppression to a Drop and Generate Events rule, the rule will *continue to drop traffic and you won't be notified*. Because of this, you should not use the suppression option for a rule that is set to drop. What you will end up with is a rule that stops generating alerts for the suppressed source or destination IP address but continues to drop packets.

One more note regarding suppression. You have the option to suppress the rule without adding a source or destination IP address. Think hard about why you would want to do this. Normally, if you don't want a rule to generate an alert, you would disable the rule. Suppression only suppresses the rule's output, but the rule continues to process traffic. Why leave the rule in the rule set, using valuable computing resources, if it's never going to generate an alert?

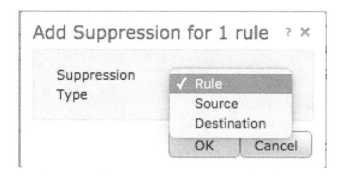

Figure 8.8: Suppression dialog

Thresholding

There are three types of thresholds to choose from: Limit, Threshold, and Both. They have a common dialog box shown in Figure 8.9, and each includes Track By, Count, and Seconds parameters. Each one is tracked based on a source or destination IP address (but not both).

Limit: Allows you to limit the number of alerts generated within a selected number of seconds. Once that limit is reached, no new alerts will occur until the time period has expired. For example, by setting Count to 10 and Seconds to 300, you will receive no more than 10 alerts every 5 minutes for the selected Source/Destination IP address.

Threshold: This will set the number of times the rule must match before generating an alert within a given time window. For example, if the count was set to 10 and the seconds set to 600, the result would be an alert for every 10 occurrences of that event within 600 seconds.

Both: This is a combination of the Limit and Threshold parameters. The count specifies the number of times the rule must match before an alert is generated. Once that count is reached, the rule will generate one alert; another alert will not be generated within the Seconds window. So a Both threshold with Count set to 10 and Seconds set to 300 means trigger an alert after seeing 10 matches within 300 seconds, and after triggering the alert, don't trigger again for 300 seconds. If the rule continues to match and exceed the threshold, you will get a maximum of one event every 300 seconds.

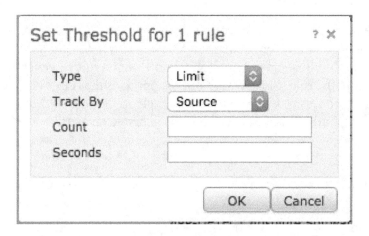

Figure 8.9: Threshold dialog

Dynamic State

Dynamic State allows the device to dynamically change the state of the rule from its current one to any of the other available states: Drop and Generate Events,

Generate Events, or Disabled. The state changes based upon the source or destination address as defined in the Track By drop-down. Another option that can appear in the Track By drop-down is Rule. If you specify Source or Destination, then the Network field must be populated. If Rule is selected in the Track By field, then the Network field does not appear. The Rate field lets you specify that the rule must fire a certain count within a given number of seconds. There's also a Timeout field that resets the rule to the previous state. The Dynamic State dialog is shown in Figure 8.10.

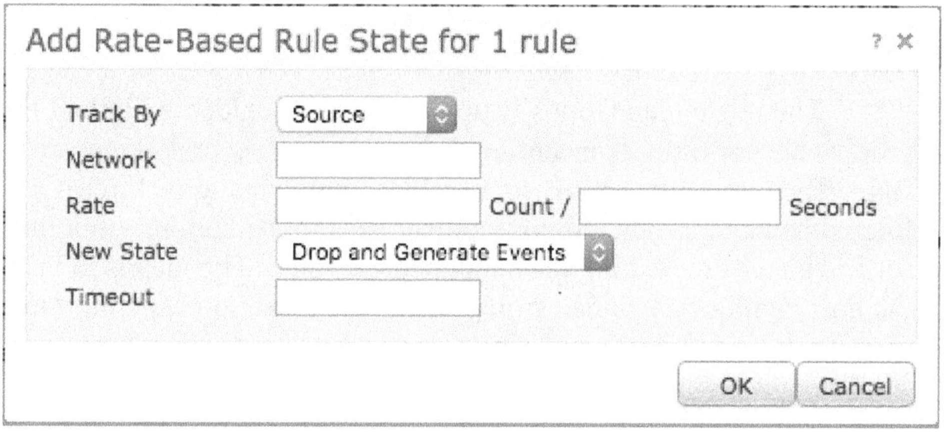

Figure 8.10: Dynamic State dialog

Alerting
To enable or disable SNMP alerts for a specific rule, use the Alerting option. You configure the SNMP destination in Advanced settings. SNMP alerts are generated by the device.

Comments
You can add comments to the individual rules that can be viewed by users of the FMC and analysts who inspect the traffic. Adding a comment automatically stamps the entry with your username and the date/time.

The Policy Drop-Down

The Policy drop-down on the far right of the button bar gives you a view of the rules based upon states set within the individual policy layers. The default view is just Policy, but you can also check out any policy layers such as My Changes, Firepower Recommendations (if used), and the base policy. Colors are important indicators here:

- All rules will appear white by default.

- When you look at individual layers, pink indicates that the rule's state has been modified in a higher layer.

- A rule highlighted in yellow means its state was adjusted in a lower layer.

- Rules highlighted in orange are ones you've clicked on.

Firepower Recommendations

The recommendations feature has been included with the Firepower product almost from its inception. It has gone by several names over the years—RNA (Realtime Network Awareness) Recommendations, FireSIGHT Recommendations, and now Firepower Recommendations—but the basic feature set and goal of the setting has remained the same. The idea is to take advantage of the host intelligence gained from the passive detection capability to provide tuning recommendations for Snort rules.

For the networks configured with host discovery in the Network Discovery policy, Firepower passively collects host information such as the following:

- IP address

- Operating system

- Applications

- Protocols

- Servers (also known as services; these are listening ports)

- Vulnerabilities based on the above information

For the Firepower Recommendations feature, the key item in the list above is vulnerabilities. By comparing the vulnerabilities present on your hosts with the vulnerabilities covered by Snort rules, Firepower can arrive at a recommended rule set tailored to your environment. Firepower can recommend which rules should be enabled. It can also recommend which rules should be disabled because they are not needed in a particular network.

When the Firepower Recommendations process is executed, recommendations are generated. Depending on the policy settings, these recommendations may be previewed or they can be implemented. If you decide to use the recommendations, a policy layer is inserted immediately above the base layer. This layer then enables or disables rules based on the recommendations generated.

To configure recommendations, click the Firepower Recommendations link on the left. If desired, you can expand the Advanced Settings item to peer a bit deeper into the internals of the process. This screen is shown in Figure 8.11.

Figure 8.11: Firepower Recommendations

Clicking the Generate Recommendations button will run the process to generate rule state recommendations but will not actually insert the recommendations layer into the policy. After you click Generate Recommendations and allow the process to complete, the screen will update with View links as shown in Figure 8.12.

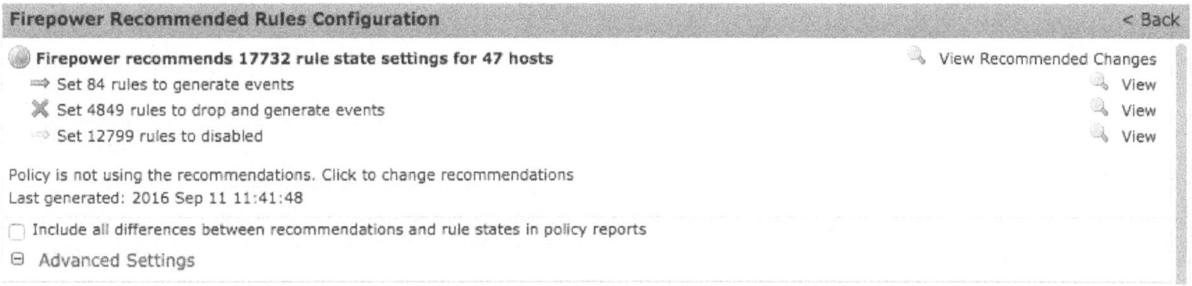

Figure 8.12: Firepower Recommendations view links

Clicking on one of the magnifying glass icons will take you to the Rules section of the policy and will insert the appropriate search into the filter bar, depending on which recommendation you select (Generate, Drop and Generate, or Disabled). This allows you to see what the rule states will be if you accept the recommendations.

After you generate recommendations once, the buttons on the page change to Use Recommendations and Update Recommendations. If you click Use Recommendations, the Firepower Recommendations layer is inserted into the policy just above the base layer. After this, the buttons change once again and you now have Do Not Use Recommendations and Update Recommendations. Clicking the former will remove the Firepower Recommendations layer from the policy, reverting back to the pre-recommendation state.

Firepower Recommendations is a useful tool, but there are a few caveats to be aware of. First of all, it depends on quality Firepower discovery data for your hosts. The system's passive detection capability functions best when devices are placed close to your hosts, which means installing Firepower/FTD devices throughout your network. However, in the real world, devices are often deployed only at the network edge. As a result, the only packets the devices process are traveling into or out of the network. This makes it difficult to collect reliable information on things like operating systems, services, and applications. The takeaway? If your deployment only includes edge devices, your host data may not be useful for Firepower Recommendations.

In addition, Firepower recommendations are not a one-shot setting. If you use them, they should be updated regularly to ensure the most up-to-date host information is being used. To assist with this, you can schedule a regular task to automatically update recommendations under System → Tools → Scheduling.

Advanced Settings

There are only a handful of advanced settings in the Intrusion policy. In fact, if you expand the Advanced Settings item, by clicking the plus icon to the left, you see only one setting, Global Rule Thresholding.

This illustrates a somewhat quirky behavior of this Advanced Settings "flattened" view. Only enabled settings will appear in the list. To see *all* the advanced settings, you have to click the Advanced Settings item itself. After this, you can see all the settings—whether they are enabled or disabled—to the right. Figure 8.13 shows all the available advanced settings.

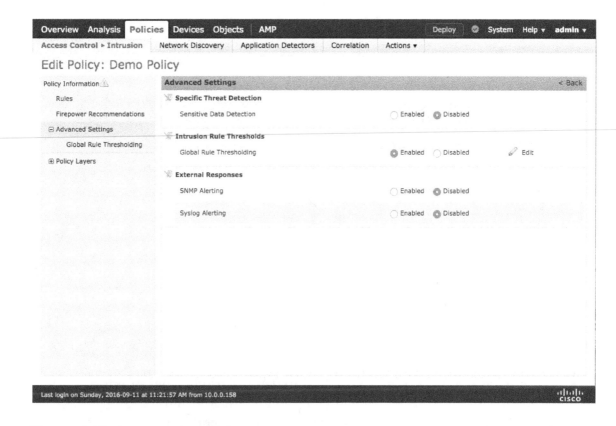

Figure 8.13: Advanced settings

Specific Threat Detection

This category of settings contains one item, Sensitive Data Detection. This feature is disabled by default. It allows searching for sensitive data within specific protocols. It has been called a "poor man's DLP" (data loss prevention) solution. The idea is you can detect when a certain volume of specific sensitive data starts flowing through the device. This may indicate a breach in progress as this data is siphoned off to some unknown evil destination.

If you enable this setting, the edit pencil icon will appear. Clicking on it will reveal the configuration options shown in Figure 8.14.

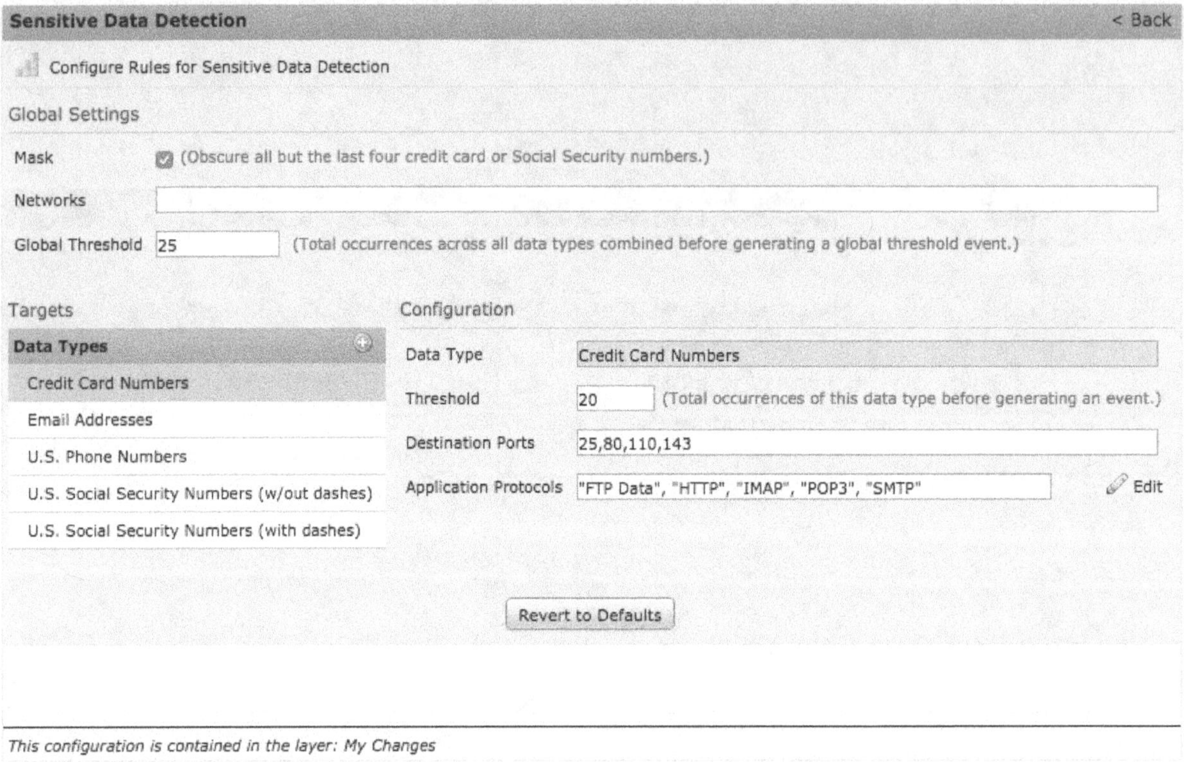

Figure 8.14: Sensitive Data Detection configuration options

There are a number of pre-built rules to detect various types of information such as credit card numbers, email addresses, and US phone and Social Security numbers. For each, you select the threshold, destination ports, and application protocols. You can also create your own custom detections using a subset of regular expression pattern matching syntax.

Each one of the data types, including any custom detections, corresponds to a Snort rule. These rules must be enabled to activate this feature. Near the top of the page you'll see this link: 📶 Configure Rules for Sensitive Data Detection Clicking this takes you to the rule management page and filters on rules that use this preprocessor. Once there, you can enabled these rules by setting them to Generate Events.

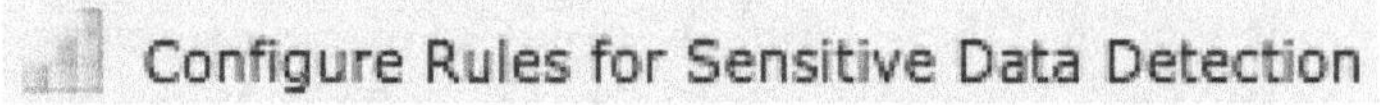

In practice, the Sensitive Data Detection feature has a couple of disadvantages. First, it has a tendency to produce false positive alerts. When you're looking for a suspicious pattern of numbers across millions or billions of packets, the chance of finding this pattern in benign data is fairly high. To combat this, the threshold for each rule can be adjusted to reduce false positive alerts as much as possible. Of course, this also reduces the sensitivity for detecting an actual breach.

Second, this feature tends to be a bad performer. Yes, this is much better than trying to use regular Snort rules with regular expression matches; however, there is still a fair amount of overhead as a result of turning on this feature.

Intrusion Rule Thresholds

As with Specific Threat Detection, the Intrusion Rule Thresholds section contains just one item, Global Rule Thresholding. This is the only advanced setting that is enabled by default. The configuration for this item is shown in Figure 8.15.

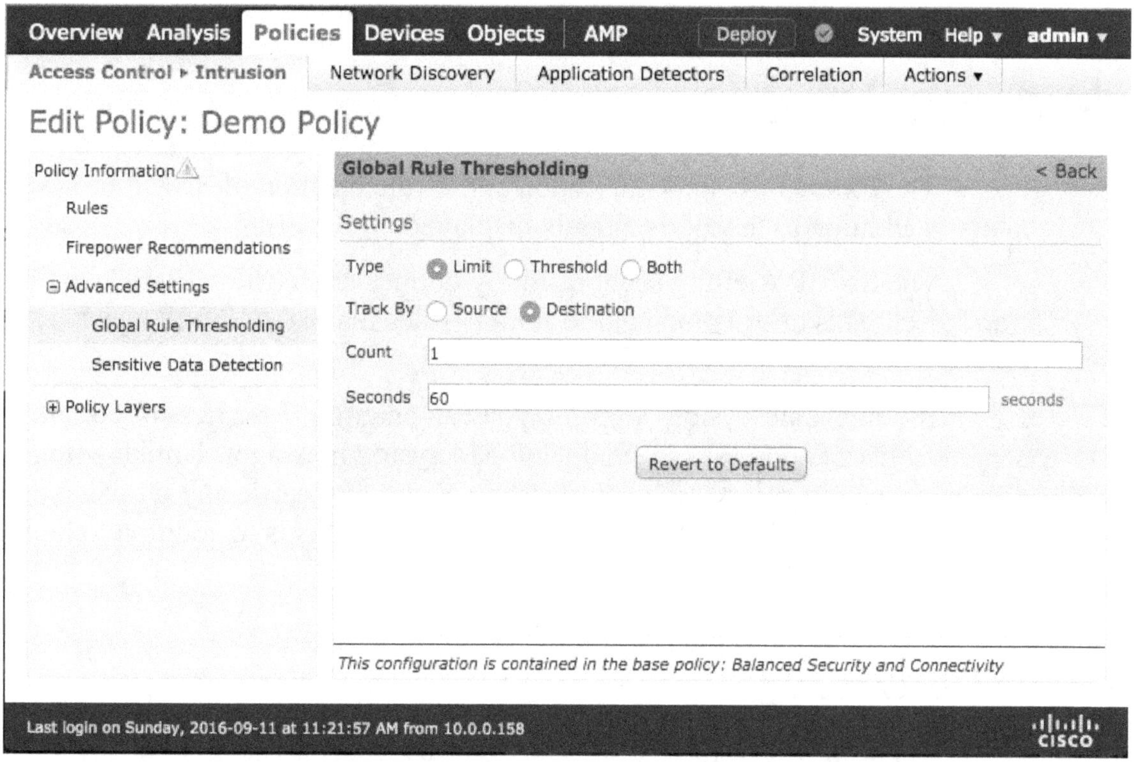

Figure 8.15: Global Rule Thresholding

This looks a lot like the same type of thresholding available in intrusion rules. That's because it is; this is a global threshold on all intrusion events. A common misconception is that when you deploy Firepower, you will get an alert every time a Snort rule matches a packet. This is not the case! Because this Global Rule Threshold setting is enabled by default, what you will actually get is one event per rule, per destination every 60 seconds.

This means if there is a situation where multiple packets traveling to a single host will match a certain Snort rule, the system will only alert on the first one over a 60 second window. If this were a long-running attack over several minutes, you would see one event every 60 seconds as the attack continued. Of course, if there were multiple destination hosts involved or multiple Snort rules matched the traffic, you would get additional alerts.

The purpose for this setting is to prevent a huge influx of events from exceeding the event processing capability of the device or the FMC. The downside is that you lose some visibility to the extent or volume of actual attack traffic. Our recommendation is to leave this enabled until you have tuned your intrusion events to a reasonable level. After this, you can disable this setting if desired. This will prevent you from being overwhelmed but also provide in-depth visibility into your network traffic.

External Responses

The External Responses section allows the creation of SNMP or syslog alerts in addition to the alerts already displayed on the FMC.

The SNMP Alerting section simply defines an SNMP v2 or v3 destination trap server. This destination is used for any rules that have SNMP alerting enabled.

If you enable Syslog Alerting, you can enter an IP address or comma-separated list of addresses to send UDP 514 syslog messages. Unlike with SNMP, which is on a per-rule basis, enabling this feature will cause any intrusion event to be sent directly to the syslog server from a device. This is in addition to being logged on the FMC.

Policy Layers

The Policy Layers section is a good way to get a visual of the layers in your policy. You can also perform other layer operations, such as the following:

- Create/delete layers
- Copy layers
- Move layers up or down
- Merge layers together
- Add shared layers from another policy
- Designate a layer as shared

Clicking the Policy Layers link displays the current layers as well as the policy summary, as shown in Figure 8.16. Here you can see that the base layer is Balanced Security and Connectivity. Immediately above that is a Firepower Recommendations layer. Then comes the My Changes layer, and at the top, the policy summary lists the enabled rules and advanced settings.

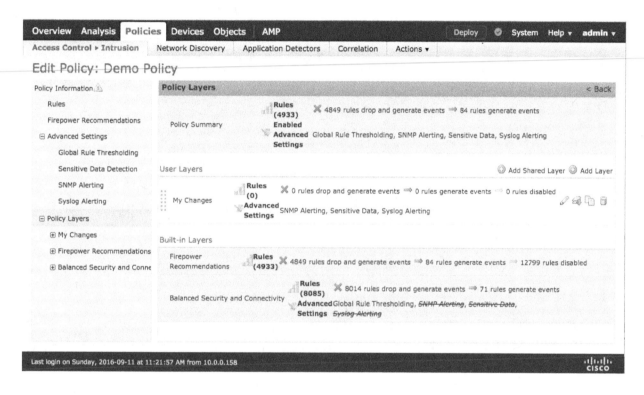

Figure 8.16: Policy Layers

Notice also that you can tell which advanced settings are enabled or disabled in each layer. If the setting is listed in normal text, it is enabled; if the text is strikethrough, the feature is disabled at that layer.

Using the Add Layer link, you can add private layers to the policy. You can designate a layer as shared after it has been created if you want to add it to other policies. The Add Shared Layer link is used to add a shared layer from another policy to this one. Clicking it loads a selection list of all of the other shared layers from Intrusion policies on the FMC. In the Figure 8.17, we created a new layer called "Demo Shared Layer 1." Initially, this is a private layer, but we want it to be shared by other policies.

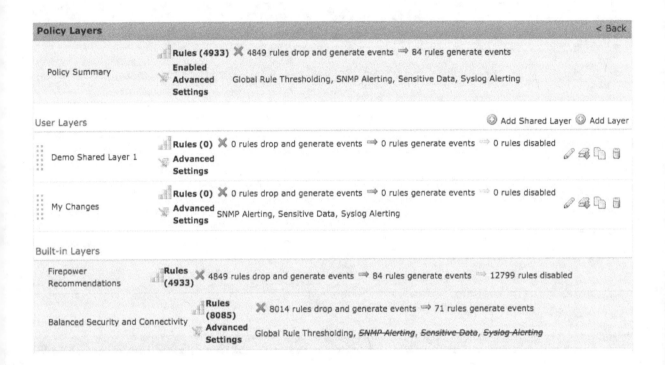

Figure 8.17: Policy layers example 1

To fix this, click the pencil icon in the new layer. This brings us to the screen in Figure 8.18. Here we can check the box marked "Allow this layer to be used by other policies." This turns the private layer into a shared layer.

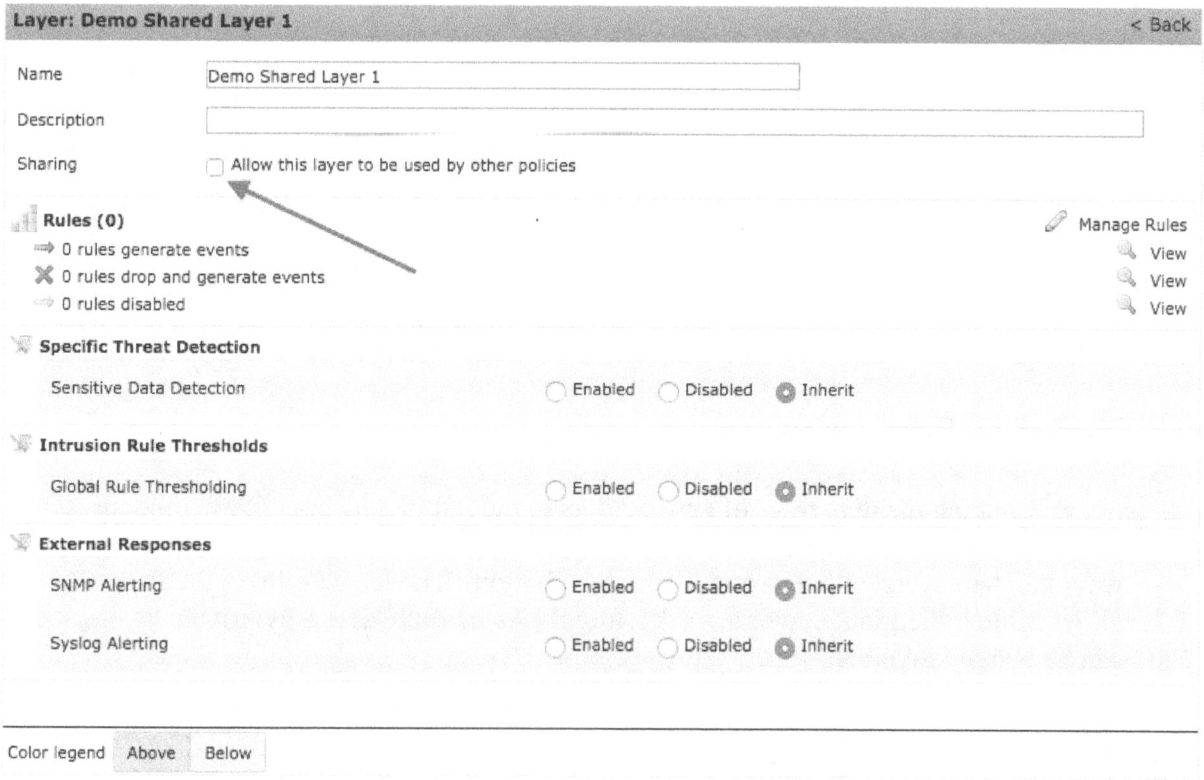

Figure 8.18: Policy layers example 2

Returning to the Policy Layers list, the layer now contains the text "Shared layer," letting us know it is no longer private. To add this layer to another policy, we must first commit changes to this policy, edit the other policy, and then add the shared layer "Demo Shared Layer 1." Figure 8.19 shows our new shared layer.

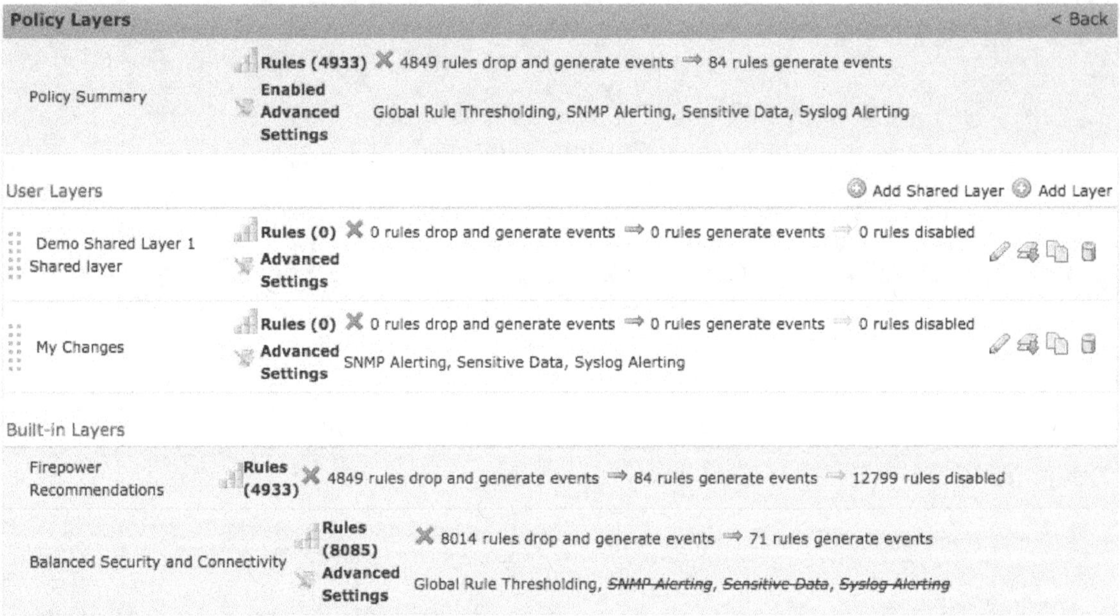

Figure 8.19: Policy layers example 3

Clicking the dual rows of vertical dots to the left of a layer and dragging up or down allows layers to be re-ordered. Only user layers can be re-ordered this way; built-in layers will always remain at the bottom. The icons to the right also allow editing, merging, copying, or deleting the layer. Note that only private layers can be merged together.

Committing Changes

When you are finished editing an Intrusion policy, it's time to commit the changes. This can only be done from the Policy Information screen. To navigate there, click on Policy Information in the upper left. You will then see the Commit Changes and Discard Changes buttons at the bottom. To save the changes, just click Commit Changes and then add any comments if prompted.

It's important to understand that as soon as you edit an Intrusion policy, it is placed into a "changed" state. It doesn't matter if you have actually changed anything or not. It doesn't matter if the yellow triangle ( ) is present next to Policy Information. Each user can only have one policy in this state at a time.

Here's why that's important. What if you see an Intrusion policy and are curious about some of the settings? You click on the policy just to look at which rules are enabled. You didn't change anything so you don't bother to commit or discard changes. You then navigate away or maybe log off of the FMC. Later, you or another administrator visits the Intrusion policy interface and see an asterisk by the policy with the text *"You have unsaved changes for this policy."* See Figure 8.20 as an example.

Intrusion Policy	Drop when Inline	Status	Last Modified	
Balanced IPS Policy based on the Talos Balanced rule set	Yes	Used by 2 access control policies Policy up-to-date on all 1 devices	2016-09-10 15:26:16 Modified by "alext"	
Demo Policy*	Yes	*You have unsaved changes for this policy* No access control policies use this policy Policy not applied on any devices	2016-09-09 21:17:53 Modified by "alext"	
Secure IPS	Yes	Used by 3 access control policies Policy up-to-date on all 2 devices	2016-09-10 16:33:10 Modified by "alext"	

Figure 8.20: Intrusion policy list

Questions begin flying. "Who changed this policy? What did you change?" Well, the truth is you didn't change anything; you merely looked at the policy. However, doing so placed the policy in a "changed" state.

In addition, if you try to create or edit another policy, you will see this dialog:

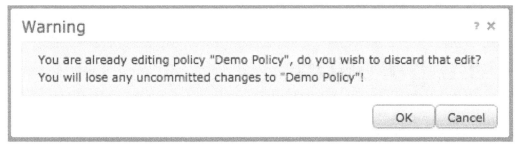

To avoid this unpleasant experience, here's some advice: Always either commit or discard changes before navigating away from an Intrusion policy. If you only looked, then click Discard Changes as you leave. Yes, we know you didn't make any changes, but trust us—it's better this way!

Chapter 9: Network Analysis Policy (NAP)

In this chapter, we will take a look at the Network Analysis policy. This policy is somewhat buried in the Firepower web user interface. In fact, it cannot be found using the menu system. You would think that Cisco doesn't want most of us messing with it—and you would be right!

This policy contains some of the most complex Snort settings. It is primarily dedicated to the configuration of Snort's preprocessors. This chapter will explain some of the history of this policy and discuss some configuration highlights.

First, let's take a step back and look at the underlying architecture of the Firepower system. Prior to its acquisition by Cisco in 2013, the Firepower IPS was a product of Sourcefire. Founded in 2001 by Martin Roesch, Sourcefire provided a commercial intrusion detection system based on the Snort open-source software.

At its inception, the commercial Sourcefire product could justifiably have been called "Snort with a pretty face." It quickly grew beyond this with enhancements in the user interface as well as features like Real-time Network Awareness (RNA). RNA was the original name for the system's ability to passively collect host information and build an internal host database. Couple this with customized high-performance hardware and you have a recipe for a successful IPS.

Snort Configuration

At the core of the system is—and always has been—the open-source Snort intrusion detection system. Snort is a network packet sniffer/analyzer with a rich rules language. It is designed to efficiently search through packets looking for attacks, malware, or anything else the rule writer is interested in. Snort software is configured in the same way as nearly all Linux software—through text configuration files.

This typically takes the form of a single file named **snort.conf**. This file contains nearly all the possible settings that control the operation of Snort's detection. The **snort.conf** file is several hundred lines long and contains **include** statements that also refer to additional configuration and rules files.

In the same manner, Snort rules are primarily found in plain text configuration files. These rules are written in the appropriately named Snort rules language. Snort can also process rules written in object code. These "shared object" rules do not use the Snort rules language and are helpful for advanced detection situations to overcome limitations with Snort keywords; however, the vast majority of rules use the rules language and are found in plain text on the Snort sensor.

Fast forward to 2016 and you can still find these same text files at the core of Snort. Yes, there have been significant improvements in speed and numerous new rule keywords added to improve detection accuracy. However, if you dig into the command line of a Firepower or FTD device, you will eventually find text files containing the familiar Snort rules and configuration parameters.

When deployed, the intrusion and network analysis policies that you create in the Firepower user interface translate to the text Snort configuration files mentioned earlier. There is actually much more going into the processing of traffic on a device as the new hardware models and FTD architecture are much more complex than just a Linux box running Snort. Firepower and FTD devices implement multiple layers of inspection and include features from the Adaptive Security Appliance (ASA) firewalls as well as malware and file inspection.

Preprocessors

Looking at the Snort configuration files, their contents can be classified into two categories:

1. Snort rules: These do most of the actual detection. In the Firepower system, you configure these rules in the intrusion policy.
2. Snort configurations: There are quite a number of other options when it comes to how Snort processes traffic. We will lump these into the configuration category. Most of these configurations can be found in the Network Analysis policy. You will also find a few of them as advanced settings in the Access Control policy.

Within the network analysis policy, you will find that most of the settings have to do with preprocessors. Preprocessors are designed to modify packet data and remove anomalies so Snort rules can function properly. Note that the packet data is not modified with the intent to change it en route to its destination. It is changed to remove conditions such as fragmentation and encoding, which can be used to obfuscate packet data in an attempt to bypass detection. This modified packet data is used for inspection but, assuming the traffic is not blocked, the original packet data will still exit the device.

Note that we will see that there are a small number of preprocessors that do actually modify network packets.

Here's the most important thing to remember about preprocessors. If the preprocessor is misconfigured, there is a good chance the rules that depend on it will not function properly. You can think of the preprocessor as being upstream of the rules when it comes to packet processing. If the stream is not preprocessed correctly, then the rules suffer.

This leads into the second most important thing to remember. If you don't know what you're doing, leave the preprocessor settings alone! These come preset from Talos to function with standard protocols and rules. They are designed to balance the needs of performance and detection. Talos rules are tested using the default base policy configuration provided. Remember, misconfiguring preprocessors will negatively impact performance or detection—or both.

Historically, this has been a bigger issue than it is today. This is largely because more intelligence has been added to Firepower to prevent users from shooting themselves in the proverbial foot. Early on, it was easy to misconfigure the system and severely impact its detection or performance. Nowadays, there is a lot more intelligence between the user interface and the actual configurations. However, don't push your luck. Before making changes to preprocessor configurations, you should make *sure* you know the impact. If you have doubts, call Cisco TAC and validate the changes you plan to make.

Preprocessor Basics

There are a few notable aspects of preprocessors that will help in understanding more about how the system operates.

Preprocessor Rules

Nearly all preprocessors have one or more alerts they can generate. These come courtesy of preprocessor rules. These rules are not like the other Snort rules you may be familiar with. There are a few major differences:

- They cannot use variables. Snort variables like HOME_NET and EXTERNAL_NET are not available to preprocessors. As a result, they are generally not aware of the direction of a connection or whether it's from client to server or vice versa.

- They don't use ports or IP addresses. Preprocessor rules do not have a traditional rule header. The rule header is basically just the rule action, which is almost universally "alert."

- Their detection is always in compiled/object code. Looking at a preprocessor rule offers little or no insight into what the rule was looking for because the actual detection is performed by compiled code. If you're good at dissecting source code, you can download the

Snort source from www.snorg.org, but beyond that there's not much to see here.

- Most of them are disabled. In the Connectivity and Balanced intrusion policies, there are no preprocessor rules enabled. The Security over Connectivity policy enables a few, but honestly, they often just generate noise. Remember, the main function of most preprocessors is to normalize traffic for the real Snort rules, not to generate events. Enabling or disabling a preprocessor rule has no impact on its normalization capabilities.

The GID

All Snort rules (preprocessor or not) have two numbers assigned. These are the Generator ID (GID) and the Snort ID (SID). The GID indicates which part of Snort will generate the event. The SID is the rule number, which is unique within a given GID. Snort rules will have a GID of 1 for a text rule and 3 for a shared object rule. Preprocessors each have one or more GIDs assigned to them; these GID numbers will be 100 or greater. When you see an intrusion event or search through the Intrusion policy for rules, you can find and identify preprocessor rules by their GID.

When you see intrusion events in the FMC interface, each one will have the GID and SID with a colon separating them. Events for rules written in the Snort rules language will start with a 1. They will have numbers like 1:1024 or 1:32230. Events generated by preprocessors will have the preprocessor GID such as 119:20 or 123:5.

As we mentioned, each Snort component has one or more assigned GIDs; a few of these, from the Firepower online help, are shown in Figure 9.1.

ID	Component	Description
1	Standard Text Rule	The event was generated when the packet triggered a standard text rule.
2	Tagged Packets	The event was generated by the Tag generator, which generates packets from a tagged session. This occurs when the tag rule option is used.
3	Shared Object Rule	The event was generated when the packet triggered a shared object rule.
102	HTTP Decoder	The decoder engine decoded HTTP data within the packet.
105	Back Orifice Detector	The Back Orifice Detector identified a Back Orifice attack associated with the packet.
106	RPC Decoder	The RPC decoder decoded the packet.
116	Packet Decoder	The event was generated by the packet decoder.
119, 120	HTTP Inspect Preprocessor	The event was generated by the HTTP Inspect preprocessor. GID 120 rules relate to server-specific HTTP traffic.
122	Portscan Detector	The event was generated by the portscan flow detector.
123	IP Defragmentor	The event was generated when a fragmented IP datagram could not be properly reassembled.

Figure 9.1: Selected Generator IDs

Snort's GID assignment makes it easy to identify and enable or disable rules for a specific preprocessor. Remember the filter search bar in the Intrusion policy? You can type in a search term such as "GID:119" and it will return only the HTTP preprocessor rules.

Configuring and enabling preprocessor rules may seem a bit convoluted. This is a by-product of the decision to split the advanced settings out of the Intrusion policy. Prior to version 5.4, preprocessors were configured within the Intrusion policy, so you could quickly jump from a preprocessor to look at its rules via a link in the Intrusion policy. Now you have to jump back and forth between the Network Analysis and Intrusion policies to configure the settings or rule states for a given preprocessor.

Global and Target Based

As you look through several of the preprocessor configurations, you will find they contain two types of settings—global and target based.

Global settings govern the overall operation of the preprocessor. You will find settings like packet depth, fragment size, maybe some options for different modes. If a preprocessor has a global configuration, it probably also has a target-based section.

Target-based settings are configured based on factors such as operating system or web server type. They allow changing Snort's normalization settings for different host protocol stacks. The need for target-based settings comes from inconsistencies between various operating systems in how they process certain types of traffic. While you can adjust these target-based settings yourself, Firepower also uses a number of techniques to automatically adjust the settings to properly normalize traffic based on the operating system or application target.

The Network Analysis Policy

Now that you have a basic understanding of Snort preprocessors, let's go over the settings in the Network Analysis policy. We're going to do this from a high level and stop only at some of the more commonly modified settings. Remember, you can always use the online help or user guide to get more detailed information about any of these settings.

The first challenge is to *find* the Network Analysis policy. There is no menu item available to navigate there. You will only find a link to this policy in two places—the Access Control policy and the Intrusion policy pages. You'll find it in the upper right in the quick links area. Figure 9.2 shows this link from the Intrusion policy page.

Figure 9.2: Network Analysis policy link

The user interface for editing the Network Analysis policy is very similar to the one for the Intrusion policy. If there are existing policies, they will appear in a list. You can create new policies or delete or edit existing policies. Clicking the Create Policy button brings up the dialog shown in Figure 9.3. Here you can give your policy a name and a description and select the inline mode. Network Analysis policies consist of layers and have a base policy just like the Intrusion policy.

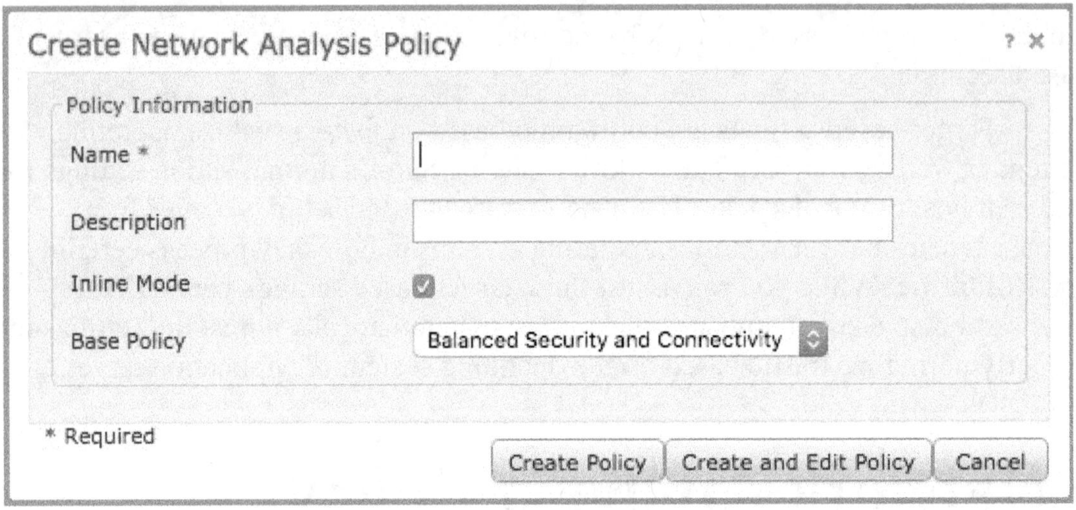

Figure 9.3: Create Network Analysis Policy dialog

The Network Analysis policy configuration also looks similar to the Intrusion policy; however, there are no rules. There is a list of settings on the left along with the two default layers, My Changes and the base layer. The policy in Figure 9.4 is using the Balanced Security and Connectivity policy as the base layer.

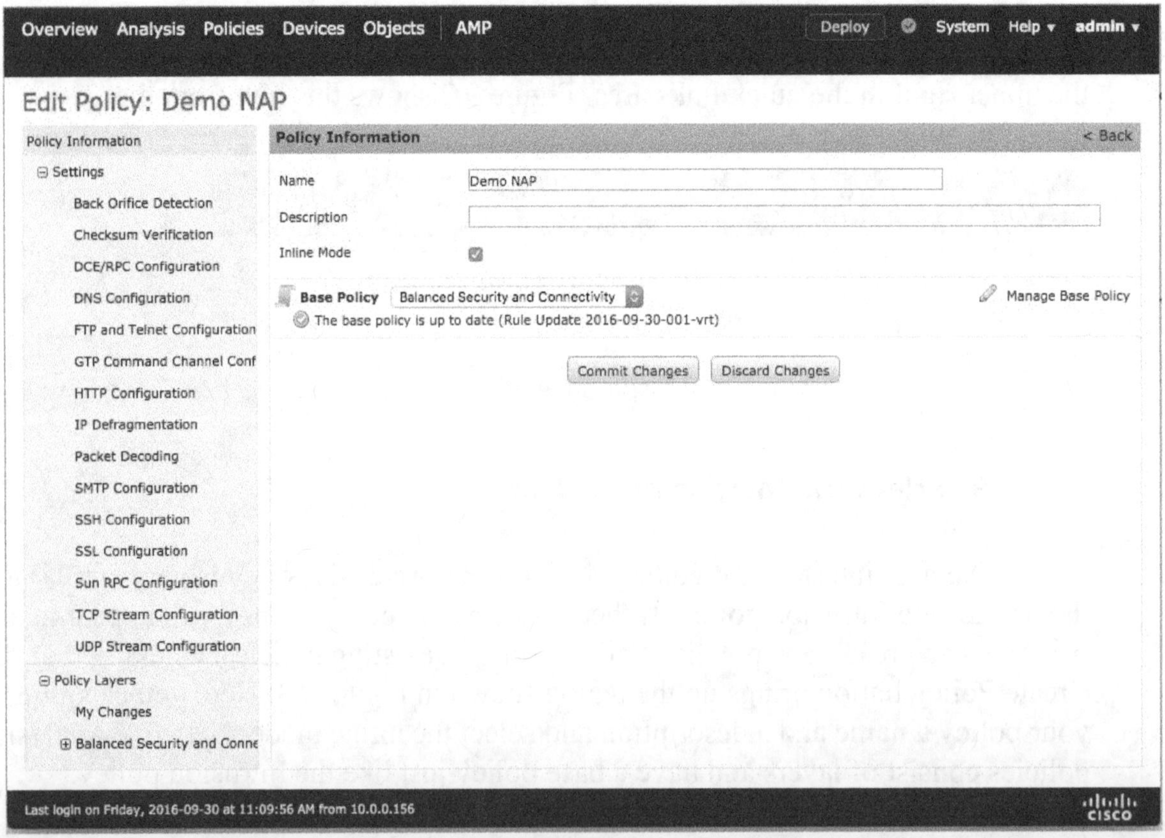

Figure 9.4: Editing the network analysis policy

Similar to working with the Intrusion policy, it's important to remember that the links on the left, showing various settings, only show the *enabled* settings in this policy. Clicking on the Settings link reveals all the policy settings whether they are enabled or not. This is illustrated in Figure 9.5. Notice that the SIP, IMAP, and POP preprocessors are not shown in the list of links on the left; that is because they are currently disabled.

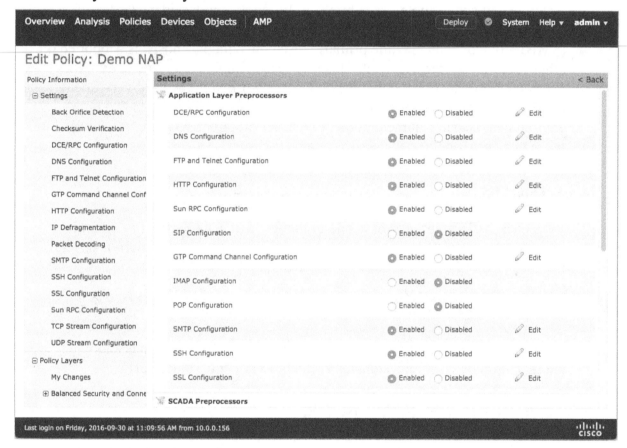

Figure 9.5: Clicking the Settings link

Looking down the list, you will see that the settings fall into several categories:

- Application Layer Preprocessors
- SCADA Preprocessors
- Transport/Network Layer Preprocessors
- Specific Threat Detection

Application Layer Preprocessors

These preprocessors are designed to normalize and inspect traffic for a number of well-known and ubiquitous applications.

DCE/RPC – GID:133

The DCE/RPC preprocessor is dedicated to Distributed Computing Environment and Remote Procedure Call traffic. In short, this means traffic to/from Microsoft Windows systems. This also includes the Server Message Block (SMB) protocol, which, while primarily used on Windows hosts, is supported on other operating systems as well. This is a fairly complex preprocessor with a number of options. It's one that we don't see modified in the field very often because of that cardinal rule we already mentioned. Unless you know your environment is using atypical ports or DCE/RPC options, you are best advised to leave this one alone.

DNS – GID:131

The DNS preprocessor is one of the few that actually doesn't do any normalization to traffic. It is an alert-only preprocessor and can alert on several irregularities if the associated rules are enabled.

FTP and Telnet GID:125,126

Two preprocessors in one, these look for specific commands and anomalous activity in File Transfer Protocol (FTP) and Telnet traffic.

HTTP Configuration GID:119,120

The HTTP inspection preprocessor is one of the most important due to the sheer volume of HTTP traffic and the attacks it carries. We will slow down a little here and point out some features.

If you compare some of the settings in the Network Analysis policies provided by Talos, you will find some differences. If you are curious, you can create a couple of policies based on different Talos policies and run a comparison report. We did this for the Balanced Security and Connectivity and Security Over Connectivity policies.

The differences in the HTTP configuration are shown in Figure 9.6. The Balanced Security and Connectivity policy is on the left and the Security Over Connectivity policy is on the right.

Demo NAP (2016-10-01 15:49:08 by admin)		SoC (2016-10-03 22:06:02 by admin)	
Settings		**Settings**	
HTTP Configuration		HTTP Configuration	
Global Settings		Global Settings	
Maximum Compressed Data Depth	1460	Maximum Compressed Data Depth	20000
Maximum Decompressed Data Depth	2920	Maximum Decompressed Data Depth	20000
Servers		Servers	
default		default	
Ports	80, 1220, 1741, 2301, 2980,	Ports	36, 80, 81, 82, 83, 84, 85, 86
Client Flow Depth	300	Client Flow Depth	0
Server Flow Depth	500	Server Flow Depth	0
Normalize HTTP Headers	No	Normalize HTTP Headers	Yes
Inspect HTTP Cookies	No	Inspect HTTP Cookies	Yes
Inspect HTTP Responses	No	Inspect HTTP Responses	Yes
		Inspect Compressed Data	Yes
		Decompress SWF File (LZMA)	Yes
		Decompress SWF File (Deflate)	Yes
		Decompress PDF File (Deflate)	Yes
Log URI	No	Log URI	Yes
Log Hostname	No	Log Hostname	Yes

Figure 9.6: HTTP configuration differences

You can see there are a number of settings that are different in the more secure policy on the right.

- Maximum compressed/decompressed data depth: We go from decompressing a single packet (1460 bytes) on the left to up to 20,000 bytes of data on the right. This is for server responses that use gzip compression.

- Ports: The list runs off the page but there are a number of additional ports in the more secure policy.

- Client and server flow depth: This determines how deep Snort will inspect an HTTP flow depending on where it's going. Notice on the left we look 300 bytes into a flow to a client and 500 bytes into a flow to a server. However, on the right, the zero indicates that the depth is unlimited; we normalize and inspect the entire flow in either direction.

- Inspect Compressed Data: Notice that we are only doing inspection of compressed data when using the Security Ofver Connectivity policy.

Like many settings within Snort, these represent the tension between performance and security. The balanced base policy must allow the Firepower device to perform at its rated throughput; however, the security base policy is weighted more toward detection at the cost of performance. The settings just noted are a perfect example of this; it is more thorough to inspect deeper into the HTTP flows and decompress more data, but this comes at a cost to device performance.

What might you want to change in the HTTP configuration? Aside from the settings just discussed, here are some common ones you may want to adjust. These are helpful for some networks and represent minimal performance impact.

- Ports: The port list is actually more dynamic than it looks. Snort can actually identify HTTP by itself and normalize the traffic even if it occurs on a port not listed here; however, to ensure that you are processing all HTTP, you should add ports where you have HTTP services not listed here.

  A note about port 443: If you are performing SSL decryption, either externally or using your Firepower device, you should add port 443 as well as any other decrypted traffic ports to this list.

- Extract Original Client IP Address: This is very handy when you have an IPS that is external to your proxy server. Snort can extract the client's original IP address if it is populated in the HTTP header by the proxy. Two of the most common fields are listed here: X-Forwarded-For and True-Client-IP. You can change their priority or add your own if your proxy uses a different header field for this information.

- Log URI and Log Hostname: These options extract the raw URI and hostname (if present) in the first HTTP header. These values are then displayed in their respective columns in intrusion events.

Sun RPC GID:106

This preprocessor reassembles fragmented Sun RPC traffic.

SIP GID:140

This allows the use of various SIP rule keywords to inspect Session Initiation Protocol (SIP) telephony traffic.

GTP Command Channel GID:143

The General Service Packet Radio (GPRS) Tunneling Protocol (GTP) preprocessor allows the use of various GTP keywords in Snort.

IMAP GID:141 and POP GID:142

These preprocessors inspect server-to-client Internet Messaging Application Protocol (IMAP) and Post Office Protocol (POP) traffic. If the associated rules are enabled, they can alert on anomalous traffic. They can also extract and decode email attachments.

SMTP GID:124

Like its IMAP and POP brethren, the Simple Mail Transport Protocol (SMTP) preprocessor can alert on anomalous traffic and extract filenames, addresses, and header data for intrusion events triggered by SMTP traffic.

SSH GID:128

The Secure Shell (SSH) preprocessor detects several types of common SSH attacks. By default, it stops inspecting SSH sessions after it sees 20 encrypted packets.

SSL GID:137

The Secure Sockets Layer (SSL) preprocessor analyzes SSL handshake messages and is required for rules that detect exploits such as Heartbleed. It stops intrusion and file inspection of packet payloads for encrypted traffic.

SCADA Preprocessors

SCADA stands for Supervisory Control and Data Acquisition. It is the term used for industrial control systems such as those used in chemical, power, manufacturing, and a host of other industries. There are two protocols supported by Snort – Modbus and DNP3. These preprocessors should be enabled if you are protecting SCADA systems along with enabling the PROTOCOL-SCADA Snort rule category. The Modbus preprocessor uses GID:144 and DNP3 uses GID:145.

Transport/Network Layer Preprocessors

The Transport/Network layer preprocessors operate at the packet layers that carry the same names. The Network layer is where we see the Internet Protocol (IP) and the Transport layer sits right on top. This is where we see the Transmission Control Protocol (TCP) and the User Datagram Protocol (UDP).

These preprocessors specialize in fragmentation reassembly. The can also trigger alerts for anomalous traffic if the associated rules are enabled.

Checksum Verification

This verifies, at a basic level, whether packets have been tampered with.

Inline Normalization

The Inline Normalization preprocessor is one of the few that is commonly modified in the Network Analysis policy. The guidance from Cisco is as follows: if your device is inline, this preprocessor should be enabled. This includes modes such as routed or switched as well—anytime the device processes packets and sends them back out.

There are numerous options that can be enabled with this preprocessor. ***Exercise extreme caution if you decide to "tweak" this!*** This preprocessor has the ability to *change* packets as they pass through the device. This can be good, but it also can be very dangerous. If you start changing flags or attributes of packets that were working just fine before, it could break a delicate business-critical application. That could ruin your whole day! If you do make changes, be sure to test thoroughly.

The reason Cisco recommends enabling this preprocessor has to do with fragmentation reassembly. The preprocessor can "clean up" malicious fragmentation, which could be used to evade detection. The discussion of malicious fragmentation could take up an entire chapter, and while it's very interesting, we're not going to cover it here. If you want to understand this in all its gory details, go to www.snort.org and look for the white paper titled "Target-Based Fragmentation Reassembly" by Judy Novak.

IP Defragmentation GID:123

This preprocessor handles packet reassembly at the IP layer. If you haven't noticed, fragmentation is a big deal when it comes to packet inspection. Fragmentation can happen at so many layers, and it's critical that fragments are properly reassembled before Snort rule inspection.

This wouldn't be so difficult except that there are seven different methods that can be used to reassemble overlapping IP fragments! This target-based preprocessor can use all of these methods depending on the operating system being targeted. Again, we're going to refer you to that Judy Novak paper on the Snort website for a detailed discussion of why this is a big deal and how Snort deals with it.

Packet Decoding GID:116

The packet decoder actually decodes the packet data before it gets sent to the other Transport/Network layer preprocessors. It decodes starting at the Data Link and on up through the Transport layer. here are numerous rules related to packet decoding, and you can alert on a variety of protocol anomalies.

TCP Stream GID:129

If you thought fragmentation was a pain at the IP layer, it just gets worse at the TCP layer. There are 13 different methods Snort can use to defragment TCP data. Some operating systems such as Microsoft Windows even change their reassembly method for different versions. Figure 9.7 shows the Policy drop-down menu on the TCP Stream settings page.

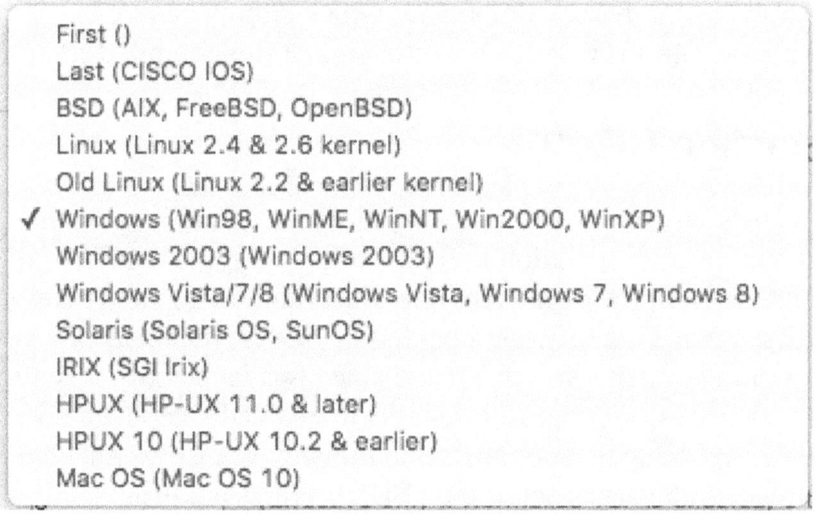

```
     First ()
     Last (CISCO IOS)
     BSD (AIX, FreeBSD, OpenBSD)
     Linux (Linux 2.4 & 2.6 kernel)
     Old Linux (Linux 2.2 & earlier kernel)
  ✓  Windows (Win98, WinME, WinNT, Win2000, WinXP)
     Windows 2003 (Windows 2003)
     Windows Vista/7/8 (Windows Vista, Windows 7, Windows 8)
     Solaris (Solaris OS, SunOS)
     IRIX (SGI Irix)
     HPUX (HP-UX 11.0 & later)
     HPUX 10 (HP-UX 10.2 & earlier)
     Mac OS (Mac OS 10)
```

Figure 9.7: TCP Stream operating system choices

Once again, we're going to refer you to the snort.org website and a paper by you-know-who—Judy Novak—this one called "Target-Based Stream Reassembly."

The TCP Stream preprocessor is important because of the huge amount of TCP traffic traversing modern networks. It also is required for multiple Snort rule keywords, including the **flow** keyword, which is used in nearly every rule. This preprocessor also maintains a state table that identifies active sessions as well as which host is the client and which is the server in a given conversation.

UDP Stream GID:129

We will finish this section with the UDP Stream preprocessor. This provides state and session tracking similar to the TCP preprocessor but for the UDP protocol. Now this may seem strange because UDP is by definition a "stateless" protocol. However, many applications use UDP as their transport protocol and maintain state at the Application layer. This preprocessor can detect this and update the state table with entries even if the session is using UDP.

Specific Threat Detection

The preprocessors in this section do not really fit the classic definition. They don't really normalize traffic for rules. Instead, they are designed to detect activity that Snort rules cannot. Detecting the activity in question may require a complex calculation or time-based component, which simply cannot be accomplished with the Snort rule language or even in a pre-compiled rule.

Back Orifice Detection GID:105

The Back Orifice preprocessor is designed to detect traffic from the similarly named remote administration tool. Calling it a remote administration tool is a bit generous since it can be installed without user interaction and takes steps to hide on the target system. This software debuted in 1998, which makes it very old! However, old operating systems still exist, and since this is the only way for Snort to detect Back Orifice, this preprocessor defaults to enabled. There are no configuration settings. Strangely enough, while the preprocessor is enabled in all of the Cisco Network Analysis policies, the GID:105 rules are disabled in the Connectivity over Security intrusion policy. Since the only function of this preprocessor is to alert on Back Orifice traffic, our advice is to either enable the rules or disable this preprocessor.

Portscan Detection GID:122

Portscan detection is a feature that looks for a large number of reset (RST) or ICMP unreachable packets coming from a host. When the sensitivity is increased, it also looks for a large number of sync (SYN) packets going to a host. Either one of these could be an indication that the host is being port scanned. This was a good idea some years ago when a Snort sensor had a single CPU; however, with modern devices and multiple instances of Snort, this preprocessor is less effective.

This has to do with Firepower's load balancing of flows across CPUs. Because no single CPU gets to "see" all the traffic, portscan activity is divided among the various Snort instances. The more CPUs, the less sensitive the device is to detecting scans. You can still try enabling this preprocessor, but your mileage may vary greatly resulting in false positives and false negatives.

Rate-Based Attack Prevention GID:135

Our last setting is Rate-Based Attack Prevention. This allows the creation of rules to detect and potentially stop rate-based attacks. These could be denial of service (DOS) attacks, which are designed to exhaust the host or network's ability to respond to legitimate requests. You can also use these rules to limit the number of established connections to a host. This prevents an attacker from using up most or all of the available connections to a single host.

Note that enabling this feature enables the appropriate GID:135 rules automatically. These rules will still show as disabled in the Intrusion policy, manually activating these rules has no effect.

One Last Thought

Before we move on, we want to tie a bow on the Network Analysis policy. We discussed a number of settings and left the majority at their defaults. Remember, misconfiguring preprocessors can have a severely detrimental effect on Snort rules. You should be aware that Firepower has gone to some lengths to minimize the potential damage an admin can do with this policy.

In previous versions of Firepower (actually back when it was FireSIGHT), if you disabled a key preprocessor such as IP defragmentation or TCP stream, you would get a warning that some rules will not operate correctly. In fact, the system would not let you save an Intrusion policy with these key preprocessors enabled.

Today, if you try to disable the key preprocessors in the Network Analysis policy, the system will not complain at all. In fact, you can disable *every one* of the preprocessors in your configuration. You can deploy policies and the system will merrily comply. You might say, "Wait, didn't I just handicap Snort rules entirely?" Actually no, the system will enable the appropriate preprocessors and your detection will likely work just fine. You can see this by going to the device and digging into the Snort configuration files. All the preprocessor settings are there!

The bottom line is that while Cisco has given you configuration options in the Network Analysis policy, you have to try really hard to shoot yourself in the foot. You *can* adjust buffer sizes or misconfigure ports or other options to the extent that Snort detection will be curtailed. But our point is, you don't have to lose sleep over it. If you only make minor tweaks and *fully understand* their ramifications, your Firepower system will do its job of detecting and stopping evil.

Chapter 10: DNS and SSL Policies

In this chapter, we will look at two of the newer features in Firepower—the DNS and SSL policies.

Both of these provide visibility beyond typical packet sniffing detection by providing additional insight into potentially compromised hosts or encrypted data.

Fun with DNS

While often taken for granted, the Domain Name System (DNS) is the glue that holds the Internet together. It provides the link between the "friendly" name of a host or website and its numeric IP address.

This is true for both legitimate and malicious sites. Malware authors and botnet herders often operate their malicious software riding on the same infrastructure protocols as everybody else. Since these protocols are well-known, we can scan them for evidence of abuse and even use them against attackers.

Now, we're not talking about retaliation against the bad guys; this is more along the lines of leveraging the existing features in the DNS protocol to identify infected hosts or malicious/compromised sites. Of course, we can also block malicious DNS activity, which provides some protection and may save a few hosts from becoming victims.

The Kill Chain

To understand why the DNS policy is so cool, we need to take a quick look at how hosts get infected with malware. The term *kill chain* comes from the military description of the progression of an attack. It goes something like this:

- Find: Locate the target.
- Fix: Make it hard for them to move.
- Track: Monitor movement.
- Target: Select the appropriate weapon system to achieve the desired effect.
- Engage: Shoot them.
- Assess: Evaluate battle damage and intelligence.

This concept lends itself nicely to cyberwarfare as well as the conventional battlefield. Here is one model of the cyber kill chain:

- Reconnaissance: Select the target, research, identify vulnerabilities

- Weaponization: Create the weapon (virus, worm, malware, etc.)

- Delivery: Transmit the weapon to the target

- Exploitation: Execute the malware code - taking action

- Installation: Take steps to stay persistent on the target

- Command and Control: Enable attacker to remotely control the malware

- Actions on Objective: Take desired action on target, such as data exfiltration, destruction, encryption (ransomware), etc.

In this cyber kill chain, we can track and possibly block some of the steps using Firepower's DNS Security Intelligence. Admittedly, our DNS capabilities for the first two are limited since much of the work there is research and development and does not require network communications with the victim. But once the actual attack is underway, there are a number of ways we can identify and/or block this activity.

A Typical Malware Infection

Let's start with a simple malware infection. A user on a corporate network clicks on a banner ad or an email link, which directs them to a website that either has been created just for this evil purpose or is a legitimate site that has been compromised to serve malware. Figure 10.1 shows how this might work.

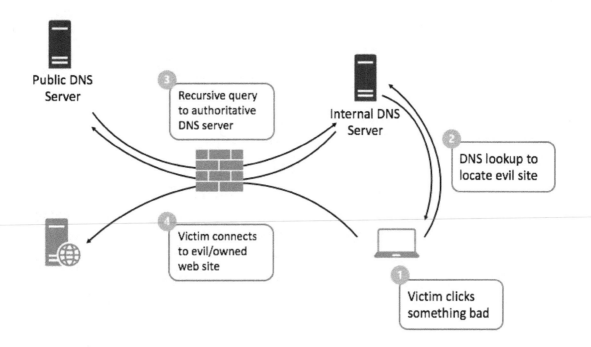

Figure 10.1: Simple malware infection

Notice the first thing that happens after the user clicks the evil content is a DNS lookup (2). This is typically routed to the organization's internal name server. Assuming the name server doesn't have the IP address cached, this request will generate a recursive lookup to the name server that is authoritative for the domain in question (3). This may require several lookups—we've just shown a single one here. The authoritative name server returns the IP address for the domain, and the IP address is then forwarded down to the victim. The victim then connects directly to the evil/compromised web server and the malware is delivered. This is analogous to the Delivery step in the cyber kill chain mentioned previously. Note that this doesn't have to be a website. The DNS lookup steps would be the same if the payload was delivered via some other method, such as the File Transfer Protocol (FTP) or even a secure protocol such as HTTPS.

Now that we have a basic understanding of how a typical malware attack begins, let's look at some of the options for stopping it.

IP Blacklists

One method of dealing with malware is to use IP blacklists. These are lists of IP addresses containing compromised or known malicious hosts. They are updated frequently as new hosts are constantly being infected and infected hosts are taken offline for cleanup. Firepower has just such a feature, which we discussed in Chapter 6, "Objects." IP blacklists provide an effective method of blocking known malicious IP addresses. Their use can cut down on new malware infections and impede communications for malware that is already running on a victim host. There are, however, some considerations that make IP blacklisting less effective.

- Fast-flux DNS: This refers to the technique used by some command and control systems to hide sites behind an ever-changing network of IP addresses. These typically have a very short time to live (TTL), creating a constantly changing list of IP addresses for a hostname.

- Update speed: IP addresses can only be blacklisted after they are known to be malicious. Once they are added to the blacklist, this list must be propagated to the various Firepower systems worldwide. The delay in updating your lists depends on the update frequency selected for the Cisco-Intelligence-Feed object. (we discussed this in Chapter 6). During this delay, victim hosts are vulnerable.

- Blacklists are not secret: Attackers also have access to the various blacklist feeds from security vendors or services. They know when one of their compromised systems has been identified and blacklisted. Chances are once they see that, they will decommission this host and bring in another pre-compromised system with a clean IP reputation.

The Proxy Problem

Another important limitation when it comes to IP blacklisting is networks using outbound web proxies. Proxying your users' web traffic is a great way to enforce organizational policies regarding non-business-related web activities. Client requests go to the web proxy where they are vetted, and if the site is allowed, the proxy initiates the session to the original server on behalf of the client. From that point all traffic to and from the original web server flows through the proxy server.

Figure 10.2 shows the original malware infection but this time the network has a proxy server implemented.

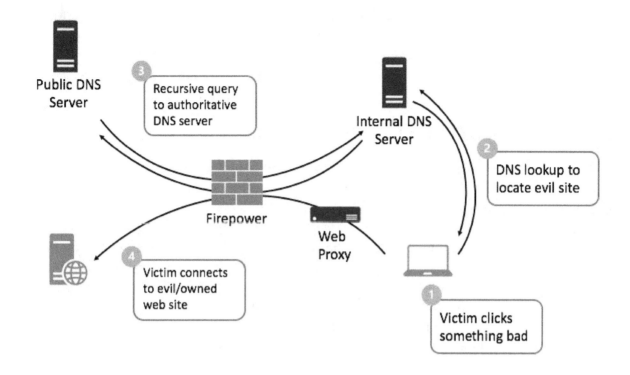

Figure 10.2: Malware through a web proxy

On the surface this seems very similar to the original malware attack. The only change we have made is to add the web proxy and also to note that the Internet firewall is actually running Firepower.

In our examples so far we've looked at the beginning of a malware attack. There is also is plenty of activity that occurs post-attack, when the host becomes part of a botnet or the malware checks into its command and control (CNC) servers. Much of that activity can also be detected by Firepower.

The presence of the proxy in this case does not impact Firepower's ability to detect or stop the attack. However, the proxy can impact Firepower's ability to identify the victim. When Firepower detects activity that indicates an active malware compromise, the real question is not, Can we stop the malware from working? We probably can't. The question is, Which host is infected? The response to a malware infected host varies somewhat, but it's often along the lines of wipe and reimage. In this case, alerting and stopping at least some of the communications is fine, but the real value is locating the infected host.

In the example in Figure 10.2, the problem is that if we detect the connection to the evil website (4), the source IP address for this traffic will be the proxy server. We need to know the address of the victim if we are going to remediate the malware infection.

What if the IP blacklist contains the public DNS server's address? In this case we detect the DNS lookup to the blacklisted IP (3), but the source IP is the internal DNS server. Once again, we need to know what client made the original DNS request, but we are being hindered by intermediate devices in the network.

The Proxy Solution

Fortunately, Firepower has solutions to these proxy and DNS issues.

X-Forwarded-For and True-Client-IP

The first solution relates to the web traffic as it exits the network through the proxy. While we have intrusion rules and/or IP blacklist entries to identify the traffic, we need to identify the original host. Most web proxies can add an optional field to the HTTP header for proxied traffic. This field contains the original client IP address of the client. You may remember that we discussed this setting in the HTTP configuration in Chapter 9, "Network Analysis Policy." By default, Snort will pull this original client IP information from the X-Forwarded-For or the True-Client-IP field if either one exists. This information is then populated in the Original Client IP field of the intrusion event.

In prior versions of Firepower, the use of these headers was limited only to intrusion events. An exciting change in Firepower 6.1 is the extension of this Original Client IP field to Connection and Security Intelligence events. This provides an even greater use-case for enabling this feature on your proxy because Firepower can now attribute most event types to the original client using this mechanism. This means that even Security Intelligence IP blacklist events can now tell you who the original client was.

DNS Sinkhole

Another new and exciting Firepower feature is the ability to respond to malicious DNS requests. With the addition of the DNS policy and the Cisco-DNS-and-URL-Intelligence-Feed, we can now quickly respond to attacks in a manner that allows identification of infected endpoints even through forwarded DNS lookups.

The feature that provides this capability is called DNS sinkhole. Through the DNS policy, Firepower can respond in a number of ways to a DNS request:

- Whitelist: Allow the request.

- Monitor the request: Allow and optionally log a security intelligence event.

- Return a "domain not found" message: Spoof a response to appear as if it came from the DNS server saying the domain name is not found.

- Drop: Silently drop the DNS query.

- Sinkhole: Return the IP address of a sinkhole object in response to the DNS query.

The last option—DNS sinkhole—is the most interesting. This can help address the situation where you have an internal DNS server forwarding external name resolution requests on behalf of your internal hosts.

As we mentioned, if you could just see or maybe block the DNS query, your event intelligence would be limited. You would see the destination IP (a public DNS server), the domain lookup (www.evilsite.com), and the source IP address (your internal DNS server). None of these give you any idea of which of your hosts tried to go to evilsite.com in the first place.

Even if you blocked the request, what if the malware retried the lookup using an alternate DNS name like www.backupevilsite.com? Unless you have DNS blacklist rules for every possible domain it might try, one request is likely to slip through. Blocking these requests is good but not foolproof. The real solution is to find the host where these requests originate and clean it up!

The DNS sinkhole can help you locate the internal host. Figure 10.3 shows how this might work.

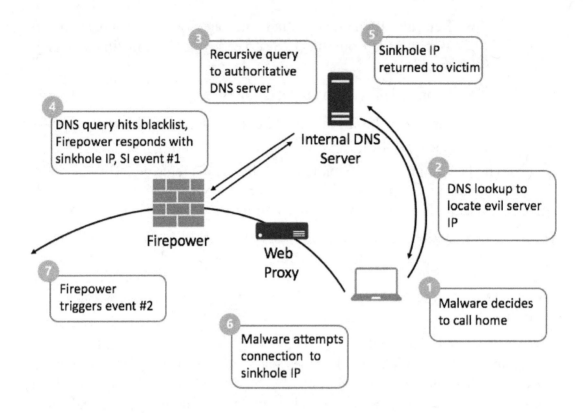

Figure 10.3: DNS sinkhole walk-through

Let's walk through the communications shown in the figure.

1. A malicious process running on the victim host decides to communicate with an external evil host such as www.badsite.com. This could be to check in with its CNC server, receive instructions, download additional malware, etc.

2. The operating system performs a DNS lookup to the local DNS server to find the IP address of this host.

3. The local server forwards the query to the authoritative name server for badsite.com.

4. Badsite.com is on a DNS blacklist. Firepower intercepts the request and returns a spoofed response containing the IP address of a DNS sinkhole object (1.1.1.1). A security intelligence event is generated noting the DNS blacklist that was matched as well as the response (sinkhole).

5. The local DNS server receives this response, adds it to its local cache, and forwards the IP (1.1.1.1) to the victim.

6. The malware attempts a connection via HTTP, FTP, HTTPS, etc. to the sinkhole IP of 1.1.1.1. This may be through the proxy or directly to the Internet, depending on the protocol and network architecture.

7. Firepower identifies the traffic going to the sinkhole, generating event #2—a connection event. You can then identify the infected host using the event Source IP or Original Client IP field.

Of course, there is room for some flexibility in the configuration and sinkhole behavior. In the diagram, the malware connection to 1.1.1.1 seems to go out to the Internet. You can choose to block the connection to the sinkhole address, ensuring none of the malware traffic actually leaves your network. The sinkhole can also resolve to an actual host if desired. If you set up your own sinkhole system, you can log connections on it as well and gain additional insight into what might be going on with your victim. Your sinkhole system should not host any services for general users. The idea is that there should never be a legitimate reason to initiate connections to the sinkhole address.

DNS Policy

The DNS policy is how we implement the protections mentioned previously. In Chapter 6, we examined how to set up and configure various security intelligence objects, including DNS sinkhole objects. In this section, we'll take a look at how to implement these in the DNS policy.

You will find the DNS policy under Policies → Access Control → DNS. You will see the Default DNS Policy. You can edit it, or, if desired, you can create a new one. To create a new policy, click the Add DNS Policy button in the upper right. You will then be prompted to enter your policy's name and an optional description. Once you load the policy, you will be greeted by the screen in Figure 10.4.

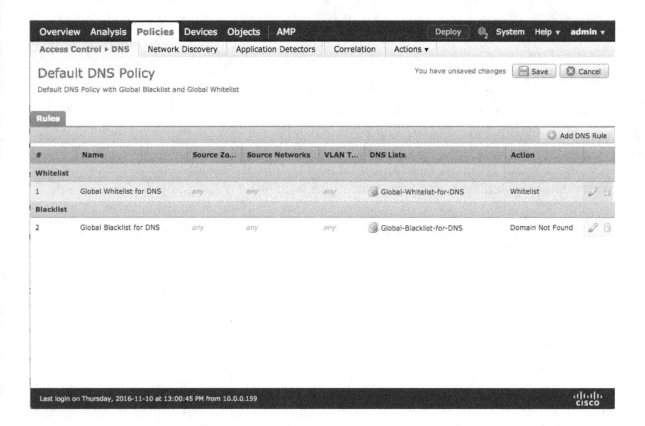

Figure 10.4: Default DNS Policy

The policy comes with two default rules for the global DNS whitelist and blacklist. The Global Blacklist for DNS returns a "domain not found" response for domains and the Global Whitelist for DNS allows the traffic, subject to further access control inspection. Notice that the Whitelist rule category is positioned above the Blacklist. This illustrates the default behavior—that is, a whitelist overrides a blacklist. These two rules can be disabled, but they cannot be modified in any other way.

To add a new rule, click the Add DNS Rule button on the right. This will display the Add Rule dialog in Figure 10.5.

Figure 10.5: Add Rule dialog

Here, you give your name a rule. Then you can select from the following actions listed in order of appearance:

- Whitelist: Allow the traffic, subject to further access control action/inspection.

- Monitor: Log a security intelligence event. Allow the traffic, subject to further access control action/inspection.

- Domain Not Found: Return a "domain not found" DNS response to the query and log beginning of connection security intelligence and connection events. The query will end with no further inspection.

- Drop: Drop the DNS query with no further inspection. Log beginning of connection security intelligence and connection events.

- Sinkhole: When you select this option, an additional drop-down appears to allow selecting a sinkhole object. Firepower returns the configured sinkhole IP address in response to the query. Logging depends on the configuration of the sinkhole object.
    - If your sinkhole object is configured to log sinkhole connections, the system logs an end of connection event for the follow-on connection.
    - If your sinkhole object is configured to log and block sinkhole connections, the system logs a beginning of connection event for the follow-on connection and blocks that connection.

Note that when using a sinkhole object, your object configuration should be different if your sinkhole is a real host versus a nonexistent one. If your host exists and you want to gain additional intelligence from the follow-on connection, your object should be configured to log but not block.

Next, you can select the zones, networks, and VLAN tags where the rule should apply.

Finally, the DNS tab allows you to select the DNS lists or feeds the rule applies to.

When you are finished, use the Save button to save your policy. DNS policy is implemented via the Access Control policy. This is explained in Chapter 13, "Access Control Policy."

SSL

The ability to decrypt Secure Sockets Layer (SSL) communications was introduced back in FireSIGHT version 5.4. Version 6.0 of Firepower then extended this capability to the ASA with the FirePOWER Services platform. With version 6.1, improvements were made to SSL processing to improve reliability and allow decryption to work in more situations. In the following sections, we will discuss some SSL basics and describe the use of the SSL policy.

Secure Sockets Primer

Over the past several years, SSL use on Internet websites has been steadily growing in popularity. If you check the various browser tabs you have open right now, it's likely that some or maybe most of them are showing the familiar "https" and associated lock icon in the site URL. From banking to web mail to your favorite social media site, everyone is getting on board with encrypted communications. It's great—unless you are using an IPS to try to inspect network traffic. Then it's terrible; it's like staring into a black hole, a lot of nothing!

Secure communications are all about privacy, integrity, and authentication. SSL helps ensure that your network traffic cannot be read, that what you send or receive has not been modified en route, and that you are really communicating with the organization or site you think you are.

Of course, SSL is not really what we are using nowadays. It's actually SSL's successor—TLS, or Transport Layer Security. However, since everyone still uses the generic term *SSL* to describe this type of encryption, we won't split hairs. Although by nature geeks love to split hairs!

While it would be fun to dive into all the nuances and intricacies of SSL, TLS, and symmetric cryptography, we are going to remain at a high level to help you understand what's important when it comes to Firepower. This will help you understand how to create your own SSL policy and rules.

First, SSL is all about certificates and keys. Certificates are (generally) used to verify the identity of the server and optionally the client. Keys are used to lock (encrypt) data prior to transmission and unlock (decrypt) data after receipt. For Firepower to transparently decrypt SSL communications, it has to be provided with this extremely confidential certificate/key data. Armed with these "secrets" and positioned properly between the client and server, it can intercept these communications and inspect their contents. This is accomplished without triggering any notifications or alarms. Sounds positively cloak-and-dagger, doesn't it?

Intercepting and decrypting these communications is successful because the organization doing the decryption owns the keys—we're the good guys, so it's okay. This is commonly referred to as a main-in-the-middle (MITM) attack. Firepower interposes itself between the client and server and pretends to be one or the other, depending on whether you are inspecting inbound or outbound connections. Being in the middle isn't always required, but you will find that attempting to perform SSL decryption in passive mode will fail for many connections. This is because newer key exchange mechanisms are designed to prevent passive decryption of SSL traffic, even if the secrets are known. The bottom line is if you plan to use SSL decryption, your device should be in routed, switched, or inline mode.

The SSL Handshake

You need to have a basic understanding of the SSL handshake to understand how Firepower performs this MITM function and some of the latest 6.1 features to improve reliability. In a typical SSL connection, there is a client and a server. Using a common example of a user connecting to a secure website, the client would be the web browser (Chrome, Firefox, Internet Explorer, etc.) and the server would be an application such as Apache or NGINX running a secure website. The two goals of SSL are (1) verify for the user sitting in front of the computer that the site that says it is www.yourbank.com is really your bank and not some imposter, and (2) ensure that communications cannot be intercepted and viewed by anyone except www.yourbank.com.

The way this is accomplished is with a carefully orchestrated handshake. This handshake process ensures that all the right conditions are present on the client and the server. When the handshake completes, you can be confident in the authenticity of the site and the security of your data. Let the banking begin! We are going to look at this handshake from a very high level. Some of the detailed information is left out so we can concentrate on what's important for configuring Firepower SSL decryption.

Here is what it looks like:

1. The client sends the "client hello." This contains the client's SSL version number, randomly generated data, and cryptographic information, including which encryption protocols the client supports. For the client and server to communicate, they must agree on a protocol or language they both understand.

2. The server responds with the "server hello." The server sends its SSL version number, cryptographic information, and its digital certificate.

3. The client uses the server's certificate information to verify the authenticity of the server. This includes whether the certificate matches the site name, whether the certificate is expired, and whether the certificate authority is trusted. If this fails, the user gets a warning that the site should not be trusted.

4. The client and server exchange secret key information. This can occur via several methods and is designed to establish and securely exchange the keys that will be used in the rest of the conversation.

5. The handshake is completed and the SSL session has begun; all further communications will be encrypted using the agreed-upon encryption algorithm.

Firepower SSL Decryption

When using Firepower to decrypt SSL traffic, the first decision is whether to decrypt inbound or outbound traffic.

Inbound SSL Decryption

Inbound traffic means SSL sessions to your servers. In this case, because you own the servers, you have both the certificate and private key information they use. This private key information is some of the most carefully protected data on the Internet. A compromise of this information would allow an attacker to impersonate your website without a user's knowledge. These keys are generally kept in offline or air-gapped systems and controlled very carefully.

When you configure inbound SSL decryption, you load this certificate and key data on the Firepower system. This allows it to perform the MITM "attack," decrypt and inspect traffic, and then re-encrypt before sending it to the actual server. This requires no changes on the web server itself or on the client making the connection. The Firepower system impersonates both sides to the other, so neither the server nor the client realize their traffic is being sniffed. As you can see, this has tremendous security implications and illustrates why these private keys are so closely guarded!

Outbound SSL Decryption

The other type of decryption you may want to implement is outbound. In this case, you are decrypting sessions that are initiated by clients within your network as they connect to external SSL servers. Since you don't own them, you do not have the secret key information for those external servers. Firepower can perform the MITM action and decrypt the session by replacing the server's certificate with its own.; however, the client (web browser) will recognize this and raise a dire warning to the user as shown in Figures 10.6 and 10.7. It is letting them know that the site they are connecting to does not have the correct certificate, which means someone is tampering with their connection.

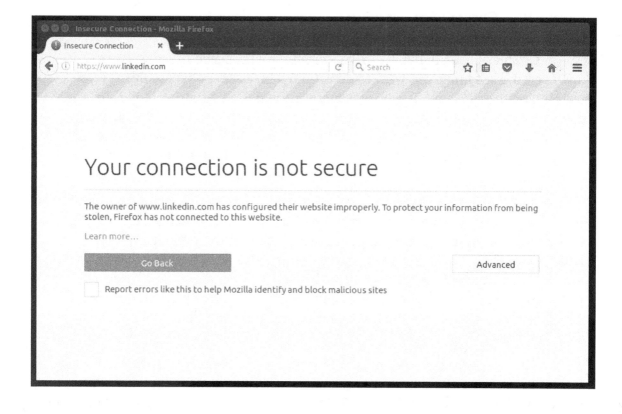

Figure 10.6: Firefox SSL warning

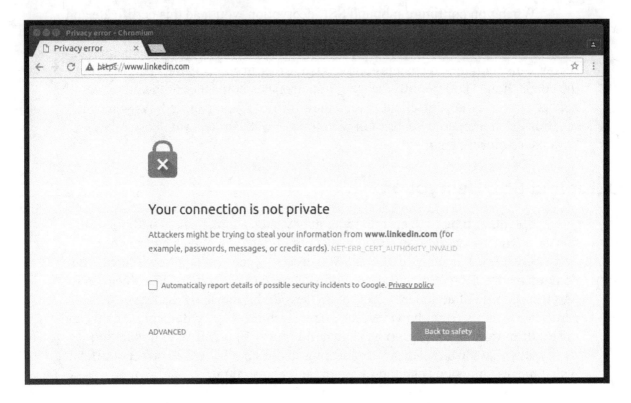

Figure 10.7: Chrome SSL warning

Users can usually bypass these warnings and proceed to the website; however, the last thing you want to do is train your users to bypass this type of warning on their system! This means there is something wrong with the site's certificate, and it could mean someone is intercepting their traffic! In the examples we see in the figures above, that's exactly what it means. These screenshots are the result of implementing an outbound SSL policy without using a trusted certificate.

It's all about the certificate chain of trust. The chain of trust is established by cryptographic signatures. Web browsers and operating systems have built-in root certificate authorities that they trust. These come from organizations you may have heard of, such as Verisign, Thawte, Entrust, etc. The concept is basically, "If the root certificate authority (CA) trusts this certificate, then so do I." Because web browsers come with these trusts built in, we can go to a well-known site, which has been vetted by a trusted authority, and trust that they really are who they say they are.

The reason your users can get the warning mentioned previously is because the certificate used by Firepower to re-sign the outbound communication was not trusted by the web browser. Since you "own" the clients in your organization, you can circumvent this warning by using your own internal certificate authority to generate and sign the certificate used by Firepower. When your clients see that the certificate Firepower is using is from your trusted certificate authority, they will treat the SSL connection as legitimate.

Because you have to add this internally generated certificate to all of your web browsers, outbound decryption is not as simple to implement as inbound. However, most of the work is done up front updating all of your client browsers with the trusted internal CA certificate. After you get over this initial speed bump, it becomes much easier. Obviously, if your organization already has deployed an internal Public Key Infrastructure (PKI), then implementing outbound SSL decryption with Firepower is much easier.

SSL Objects

Once you decide what type of SSL decryption you want to use, you may want to configure the appropriate objects. These are found in the Objects menu. There are three that relate to SSL decryption. We discussed these in some detail back in Chapter 6. They are as follows:

- Cipher Suite List: If you want to customize your SSL rules to match a subset of the complete list of supported ciphers, you can create a custom object and add specific cipher suites.

- Distinguished Name: This object matches the distinguished name field in a server's certificate. You can use this in rules to enable or disable decryption for the specific site name.

- PKI: This contains the various certificates that have been either generated or imported/signed by external authorities. These are used to sign or re-sign communications as part of the MITM function.

SSL Policy

Decryption, logging, and blocking of SSL traffic is implemented in the SSL policy. An SSL policy is associated with an Access Control policy. It has its own set of traffic processing rules, which are implemented before the traffic is processed by access control rules.

You will find the SSL policy along with the rest of the detection policies under Policies → Access Control → SSL. There are no SSL policies by default. To create one, click the New Policy button in the upper right. This will bring up the dialog shown in Figure 10.8.

Figure 10.8: New SSL Policy dialog

Here, you enter the name, an optional description, and the default action for your policy and click the Save button.

After saving, you are brought to the main policy editing interface. Here you have three tabs: Rules, Trusted CA Certificates, and Undecryptable Actions.

The Trusted CA Certificates tab (the *CA* stands for *Certificate Authority*) contains the trusted root certificates we mentioned earlier in the section on outbound SSL decryption. The list is very similar to the ones you will find in your own web browser and contains the various trusted certificate services. By default, the trusted CA group named Cisco-Trusted-Authorities is selected. This contains nearly every item from the Available Trusted CAs column on the left. The exception is any CAs you have added yourself. If you want them to be trusted, you will have to add them yourself, to the Cisco-Trusted-Authorities group, via another group, or by adding a specific entry. The Trusted CA Certificates tab is shown in Figure 10.9.

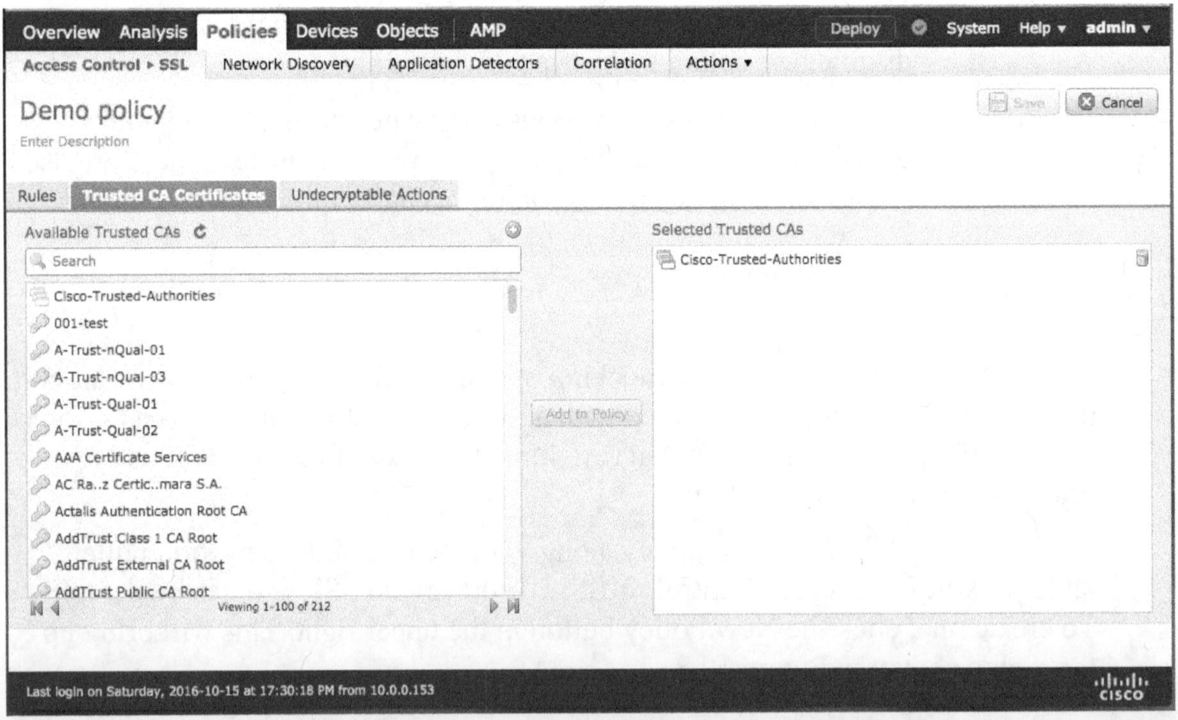

Figure 10.9: Trusted CA Certificates tab

The Undecryptable Actions tab determines what action should be taken if the SSL traffic is undecryptable. There can be a number of reasons for this, which are listed on this tab. They vary from errors to unknown or unsupported cipher suites. Your choices on how to handle this traffic are fairly straightforward.

- Inherit Default Action: Do whatever the default action in the policy is set to.

- Do not decrypt: Allow the session to pass encrypted. This means you will have limited visibility into the session.

- Block: Block the traffic without resetting the session.

- Block with reset: Block the traffic and send a TCP reset to the client and server.

Figure 10.10 shows the defaults for the Undecryptable Actions tab.

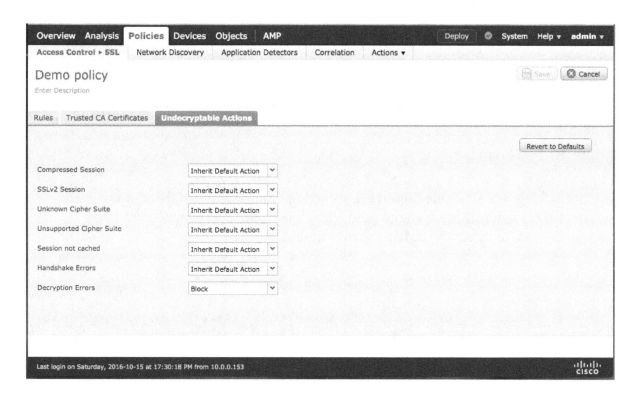

Figure 10.10: Undecryptable Actions tab

The Rules tab is where you will spend most of your time configuring this policy. Here you have three categories: Administrator, Standard, and Root. These are honestly not all that useful and appear to be somewhat of a throwback to the pre-6.x versions of Firepower. The default is to add rules into the Standard category, which works just fine.

Here you can configure the default action at the bottom of the rules list and enable logging using the scroll icon to the right. The Rules tab is shown in Figure 10.11.

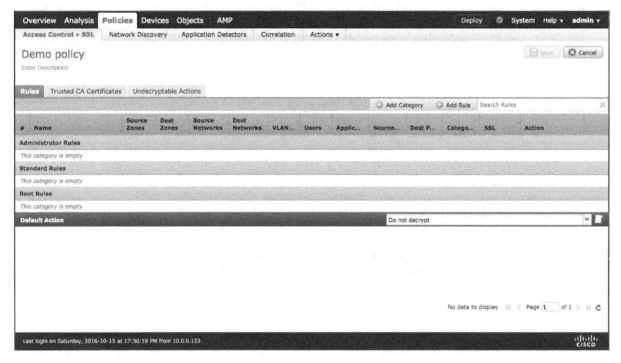

Figure 10.11: Rules tab

Clicking the Add Rule button brings up the Add Rule dialog shown in Figure 10.12. Each rule has a Name field, an Action field, and a number of tabs that can be used to select the traffic the rule should apply to.

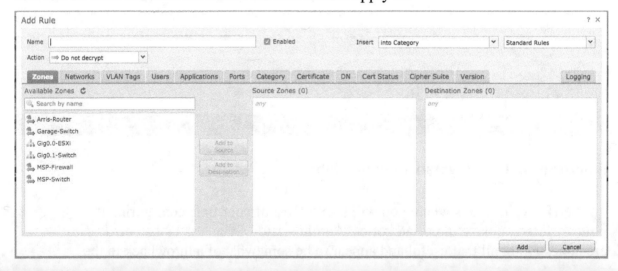

Let's take a look at the SSL rule options:

- Name: Pretty self-explanatory. The name for your rule, 30 characters or less.

- Insert: Where you want the rule inserted. Can be into a category or above/below an existing rule.

- Action:
  - Decrypt – Resign: Decrypt the traffic and re-sign with a previously uploaded CA certificate. This is typically used for outbound decryption. A drop-down list appears for selection of an internal or uploaded CA certificate.

  - Decrypt – Known Key: Match the server certificate data to a previously uploaded server certificate. If it matches, use the uploaded private key to decrypt and re-encrypt the application data. This is used for inbound decryption. A drop-down list appears to select an available certificate.

  - Do not decrypt: Do not decrypt the data in the SSL session.

  - Block: Block the traffic without sending a TCP reset.

  - Block with reset: Block the traffic and send a TCP reset to the client and server.

  - Monitor: Do not decrypt but log a connection event for the traffic.

- Rule Conditions: Most of the tabs (except the Logging tab) are used to limit the traffic a rule applies to. Leaving all of these tabs at their defaults will cause the rule to match *all* traffic. Many of these tabs are the same as those found in the Access Control policy. Because of this, we will limit the discussion to just those that are specific to SSL rules.

  - Certificate: If you have uploaded an external certificate, you can add it here. Only traffic encrypted with this certificate will match the rule.

  - DN: Distinguished name, a site name, or part of a site name with a wildcard, such as, for example, CN=*.mozilla.org. The rule will match traffic that contains the value in the specified attribute. You can add up to 50 conditions in a single rule.

Note: The Certificate and DN tabs are not available for the Decrypt – Known Key action because this information is already in the certificate object.

- o Cert Status: Look for the presence or absence of various certificate attributes. For example, to block sessions using expired certificates, you can select Yes for the Expired status in a block rule.
- o Cipher Suite: Match sessions using specific cipher suites.
- o Version: Restrict the rule to only match selected SSL/TLS versions.

SSL Rule Examples

Here are some examples of practical SSL rules.

Outbound Decryption

If you want to decrypt outbound SSL, there are a number of items you should remember.

First, you don't want your users to get the browser warnings we saw previously in the chapter. This means you will need you own internal certificate authority (CA). Then you will need to include the CA certificate in the trusted certificates store on all your users' computers.

Next, you need to configure Firepower to re-sign SSL communications using a certificate signed by your CA. To do this, you would go to Objects → PKI and select Internal CAs. Then click the Generate CA button. This will show the dialog in Figure 10.13.

Generate Internal Certificate Authority   ? ×

Name:

Country Name (two-letter code):

State or Province:

Locality or City:

Organization:

Organizational Unit (Department):

Common Name:

[Generate CSR]   [Generate self-signed CA]   [Cancel]

Figure 10.13: Generate Internal Certificate Authority dialog

Notice the Generate CSR and Generate Self-Signed CA buttons at the bottom. For testing, you may want to generate a self-signed CA, but this will cause your browsers to warn you that the site is insecure. For production, you want to generate a certificate signing request (CSR). This is a file you would then have your CA sign and then import back into your FMC. Now your devices can sign communications under the authority of your internal CA, which is trusted by all of your browsers.

Now that you have the properly signed internal CA, you can proceed with the SSL rules.

Before you add rules to decrypt outbound sessions you should consider the types of traffic you should *not* decrypt. Do your users do online shopping? What about banking or logging into their healthcare provider's website? These are all examples of communications you probably should not be inspecting. You may want a do not decrypt rule, which identifies the various sites you want to avoid decrypting. You can do this with the DN, or if you have the URL Filtering license, you could do it by the site category.

Other sites that may fall into the do not decrypt category are those that are known to have issues when decrypted. For these, Cisco has created a group of Distinguished Name objects you can easily plug into your rules. The Object Group named Cisco-Undecryptable-Sites contains site CNs for sites where attempting to decrypt the traffic will break the underlying application. This is usually because the application uses non-standard SSL parameters or other modifications. You are likely to discover more of these specific to your own organization, which you can add to this rule later on.

Next, think about any sites where you don't want users to go. Maybe add a Block or Block With Reset rule to prevent users from connecting to sites with self-signed or expired certificates.

Finally, add your Decrypt – Resign rule and select the signed internal CA you created.

An example policy with these rules is shown in Figure 10.14. In this policy, the default action is set to Do Not Decrypt, which will allow traffic to pass if Firepower cannot decrypt it. This is done in the interest of providing connectivity over security. Your organization may dictate a stricter standard, in which case you should select one of the block actions as your default.

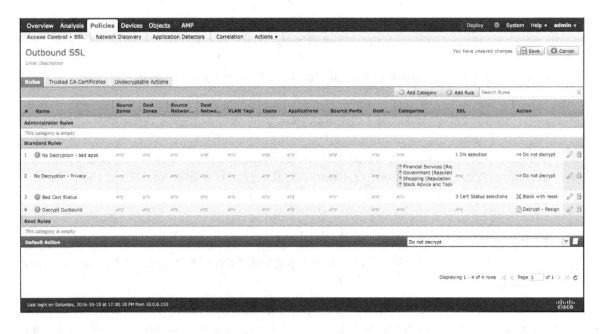

Figure 10.14: Example outbound rules

Inbound Decryption

Decrypting inbound SSL is a much simpler configuration. You don't need to worry about decrypting private information from your users or installing new root certificates on all of your web browsers. All you need to do is convince the keepers of your web server's secret keys to share them with you.

As with outbound SSL, your journey starts in the Objects menu. Go to Objects → PKI → Internal Certs. Here you will click the Add Internal Cert button and import the certificate and private key from each of the websites you want to decrypt. These can be files (in DER or PEM format) or the cert and key data can be pasted into the appropriate fields. The Add Known Internal Certificate dialog is shown in Figure 10.15.

Figure 10.15: Add Known Internal Certificate dialog

After this, you can create rules in your SSL policy to decrypt the inbound traffic. Your rule or rules will use the Decrypt – Known Key action, as shown in Figure 10.16.

Figure 10.16: Inbound decryption rule

When using this rule action, you must select one or more internal certificate objects. Clicking the field to the right of the action or the Edit link will bring up the Select Internal Certificate Objects dialog in Figure 10.17.

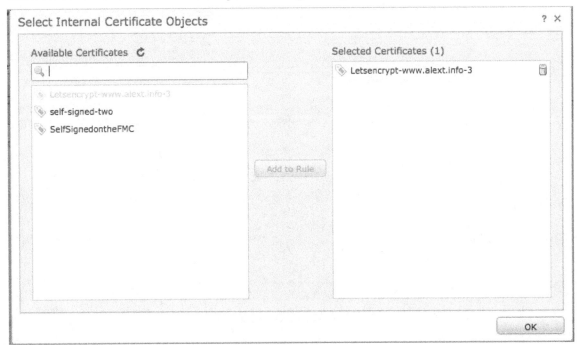

Figure 10.17: Select Internal Certificate Objects dialog

You can create several rules or add multiple certificates to a single rule. The rule will only match SSL sessions using the selected certificates. However, you may want to restrict the rules further by using options on the Networks or Ports tabs. Unless you are decrypting all inbound SSL, you will probably leave the default action in this policy to Do Not Decrypt. Figure 10.18 shows a simple rule for a single SSL website.

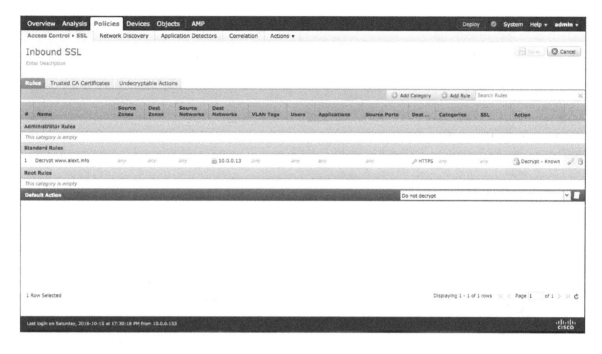

Figure 10.18: Inbound decryption policy

SSL Troubleshooting

Once you have deployed your SSL policy, you can view your logged events to determine if it is working. This requires logging to be enabled (the Logging tab in your rules) in the SSL or Access Control policy. Don't worry, if you enable it in both policies; you will not see multiple connection events.

Navigate to Analysis → Connections → Events to view your connection data. The default workflow and table view do not show the SSL information columns. To see this information, you can enable the various SSL fields using the following procedure.

First, click on the Table View of Connection Events link near the upper left of your connection event view. This is shown in Figure 10.19.

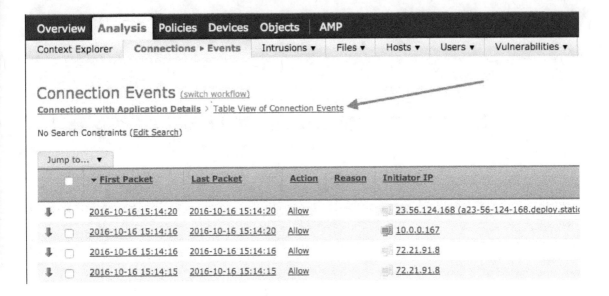

Figure 10.19: Connection events table view link

This will take you to a table view of your connections which shows numerous additional columns. However, the SSL data you are looking for is still hidden. One way to reveal it is to click on one of the grey X icons to the right of a column heading, as shown in Figure 10.20.

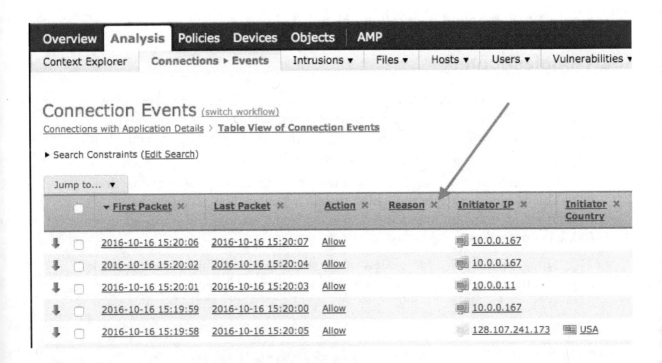

Figure 10.20: Connection event column icon

Clicking this X by a column will bring up a list of all the columns that are available in the table view. Here, you can pick and choose which columns you want to add or remove. Figure 10.21 shows what this list looks like. If you scroll down in the list, you will find a number of columns that show SSL information about the connection.

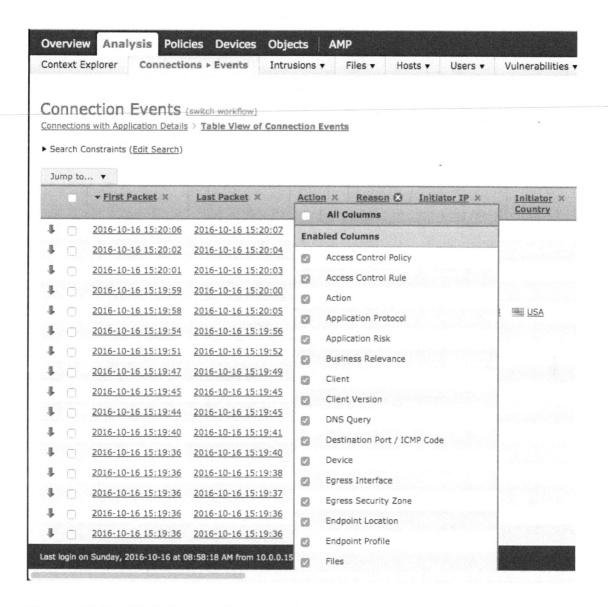

Figure 10.21: All Columns list

You will find the SSL columns way at the bottom of the list and all unchecked. To get all the information there is about an SSL connection, check these and click the Apply button. You may find that some columns like the ticket and session ID are of limited value. This list is shown in Figure 10.22

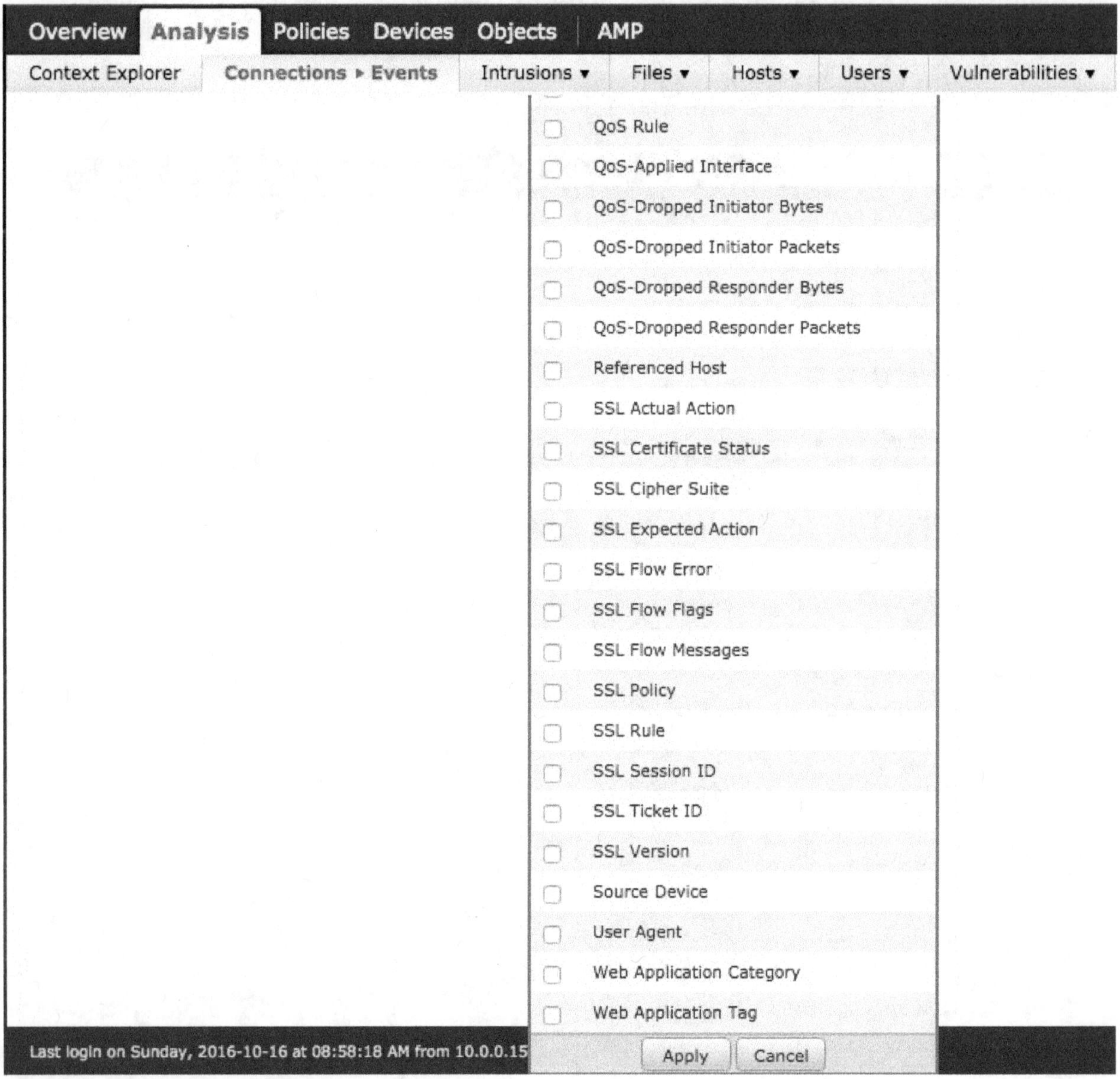

| Overview | **Analysis** | Policies | Devices | Objects | AMP |

| Context Explorer | **Connections ▸ Events** | Intrusions ▾ | Files ▾ | Hosts ▾ | Users ▾ | Vulnerabilities ▾ |

☐ QoS Rule

☐ QoS-Applied Interface

☐ QoS-Dropped Initiator Bytes

☐ QoS-Dropped Initiator Packets

☐ QoS-Dropped Responder Bytes

☐ QoS-Dropped Responder Packets

☐ Referenced Host

☐ SSL Actual Action

☐ SSL Certificate Status

☐ SSL Cipher Suite

☐ SSL Expected Action

☐ SSL Flow Error

☐ SSL Flow Flags

☐ SSL Flow Messages

☐ SSL Policy

☐ SSL Rule

☐ SSL Session ID

☐ SSL Ticket ID

☐ SSL Version

☐ Source Device

☐ User Agent

☐ Web Application Category

☐ Web Application Tag

Apply   Cancel

Figure 10.22: Enabling SSL columns

Viewing the information in these columns will help you understand if your SSL decryption is working as you expected and help locate any issues you may need to address. Figures 10.23 and 10.24 show some of the information in these columns.

SSL Status ✕	SSL Flow Error ✕	SSL Actual ✕ Action	SSL Expected Action	SSL Certificate Status	SSL Version	SSL Cipher Suite ✕	SSL Policy
Decrypt (Resign)	Success	Decrypt (Resign)	Decrypt (Resign)	Valid	TLSv1.2	TLS_ECDHE_RSA_WITH_AES_128_GCM_SHA256	Outbound SSL
Decrypt (Resign)	Success	Decrypt (Resign)	Decrypt (Resign)	Valid	TLSv1.2	TLS_ECDHE_RSA_WITH_AES_128_GCM_SHA256	Outbound SSL
Decrypt (Resign)	Success	Decrypt (Resign)	Decrypt (Resign)	Valid	TLSv1.2	TLS_ECDHE_RSA_WITH_AES_128_GCM_SHA256	Outbound SSL
Decrypt (Resign)	Success	Decrypt (Resign)	Decrypt (Resign)	Valid	TLSv1.2	TLS_ECDHE_RSA_WITH_AES_128_GCM_SHA256	Outbound SSL
Do Not Decrypt (Handshake Error)	MASTER_KEY_INVALID (0xb900035d)	Do Not Decrypt	Unknown	Not Checked	TLSv1.2	TLS_ECDHE_ECDSA_WITH_AES_128_GCM_SHA256	Outbound SSL
Do Not Decrypt (Handshake Error)	MASTER_KEY_INVALID (0xb900035d)	Do Not Decrypt	Unknown	Not Checked	TLSv1.2	TLS_ECDHE_ECDSA_WITH_AES_128_GCM_SHA256	Outbound SSL
Do Not Decrypt (Handshake Error)	MASTER_KEY_INVALID (0xb900035d)	Do Not Decrypt	Unknown	Not Checked	TLSv1.2	TLS_ECDHE_ECDSA_WITH_AES_128_GCM_SHA256	Outbound SSL
Do Not Decrypt (Handshake Error)	MASTER_KEY_INVALID (0xb900035d)	Do Not Decrypt	Unknown	Not Checked	TLSv1.2	TLS_ECDHE_ECDSA_WITH_AES_128_GCM_SHA256	Outbound SSL
Do Not Decrypt (Handshake Error)	MASTER_KEY_INVALID (0xb900035d)	Do Not Decrypt	Unknown	Not Checked	TLSv1.2	TLS_ECDHE_ECDSA_WITH_AES_128_GCM_SHA256	Outbound SSL

Figure 10.23: Interesting SSL columns

SSL Rule ✕	SSL Flow Flags ✕	SSL Flow Messages ✕
LinkedIn	VALID, INITIALIZED, SSL_DETECTED, CERTIFICATE_DECODED, FULL_HANDSHAKE, SERVER_SESSION_ID_SEEN, CLIENT_HELLO_SESSTKT, CH_PROCESSED, SH_PROCESSED, CH_CIPHERS_MODIFIED, CH_CURVES_MODIFIED, CH_EXTENSION_REMOVED, CH_ALPN_HAS_H2	CLIENT_HELLO, SERVER_HELLO, SERVER_CERTIFICATE
LinkedIn	VALID, INITIALIZED, SSL_DETECTED, CERTIFICATE_DECODED, FULL_HANDSHAKE, SERVER_SESSION_ID_SEEN, CLIENT_HELLO_SESSTKT, CH_PROCESSED, SH_PROCESSED	CLIENT_HELLO, SERVER_HELLO, SERVER_CERTIFICATE
LinkedIn	VALID, INITIALIZED, SSL_DETECTED, CERTIFICATE_DECODED, FULL_HANDSHAKE, SERVER_SESSION_ID_SEEN, CLIENT_HELLO_SESSTKT, CH_PROCESSED, SH_PROCESSED	CLIENT_HELLO, SERVER_HELLO, SERVER_CERTIFICATE
LinkedIn	VALID, INITIALIZED, SSL_DETECTED, CERTIFICATE_DECODED, FULL_HANDSHAKE, SERVER_SESSION_ID_SEEN, CLIENT_HELLO_SESSTKT, CH_PROCESSED, SH_PROCESSED	CLIENT_HELLO, SERVER_HELLO, SERVER_CERTIFICATE
Default Rule	VALID, INITIALIZED, UNDECRYPTABLE, PRE_DECISION_ERROR, SSL_DETECTED, CLIENT_HELLO_SESSTKT, CH_PROCESSED, SH_PROCESSED	CLIENT_HELLO, SERVER_HELLO
Default Rule	VALID, INITIALIZED, UNDECRYPTABLE, PRE_DECISION_ERROR, SSL_DETECTED, CLIENT_HELLO_SESSTKT, CH_PROCESSED, SH_PROCESSED	CLIENT_HELLO, SERVER_HELLO
Default Rule	VALID, INITIALIZED, UNDECRYPTABLE, PRE_DECISION_ERROR, SSL_DETECTED, CLIENT_HELLO_SESSTKT, CH_PROCESSED, SH_PROCESSED	CLIENT_HELLO, SERVER_HELLO
Default Rule	VALID, INITIALIZED, UNDECRYPTABLE, PRE_DECISION_ERROR, SSL_DETECTED, CLIENT_HELLO_SESSTKT, CH_PROCESSED, SH_PROCESSED	CLIENT_HELLO, SERVER_HELLO
Default Rule	VALID, INITIALIZED, UNDECRYPTABLE, PRE_DECISION_ERROR, SSL_DETECTED, CLIENT_HELLO_SESSTKT, CH_PROCESSED, SH_PROCESSED	CLIENT_HELLO, SERVER_HELLO

Figure 10.24: More interesting SSL columns

SSL decryption is an extremely complex process and there are a number of things that can go wrong. We can't go into all of them here, but we can illustrate one of the new features of Firepower version 6.1. If you remember, during the SSL handshake one of the items that is established is which cipher suite will be used. It has to be one that the server accepts and the client also supports. During the client hello, the client transmits the list of cipher suites it knows to the server. The server then selects one of these and the session proceeds.

One problem that can arise is if the client and server agree on a cipher suite that Firepower does not support. In previous versions of Firepower, this meant the session could not be decrypted. In version 6.1, a new feature was introduced to modify the client hello and remove any cipher suites or other features that Firepower doesn't support. In this way, we are ensuring that the agreed-upon encryption method is one that we can decrypt. The result is more decrypted sessions and fewer undecryptable ones.

You can see this happening in the messages in Figure 10.24. Since this may be difficult to read, Figure 10.25 is an expanded view of the SSH Flow Flags column. Here you can see the various flags Firepower has noted in this session. Of particular interest are any that start with *CH*. This means they were part of the client hello. Notice the "MODIFIED" flags. These indicate that we modified the client hello on its way back to the server and removed some data that might have caused the session to be undecryptable.

SSL Flow Flags ✕

VALID, INITIALIZED, SSL_DETECTED, CERTIFICATE_DECODED, FULL_HANDSHAKE, SERVER_SESSION_ID_SEEN, CLIENT_HELLO_SESSTKT, CH_PROCESSED, SH_PROCESSED, CH_CIPHERS_MODIFIED, CH_CURVES_MODIFIED, CH_EXTENSION_REMOVED, CH_ALPN_HAS_H2

Figure 10.25: SSL Flow Flags

This is pretty cool stuff!

We're going to stop our troubleshooting section here, but hopefully you now have more information you can use to determine why SSL decryption might not be working as you had hoped and fix it. Don't forget the online help as well; it contains a ton of useful information regarding SSL decryption with Firepower.

Chapter 11: Identity

This chapter covers identity—this translates to the ability for Firepower to take different actions depending on the user associated with a connection.

The concept of using Firepower to block or allow traffic based on users or groups is one that appeals to many organizations. It sounds like a great way to keep employees more productive and allow or block access to websites or services based on job function.

Implementing user-based control is a bit more complex, as you will see in this chapter.

Identity with Firepower

The basic purpose of identity with Firepower is to provide the ability to tailor the actions taken on the network to the user. This allows you as an administrator to control which users or groups are allowed or denied access to network services or applications.

To facilitate this, some type of mapping must occur between the traffic that passes through the device and the user sending it. This takes the form of associating an IP address with a user. There are several ways to accomplish this. The method you select will depend on several factors, including the type of directory services you use, the location of your devices, and interface types.

Identity Sources

The first thing to decide is which identity sources you will use. There are two broad categories, non-authoritative and authoritative.

Non-authoritative

There is only one non-authoritative identity source available in Firepower. It is called traffic-based detection. This is the user information gained from passive detection through the various supported applications and protocols. These are configured in the Network Discovery policy as described in chapter 7: "Firepower Network Discovery". The protocols supported are LDAP, AIM,

IMAP, Oracle, SIP (VoIP), FTP, POP3, HTTP, MDNS, and SMTP. Both successful and failed login attempts can be recorded.

Traffic-based detection provides user information based on logins using the above protocols. This information is then saved in the Firepower Management Center (FMC) database. As events occur, Firepower associates this user information, providing analysts with another data point when investigating a possible incident. The username is pulled directly from logins in the network traffic. Additional information on the username can also be stored by querying a Lightweight Directory Access Protocol (LDAP) directory.

When a device detects a login using one of the supported services or applications, it sends the following information to the FMC:

- The username identified
- Time of the login
- IP address involved
- For POP3, IMAP and SMTP, the user's email address
- The name of the device detecting the login

If the user was previously detected, the user's login history is updated with the new event. If the user was previously undetected, the FMC adds the user to the users database.

To configure traffic-based detection, you must enable user discovery in your discovery policy rule or rules. You can find this on the FMC under **Policies → Network Discovery.** Check your network discovery rules and ensure that both the Hosts and Users boxes are selected, as shown in Figure 11.1

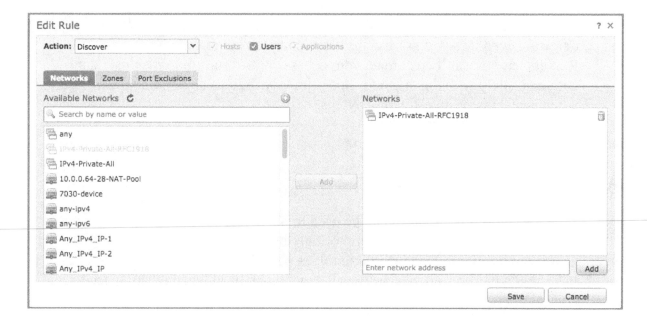

Figure 11.1: User discovery rule

After editing your discovery rules, return to the discovery policy and click the Users tab. Configure the services and applications where you will be performing this detection, by default these are all enabled. Also, determine whether you want to capture failed logging attempts. Click the pencil icon to enable or disable the various settings. The Users tab is shown in Figure 11.2.

Networks	**Users**	Advanced
Traffic-Based Detection		🖉
aim		Yes
imap		Yes
ldap		Yes
oracle		Yes
pop3		Yes
sip		Yes
ftp		Yes
http		Yes
mdns		Yes
Capture Failed Login Attempts		Yes

Figure 11.2: Users tab

That's all there is to it! Most deployments leverage this traffic-based user detection even if they don't use the more complex authoritative sources. Remember, you can't customize your access control rules based on user data gathered solely with this method. It is primarily used as an additional data point when analyzing or investigating events.

Authoritative Sources

Authoritative sources can be used to positively associate a username with an IP address. You must use an authoritative source if you want to use user-based access control rules. This method involves periodically updating the FMC with a list of known users and groups, which can then be used when creating access control rules. You then use one of the supported authoritative sources to associate an IP address with a username. In this manner, the access control rules can be selectively enforced based on this user-to-IP mapping.

Two of the sources we will discuss are the User Agent and Identity Services Engine (ISE). As we are discussing these, one important thing to remember is you *cannot* use both the User Agent and ISE sources simultaneously. You must select one for your deployment.

The Firepower User Agent

The Firepower User Agent—formerly called the Sourcefire User Agent (SFUA)—is one type of authoritative source. This is an agent that reads the login events from a Microsoft Active Directory server and forwards them to the FMC. The agent is a Windows service that can be installed locally on an Active Directory server or on a separate Windows computer. When installed on a separate Windows machine, the agent can query up to five Active Directory servers and update up to five Firepower FMCs. You will want to cover all your Active Directory servers with either local or remote agents. This ensures that a user login will be reported regardless of the server where they are authenticated.

To setup a User Agent connection, navigate to System → Integration → Identity Sources on the FMC. You will see three choices for Identity Sources on this page: None, Identity Services Engine, User Agent (Figure 11.3).

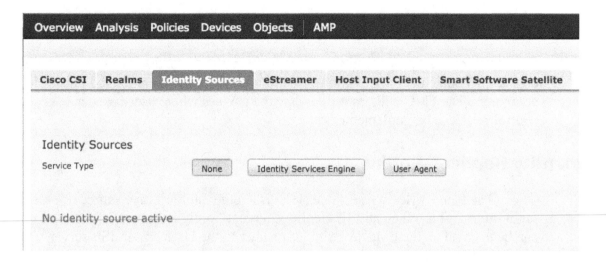

Figure 11.3: Identity Sources

Clicking the User Agent button will bring up the list of hosts that are currently configured. To add a new User Agent, click the New Agent button.

You will then be prompted for the host name or IP address of the agent, as shown in Figure 11.4.

This is the Windows computer or directory server where you will install the User Agent software.

Figure 11.4: Add User Agent

After adding all of your User Agents here, click the Save button in the upper right. This tells the FMC that you will be using this method of authoritative user identification.

The next step is to download the User Agent installer from the Cisco support site and install it on your Windows computers. During the installation process, you will point the agent to your FMC. Cisco has a separate guide (the *Firepower User Agent Configuration Guide*) to assist with installing and configuring the User Agent.

Later, when your identity configuration is complete, these User Agents will constantly update the FMC with information on which users are logged into which computers. The FMC will, in turn, update the devices where user-based access control rules can be implemented.

Identity Services Engine

The Identity Services Engine (ISE) is another authoritative source of user login information. When an ISE identity source is configured, user information can be updated on the FMC in a similar manner to the User Agent. ISE server provides the same user-to-IP mapping as the User Agent.

In addition, ISE can use Security Group Tags (SGTs) to tag packets as they traverse the network. These SGTs can be used as conditions in access control rules. So, with ISE you have two methods of controlling access, through the user/group and/or through the SGT in the packet.

To configure an ISE server connection, navigate to System → Integration → Identity Sources on the FMC. Then click the Identity Services Engine button. This displays the ISE settings, shown in Figure 11.5.

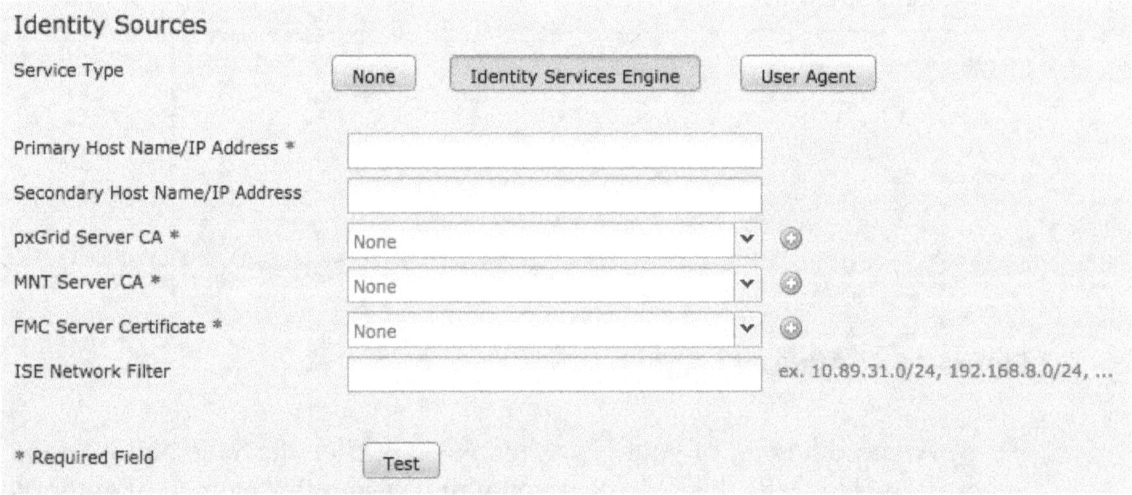

Identity Sources

| Service Type | None | Identity Services Engine | User Agent |

Primary Host Name/IP Address *

Secondary Host Name/IP Address

pxGrid Server CA *   None

MNT Server CA *   None

FMC Server Certificate *   None

ISE Network Filter   ex. 10.89.31.0/24, 192.168.8.0/24, ...

* Required Field   Test

Figure 11.5: Identity Sources settings

You will need the necessary certificates to enable communication with the ISE server. See your ISE documentation for these certificate requirements.

The Terminal Services Agent

While the Terminal Services Agent is mentioned in the FMC documentation, you must have at least Firepower 6.2, or better 6.2.1 at a minimum to run this.

This agent is required if you want to perform user identification in a terminal services environment. This is because a simple IP-to-user mapping won't work when multiple users log in to a single host.

The Terminal Services Agent assigns port ranges to each user for various applications, thereby allowing the FMC to identify users by IP and source port. Contact your Cisco account management representative if you would like access to this feature. It will be included in a future Firepower version.

Captive Portal Authentication

Captive portal is another authoritative identity source that can be leveraged in Firepower. This requires users to authenticate to the network through a managed device. It can also optionally allow guest access. Active authentication is performed only on HTTP and HTTPS traffic. To perform active authentication on HTTPS traffic, you must use an SSL policy to decrypt the traffic from users you want to authenticate. If this sounds like a lot of work—it is!

Your Identity policy can be configured to first look for passive authentication via the User Agent or ISE. It can then redirect the user to a captive portal authentication page if there is no user associated with the traffic.

To perform captive portal authentication, your device must serve up the portal page to your users. Because of this, you can't use a passive or inline device since they do not have IP addresses assigned to their sensing interfaces. Captive portal is supported on the following device configurations:

- Virtual routers on 7000 and 8000 series devices
- ASA FirePOWER devices in routed mode running version 9.5(2) or higher
- Firepower Threat Defense devices in routed mode

Realms

If you're going to do identity right, you need a realm. A realm consists of one or more LDAP or Microsoft Active Directory servers. You must configure a realm if you want to leverage user-based control or configure an authoritative identity source. In fact, you cannot configure an identity policy until you have configured one or more realms. Think of the realm as the connection to your user directory. There is very little that can be done without this connection. All you can really do is glean a few usernames via Firepower's passive discovery of login traffic.

Add Realm

To create a realm, navigate to System → Integration → Realms. When you click the New Realm button, you will be greeted by the screen in Figure 11.6.

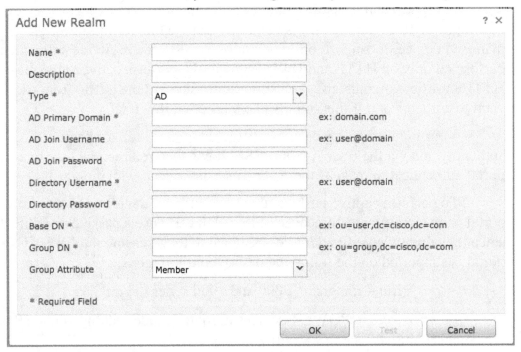

Figure 11.6: Add New Realm

Here you will enter the realm-specific information such as type (AD or LDAP), domain, username, password, and distinguished names (DNs). Notice there is no information on the hostname or IP address of the directory server. That is because you can have multiple directory servers in a realm as long as they host the same directory.

The AD Join Username and Password fields are only needed if you will be configuring Kerberos captive portal active authentication. The Test button is greyed out unless you fill in these two fields.

Add Directory

After adding your realm, you will be taken to the Directory tab. Here is where you point to your actual directory servers. Click the Add Directory button on the right to add a new entry. This brings up the page in Figure 11.7.

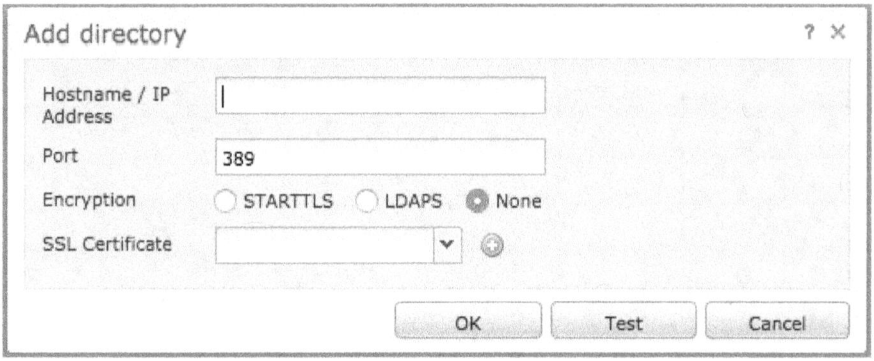

Figure 11.7: Add Directory

You can repeat by adding as many directory servers as desired. If there are multiple directory server entries, Firepower will use the top entry. If the server is down, it will proceed down the list until it finds a responsive server or runs out of entries. You can drag servers up and down this list to change their priority.

User Download

After adding and activating the realm, you could stop there but you wouldn't accomplish all that much. Firepower will begin looking up usernames discovered through passive traffic analysis in your directory. If available, additional information such as first name, last name, email, department, and phone number will be populated in the FMC user database. However, you probably don't want to just stop with the realm. To configure user-based control in your Access Control policy, you will need to proceed with user download.

After adding the directory as we mentioned earlier, click the User Download tab. As soon as you do this, Firepower will attempt to connect to the directory and enumerate the groups available. If there's a problem with your realm or directory configuration, you'll find out right away as your user download will fail.

If everything was entered correctly, you will see a screen similar to the one in Figure 11.8.

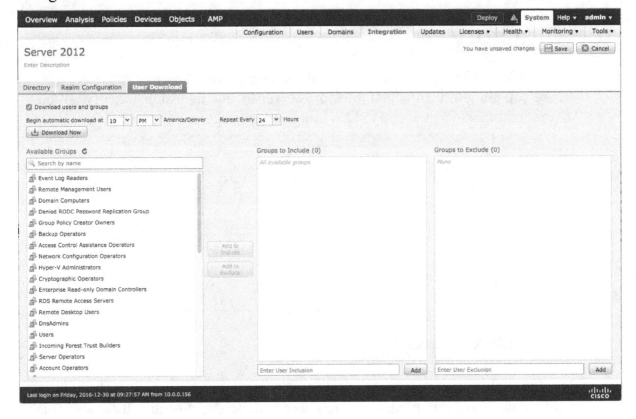

Figure 11.8: User Download

On this page the available groups are shown in the left column. By default, no groups are added to the Groups to Include column. You may not want to pull down all the users/groups in your entire directory to the FMC. To populate users on your FMC, select the groups on the left and click the Add to Include button. If you have larger groups but want to exclude some sub-groups, you can add these to the Groups to Exclude column.

By default, the users are updated on your FMC every 24 hours. You can modify the start time and interval of this update with the settings at the top of the page.

When finished, click the Save button in the upper right. This will return you to your Realms list. The final—and very important—step is to enable the realm by clicking the slider in the State column. Once your realm is enabled, Firepower will use it for user identity and optionally download users at the interval specified.

Identity Policy

After setting up your realm, directory and authoritative user sources, you can finally proceed with the identity policy! The identity policy brings together all the various components and associates traffic on your network with an authoritative identity source and a realm. Remember that you must have already configured at least one realm before the system will allow you to create an identity policy.

You will find the identity policy on the FMC under Policies → Access Control → Identity. Clicking New Policy brings up the dialog in Figure 11.9, where you simply give your policy a name and optional description.

Figure 11.9: New Identity Policy

Your new policy contains no rules by default. To add an authentication rule, click the Add Rule button. This brings up the page shown in Figure 11.10.

Figure 11.10: New identity policy

First, give your rule a name. You can then use the four tabs on the left to configure the traffic that will match this rule. By default, the rule will match all traffic.

The Realm & Settings tab on the right determines how to authenticate users for traffic matching the rule. If you click this tab, you can select the realm you will use to authenticate traffic matching the rule (Figure 11.11).

Figure 11.11: Realm & Settings tab

To perform passive authentication using a realm, simply select the realm from the drop-down list. The configured identity source and realm will then be used (User Agent or ISE). Note that if passive authentication fails—there is no user associated with the IP address—then the traffic will not be associated with a user. Any user-based access control rules would then fail to match the traffic.

When configuring user-based control, it's important to understand the preceding statement. In order to allow or block connections based on user identity, the traffic must be associated with a user account before it's processed through the Access Control (AC) policy. If an AC rule contains a user or group criteria but the traffic is not from a known user, the rule will not match the traffic.

This may be acceptable. If you only want to allow a given group of users access to a given application or website, then they must be authenticated to gain that access. Any other unauthenticated traffic would be blocked by another AC rule. However, if you want to authenticate *all* traffic passing through your device then you may need to actively authenticate unknown connections.

To augment your passive authentication with active authentication, check the "Use active authentication if passive authentication cannot identify user" check box. When you check this box, you see a number of additional options, as shown in Figure 11.12.

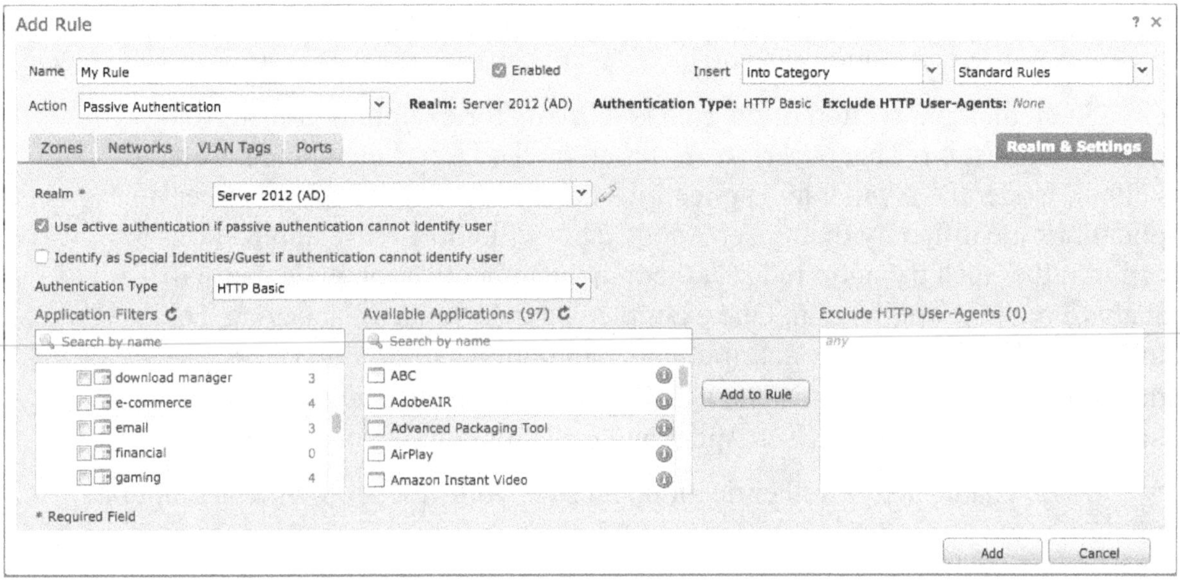

Figure 11.12: Active authentication options

Let's take a look at some of the options on this page.

There is a check box to automatically identify the connection as guest if authentication doesn't successfully identify the user. This is fairly self-explanatory; there are several special identities you can choose in your AC rule matching criteria:

- Failed Authentication

- Guest

- No Authentication Required

- Unknown

There is an Authentication Type drop-down that contains several options:

- HTTP Basic: This uses standard fields in the HTTP header of each HTTP request

- NTLM: Requires a browser that supports this type of authentication.

- Kerberos: This is the same as NTLM; it must be enabled in the browser

- HTTP Negotiate: Yet another method that can be used on supported browsers. It allows the browser to choose between HTTP Basic, Kerberos, and NTLM.

- HTTP Response Page: Unlike the preceding options, this is a web page served by the Firepower device. Instead of using the credentials from the browser/operating system, this page prompts for a username and password.

The remaining section of the rule is to allow for excluding traffic from active authentication. This is performed based on the User Agent being used by the client. Under the Available Applications column, you will find a number of applications identified by their User Agent. This will allow these applications to function rather than trying to redirect them to an authentication page that will probably break the application. One example is the Advanced Packaging Tool, which is used by some Linux distributions, including Ubuntu's **apt-get** command. Keep in mind that if you use this feature, it would be trivial for a mischievous user to spoof a User Agent and possibly bypass your AC rules.

If you enable active authentication and save your rule, you will encounter a warning, shown in Figure 11.13

Error

Please provide server certificate, redirect port, and maximum login attempts in Active Authentication tab when using Active Authentication

Figure 11.13: Active authentication error

The reason for this is that we have not configured the Active Authentication tab yet. Clicking this tab shows the page in Figure 11.14.

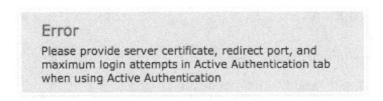

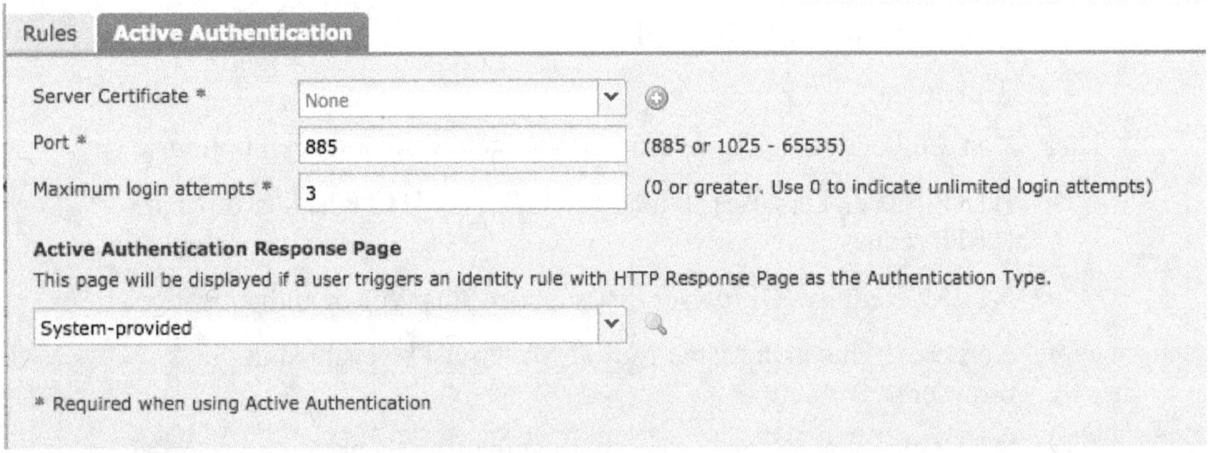

Figure 11.14: Active Authentication settings

Notice that we have one red asterisk item that is not configured. We must have a server certificate because the authentication mechanism used will be SSL encrypted. There are no certificates included with Firepower by default. You can create your own certificate authority (CA) and server certificate; however, this will be a self-signed certificate and will alert users that there is a problem. It's probably not a good practice to implement authentication this way as you would be training users to ignore these SSL errors. What you really need is a server certificate that is generated or signed by your own CA and trusted by your users' web browsers. This will allow your devices to serve up this secure web page without forcing users to deal with certificate errors.

To add the certificate used here you can navigate to Objects → PKI → Internal Certs and add the certificate. Or—even easier—you can click the green plus icon (⊕) to the right of the Server Certificate drop-down and go directly to the Add Known Internal Certificate dialog, as shown in Figure 11.15.

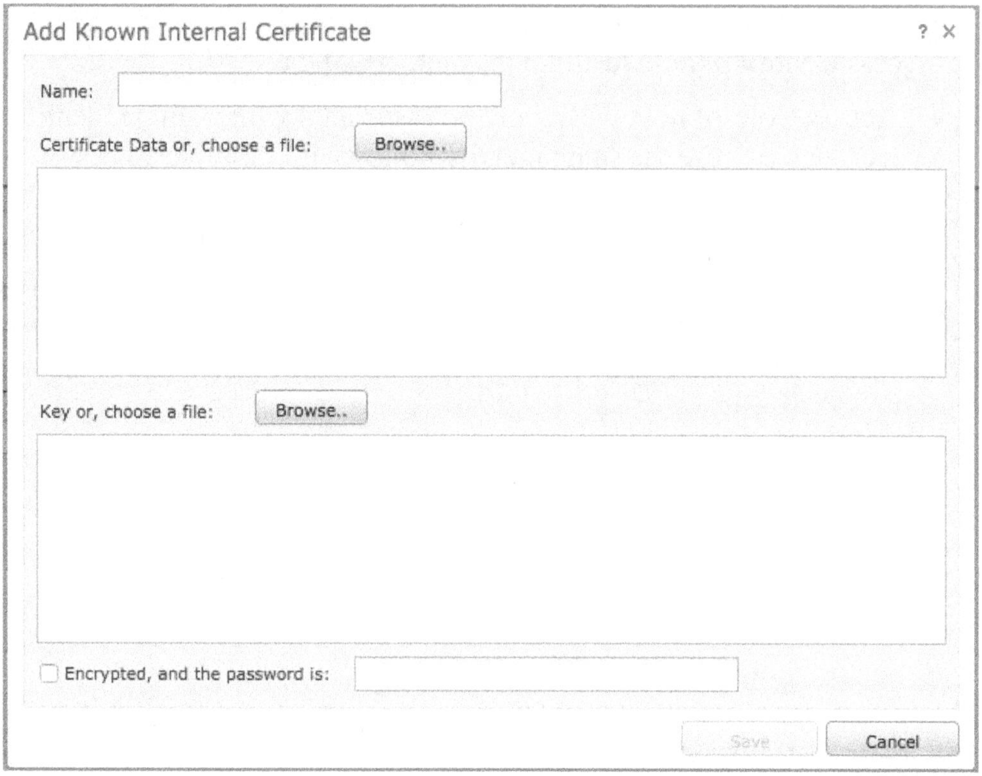

Figure 11.15: Add Internal Certificate

Before we finish with identity policy, we should note that there are two more rule types in addition to passive. The three rule types available are as follows:

- Passive Authentication: This is the one we discussed in detail earlier.

- Active Authentication: This provides for active authentication instead of passive. The active methods are the same as discussed earlier.

- No Authentication: This rule simply disables the Realm & Settings tab. Any traffic matching these rules is exempt from authentication.

Note that while identity rules will allow you to select UDP ports for active authentication rules, the system cannot enforce active authentication on non-TCP traffic. You can use Passive Authentication or No Authentication rules for non-TCP traffic.

Implement your Identity Policy

Once you have your identity policy configured, the last step is to implement it via the Access Control policy, just like most other policies.

Each Access Control policy can only be associated with a single identity policy; however, you can use the same identity policy with multiple Access Control policies.

Adding this to the ACP is a fairly simple step, which will be discussed in Chapter 13, "Access Control Policy. Doing this will show users and groups in the Users tab when creating a rule. Nice!

Chapter 12: Malware & File Policy

One of the handy features of Firepower is the ability to carve out files from network flows, reassemble them, and then perform an action. This feature is divided into two capabilities, both controlled by a single policy type. These are Advanced Malware Protection (AMP) and file control.

AMP is designed to address what may be the most prevalent threat vector in use today. That threat vector is what we call malware. Simply put, malware is software intended to damage or disable a computer system, steal data, or perform some other nefarious function not intended by the victim. The term *malware* is a shortened version of *malicious software*. While malware can take advantage of a software bug or weakness, many times the vulnerability attacked is the user. Cisco has integrated AMP capabilities into several products, including Firepower, AMP for Endpoints, and the email (ESA) and Web (WSA) security appliances. These have many similarities in their methods of detection and all use the centralized Cisco Collective Security Intelligence (CSI) cloud as their main source of information.

The second capability—file control—gives Firepower the ability to perform actions on files based on the file type. An example might be blocking executable file types transferred via HTTP. Unlike malware detection, this does not require reassembling the entire file, just the first part of the file containing the header information.

AMP Basics

Modern networks make it extremely easy to communicate, share information, and collaborate with other users and businesses. The ability to download and run software with a single mouse click breaks down many barriers that existed before this age of connectivity; however, these benefits also come with significant risks. To coin a popular phrase, "With great power comes great responsibility." Many users are not aware that there is no way to tell what a binary executable program will do before executing it. When we execute software, we are trusting that it will do what it is supposed to and nothing else. The program can typically do anything within the context of the user's permissions. If that user has root or admin privileges, then there is practically no limit on what the software can do on the system.

A key component of AMP is cloud intelligence. The Collective Security Intelligence cloud continuously processes samples of files received from various sources. These files are run through a series of checks comparing them to known malware or executing them in a sandbox environment. The files are then assigned a disposition. In addition, third-party intelligence feeds may provide hash values and dispositions for malicious software without the actual files themselves. For these trusted sources, the AMP cloud may convict the file without actually testing and analyzing it in a sandbox environment.

File Analysis

AMP uses this cloud intelligence to block and/or alert on known malicious software before it reaches the endpoint target. It does this using several techniques:

- SHA-256 hash
- Static file fingerprint (Spero)
- Local malware analysis
- Dynamic analysis

SHA-256

The first technique used is to calculate the SHA-256 hash for the file in question. Each file has a unique hash value. The Firepower/FTD device carves the file out of the network flow, calculates the SHA-256, and transmits it to the FMC, which in turn checks its local cache and if necessary transmits the hash to the Cisco CSI cloud. A disposition is then returned to the FMC, which forwards this to the device. If the disposition is malware, the device may block the file and could store it on the device, depending on the file policy settings. This lookup is very fast, usually under 600 milliseconds (ms). It is important to note that the file itself never leaves the device in this case—only the SHA-256 hash is transmitted.

Spero Analysis

The second technique is a static file analysis known as Spero. Spero analysis collects a number of file attributes and generates a signature of these values. These include file header information, DLLs called, and other static metadata information. The idea is that even if the file isn't exactly the one we are looking for, there may be signs within the file that it is malware. The Spero signature is analyzed and the Cisco cloud arrives at a malware score. This score is returned to the FMC, which forwards it to the device. If this score is high enough, the file may be convicted as malware. As with the SHA-256 method, Spero analysis does not require the file itself to be transmitted to the cloud.

Local Malware Analysis

This method involves the device inspecting a file using a local malware inspection engine. This local engine is actually ClamAV, an open source antivirus and anti-malware toolkit maintained by Cisco. This is not a full implementation of ClamAV. Files are run through a number of high-confidence checks. Local malware analysis may generate a malware alert and block the file if determined to be malware. In addition, a file composition analysis is performed detailing a file's properties, embedded objects, and possible malware characteristics. This report is available via the FMC analysis user interface.

Dynamic Analysis

The last technique differs from those above in several ways. First of all, it takes time. This technique can take 10 minutes or more to return a disposition. In addition, dynamic analysis requires that the file be uploaded to the Cisco cloud. This technique involves executing the file in a sandbox virtual machine environment. As the file executes, its actions are analyzed. This includes behaviors like the following:

- Host IPS/firewall/operating system protection evasion
- Persistence and installation behavior
- Anti-debugging
- Boot survival
- Data obfuscation
- Remote access functionality
- Virtual machine detection
- Network connections

If the analysis score is high enough, then the file is convicted as malware. By this time the file has already passed through the device, so it obviously cannot be blocked; however, because the hash is now classified as malware, any future detections of this file will immediately return a malware disposition. If the score is high enough, the conviction will be universal within the Cisco cloud. So if this file is seen by any AMP-enabled product in the future, a malware disposition will be returned. In this way, the power of the cloud provides protection across the Cisco customer base even for customers who have not actually encountered a specific piece of malware.

Retrospective Events

Another interesting feature of AMP is known as the retrospective event. This occurs when the malware disposition for a previously detected file changes. This virtually always means a file, previously assigned the disposition of unknown, is discovered to be malicious. This after-the-fact detection generates a special type of event called a retrospective event, which can occur minutes or even days after a file is first detected. This change is reported to the FMC from the Cisco Security Intelligence cloud. The FMC then updates all previous detection events for this SHA-256 value with the new disposition.

Retrospective detection is a powerful feature of the AMP product. It means that even if a new piece of malware escapes detection initially, once its true nature is determined, you will be alerted and can go back and identify where it has traversed your network. If the disposition of the file changes to malicious, it can be blocked on all your Firepower devices. If you are using the ESA, WSA, or endpoint AMP products, malicious files can then be respectively blocked or quarantined. This feature is available because of the AMP cloud database. This database knows every network or endpoint that has encountered a particular file. When a file moves from an unknown to malicious disposition, the cloud can then send that information to all affected customers. With AMP, malware doesn't stand a chance! *

*Yes we realize AMP is not the silver bullet to kill all malware but couldn't resist a little hyperbole.

File Dispositions

The purpose of these techniques is to arrive at a file disposition. There are five possible dispositions that can be returned.

- Clean: The file is benign. This indicates that it is a known good file. Either the clean disposition is returned by the AMP cloud or the file may have been manually added to the Clean-List.

- Unknown: A definitive disposition could not be determined. It could be that this file has not been seen anywhere else or a sandbox score was not high enough to convict it.

- Malware: The file has been categorized as malware by the cloud or by local malware analysis, or it has exceeded the malware score threshold in the file policy.

- Unavailable: This is not actually a disposition returned from Cisco but means something prevented the cloud lookup. Cisco says a small percentage of lookups may return this disposition.
- Custom detection: The user has added the file to the Custom-Detection-List

Archive files receive the disposition of the lowest rated file in the archive. For example, an archive containing all clean files will be marked a clean. However, if the archive has several clean files and one unknown file it will be marked as unknown. An archive with a single malware file will be marked as malware regardless of the other files it contains.

File Disposition Caching

To minimize the number of cloud lookups, file dispositions are cached on the FMC. Once a file disposition is returned from the cloud, this disposition is cached so that subsequent lookups of this same hash value do not result in repeated cloud communications. The cache time-to-live values are shown below.

- Clean: 4 hours

- Unknown: 1 hour

- Malware: 1 hour

- Unavailable: Not cached

- Custom Detection: This disposition never results in a cloud communication since the FMC maintains the Custom-Detection-List locally.

Cloud Communications

The communications architecture for this process is fairly simple. Nearly all cloud communications are initiated by the FMC. By default, this communication takes place over port 443. You can change this port on the FMC under System → Integration → Cisco CSI. Figure 12.1 shows the options available for AMP network communications.

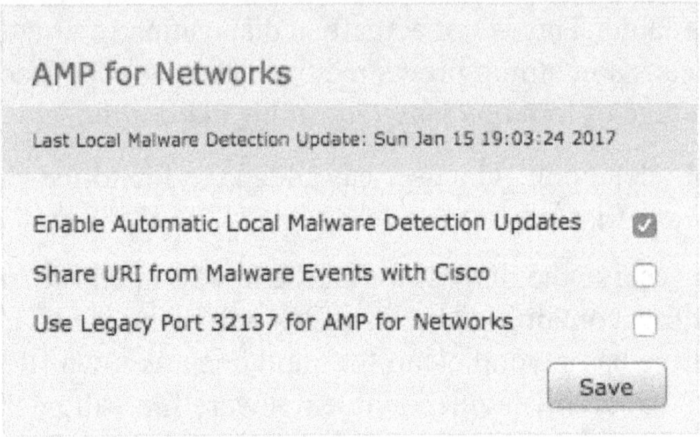

Figure 12.1: AMP CSI options

You can change the cloud communications port to 32137 if desired. While this port is an unusual one and may require a special firewall rule, there is a reason for this option. Cloud communications are encrypted end-to-end by the FMC. When using port 443, this encrypted traffic is encrypted a second time with Secure Sockets Layer (SSL). Encrypting traffic that is already encrypted introduces additional overhead. If you want the most efficient cloud communications, then using port 32137 is the best option; however, keep in mind that you cannot proxy communications on port 32137. If your FMC communicates to the Internet via a proxy, then you will have to use port 443. Note that the Cisco cloud infrastructure is moving away from the use of port 32137. We recommend using port 443 for new installations to avoid having to change this later.

Earlier we said *nearly* all communications are initiated by the FMC. There is one exception to this. If you enable Dynamic Analysis in your file policy, files are uploaded directly from the device to the cloud. This means you will have to open outgoing ports on the firewall for your Firepower/FTD devices. Devices can connect directly or through a proxy.

Malware & File Policy

The policy controlling this behavior is called the Malware & File policy. we will just call it file policy for short. This policy controls which application protocols will undergo file inspection, the direction of file transfer, the type of files to inspect, and the action. File policy is not applied directly to managed devices. Instead it is applied to traffic via a rule in the Access Control policy. You typically add file inspection to the same rule or rules where you specify an intrusion policy. We will expand on this in Chapter 14, "Access Control Policy."

There are no policies created by default. To create a new file policy, navigate to Policies → Access Control → Malware & File. Click the New File Policy button to start a new policy. Fill in the policy name and optional description in the dialog as shown in Figure 12.2.

Figure 12.2: New File Policy dialog

Advanced Settings

There are two tabs in the file policy, Rules and Advanced. Let's start with the Advanced settings. Clicking the Advanced tab displays the options shown in Figure 12.3.

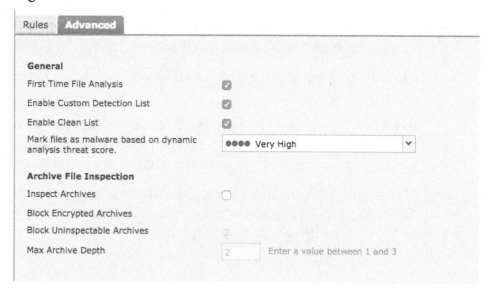

Figure 12.3: Advanced options

The settings shown in Figure 12.3 are the defaults. You may want to modify these based on your requirements.

- First Time File Analysis: Submit for file analysis a file that is detected on the system for the first time. This corresponds to a file having an unknown disposition. For this to work, the file must match a rule configured to perform malware cloud lookup as well as Spero, local malware, or dynamic analysis. If you disable this option, files that are detected for the first time are given an unknown disposition.

- Enable Custom Detection List: Check this box to use your Custom-Detection-List object. This contains a list of SHA-256 values that will be considered malware.

- Enable Clean List: Selecting this box enables your Clean-List object. These SHA-256 values will always be considered clean regardless of their cloud disposition.

- Mark files as malware based on dynamic analysis threat score: This option has four settings:
  - Disabled (Files will not be considered malware based on Dynamic Analysis.)
  - Medium
  - High
  - Very High

  Medium, High and Very High are the Dynamic Analysis scores that will result in marking a file as malware. This applies to any files analyzed in the Cisco Intelligence Cloud.

- Block Encrypted Archives: Block archive files that have encrypted contents (password protected).

- Block Uninspectable Archives: Block archive files that cannot be inspected for reasons other than encryption. This usually applies to corrupt files or files that exceed your maximum archive depth.

- Max Archive Depth: Block nested archives exceeding the specified depth. The top-level archive is not counted, so an archive with one nested archive file would be a depth of one.

File Rules

File policy rules are configured on the Rules tab. To create a rule, click the Add File Rule button. This brings up the View Rule dialog, shown in Figure 12.4.

View Rule   ? ✕

Application Protocol   [Any   ▾]   Action   [✓ Detect Files   ▾]   ☐ Store files

Direction of Transfer   [Any   ▾]

File Type Categories		File Types	Selected File Categories and Types
☐ Office Documents	20	🔍 Search name and description	
☐ Archive	18	📄 **7Z** (7-Zip compressed file)	
☐ Multimedia	30	📄 **9XHIVE** (Windows 9x registry hive (REG)	
☐ Executables	11	📄 **ACCDB** (Microsoft Access 2007 file)	
☐ PDF files	2	📄 **AMF** (Advanced Module Format for digital	[Add]
☐ Encoded	2	📄 **AMR** (Adaptive Multi-Rate Codec File)	
☐ Graphics	6	📄 **ARJ** (Compressed archive file)	
☐ System files	12	📄 **ASF** (Microsoft Windows Media Audio/Vide	
☐ Dynamic Analysis Capable	4	📄 **AUTORUN** (Windows Autorun setup file)	
☐ Local Malware Analysis Capable	5	📄 **BINARY DATA** (Universal Binary/Java Byt	

[Save]   [Cancel]

Figure 12.4: View Rule dialog

Application Protocol

The first item on this screen is Application Protocol. Clicking this drop-down reveals the protocols available for file inspection. See Figure 12.5 for the supported protocols.

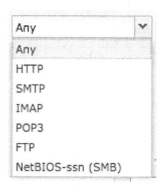

Figure 12.5: Application protocol list

These are fairly self-explanatory and encompass the most common protocols associated with file transfers. Notice that these are not encrypted protocols. Without the help of a separate decryption solution, Firepower cannot peer into connections using protocols such as SCP, SFTP, SSL, and TLS.

Application protocol selection is provided to help you improve performance by only inspecting a certain protocol with your rule. Selecting Any will detect files over multiple protocols regardless of the file transfer direction.

Direction of Transfer

Below the Application Protocol option you will see the Direction of Transfer option. The values available in this drop-down depend on what is selected in the Application Protocol option above it. If Any is selected for a protocol, then the options here are as follows:

- Any

- Upload

- Download

Not all application protocols are treated equally. Some protocols are restricted in the direction of file transfer supported. You will notice that the protocols dealing with email (SMTP, POP, IMAP) are restricted to upload or download. The following table shows what directions are supported for each protocol.

Application Protocol	Direction of Transfer
Any	Any, Upload, Download
HTTP	Any, Upload, Download
SMTP	Upload
IMAP	Download
POP3	Download
FTP	Any, Upload, Download
NetBIOS-ssn (SMB)	Any, Upload, Download

Action

Next is the Action drop-down. This is where you select the action to take on the traffic matching the rule. The default is Detect Files but there are several other options you can select:

- Detect Files: Log the detection of the file while still allowing it to be transmitted.

- Block Files: Block the file type.

- Malware Cloud Lookup: Calculate the SHA-256 hash value and also use any additional methods selected to check if the file is malicious. This action will log files with a malware disposition while still allowing their transmission.

- Block Malware: Same as Malware Cloud Lookup, but this rule will block transmission of files marked as malicious.

Each of the actions selected will display additional option check boxes. Let's look at the options for each.

Detect Files

The Detect Files action merely logs the passage of the file type through the device. It does not perform any malware or other analysis of the file. This action also does not collect the entire file as it passes through the device. Only the first 1460 bytes are collected and examined for file header information. This is the information used to determine the file type. Selecting this action gives the option of storing the files. If this is checked, files matching the rule are stored on the device.

Block Files

The Block Files action blocks files based on the file type. As with the Detection action, it does not collect the entire file. It also allows storing the file and gives the option to reset the connection. These options are shown in Figure 12.6.

Figure 12.6: Block Files options

Malware Cloud Lookup

The Malware Cloud Lookup action adds a number of options, as shown in Figure 12.7.

Figure 12.7: Malware Cloud Lookup options

The options are as follows:

- Spero Analysis for MSEXE: Checking this box causes the device to send the Spero signature to the FMC if the initial SHA-256 comes back as unknown. This only applies to MSEXE (Microsoft Windows executable) file types.

- Dynamic Analysis: Checking this box tells the device to upload the file to the cloud for dynamic analysis. This is only for certain file types and applies to files that have an Unknown file disposition.

Did you know that you can only send 100 files to the dynamic cloud a day? It's true. If money is no object, call Cisco and tell them you want more!

- Capacity Handling: This option is grayed out unless the Dynamic Analysis option is selected. Hovering over the information icon displays this note:

> Capacity Handling will attempt to store files that cannot be submitted for dynamic analysis to disk for later submission. Selecting this option will use disk space that is available for file storage.

This can be a bit confusing but it has to do with the action taken when a file cannot be submitted for Dynamic Analysis. This may be due to a cloud communication issue or it could be because you have exceeded the file submission limit. If this happens and this option is not checked, the file will not be saved and will not be submitted for analysis. Checking this box will cause the device to save the file so it can be submitted later. The device will resubmit files to the cloud if either of the following conditions are present:

- The device could not communicate with the cloud and later reestablishes cloud communications.

- The device reached the maximum number of submissions and a sufficient time has passed.

- Local Malware Analysis: Runs ClamAV local malware checks on the file. This also provides information used for the file composition analysis. This is a report that is available in the file analysis screen on the FMC.

- Store Files: This option allows for storage of files based on their disposition. Note that storing all file types is not recommended as it can impact device performance and storage.

Block Malware

The Block Malware action is the same as Malware Cloud Lookup but adds the option to reset the connection, as shown in Figure 12.8.

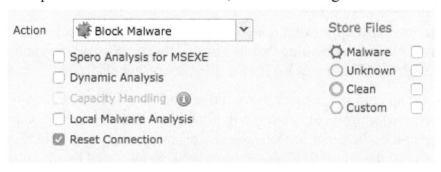

Figure 12.8: Block Malware options

Resetting the connection is recommended to prevent blocked sessions from remaining open until the TCP connection resets itself. This generally results in a poor user experience.

File Blocking Behavior

We should probably discuss how Firepower blocks files that are classified as malware. It is important to understand this when troubleshooting or observing packet flows on the network.

Blocking a file type is fairly straightforward. As we already mentioned, the file type is identified by the first 1460 bytes and Firepower knows right away if it should block the file transfer. If the file type is blocked, all subsequent packets in the file transfer fail and an optional but recommended TCP reset is sent to both the source and destination hosts.

Blocking malware is not so simple. First, we have to collect the entire file to analyze it. This means Firepower must allow the transfer to continue until the file is complete. However, if we allow the transfer to complete, how can we block the file? The answer is allowing the file to *almost* complete. Firepower watches the file transfer, and when the end-of-file marker is observed, the packet containing it is held. The Firepower/FTD device then completes the file reassembly, calculates the SHA-256, and transmits it to FMC, which forwards it to the Cisco CSI cloud. The file disposition is returned and the device can then make a decision on what to do with the last packet. If the file is malware, the packet will be dropped. The file transfer will not complete successfully and the endpoint will never receive the complete malicious file. For most protocols, any remaining fragments are removed from the destination host.

The process just described is fairly fast. By default, the device will wait no longer than two seconds for a file disposition. If it does not receive anything in this timeframe, the last packet is released and the file transfer completes.

File Blocking Notes and Limitations

The following file blocking notes are quoted from the Firepower online help. They're included to illustrate that this is a fairly complex process and there are nuances with the blocking behavior for different protocols.

- If an end-of-file marker is not detected for a file, regardless of transfer protocol, the file will not be blocked by a Block Malware rule or the Custom-Detection-List. The system waits to block the file until the entire file has been received, as indicated by the end-of-file marker, and blocks the file after the marker is detected.

- If the end-of-file marker for an FTP file transfer is transmitted separately from the final data segment, the marker will be blocked and the FTP client will indicate that the file transfer failed, but the file will actually completely transfer to disk.

- File rules with Block Files and Block Malware actions block automatic resumption of file download via HTTP by blocking new sessions with the same file, URL, server, and client application detected for 24 hours after the initial file transfer attempt occurs.

- In rare cases, if traffic from an HTTP upload session is out of order, the system cannot reassemble the traffic correctly and therefore will not block it or generate a file event.

- If you transfer a file over NetBIOS-ssn (such as an SMB file transfer) that is blocked with a Block Files rule, you may see a file on the destination host. However, the file is unusable because it is blocked after the download starts, resulting in an incomplete file transfer.

File Types and Categories

The final criteria for a file rule is the file type. There are three columns in the rule related to file types, as shown in Figure 12.9.

Figure 12.9: File types

The File Types list is in the center column. This shows all the supported file types that can be inspected with a file rule. If you know the specific files you want to inspect, you can select one or more from this column and click the Add button to add them to the Selected File Categories and Types column; however, the File Type Categories column on the left is provided to make this selection easier. By checking the boxes on the left, you can select all the file types matching a given category. The number to the right of each category indicates how many file types are currently in this category. Note there may be some overlap with File Type Categories. For example, the MSEXE file type is present in both the Dynamic Analysis Capable and Executables categories.

Of particular interest is the Dynamic Analysis Capable file category. This contains file types that are eligible for upload to the Cisco cloud for Threat Grid sandbox analysis. The file types are as follows:

- MSEXE (Windows/DOS executable file)

- MSOLE2 (Microsoft Office applications OLE document)

- NEW_OFFICE (Microsoft Office Open XML document format, DOCX, PPTX, XLSX)

- PDF (Adobe Portable Document Format)

To upload a file for dynamic analysis, it has to be preclassified as malware. This could be through the local malware analysis or through its Spero score. What this means is that if you enable dynamic analysis and include all the file types above, Firepower will *not* upload all of the Office documents or PDF files it sees.

But, the system still may *automatically* upload some files containing information that is confidential or sensitive. Before you enable dynamic analysis for all of these file types, make sure your organization understands any privacy ramifications of automatically uploading these documents.

Enabling the MSEXE file type for dynamic analysis is generally much less risky. Executable files normally do not contain any type of sensitive or confidential data. In addition, unknown executables represent a serious risk and are therefore prime candidates for dynamic analysis.

Once you have selected the criteria for the rule, you are ready to add it to your policy. The rule shown in Figure 12.10 is configured to inspect executables and system files within all supported protocols in all directions for malware. It will perform Spero and local malware analysis and upload the file for dynamic analysis if required. Files that exceed the threat score or return a malware disposition from the cloud will be blocked and the connection reset. Just for fun, we're also storing any file classified as malware so we can analyze it ourselves later if desired. Depending on the Access Control policy rule, a file/malware event will also be logged to the FMC.

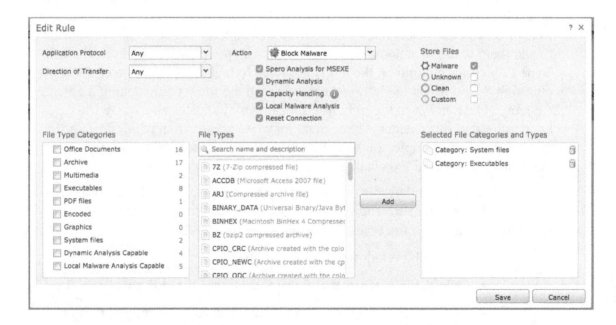

Figure 12.10: Sample rule

Rule Precedence

File rules are unordered. They will be placed into the policy in the order they are created; however, this order has no effect on how they operate. It is possible to have conflicting file rules. For example, if a file policy includes a rule to inspect a given file type and another rule blocks the same file type, these rules are in conflict. The example in Figure 12.11 shows such a file policy.

Figure 12.11: Conflicting rules

Note the warning triangles to the left of the rules. The problem with this policy is that MSEXE files will be blocked; however, they are included in the Executables category. The first rule says to inspect these files for malware and the second rule says to block the MSEXE file type.

Remember, we said file type analysis only requires the first 1460 bytes of the file. By examining the file header, Firepower can determine what type of file is being transferred. This is enough to make the decision to block a file based on file type. Once the transfer is blocked, the rest of the file does not pass and therefore we can't calculate the SHA-256 for malware analysis. Simply stated—you can't block a file and also analyze it for malware.

Hovering over the warning icon for the first rule brings up a help balloon explaining this conflict:

Malware lookups won't occur on MSEXE files because the rule marked with 'Warning 1' will block these files.

You can still apply and use a file policy with warnings as long as you understand how the policy will behave.

Sample Policy

Let's create a basic File & Malware policy. For this policy, we will use the following business requirements:

- Maximize malware detection and blocking capabilities by using all available detection methods.

- Disallow transfer of executable or system files via HTTP.

- Block encrypted archive files.

- Store malicious files for internal investigation.

- Company policy does not allow sending potentially sensitive files to offsite storage locations.

Our business requirements have a slight conflict. The first one says we want maximum detection. However, the last one says we can't send potentially sensitive files off-site. We're going to assume that the privacy requirement trumps the detection requirement as this is often the case. This means we can't use dynamic analysis on all the possible file types. The policy shown in Figures 12.12 and 12.13 is one way to address these requirements.

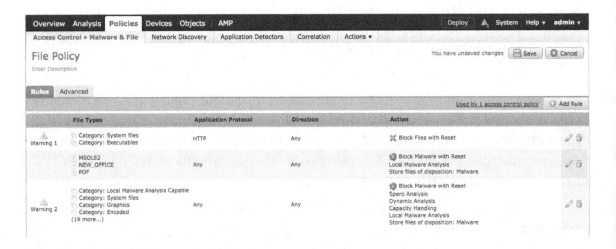

Figure 12.12: Sample policy rules

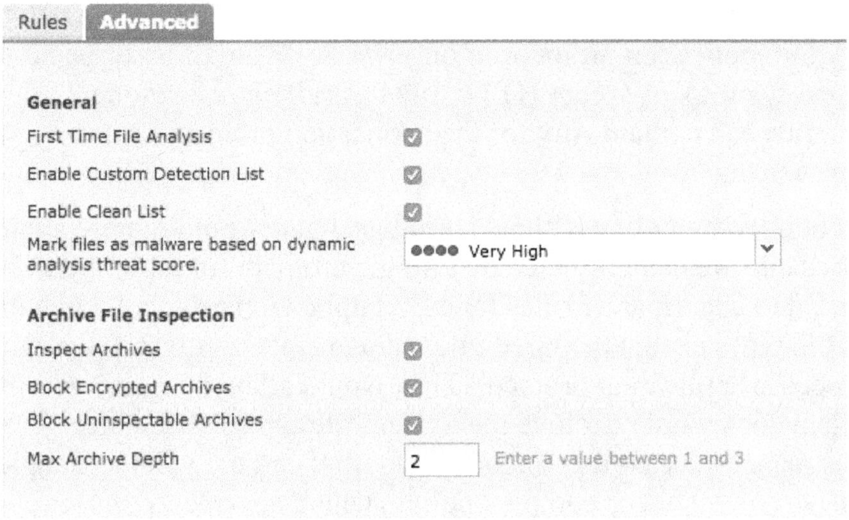

Figure 12.13: Sample advanced settings

Our file policy is set up like this:

- On the Advanced tab, the default settings already include blocking encrypted archives. We also checked Inspect Archives and Block Uninspectable Archives. We left the default Max Archive Depth value at 2.

- Rule 1 blocks the System files and Executables categories for the HTTP protocol.

- Rule 2 performs malware analysis for the MSOLE2, NEW_OFFICE, and PDF file types. This rule does not perform Spero (only for MSEXE) or dynamic analysis. This addresses the privacy requirement by disabling dynamic analysis for these file types.

- Rule 3 performs malware analysis including Spero, local malware, and dynamic analysis for all file types except the three document file types in rule 2.

Ah, you have noticed the warning triangles. They are warning us that we have told the policy to block some file types in the first rule and inspect them in the third rule. Is this a bad thing? Not really. In the first rule we are only blocking the System files and Executables categories transferred via HTTP. Of course, the protocol of Any in the third rule also includes HTTP, meaning we are telling this rule to inspect the files that were blocked in the first rule. However, the fact that the third rule will never inspect these file types is something we're willing to accept in the interest of a simpler policy.

The limitation that is causing this conflict is the fact that a rule can only contain one entry for application protocol. If only we could create an inspection rule and specify every protocol except HTTP. It's basically an all-or-one proposition. Each rule can contain Any for the application protocol or it can contain a single protocol.

We could build a file policy with no warnings, but it would require about six more rules. Because we can only include a single protocol (or all of them) in a rule, we would need to add separate rules for each application protocol. Each one must include all file types except the three office documents in rule 2. Each rule would be for a specific application protocol. They would all be the same except for the HTTP rule, which would exclude the System files and Executables categories. In this manner, we could remove the conflict and the yellow triangles. We would also have a much more complex policy, which provides a greater margin for error and confusion down the road.

The sample policy illustrates one way to go about addressing the business requirements. Another way is to use the Access Control Policy to apply one file policy to HTTP traffic and another one to all other traffic, but this would require two file policies. You could also add the additional six rules to this file policy if you want to eliminate the warnings. The idea is to show you that there are often several ways to address a situation with Firepower. Use the one that makes the most sense in your situation.

Chapter 13: Prefilter Policy

While it's not actually part of the Access Control policy, the Prefilter policy actually processes traffic first. It should be noted that **this policy only applies to Firepower Threat Defense (FTD) devices**.

Firepower devices do not use any of the rules in this policy. As with many other policies, the Prefilter policy is implemented through a setting in the Access Control policy.

Overview

Each Access Control policy has a Prefilter policy associated with it. That's right, even Access Control policies targeted for Firepower devices have a Prefilter policy, even though it is not used for these devices.

There is a default Prefilter policy included; this is the one assigned to any new Access Control policies. If you use a custom Prefilter policy with an Access Control policy targeted for Firepower devices, you will receive a warning when you deploy the policy, as shown in Figure 13.1.

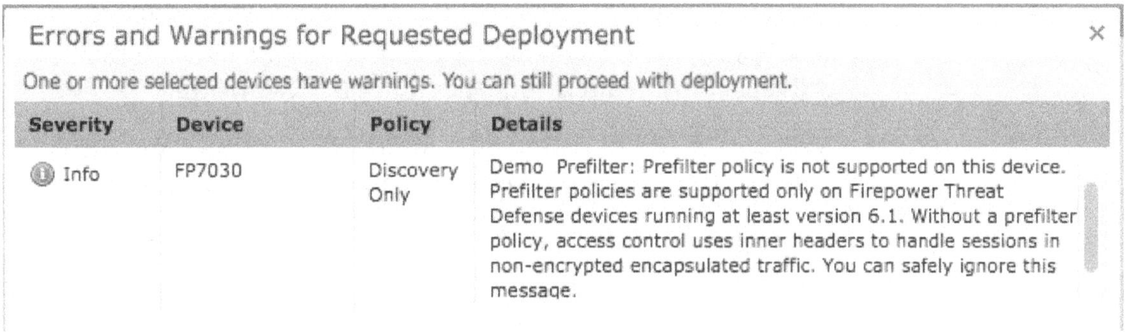

Errors and Warnings for Requested Deployment   ✕

One or more selected devices have warnings. You can still proceed with deployment.

Severity	Device	Policy	Details
ⓘ Info	FP7030	Discovery Only	Demo Prefilter: Prefilter policy is not supported on this device. Prefilter policies are supported only on Firepower Threat Defense devices running at least version 6.1. Without a prefilter policy, access control uses inner headers to handle sessions in non-encrypted encapsulated traffic. You can safely ignore this message.

Figure 13.1: Prefilter warning

Prefilter Uses

The Prefilter policy can be broken down into three functions.

- Block traffic

- Fastpath traffic

- Rezone tunneled traffic

The first two are fairly easy to understand. If we want to block traffic based on criteria such as interface, source/destination IP address, port, or VLAN tag, this is the place to do it. This also applies to traffic we do not want to inspect at all. Passing traffic without inspection using the Prefilter policy is called fastpath.

While blocking traffic is one of the options, probably the more common use of Prefilter rules is to fastpath traffic. This is usually done because there is certain traffic passing through our device that we do not want to inspect or impact in any way. Here are some common use cases for fastpathing traffic:

- Backup applications: They typically transfer high volumes of traffic over long-running connections. Inspecting these flows provides no security benefit and can impact backup speeds as well as device utilization.

- Replication traffic: Database or other replication traffic is often encrypted or uses encoding that Snort does not understand. These are also long-running high-volume flows that do not need to be inspected.

- Antivirus signature updates: While these may not be long-running flows, they contain data that does not lend itself to inspection. In addition, we often see false positive alerts from Firepower's Advanced Malware file inspection on these flows.

- Voice over IP (VOIP) traffic: While not a significant burden to detection, sometimes latency is an issue with this type of traffic.

- Any other traffic you don't want to inspect.

Policy Creation

Creating rules to fastpath traffic for the examples above is generally fairly straightforward. If we know which hosts are sending/receiving this traffic as well as their TCP ports, it's easy to create rules to match. Before we go on and discuss tunneled traffic, let's take a look at the policy itself.

You will find the Prefilter policy under Polices → Access Control → Prefilter. If this is your first visit you will notice there is already a default Prefilter policy here. As mentioned previously, this policy is used by default for all new

Access Control polices. If you click the edit pencil icon by this policy, you will see the screen shown in Figure 13.2.

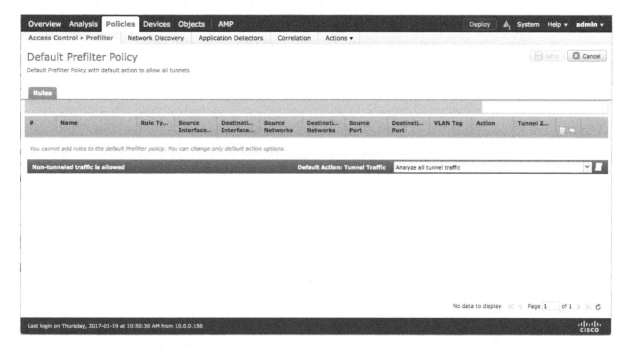

Figure 13.2: Default Prefilter policy

This policy has a Rules tab as well as a default action. Notice there is no Add Rules button. This is because you cannot add rules to the Default Prefilter Policy. You also cannot delete the default Prefilter policy. All you can do is change the Default Action and logging options.

Your options for the default action are as follows:

- Analyze all tunnel traffic

- Block all tunnel traffic

Speaking of tunneled traffic, what exactly is this? Tunneled traffic is IP traffic encapsulated within a tunneling protocol. The following protocols are supported by the Prefilter policy:

- GRE: Generic Routing Encapsulation, IP protocol 47. This is a Cisco protocol used to encapsulate a wide variety of Network layer protocols inside virtual point-to-point links over an IP network.

- IP-in-IP: Encapsulating an IP packet in another IP packet. This is covered by RFC 2003.

- IPv6-in-IP: Allows tunneling of IPv6 traffic over an IPv4 network.

- Teredo: Encapsulating IPv6 packets within IPv4 User Datagram Protocol (UDP) packets.

In the default Prefilter policy, you have the option to analyze traffic within these tunnels or block it. When we say "analyze," we mean pass the traffic on to the Access Control policy. Of course, block means... block.

But why do we need a Prefilter policy for this? The reason is that the Access Control policy has no concept of tunnels. As traffic is processed, the tunneling protocol is stripped so the access control, intrusion, and file/malware rules can access the underlying network and application traffic. The Prefilter policy gives you access to these tunneling protocols so you can make decisions on whether to block tunneled traffic or perform some type of Access Control action based on the tunnel characteristics.

You may still be a little fuzzy on the whole Prefilter policy thing, but bear with us for a while. To understand this more fully, let's create a new Prefilter policy and look at the available rules.

Prefilter Rules

First navigate back to Policies → Access Control → Prefilter. This time, click the New Policy button to create your own custom Prefilter policy. Give the policy a name and optional description in the New Policy dialog, shown in Figure 13.3. Then click Save.

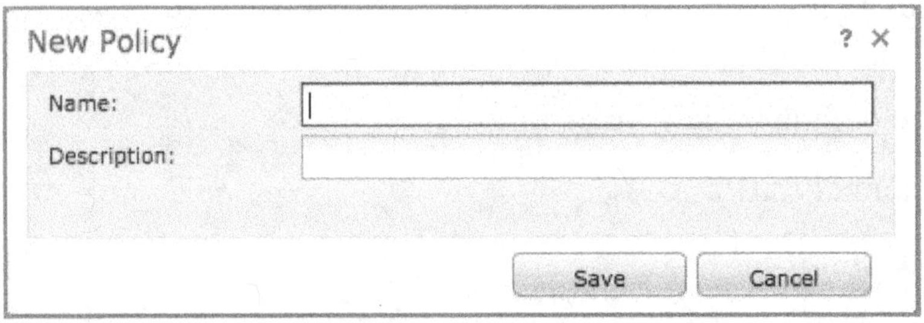

New Policy	? ×
Name:	
Description:	
	Save Cancel

Figure 13.3: New Prefilter policy dialog

The Default Action settings are the same as the settings for the default Prefilter policy, but we now have the option to add rules, as shown in Figure 13.4.

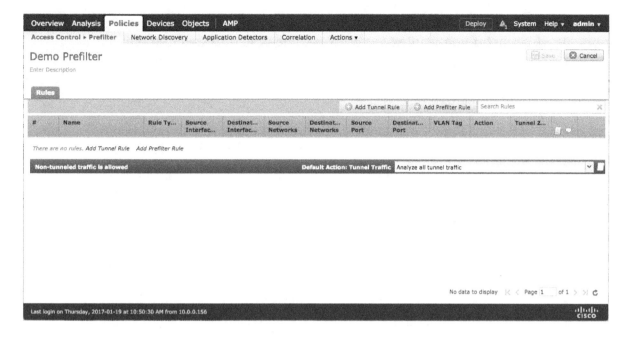

Figure 13.4: Custom Prefilter policy

There are two types of rules we can add, tunnel rules and prefilter rules. Rather than try to restate what is already explained in the Firepower help, we have included the explanations from the help page, shown in Figure 13.5. This shows the differences between tunnel and prefilter rules.

Characteristic	Tunnel Rules	Prefilter Rules
Primary function	Quickly fastpath, block, or rezone plaintext, passthough tunnels.	Quickly fastpath or block any other connection that benefits from early handling.
Encapsulation and port/protocol criteria	Encapsulation conditions match only plaintext tunnels over selected protocols, listed in Encapsulation Conditions.	Port conditions can use a wider range of port and protocol constraints than tunnel rules; see Port and ICMP Code Conditions.
Network criteria	Tunnel endpoint conditions constrain the endpoints of the tunnels you want to handle; see Tunnel Endpoint Conditions.	Network conditions constrain the source and destination hosts in each connection; see Network Conditions.
Direction	Bidirectional or unidirectional (configurable). Tunnel rules are bidirectional by default, so they can handle all traffic between tunnel endpoints.	Unidirectional only (nonconfigurable). Prefilter rules match source-to-destination traffic only.
Rezone sessions for further analysis	Supported, using tunnel zones; see Tunnel Zones and Prefiltering.	Not supported.

Figure 13.5: Tunnel vs. prefilter rules

We've discussed the concepts of blocking and fastpath, but what is this "rezone" that's mentioned in Figure 13.5?

Remember we said the Access Control policy has no concept of tunnel protocols. But what if you wanted to perform some type of inspection only on traffic within certain tunnel links? You need a way to tell the Access Control policy which traffic is within a tunnel. This is what tunnel rules are for! The process goes something like this:

1. Define a tunnel zone object. This is a specific object type that contains your tunnel name and optional description.

2. Create a tunnel rule to match traffic for this tunnel. Define tunnel encapsulation and optionally interfaces, endpoints, and VLAN tags.

3. Assign your tunnel zone object to the rule.

4. After saving your Prefilter policy, associate it with your Access Control policy and create rules using your tunnel zone object.

You can now specify Access Control actions based on your tunnel object. The Access Control rule will have access to the underlying network/application protocols. It still doesn't know what a tunneling protocol is, but you have identified your tunnel traffic, allowing you to customize your Access Control actions.

Let's take a look at some examples.

We want to create a rule to fastpath traffic to our antivirus update servers. When our clients connect to these servers to download updates, we are getting false positive malware events. Clicking the Add Prefilter Rule button displays the dialog in Figure 13.6.

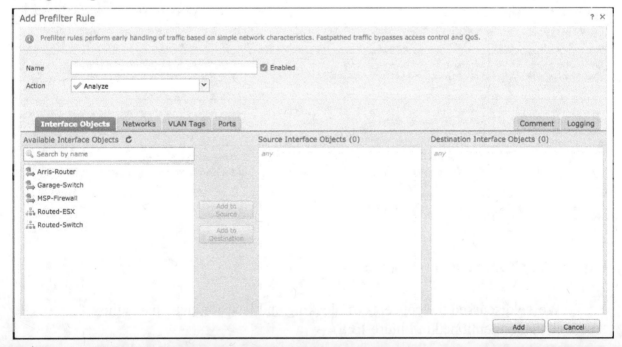

Figure 13.6: Add Prefilter Rule dialog

In this dialog, we need to give our rule a name and select an action. The actions available are as follows:

- Analyze: Send the traffic on to the Access Control policy; inner headers will be used for analysis.

- Block: Block the traffic.

- Fastpath: Allow the traffic without sending it through the other policies (Access Control, Intrusion, File, etc.).

In our case, we will select Fastpath to allow our antivirus updates to pass without inspection. Using the Interface Objects, Networks, VLAN Tags, and Ports tabs, we will specify the criteria for the traffic. Be as specific as possible here as this fastpath rule is creating a hole in the detection of your Firepower system. We want to make sure we pass only the traffic we intend to with this rule. In Figure 13.7, we have clicked the Rules tab and added our AV-servers network object to the Destination Networks column.

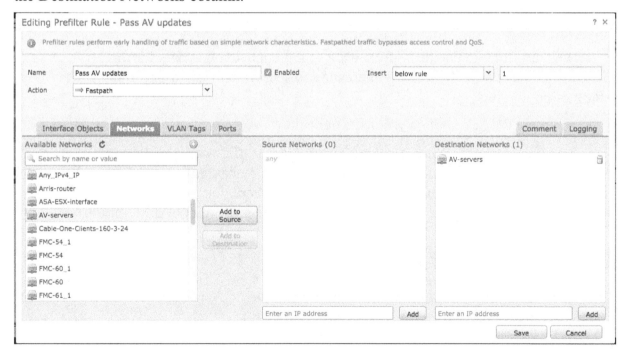

Figure 13.7: Networks tab

Finally, let's add the port used by the antivirus application—8014/tcp. In Figure 13.8, we used a port object created for this purpose and added the destination port to our rule.

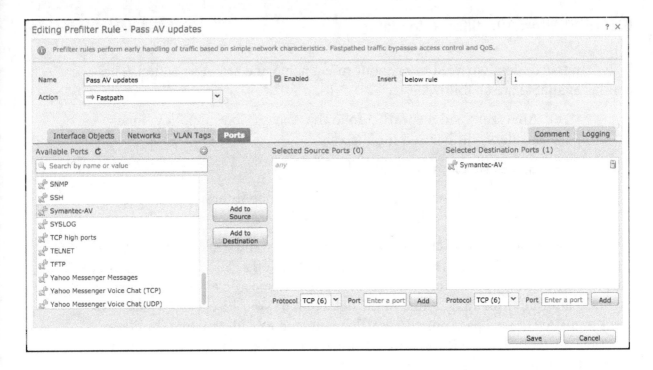

Figure 13.8: Ports tab

The last thing to decide is if we want to log connection events for this traffic. Since there's really nothing interesting to see, we will leave this at the default of no logging.

Clicking the Save button will save our rule.

Next, let's create a sample rule to tag all GRE traffic with a custom tunnel zone. You can create your tunnel zones ahead of time by navigating to Objects → Object Management, as shown in Figure 13.9. From there you can click on Tunnel Zone from the list on the left. Give your object a name and optional description.

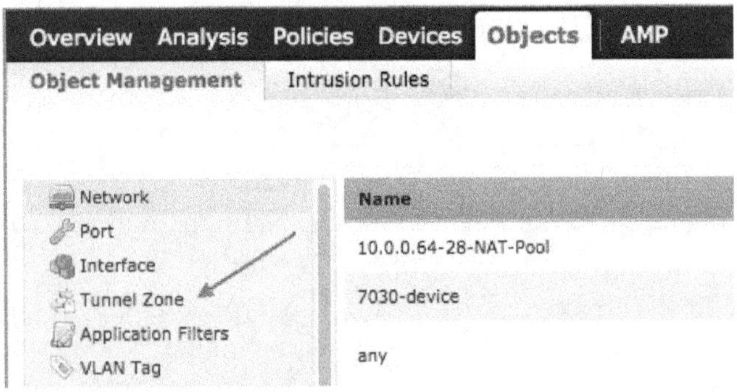

Figure 13.9: Tunnel Zone objects

You can also add this object on the fly without the need to leave your Prefilter policy and visit the Objects menu.

To add a tunnel rule, click the Add Tunnel Rule button. This displays the dialog shown in Figure 13.10.

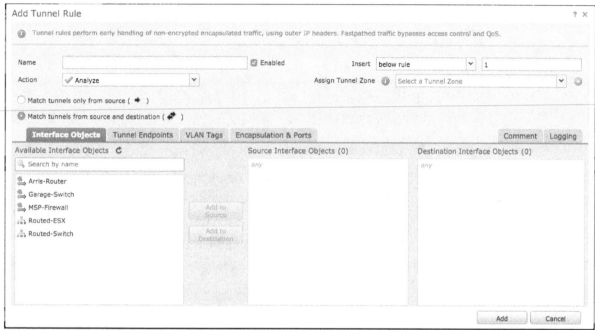

Figure 13.10: Add Tunnel Rule dialog

There are several options available for a tunnel rule:

- Name: Descriptive name for your rule.

- Action: Same as a Prefilter rule; actions are Analyze, Block, Fastpath.

- Match tunnels only from source: For the rule to match, traffic must originate from one of the source interface objects or tunnel endpoints and leave through one of the destination interface objects or tunnel endpoints. This refers to the session initiation (who sent the SYN). All Prefilter rules are bidirectional, so matching return traffic for established connections is assumed.

- Match tunnels from source and destination: Match traffic from source to destination and destination to source. This means the rule will match sessions initiated in either direction.

- Assign Tunnel Zone: Select a tunnel zone object previously created or create a new one on the fly by clicking the green plus icon to the right.

- Interface Objects: Optional source and destination interface objects.

- Tunnel Endpoints: Optional source/destination IP addresses.

- VLAN Tags: Optional VLAN tags.

- Encapsulation & Ports: – This option is required. Check one or more tunnel types to match traffic.

  - GRE

  - IP-in-IP

  - IPv6-in-IP

  - Teredo Port (3544)

- Comment: Optional rule comment.

- Logging – Only available for the Block or Fastpath actions. Will log a connection event if traffic is fastpathed or blocked.

To add a simple rule to tag all GRE tunnel traffic, we will leave the Interface Objects, Tunnel Endpoints, and VLAN Tags tabs at their default settings. On the Encapsulation & Ports we will check GRE and assign our GRE-tunnel tunnel zone object. This rule is shown in Figure 13.11.

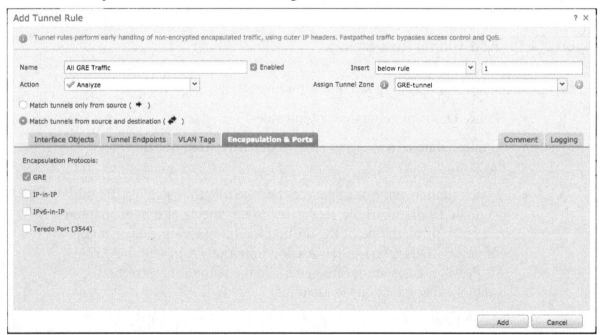

Figure 13.11: Simple GRE tunnel rule

When finished, we click the Add button to add the rule to our custom Prefilter policy.

We now have two rules in our sample policy, as shown in Figure 13.12. The Prefilter policy processes rules in order from top to bottom. Rules evaluate traffic until there is a match. Once a rule matches traffic, that traffic is not processed by subsequent rules. In our case, the rules will never conflict so the order is not important. However, if you do have multiple rules that could match the same traffic you will want to place the more specific rules higher in your policy. This works just like a firewall rule set or router access control list (ACL). These are familiar concepts in networking and security.

Figure 13.12: Demo Prefilter policy

Rule order can be changed by clicking and dragging a rule up or down in the policy. It can also be changed by editing the rule and modifying the rule number in the upper-right corner.

Chapter 14: Access Control

If there is one policy that is at the heart of the Firepower system, it is the Access Control policy. Virtually all traffic entering a Firepower or FTD device will be processed through one or more rules in this policy. This truly is Firepower's central traffic cop.

The Access Control policy determines what traffic will be logged, allowed or blocked. It is also used to implement Security Intelligence lists, IPS rules and File policies, as well as SSL, Identity, DNS and your NAP.

. All traffic passing through a device is processed through the AC policy. If your background includes experience with packet filtering firewalls this may look familiar to a traditional firewall Access Control List (ACL). However, in addition to allowing/blocking connections based on IP address, port and protocol, the AC policy offers several additional methods of traffic inspection.

You can deploy your Access Control policies in a number of ways. For example you could create a single policy and deploy it to all your devices. Or you could create a separate policy for each device or group of devices. However, only one policy can be applied to a device at a time. Applying a policy replaces any existing policy with the new one.

Overview

If the Access Control policy is so important, why did we wait until Chapter 14 to discuss it? This is a valid question, and it also relates to the order in which you might go about setting up policies in your new Firepower system. Because the Access Control (AC) policy is the central hub, it has dependencies on a number of other policies. Let's look at some examples:

- Prefilter policy (FTD only): Prefilter rules may block or trust traffic prior to the AC policy. In addition, we may assign tunnel zone names to various tunneled traffic and then create AC rules to deal specifically with this traffic.

- Identity policy: AC rules can be created to match traffic based on user identity. For these rules to function, an Identity policy is associated with an AC policy.

- SSL policy: If we are performing SSL decryption, this must be done before processing by the AC policy. This is important especially when it comes to identifying applications within encrypted sessions.

- DNS policy: Each AC policy has a DNS policy associated with it. This policy inspects traffic prior to processing by AC rules and can be configured to allow, block, or sinkhole DNS traffic.

- Intrusion policy: Certain rules in the AC policy may send traffic for inspection by the Snort engine via an Intrusion policy.

- Network Analysis policy: The AC policy specifies one or more Network Analysis policies with settings that impact Snort preprocessors and subsequent Intrusion policy processing.

- File & Malware policy: Traffic can also be routed for file and malware inspection through one or more AC rules.

Through the Access Control policy, Firepower can invoke one or more of the above policies to process network traffic. For example, we might decrypt an SSL session, identify the application protocol, then inspect the application traffic via Snort and Advanced Malware Protection (AMP) before allowing it to proceed to its destination.

This is why we don't start with the Access Control policy. Once the dependent policies are configured, they are then glued together with this policy.

Each Firepower/FTD device can only have a single AC policy deployed to it at a time. However, a single policy can be targeted for one or more devices. This means you may deploy one policy per device or assign the same policy to multiple devices. If your deployment is fairly basic and you are simply performing intrusion inspection on all traffic, then a single AC policy across all your devices may be all you need. Remember, complexity is the enemy of security; using fewer policies will make the tasks of configuration and maintenance easier down the line.

You can also use policy hierarchy to aid in keeping settings consistent between policies. By using a master/child policy design, you can enforce certain settings in your child policies by defining them in the master. You can even decide if you want to allow child policies to override various settings from the master.

Policy Creation

Let's dive into the Access Control policy!

To start, navigate to Policies → Access Control → Access Control. There is no default AC policy. To create one, click the New Policy button. You will be presented with the dialog shown in Figure 14.1.

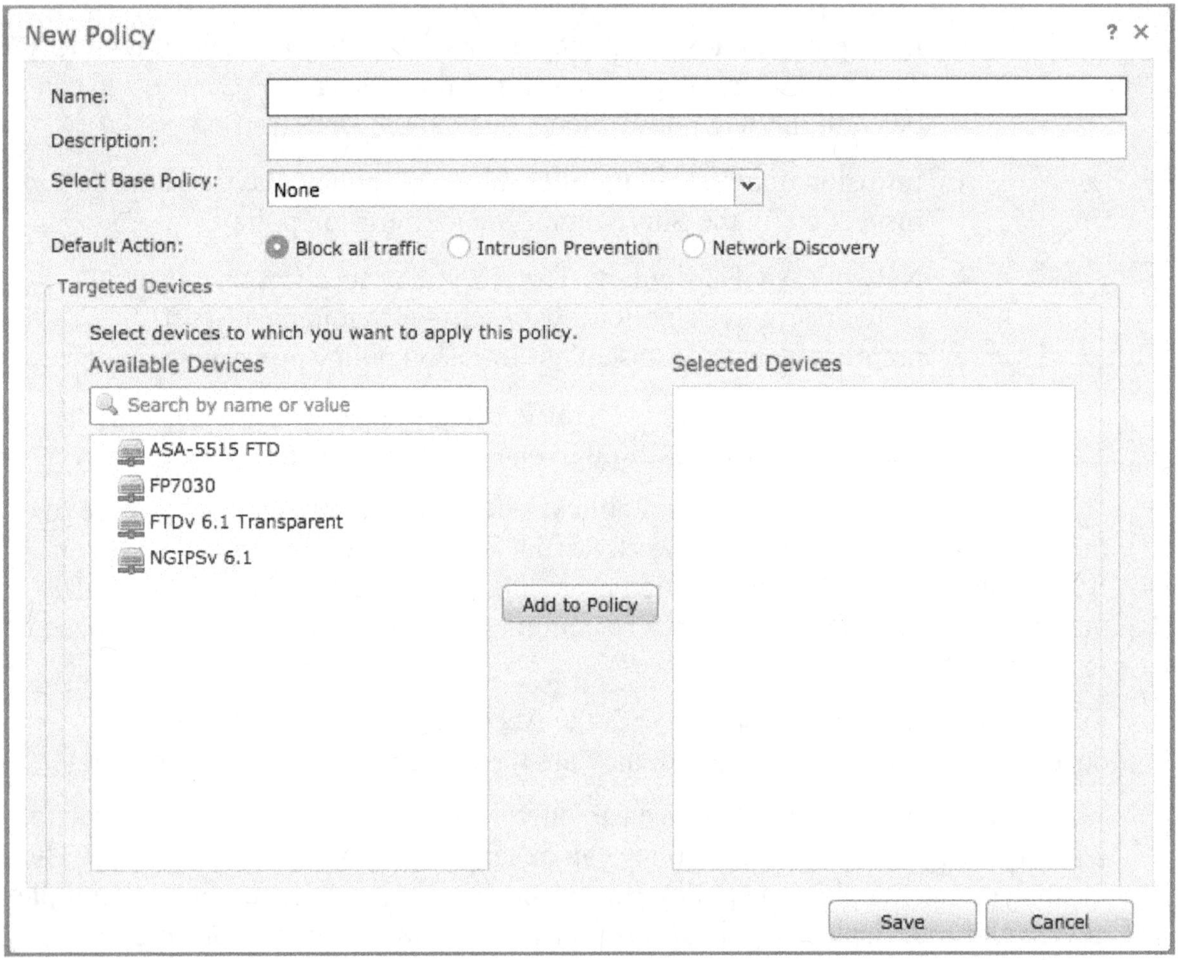

Figure 14.1: New Policy dialog

Here, you can insert your policy name and an optional description and select a base policy if desired. If this is your first policy, leave the Select Base Policy option at None.

Next you have three choices for your policy default action. These are as follows.

- Block All Traffic: If traffic doesn't match any AC rules, it will not be allowed to pass through the device.

- Intrusion Prevention: Traffic not matching any rules will be processed through Snort rules in an Intrusion policy.

- Network Discovery: Traffic not matching any rules will be allowed through the device and may be subject to analysis via the Network Discovery policy.

Note that there are a couple of options not available on this screen. The first is which Intrusion policy will be used; the second is the trust action. Both of these can be configured from the main policy configuration screen.

After configuring the settings above, you have the option of targeting the policy for one or more devices. Select one or more devices on the left and click the Add To Policy button.

If you target a device that already has an AC policy defined, when you click Save you will see a dialog similar to Figure 14.2.

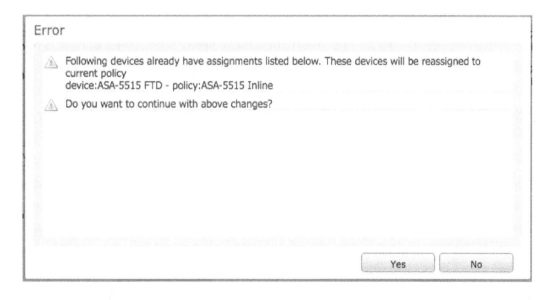

Figure 14.2: Policy assignment error

Clicking Yes will move the device assignment from the existing policy to your new policy. Rest assured, this isn't really an error as long as you actually meant to remove an existing device from another AC policy and add it to your new one.

This behavior stems from the fact that Firepower will not allow you to configure a device with no Access Control policy. As a result, the system will not let you simply remove a device from an AC policy. The only way to do so is to add the device to another AC policy, which will in turn remove it from the old policy assignment. Call it a "positive handoff" if you like; this results in a message similar to the one shown in Figure 14.2.

After you have assigned your devices, click the Save button to begin editing your new policy.

Policy Editing

When you start editing a policy, the first screen you are presented with shows the empty rule set along with tabs for the various policy settings. This is shown in Figure 14.3. Before we dive into Access Control rules, let's look at some of the other policy settings available. Again, this follows our methodology of ensuring that all the dependent settings and policies are in place before we get to the heart of the policy—the rules. Remember, it's tempting to dive straight into the AC rules, but exercise some self-control and make sure all your ducks are in a row first!

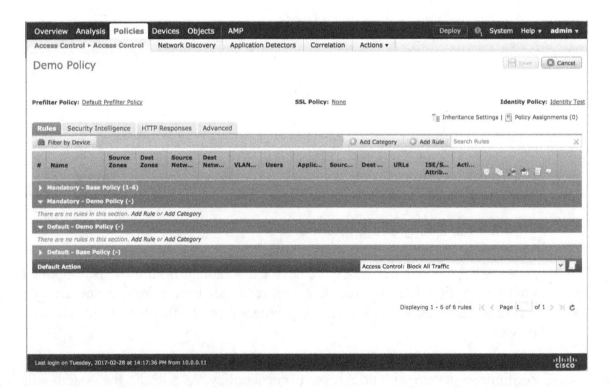

Figure 14.3: Initial AC policy screen

General Settings

Let's look at some of the settings across the top of the Access Control policy page. These settings are not specific to the tab that is selected.

Prefilter Policy

This link allows selecting a Prefilter policy. This policy will be applied to the devices targeted by this Access Control policy. Even though this setting only applies to Firepower Threat Defense (FTD) devices, you still have to select a policy here. Every policy starts with the Default Prefilter Policy selected and you can simply leave this as-is if you are not using FTD.

SSL Policy

This link allows you to select your SSL policy. Of course, if you are not performing SSL decryption, you can leave this at the default setting of None. SSL decryption is performed before traffic is processed through Access Control rules.

Identity Policy

As with Prefilter and SSL, this allows you to select an Identity policy to deploy to your devices. The default is None.

Inheritance Settings

Clicking Inheritance Settings displays the dialog shown in Figure 14.4. Inheritance allows nesting of multiple Access Control policies. You select a base policy and optionally select Child Policy Inheritance Settings. Leaving these boxes unchecked means child policies can accept or override the various settings in the base policy. By checking a box, you are forcing the child policy to use the settings for that particular area.

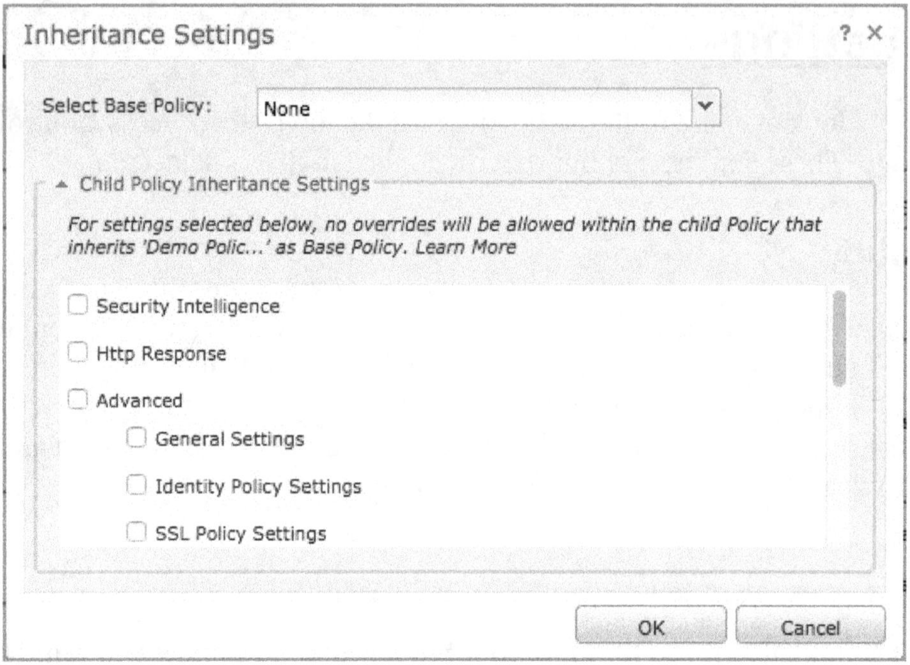

Figure 14.4: Inheritance Settings dialog

When policies are nested, rules in the base policy are inherited by the child policies. The Mandatory and Base rule categories are placed at the beginning and end of the child policy rule set. More on this when we get to rules later in this chapter.

Policies can be nested up to 10 levels deep. However, this could wind up being an administration nightmare as the various rule layers are nested within each other. One of the most effective uses of policy nesting is to maintain consistency in the Advanced and Security Intelligence settings across your policies. These settings can tend to drift over time. Maintaining them in the single base layer is a good way to keep all of your policies synchronized. Also, if you decide to modify these settings, you only have to do it in the base policy.

Policy Assignments

The Policy Assignments link is used to modify the device assignments of the policy. This is the same setting used when we first created the policy. Figure 14.5 shows an example of the Policy Assignments dialog.

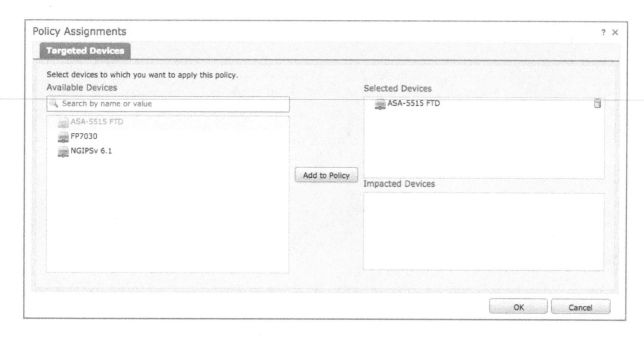

Figure 14.5: Policy Assignments dialog

Selected Devices shows the devices where the policy is currently assigned. If this policy is used as a base for others, then the Impacted Devices section lists the policies that would be impacted by changing this one.

Because each device must always have an Access Control policy assigned, the system will not allow you to remove a device from a policy and then save that policy. To assign a different policy to a device, you have to edit your target policy and *pull* the device from the previous policy into the new one. When you do this, you will receive a confirmation dialog similar to the one shown in Figure 14.6. This is nothing to be worried about; it is just confirming that you meant to remove this device from the previous policy assignment.

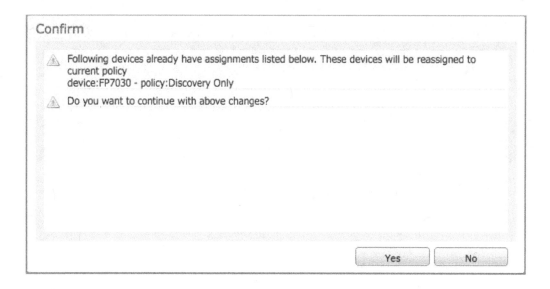

Figure 14.6: Confirmation dialog

Security Intelligence

Before we dive into AC rules, it is helpful to first review some of the other configuration tabs. One that you should always consider is the Security Intelligence tab. This tab is where you configure the behavior of the various Security Intelligence lists. The primary purpose of a Security Intelligence list is to blacklist or block something. This capability has been expanded over various Firepower versions and now includes DNS, URL, and IP address lists.

Blacklists and Whitelists

Using Security Intelligence, you have the option of adding a given DNS request, URL, or IP address to either a blacklist or a whitelist. The blacklist is fairly self-explanatory. Adding an entry to a blacklist means the system will generate a Security Intelligence event and optionally block the traffic. But what does a whitelist do?

The easiest way to think about a whitelist is that a whitelist entry exists only to override a blacklist entry. The purpose of a whitelist is to prevent a blacklist entry from negatively impacting critical traffic. In the case of an IP list, imagine what would happen if the IP address of a core router on your network was inadvertently blacklisted. If your IPS started blocking all traffic to and from that router, it could cause the entire network to grind to a halt! To prevent this, you can add the IP addresses of key systems to a whitelist.

The reason this works is that whitelist entries always override blacklist entries. So, if there is ever a conflict, the whitelist will prevail. Keep in mind that whitelist entries only override blacklist entries. Putting an entry into a whitelist does not mean Firepower will give that traffic a free pass. It only means Firepower won't blacklist the traffic. It will still be processed by the appropriate access control rules and possibly undergo intrusion and/or file inspection. It could also be blocked by an AC rule.

The Security Intelligence Tab

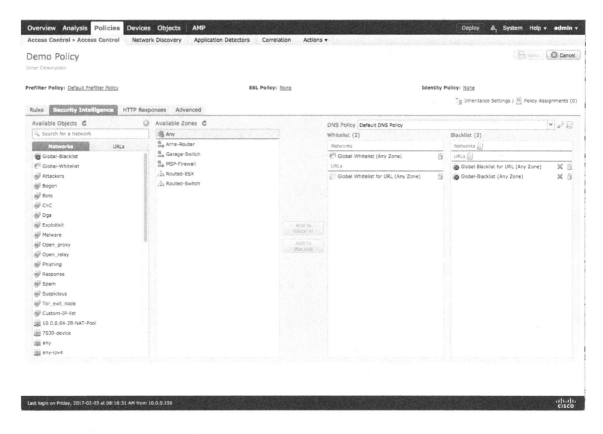

Figure 14.7: Security Intelligence tab

The Security Intelligence tab, shown in Figure 14.7, looks a bit busy when you first see it. On the left, you will see the Available Objects and Available Zones columns. This is where you select your network or URL objects. You can optionally add a zone qualification to your object. This means the traffic must match the object (IP address or URL) and also be traveling to or from the selected zone. You do not have to select a zone; if you don't, the default zone of Any will be used.

On the right, you see the Whitelist and Blacklist columns. These two columns are also divided horizontally into Networks and URLs sections. Adding a Network or URL object will cause it to appear in the appropriate section within each list.

Available Objects

Let's take a closer look at the Available Objects column in Figures 14.8 and 14.9. This column is further divided into two sub-tabs, one for networks and one for URLs.

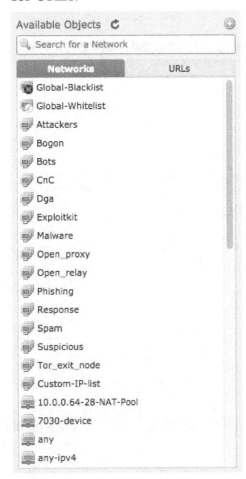

Figure 14.8: Available Objects Networks sub-tab

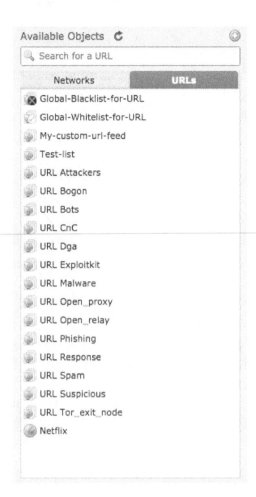

Figure 14.9: Available Objects URLs sub-tab

You will notice that each of these lists contains various Security Intelligence categories. These categories are populated as a result of the Cisco Security Intelligence feed. Your FMC downloads the feed periodically and populates these Security Intelligence categories. While you cannot view the individual entries from here, you can see how many entries are in a given category. Hovering your mouse over a given category will cause a pop-up to appear listing the number of entries in the category, as shown in Figure 14.10.

Figure 14.10: Object count pop-up

Keep in mind that this feed is updated constantly and this count is likely to change within minutes or hours, depending on the update frequency selected in the intelligence feed object. For more information, see Chapter 6, "Objects."

The Available Objects column will also show all of your custom Network or URL objects as well as custom feeds. Any of these can be added to either the Whitelist or Blacklist column by selecting them and clicking either Add to Whitelist or Add to Blacklist. You will also notice the green plus icon above the search field. This allows you to add a Security Intelligence feed or list on the fly without having to navigate back to the Objects menu. If you do add an object in this manner, use the refresh icon (↻) to refresh the list and show your new entry.

Blacklist Actions

When you first add entries to your Blacklist column, they will default to a drop action. This is indicated by the red X next to the list. However, for some lists you may only want to be notified of a connection rather than blocking it. Right-clicking on an entry will bring up a context menu that will allow you to select an action of Monitor-only (do not block) instead. Doing so will change the action of the list to logging an event without blocking the traffic. The icon will also change to a green arrow. This is shown in Figures 14.11 and 14.12.

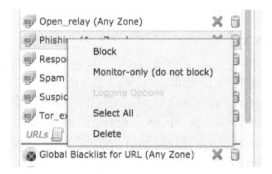

Figure 14.11: Blacklist action menu

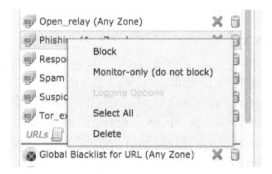

Figure 14.12: Monitor-only icon

Logging Options

There are three blue scroll icons on the page that control the logging for each type of Security Intelligence list. These are shown in Figure 14.13. The default setting for each type of Security Intelligence is to log the connection. This means any matching traffic will be logged as Security Intelligence events. These can be viewed by navigating to Analysis → Connections → Security Intelligence Events.

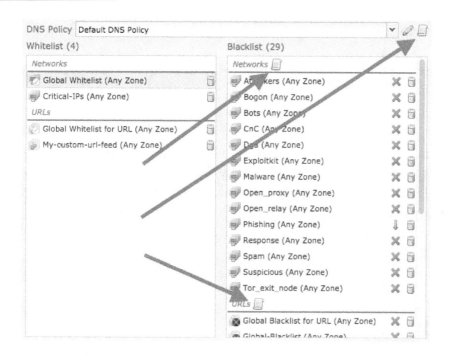

Figure 14.13: Logging icons

Clicking on any of the icons displays the logging options dialog, shown in Figure 14.14.

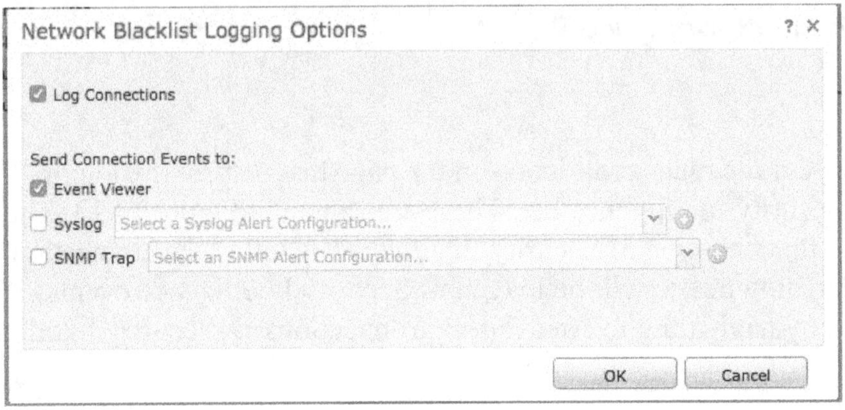

Figure 14.14: Logging options

This allows you to disable logging if desired, or direct the logging to a syslog or SNMP destination.

DNS Policy

DNS Security Intelligence is controlled by the DNS policy. We discussed this back in Chapter 10, "DNS and SSL Policy." Selecting a DNS policy is as easy as clicking the DNS Policy drop-down (shown at the top of Figure 14.13) and selecting your previously created policy. You can also edit the DNS policy directly from here by clicking the pencil icon. This will open your DNS policy in a new browser tab.

HTTP Responses

The HTTP Responses tab has not changed since version 5 of the Sourcefire System was first introduced. This tab is used to configure the web page returned when a user attempts to visit a blocked website. When using the URL Filtering feature, it is generally a good idea to present the user with a web page explaining why a particular site is blocked. The alternative—simply dropping their HTTP request—will usually leave the user wondering if there is something wrong with their Internet connection. Attempting to visit a page and experiencing a time-out or an unfriendly browser error message is sure to increase help desk calls. Instead, Firepower can return a web page notifying the user that their attempt was blocked.

There are two available options for configuring the HTTP response on this tab: Block Response Page and Interactive Block Response Page. These are shown in Figure 14.15.

Figure 14.15: HTTP Responses tab

Block Response Page

The Block Response page will be returned anytime a user's HTTP request is blocked by a rule using the Block or Block with Reset action. For this page, you have three options: None, System-Provided, or Custom. The default is None. This means that if you use an access control rule to block a user's HTTP request, they will not receive information as to why the page will not display. If the rule does not include the reset action, the user will probably see their browser spin for some time before returning a browser-specific message indicating the site could not be loaded.

Instead, you can send the user a generic notification that the site was blocked or return a customized response page. The default system-provided response page is shown in Figure 14.16.

Figure 14.16: Access Denied response page

To select the standard response page, select System-Provided from the pull-down list. To view the page source, click the magnifying glass icon next to the field.

To customize the HTTP response, select Custom. This will load the existing page (system-provided by default) and allow editing or pasting the HTML code you choose.

Interactive Block Response Page

The Interactive Block Response Page will be returned anytime a user's HTTP request is intercepted by a rule using the Interactive Block or Interactive Block with Reset action. This page functions similarly to the Block Response Page above. The only difference is that the interactive rules give the user the option of proceeding to the site anyway. The Interactive Block Response page includes a JavaScript-driven button that, if clicked, allows the user to proceed to the blocked website. The default System-Provided Interactive Block response page is shown in Figure 14.17.

Figure 14.17: Access Denied interactive block response page

Once the user clicks the Continue button, they can load the blocked website. By default, the duration of this access is 600 seconds (10 minutes). After this period, the interactive block page will appear again.

Note: Without the use of SSL decryption, neither of the HTML response pages will work if the site blocked is using HTTPS.

Advanced

The Advanced tab has a plethora of settings that can be modified. Figure 14.18 is provided for your reference. Settings are grouped into various sections on the page. Most of these settings can be left at their defaults. Several, such as the Identity, SSL, and Prefilter policies, can be set at any time by clicking the links near the top of the page.

Figure 14.18: Advanced settings

General Settings

The General Settings section is a catchall of settings that don't fit into the other categories. This section is shown in Figure 14.19.

General Settings ?

Maximum URL characters to store in connection events	1024
Allow an Interactive Block to bypass blocking for (seconds)	600
Retry URL cache miss lookup	☑
Inspect traffic during policy apply (If this option is enabled and you continue to inspect traffic during the policy deploy process, depending on the load and capacity of the ASA FirePOWER modules, packets may be dropped, causing latency on the network)	☑

Revert to Defaults   OK   Cancel

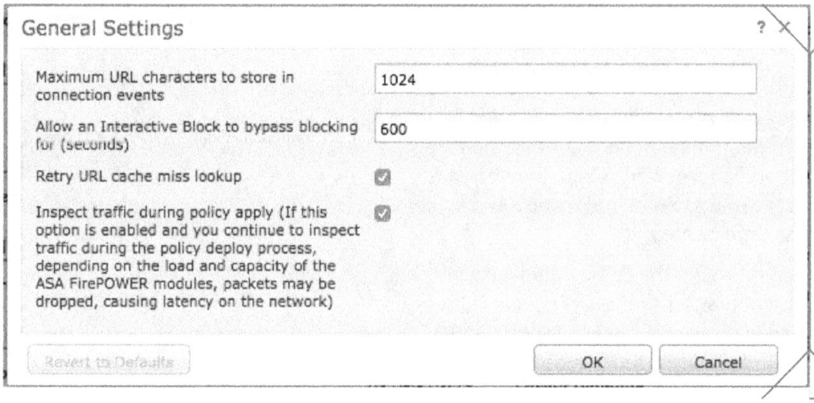

Figure 14.19: General settings

Maximum URL characters to store in connection events

Default: 1024

Maximum: 4096

This defines the maximum length of the field used to store URLs in connection events for HTTP. Setting this value to zero disables storing of URLs in connection events. Reducing or disabling this setting may improve performance if the system logs a high number of HTTP connections.

Allow an Interactive Block to bypass blocking for (seconds)

Default: 600 (10 minutes)

Maximum: 31536000 (365 days)

This is the default time during which a user can access a URL that triggered an Interactive Block rule. This time starts when the user clicks the Continue button. Setting this value to zero requires the user to bypass the block using the Continue button for each request.

Retry URL cache miss lookup

Default: Checked

When this is disabled, the system will immediately allow traffic to a URL when the URL category is not in the cache. A cloud lookup to determine the URL category then takes place in the background. The URL is treated as uncategorized until the cloud lookup completes with a different category. In short, unchecking this will result in a faster user experience at the cost of some accuracy and timeliness in URL categorization. Note that this only applies if the URL Filtering license is in use.

Comment [ABT]: Note to self, this gets even harrier in v 6.2

Inspect traffic during policy apply

Default: Checked

When policies are deployed, the Snort process may either be reloaded or restarted, depending on the type of changes in the policy. When Snort is reloaded, traffic will continue to pass and will continue to be inspected. There may be some increased packet latency as the system works to reload Snort and inspect traffic at the same time. However, no packets will pass uninspected.

When Snort is restarted, traffic will pass through the device uninspected between the time Snort is stopped and the time the Snort process is up and running again. This is normally just a matter of seconds but there will be *some* traffic that passes through the device uninspected.

This setting allows you some control over how this restart/reload takes place. When you leave this setting at its default state of checked, the Snort process will be reloaded if possible. However, certain policy setting changes will still cause Snort to restart.

If you uncheck this setting, Snort will always restart when policies are deployed. The effect is that there will always be some packets that pass uninspected, but you will not experience the increased latency that is the result of a Snort reload.

The list of policy changes that cause a Snort restart is quite long and there is no reliable rule of thumb that will help to determine if a given policy change will cause a reload or a restart. What's that? You want to see the list? Okay, here goes.

1. Add a custom Network Analysis policy to AC policy
2. Add URLs the first time to an AC rule
3. Add/delete a File policy to/from an AC rule
4. Add/delete Intrusion policy to/from an AC rule
5. Deploy a new AC policy
6. Enable/disable adaptive profiles in AC policy
7. Enable/disable Identity policy in AC policy
8. Enable/disable SSL policy in AC policy
9. Make changes to default values under File and Malware Settings
10. Change IMAP preprocessor depth in Network Analysis policy

11. Change POP preprocessor depth in Network Analysis policy

12. Change SMTP preprocessor depth in Network Analysis policy

13. Enable/disable Inspect Archives in File policy

14. Enable/disable Store Files in File policy

15. Add custom DNS policy to AC policy

16. Modify the MTU size on device interfaces

17. Activate or deactivate an existing application detector

18. Create a new application detector

19. Install a vulnerability database (VDB) update

20. Install a Snort rule update (SRU)

21. Deploy new shared object rules in the Intrusion policy

22. Create an identity rule with an action of passive authentication

23. Add/remove a URL category/reputation condition in an AC rule

24. Revert to default values under File and Malware Settings on the Advanced tab of AC policy

25. Restore a single default value under File and Malware Settings on Advanced tab of AC policy

Note that this list is not exhaustive as there are likely several other modifications—especially in the Network Analysis policy—that will precipitate a Snort restart.

The setting you select here is largely a trade-off of detection versus connectivity. To get the best detection at the expense of a little latency during policy deployment, keep the default setting. To ensure minimum latency at the cost of some detection, disable the setting.

Identity, SSL and Prefilter

These three are fairly straightforward. Each offers a simple drop-down menu to select the associated Identity, SSL or Prefilter policies.

Network Analysis and Intrusion Policies

These settings affect how intrusion rules are processed as well as which Network Analysis policy settings are in effect. This is shown in Figure 14.20.

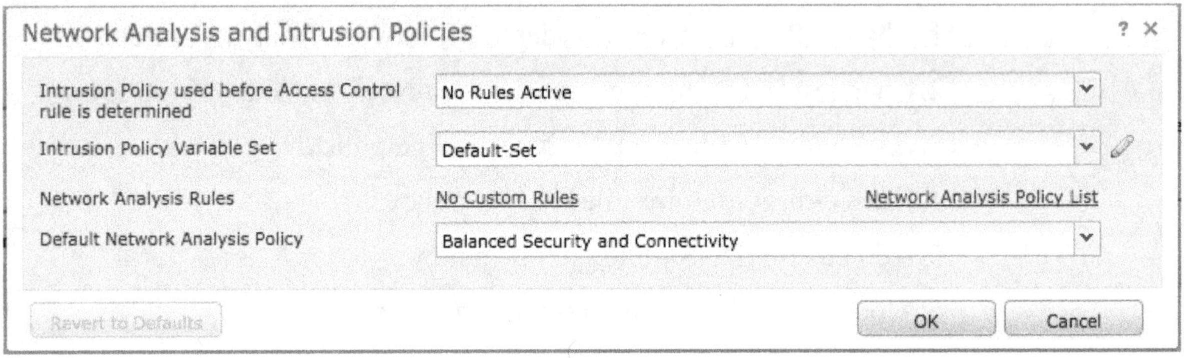

Figure 14.20: Network Analysis and Intrusion Policies

Intrusion Policy used before Access Control rule is determined

Default: (Depends on default action)

This setting determines what will happen to traffic that matches an AC rule containing an application or URL condition. The challenge in application identification is that it cannot be accomplished by inspecting just a single packet. The number of packets required depends on the application detector, but the system must allow at least some of the traffic to pass until it can come to a determination of whether a given application is present. Once the application has been identified, the AC rule or rules designed to take an action will then be enforced.

This setting determines what happens to these packets that are allowed to pass prior to application detection. The default setting is to simply allow them to pass using the No Rules Active intrusion policy (an empty intrusion policy).

It would probably be advisable to perform intrusion inspection on this traffic. To do so, use the drop-down to select an Intrusion policy with your preferred rule set.

There is another consideration here when determining which rule set to use. Say you have created a custom intrusion policy that you plan to use in your AC rules. We'll call it My IPS Policy. When you deploy policies to your devices, your custom intrusion policy will be applied. If you select a different policy, such as Balanced Security and Connectivity, in this setting this will result in two intrusion policies being applied to your devices. Each of these policies will use system resources (CPU and memory). To increase the efficiency of your policy and reduce some overhead, you should apply only as many different intrusion policies as you really need. Because of this, we recommend using an intrusion policy you are already using in your AC rules for this setting. In our example, here, you would select My IPS Policy from the drop-down.

The default setting for this item depends on the policy default action you selected when you first created this AC policy. If you selected Intrusion Prevention, this will be set to Balanced Security and Connectivity. If you selected block or network discovery, this will be set to No Rules Active.

Intrusion Policy Variable Set

Default: Default-Set

This is the variable set object that will be used in conjunction with the Intrusion policy immediately above it. Recall from Chapter 6 that this is what determines the values for the variables used by Snort in intrusion rules.

Network Analysis Rules and Default Network Analysis Policy

Default: Balanced Security and Connectivity

These two settings are closely related so we will discuss them together. One way to look at the Network Analysis policy is that it contains advanced Snort settings. Most of the settings in this policy should not be changed from their defaults as this could have a negative impact on detection, performance, or both! However, there are a few settings that Cisco recommends adjusting, largely based on whether the device will be used in passive or inline mode. When we say inline, here this also includes transparent, switched, or routed mode.

We spent a lot of time in Chapter 6 explaining how the Network Analysis policy works and warning you about making modifications. Here is our guidance for the Network Analysis policy:

- Start with the Talos base policy that corresponds to your Intrusion base policy (Connectivity, Balanced, Security).

- Enable inline mode and the inline normalization preprocessor if your device is inline (including switched or routed).

- Restrain yourself from making other changes unless you know *exactly* how they will impact detection and performance.

What this means is if your device uses only inline interfaces, you probably only need one Network Analysis policy for that device. The same applies if your device uses all passive interfaces. If this is the case, *select your customized Network Analysis policy here and move on.* You do not need any network analysis rules—these are not the droids you are looking for! The vast majority of deployments fall into this category.

The purpose of network analysis rules is to allow you to specify a different Network Analysis policy for traffic in different zones, networks, or VLANs. This means that if you have both inline and passive interfaces on the same device, you may want to specify two different Network Analysis policies. In this case, using zones is probably the best idea. Zones translate to physical interfaces, so these are natural traffic delineators between passive and inline interfaces. To specify these different policies, you need custom rules.

To create custom rules, click the No Custom Rules link in Figure 14.20. This expands the dialog as shown in Figure 14.21.

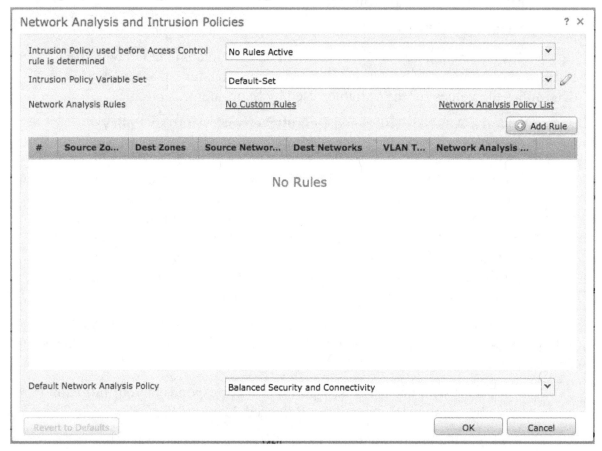

Figure 14.21: Network analysis rules

This allows you to create rules based on zone, source/destination network, and/or VLAN tag. These rules each have an associated Network Analysis policy. So, you might specify your inline Network Analysis policy as the default and then add a rule that includes all of your passive zones. In that rule you would specify your passive Network Analysis policy (the one without the inline preprocessor enabled).

Honestly, even if you had both inline and passive interfaces, it probably would make little difference if you just used a Network Analysis policy with inline mode enabled for all the traffic. In security, we have to pick our battles, and you need to decide how much time you have to tweak your policies and settings and whether that time could be used more effectively somewhere else. Also, consider that adding these rules increases the complexity of your policy—this is generally not a good thing.

But, if you really want to dial in your detection and take advantage of all the flexibility that Firepower has to offer, custom analysis policy rules are one way to do this.

Files and Malware Settings

The Files and Malware Settings section allows you to tweak the behavior of your Advanced Malware Protection (AMP) and file detection. Most of the settings here are designed to balance performance and detection. Be very careful, especially when it comes to increasing these values. They were set by folks who know an awful lot about how malware behaves and how to squeeze the most performance out of the system while still providing the maximum detection possible.

The Files and Malware Settings dialog is shown in Figure 14.22.

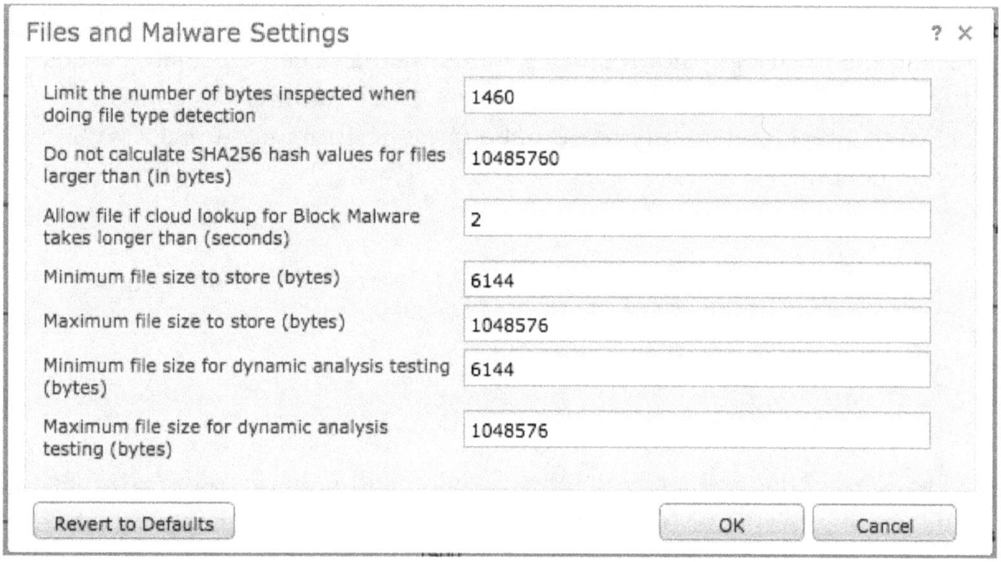

Files and Malware Settings	? ✕
Limit the number of bytes inspected when doing file type detection	1460
Do not calculate SHA256 hash values for files larger than (in bytes)	10485760
Allow file if cloud lookup for Block Malware takes longer than (seconds)	2
Minimum file size to store (bytes)	6144
Maximum file size to store (bytes)	1048576
Minimum file size for dynamic analysis testing (bytes)	6144
Maximum file size for dynamic analysis testing (bytes)	1048576
Revert to Defaults	OK Cancel

Figure 14.22: Files and Malware Settings dialog

Limit the number of bytes inspected when doing file type detection

Default: 1460 bytes

Range: 0–4294967295 (4 GB)

When performing file type detection Firepower looks for a signature near the beginning of the file. For example, a GIF file will always begin with the string "GIF8." Other file types, such as EXE or PDF, also have similar telltale strings or byte patterns. This setting limits how many bytes will be inspected to make this determination. The default size of 1460 is equivalent to the data segment of a typical Ethernet TCP packet. A value of zero removes the restriction altogether.

Do not calculate SHA256 hash values for files larger than (in bytes)

Default: 10485760 (10 MB)

Range: 0–4294967295 (4 GB)

This setting will prevent the system from storing, performing malware cloud lookup for, or blocking files larger than this size. This value must be greater than or equal to the settings for "Maximum file size to store (bytes)" and "Maximum file size for dynamic analysis testing (bytes)." Setting this value to zero will remove this size restriction.

At first this may look like a good number to increase. After all, it seems like we are allowing malware larger than 10 MB to traverse our network. Isn't this opening up a hole in our detection? Well, the answer is yes and no. Yes, this does mean we do not do malware lookup on files larger than 10 MB. However, it turns out that 99.9% of all malware is under 10 MB. This helps preserve the detection resources of the devices by not requiring them to collect and calculate hashes for large files. Statistically, these large files are extremely unlikely to contain malware, so it would potentially represent a large performance impact with virtually no benefit.

Allow file if cloud lookup for Block Malware takes longer than (seconds)

Default: 2 seconds

Range: 0–30 seconds

This setting determines how long a device will hold on to the last piece of a file while waiting for the FMC to perform a malware cloud lookup on the SHA-256. This setting prevents a large delay in a file transfer in case there is latency in performing the cloud lookup. If this time elapses with no response from the FMC, the device will allow the file transfer to complete and register a disposition of Unavailable for the file's status. As with most settings, Cisco recommends leaving this at the default.

Minimum file size to store (bytes)

Default: 6144 (6 KB)

Range: 0–10485760 (10 MB)

The minimum file size that can be stored using a file rule. A setting of zero disables file storage. Again, storing tiny files is a potential drain on system resources with dubious benefits. This field must be less than or equal to "Maximum file size to store (bytes)" and "Do not calculate SHA256 hash values for files larger than (bytes)."

Maximum file size to store (bytes)

Default: 1048576 (1 MB)

Range: 0–10485760 (10 MB)

The maximum file size that can be stored using a file rule. A setting of zero disables file storage. Must be greater than or equal to "Minimum file size to store (bytes)" and less than or equal to "Do not calculate SHA256 hash values for files larger than (bytes)."

Minimum file size for dynamic analysis testing (bytes)

Default: 6144 (6 KB)

Range: 6144 (6 KB) – 2097152 (2 MB)

The minimum file size the system will submit to the cloud for dynamic analysis. This field must be less than or equal to "Maximum file size for dynamic analysis testing (bytes)" and "Do not calculate SHA256 hash values for files larger than (in bytes)."

Maximum file size for dynamic analysis testing (bytes)

Default: 1048576 (1 MB)

Range: 6144 (6 KB) – 2097152 (2 MB)

The maximum file size the system will submit to the cloud for dynamic analysis. This field must be greater than or equal to "Minimum file size for dynamic analysis testing (bytes)" and less than or equal to "Do not calculate SHA256 hash values for files larger than (in bytes)."

Intelligent Application Bypass Settings

Intelligent Application Bypass (IAB) is a cool new-ish feature in Firepower. It was first introduced in version 6.0. It allows the system to automatically bypass or trust traffic flows based on criteria you set. The idea is that large flows such as a nightly backup can cause excessive utilization and increase packet latency through the device. This will not only affect the backup, but other traffic can also be impacted. It would be better not to inspect these backups since there is no security value in doing so anyway.

You can trust these flows with explicit trust rules or you can do it automatically using IAB. Even if you do add manual trust rules, IAB can help by automatically trusting other flows you may not have anticipated. Figure 14.23 shows the available IAB settings.

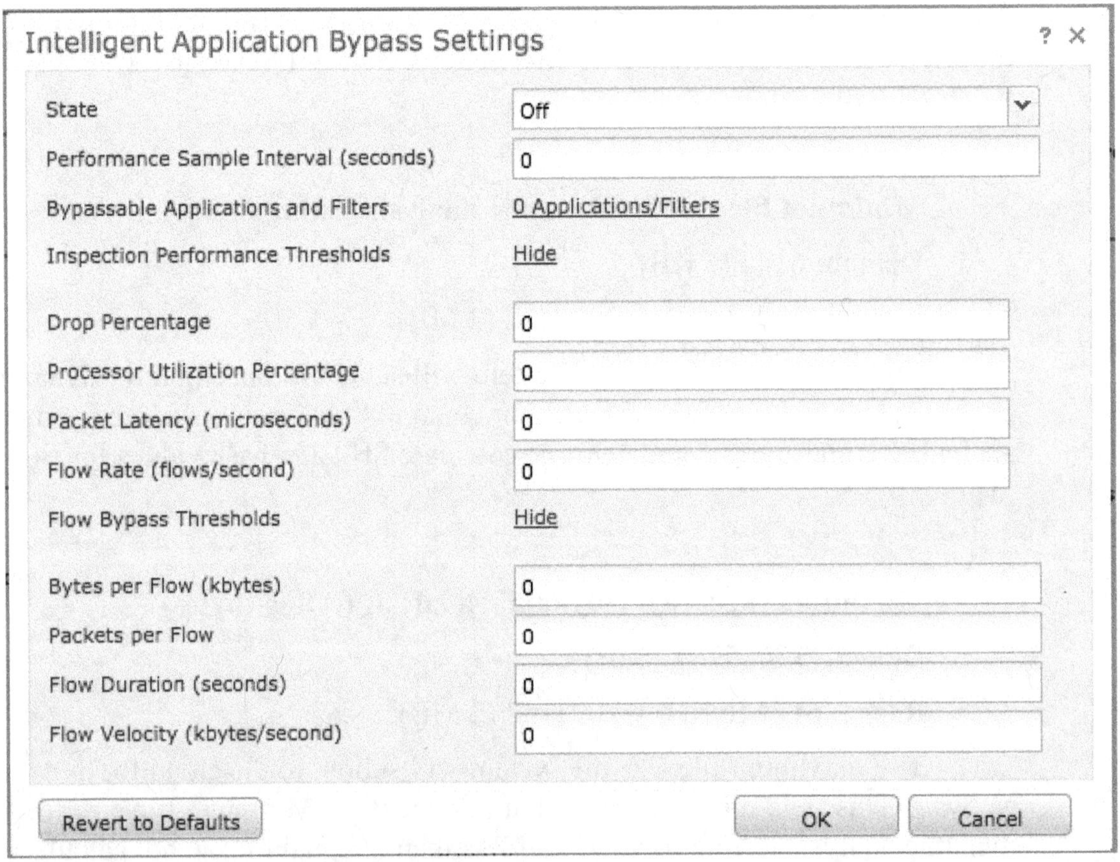

Intelligent Application Bypass Settings	? ✕
State	Off
Performance Sample Interval (seconds)	0
Bypassable Applications and Filters	0 Applications/Filters
Inspection Performance Thresholds	Hide
Drop Percentage	0
Processor Utilization Percentage	0
Packet Latency (microseconds)	0
Flow Rate (flows/second)	0
Flow Bypass Thresholds	Hide
Bytes per Flow (kbytes)	0
Packets per Flow	0
Flow Duration (seconds)	0
Flow Velocity (kbytes/second)	0

Revert to Defaults   OK   Cancel

Figure 14.23: Intelligent Application Bypass settings

To use IAB, first set the **State** option to Test or On. Then select a non-zero **Performance Sample Interval (seconds)** value. After this, click the link next to **Bypassable Applications and Filters** and add the applications you want to be eligible for bypass. Then, adjust the **Inspection Performance Thresholds** and **Flow Bypass Thresholds** settings. You must set at least one condition in each of these two categories. Both conditions must be exceeded for bypass to kick in on a given flow.

It is a very good idea to start in Test mode. In this mode, no traffic will be bypassed but connection events will indicate any flows that would have been bypassed using the current settings. You should confirm that these flows *should* have been bypassed prior to enabling this feature.

Transport/Network Layer Preprocessor Settings

These settings control some seldom-used behaviors of Snort's transport/network layer preprocessor (stream5). Figure 14.24 shows the Transport/Network Layer Preprocessor settings. The first check box is **Ignore the VLAN header when tracking connections**. Check this if your device might process packets that are part of the same TCP connection but have different VLAN tags. This would be an unusual occurrence, but if you don't check this, these connections would not be correctly reassembled.

The next two items have to do with Snort's active response capability. The **Maximum Active Responses** setting limits the number of responses Snort will generate for a specific connection. **Minimum Response Seconds** determines the minimum number of seconds to wait before initiating subsequent active responses for a connection. There are two situations that are being addressed here.

The first is drop rules. When deployed inline (including switched or routed), Snort will actively terminate a connection in the case where a drop rule matches a packet. It does this by silently dropping the offending packet and then continuing to drop subsequent packets in that same connection by sending a RST.

The second is Snort rules written with the **resp** or **react** keywords. These keywords can be used in rules to tell Snort to take an active role in terminating the connection. It does this by sending a TCP RST or ICMP port unreachable (type 3) packet to the source host. Rules with either of these keywords will reset the connection regardless of the settings selected here. However, these settings determine whether Snort continues to initiate additional active responses like it does for drop rules.

If you want to disable Snorts active responses altogether, enter a zero in the **Maximum Active Responses** field. This will cause drop rules to silently drop only the offending packets that they match. It will also disable active responses for the **resp** and **react** keywords.

Note that the active response settings do not apply to ASA with FirePOWER Services modules.

Do not attempt to make adjustments to the Troubleshooting Options. These settings should only be changed when advised by Cisco TAC.

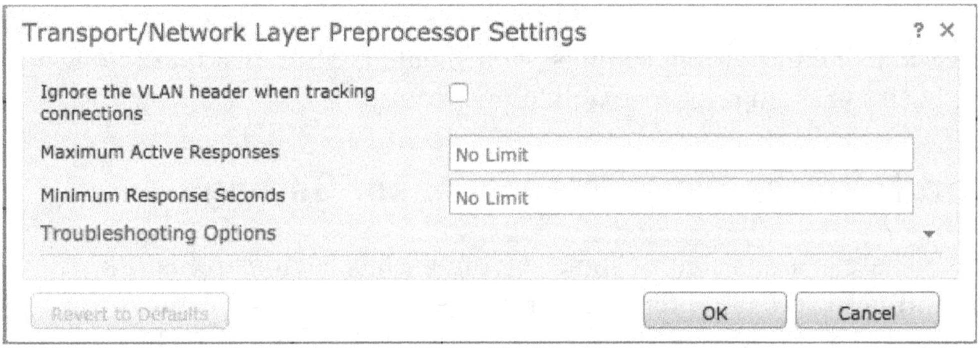

Transport/Network Layer Preprocessor Settings ? ×

Ignore the VLAN header when tracking connections ☐

Maximum Active Responses — No Limit

Minimum Response Seconds — No Limit

Troubleshooting Options ▼

Revert to Defaults | OK | Cancel

Figure 14.24: Transport/Network Layer Preprocessor Settings dialog box

Detection Enhancement Settings

Detection Enhancement Settings has been updated a bit for version 6.1. Previously, this setting was only used to enable adaptive profiles and set the update interval. The default was to disable adaptive profiles. With 6.1, we now have an Enable and an Enable Profile Updates check box. The former is enabled by default and the latter is disabled. What does it all mean? See Figure 14.25 for an example of the Detection Enhancements Settings dialog.

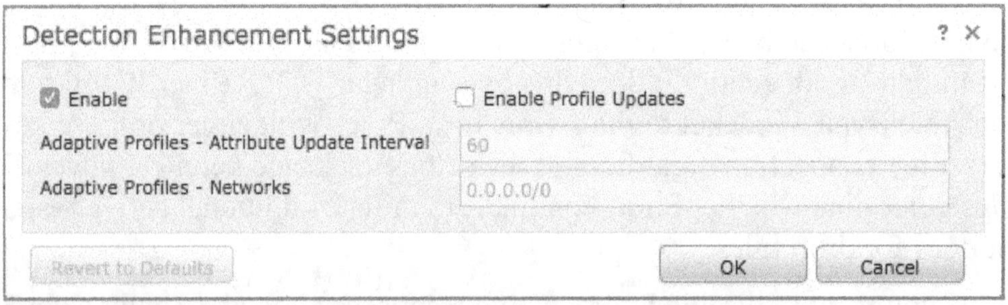

Detection Enhancement Settings ? ×

☑ Enable ☐ Enable Profile Updates

Adaptive Profiles - Attribute Update Interval — 60

Adaptive Profiles - Networks — 0.0.0.0/0

Revert to Defaults | OK | Cancel

Figure 14.25: Detection Enhancement Settings dialog

First, let's discuss the classic definition of adaptive profiles in Firepower. The purpose is to allow the device to "adapt" its traffic processing based on the various packet reassembly behaviors of different operating systems. Different operating systems perform both TCP and IP fragment reassembly differently. This is especially true when there are overlapping data offsets in the packets. Never mind that this should never happen; the fact that it can happen opens the possibility that an attacker could evade detection by fooling the IPS into reassembling packets incorrectly. If you are curious how this works, you can check out the 1998 paper by Thomas Ptacek and Timothy Newsham called "Insertion, Evasion, and Denial of Service: Eluding Network Intrusion Detection". To see how this is implemented in Snort, you can read "Target-Based Fragmentation Reassembly," written in 2005 by Judy Novak (both of these papers can be found online by searching for their titles).

The bottom line is, if we know the operating system that is performing the reassembly, we can predict what the resulting data will be. The Adaptive Profiles feature allows Firepower to do this. Because Firepower passively builds a host database, it presumably knows the operating systems of all the hosts in the protected network. This information is saved on the FMC. By enabling Adaptive Profiles and sending periodic updates to the managed devices, Snort can leverage this intelligence when performing packet and stream reassembly.

So, in previous versions of Firepower, we only enabled Adaptive Profiles if we had passive devices. When the devices are inline, the inline normalization preprocessor handles this without being updated with information from the FMC's host database.

In version 6.1, we have a new **Enable** check box, which is checked by default. What does this mean? This box must remain checked for access control rules to perform application and file control, including AMP, and for Snort rules to use service metadata. In short, this box is huge! *Unchecking it turns off most of the valuable features you bought Firepower for in the first place*—don't do it. would you want to disable this? Perhaps if your system is deployed in a very limited environment with no application control, no AMP, and you don't use any of the most well-known protocols like HTTP, FTP, and SMTP, then yes, and maybe I'm a Chinese jet pilot!

You still have the **Enable Profile Updates** option if your policy is deployed to passive devices. You can also set **Adaptive Profiles – Attribute Update Interval** if desired. This is the interval (in minutes) at which the FMC updates the managed device with new profile data from the host database. To be more efficient, you should also use the **Adaptive Profiles – Networks** setting to define a subnet range or variable where the protected hosts are for this device. Otherwise, information on all the hosts in the database will be pushed to the target device or devices.

Performance Settings

Okay, we have to draw the line somewhere. These performance settings (Figure 14.26) are something that users should simply not adjust. If you are dying to know what these settings do, please consult the online help. Just be aware that changing parameters in areas such as regular expression or pattern matching limits can create detection issues that are extremely difficult to troubleshoot. Enough said!

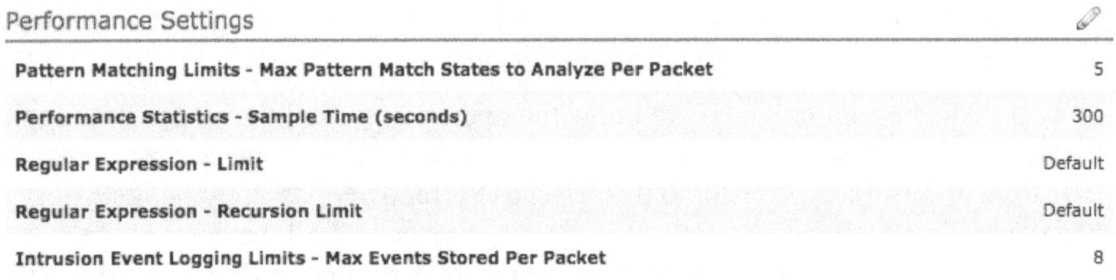

Performance Settings	
Pattern Matching Limits - Max Pattern Match States to Analyze Per Packet	5
Performance Statistics - Sample Time (seconds)	300
Regular Expression - Limit	Default
Regular Expression - Recursion Limit	Default
Intrusion Event Logging Limits - Max Events Stored Per Packet	8

Figure 14.26: Performance Settings options

Latency-Based Performance Settings

Latency-Based Performance Settings control Snort's behavior in cases where packet processing is slowing down. These settings determine how Snort behaves when there is some problem causing packets to move through the inspection process too slowly. There are two tabs available: Packet Handling, shown later in Figure 14.28, and Rule Handling, shown in Figure 14.29.

Latency-Based Packet Handling

The Packet Handling tab controls the per-packet latency threshold. Each packet is timed as it is processed through Snort's preprocessors and intrusion rules. The timer starts at zero and is checked at various points throughout the inspection process. If at any time the latency number exceeds the microsecond setting here, the packet is released to exit the device.

The purpose of this setting is to reduce or prevent negative impact on applications. The default setting is 256 microseconds and, according to the

Firepower help, equates to a traffic flow of about 100 Mbps. Table 14.1 shows the recommended minimum packet latency settings.

Data Rate	Microsecond Threshold
1 Gbps	100
100 Mbps	250
5 Mbps	1000

Table 14.1: Recommended minimum packet latency

By default, packets that exceed this threshold pass out of the device without generating any alerts. Hearing for the first time that you may have packets slipping through your devices can be a bit unnerving. However, there is something you can do to know for sure.

To view alerts for packets triggering the packet latency threshold, enable Snort rule 134:3. The easiest way to find this is to go to your Intrusion policy and search for "GID:134" in your rule filter bar. This is shown in Figure 14.27. Set the rule state for 134:3 to Generate Events and stand back. We say this because if you have a lot of traffic and you are hitting this threshold repeatedly, you may see a large number of events generated from this rule. Be ready to disable it if it sends your event analysis group into a tizzy!

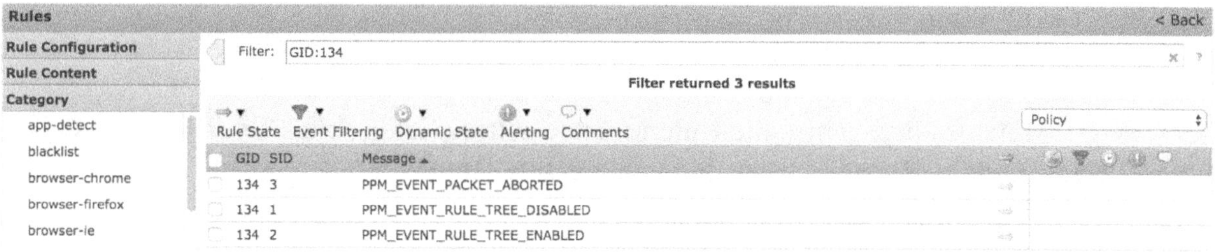

Figure 14.27: Searching for GID:134 rules

We have found that the default tends to favor application performance. This means when utilization spikes and latency numbers climb, there will likely be some packets that are not fully inspected as they pass through the device. Because of this, you may find yourself raising the default number, which will potentially increase packet latency but also reduce the number of packets that exit the device prematurely.

The idea is to adjust this number through trial and error until you arrive at a happy medium where you obtain maximum traffic visibility with minimal (or no) impact on applications. Unless your devices are woefully underpowered, you should be able to perform 100% inspection with no application impact.

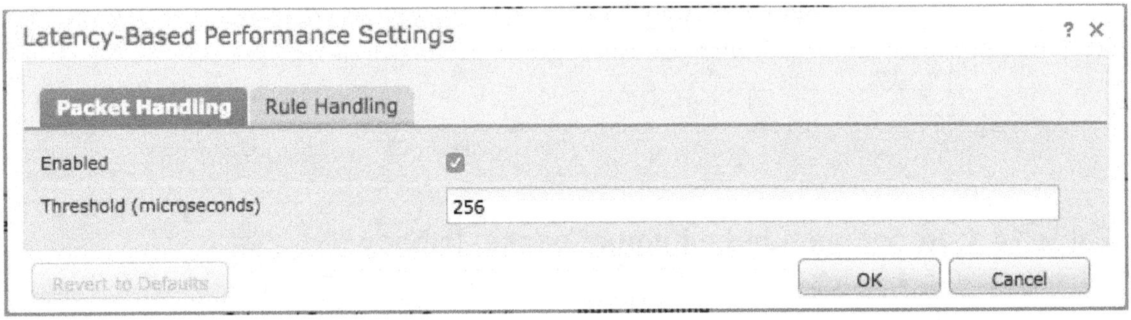

Latency-Based Performance Settings   ? ×

Packet Handling   Rule Handling

Enabled   ☑
Threshold (microseconds)   256

Revert to Defaults   OK   Cancel

Figure 14.28: Packet Handling parameters

Latency-Based Rule Handling

The Rule Handling tab controls Snorts behavior when there are specific rule groups that are introducing excessive latency. Figure 14.29 shows the options available here.

Like Packet Handling, this setting is designed to prevent Snort from causing application impact due to poor performance. In this case, we are zeroing in on poor performing rules. There are four parameters that can be configured here.

Enabled

Default: On

Enables or disables the Rule Latency setting. If disabled, Snort will never disable poor-performing rules due to excessive latency.

Threshold (microseconds)

Default: 512

The default microsecond threshold allowed for a rule group to process a single packet. Exceeding this threshold will increment the violation count for the group.

Consecutive Threshold Violations Before Suspending Rule

Default: 3

The number of consecutive threshold violations before the rule group is automatically disabled.

Suspension Time

Default: 10 seconds

The number of seconds a rule group will be disabled if the consecutive violation threshold is met.

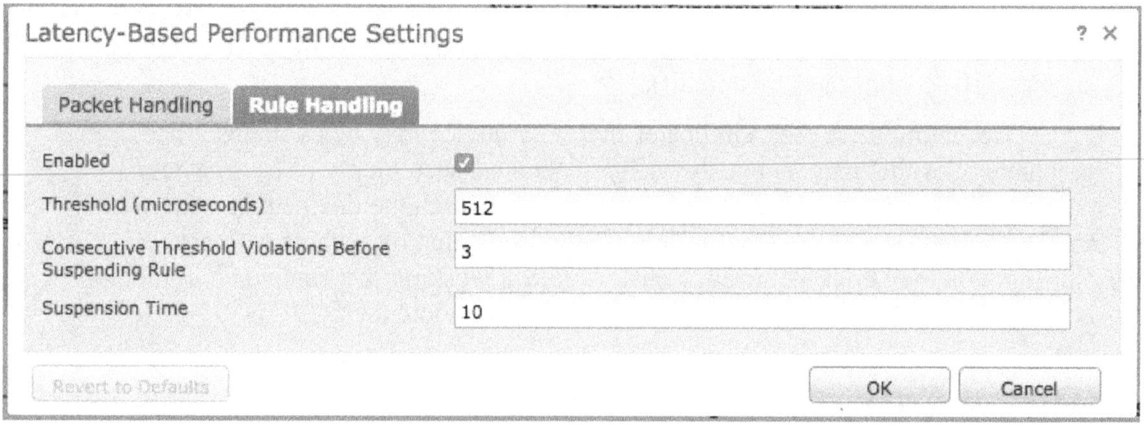

Latency-Based Performance Settings ? ✕

| Packet Handling | **Rule Handling** |

Enabled	☑
Threshold (microseconds)	512
Consecutive Threshold Violations Before Suspending Rule	3
Suspension Time	10

Revert to Defaults   OK   Cancel

Figure 14.29: Rule Handling parameters

The documentation for this setting speaks of "rule groups." What are these groups they speak of? When Snort first starts up, it builds decision trees from the rule set. The purpose of these trees is to leverage the fact that many rules look for similar packet conditions. For example, if a number of rules are looking for the same content, it would be inefficient to continually check for this content as Snort evaluates rules against a given packet. By grouping similar rules together, Snort can inspect more efficiently by qualifying or eliminating a number of rules with a single content check. To accomplish this, Snort builds rule trees or groups with similar rules grouped together for inspection. This process is completely transparent and occurs in the Snort start-up process, which typically lasts just a few seconds. A thorough understanding of this rule grouping behavior is beyond the scope of this discussion. However, understanding this can be very valuable for rule writers who want to create more efficient Snort rules.

During packet inspection, if a rule group exceeds the rule handling latency threshold, the violation counter for that group is incremented. If the violation count meets the consecutive violations number, the rule group is temporarily disabled. This means packets are not inspected by this group. At the end of the time specified in the Suspension Time setting (in seconds), the rule group is re-enabled.

For a rule group to be disabled, the violations must be consecutive. Any packets inspected by the rule group that do not exceed the threshold will reset the violation counter to zero. This means a stray packet or two that exceed the threshold will not trigger any change in Snort's inspection.

Like packet latency, the default setting is silence if a rule group is disabled. To enable event logging for this setting, you should enable events 134:1 and 134:2 using the technique mentioned previously. The 134:1 intrusion event will trigger when a rule group is disabled, and 134:2 will trigger when the rule group is re-enabled (10 seconds later by default).

Receiving these alerts indicates that your device may be oversubscribed or you have rules that may be poorly written. We have seen plenty of cases where poorly written rules are repeatedly disabled even though the device may otherwise be functioning smoothly. Because this setting is enabled by default with no alerting, you may think your fancy custom rule is working just fine when in fact it is being disabled nearly 100% of the time due to high latency!

The Rules Tab

If Firepower has one location that could be considered the heart of the system, that location is the Access Control Rules tab (Figure 14.30). This is the central rule set determining what happens to traffic as it is processed through the devices.

Figure 14.30: Rules tab

Rule Categories

Access control rules are evaluated from top to bottom. By default, there are two rule categories—Mandatory and Default. These can be used to group similar types of rules together. Additional categories can be added by clicking the Add Category button. For example, you may have a Trust category that you place near the beginning of your rule set. The Add Category dialog is shown in Figure 14.31.

Adding additional categories may be helpful for organizing rules. Keep in mind, however, that the category has nothing to do with the order rules are processed. Traffic is always processed from top to bottom regardless of whether you use multiple categories or place all you rules into a single category. When adding a custom category, you have the option to select the existing category where it will be inserted. Choose carefully—while you can reorder individual rules, you cannot reorder categories.

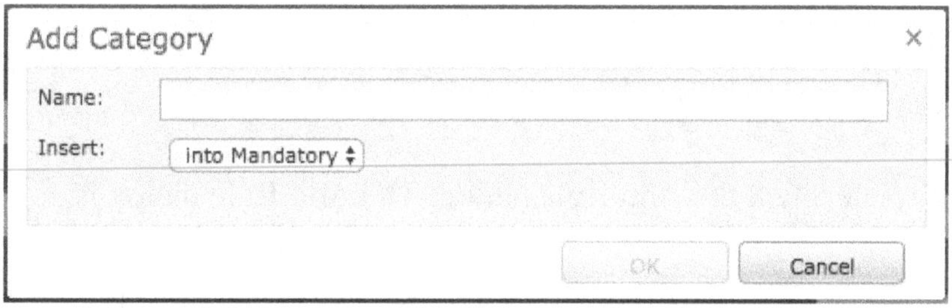

Figure 14.31: Add Category dialog

Figure 14.30 is an example of a child policy that is inheriting settings from a base policy named Base Policy. Any rules in the base policy are added to Mandatory and Base categories at the beginning and end of the child policy. The effect is to give the base policy the first and last word when it comes to rules. Clicking the white triangle icon next to the category name will expand or collapse the rule listing in that category.

Default Action

The Default Action is the action that the device takes if none of the access control rules match a given traffic flow. Clicking the drop-down field displays the available actions:

- Inherit from base policy: This option only appears if this is a child policy. The default action becomes whatever is configured in the base or master policy.

- Access Control: Block All Traffic: Simply stated, if traffic makes it this far, we block it. This is typical for a device deployed as a firewall.

- Access Control: Trust All Traffic: If traffic makes it this far, we let it pass through the device with no further inspection performed.

- Network Discovery Only: Traffic is inspected via the Network Discovery policy only.

- Intrusion Prevention: Allow the traffic but first inspect it with Intrusion and Network Discovery policies. All of the Cisco-provided and user-created policies are listed here. Depending on the Intrusion policy, some traffic could still be dropped if it matches a Snort rule with the "Drop and generate" action.

It's worth noting that you cannot perform file and malware inspection with the default action. This has to be performed in an access control rule.

Rules

To add a new rule, click the Add Rule button. The Add Rule dialog is shown in Figure 14.32.

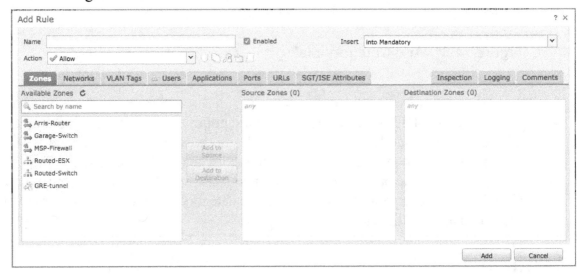

Figure 14.32: Add Rule dialog

Name

Your rule deserves a name but keep it succinct. You only get 30 characters here! The name field will turn red if you enter too many characters.

Enabled

New rules are enabled by default. Unchecking this box will leave the rule in its current location but it will not process traffic.

Insert

Select the category or position of the rule here. If this is the first rule, you will only have category choices. If there are other rules in your policy already, you can also insert your rule above or below an existing rule number.

Rule Actions

Allow

Use this action for AMP or Snort inspection. Traffic matching Allow rules is allowed to pass through the device after being inspected by the appropriate policies. You can inspect this traffic using an Intrusion policy, a File policy, or both. Depending on the rules in these policies, traffic could be blocked. You can technically use an Allow rule with no inspection, but this makes little sense— that's what a Trust rule is for.

Trust

The Trust action allows traffic to pass through the rule set unmolested. It is typically used for network communications you don't want to inspect because of an impact to either the device or the application. Trust rules are typically inserted early in the rule set.

Monitor

This is the only action that does not affect traffic flow. The only purpose of a Monitor rule is to log a connection event. Traffic matching a Monitor rule continues to be processed by subsequent rules. You may decide to insert a Monitor rule early in the rule set to ensure connection events are generated. This prevents the need to remember to check the logging option for some of your other rules.

Block and Block with Reset

These two actions deny traffic without further inspection. The Block action simply stops the traffic from passing while Block with Reset also resets the connection. Blocked traffic is not inspected by Intrusion, File, or Discovery policies. Note that even if you have a Monitor rule upstream, you will probably still want to enable logging for this rule type.

Interactive Block and Interactive Block with Reset

In the case of HTTP traffic, these actions allow users to bypass a website block by clicking through a warning page. If the user elects not to bypass the block, the rule functions like a Block rule in that traffic is denied without further inspection. However, if a user does bypass the block, then the rule functions like an Allow rule and can perform intrusion, file, and discovery inspection. These rules can be associated with Intrusion and File policies in the same manner as Allow rules. For non-HTTP traffic, these rules function just like a Block or Block with Reset rule.

Rule Criteria

The group of eight tabs to the left of the dialog is used to determine the criteria for matching traffic. By default, all of the tabs are empty, meaning your rule will match all traffic.

Zones

The Zones tab, shown in Figure 14.33, allows you to select the source or destination zone or tunnel tag. This is helpful when your rule is designed for traffic to or from a certain interface or tunneled traffic type. Select the applicable zone or zones and use the Add to Source or Add to Destination button as appropriate.

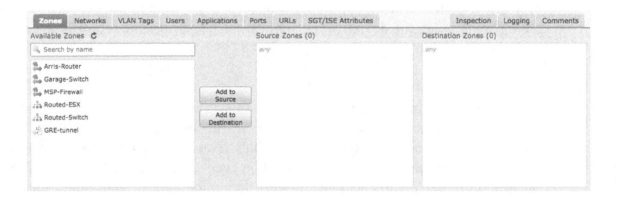

Figure 14.33: Zones tab

Networks

The Networks tab, in Figure 14.34, offers several options. First, you can select an existing network object from the left and add that to the source or destination networks column. You can also enter an IP address or netmask manually below either the source or destination column. If you want to add a new network object from here, use the green plus icon (⊙) to add an object on the fly. After you do so, the object will appear in the Networks column.

The Geolocation sub-tab provides access to all available locations as well as any Geolocation objects you have created. This can be used instead of or in addition to the other network criteria.

There is also a very cool sub-tab in the Source Networks column. The default setting of Source simply matches the IP address of the packet's source IP field in the header. However, the Original Client tab allows matching on the original client IP address. This applies to HTTP traffic only and equates to the X-

Forwarded-For, True-Client-IP, or other HTTP header fields as configured in the Network Analysis policy HTTP Configuration settings. This means if your device is positioned outside your outbound web proxy, you can still take action on traffic based on the IP address of your internal hosts.

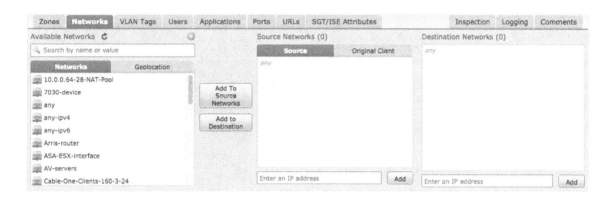

Figure 14.34: Networks tab

VLAN Tags

VLAN Tags allows you to specify a number from 0 to 4094 to identify a network by VLAN. You can use objects you have created, add on the fly using the green plus icon, or enter VLAN numbers directly below the Selected VLAN Tags column. See Figure 14.35.

Figure 14.35: VLAN Tags tab

Users

This tab, shown in Figure 14.36, allows you to specify the users your rule should apply to. These users and groups are retrieved from a Microsoft Active

Directory server. Before you can use this condition, you must configure an Identity policy and it must be selected using the Identity Policy link near the upper right of the main Access Control policy screen.

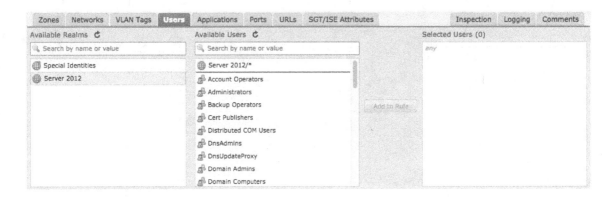

Figure 14.36: Users tab

Applications

The Applications tab (Figure 14.37) allows filtering your rule based on built-in applications, user-defined applications, and application filter objects you have created. You will find the same application criteria (Risks, Business Relevance, Types, etc.) available here as you saw under Application Filters on the Object Management page (Chapter 6). You will also see any user-created filters previously added.

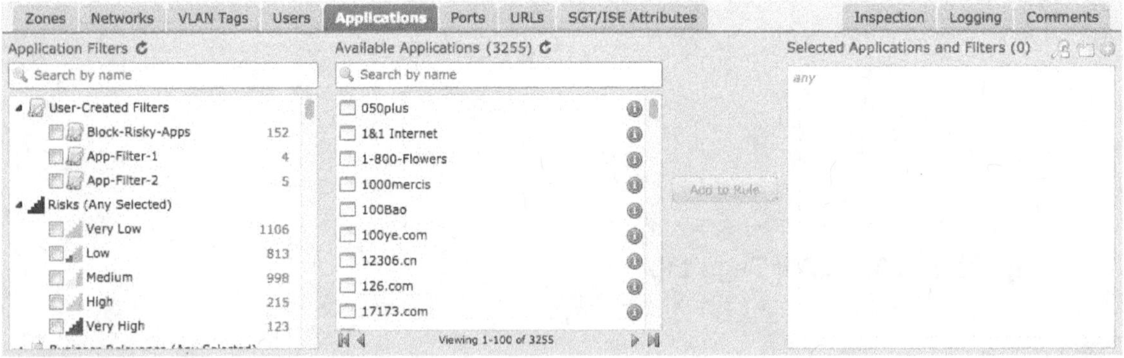

Figure 14.37: Applications tab

In the upper right corner of Figure 14.37 there are two icons that control the Safe Search and YouTube EDU settings. These icons are only clickable for rules with the Allow action. They are visible but disabled for other rule actions.

Safe Search

Safe Search is supported by major search engines. It involves filtering out explicit and adult-oriented content that businesses and education environments may find objectionable. The way this works is by communicating the restricted status to the search engine via the request URI, cookie, or a custom HTTP header element. When you configure this in an AC Allow rule, Firepower makes the appropriate modifications to traffic matching the rule.

Clicking Safe Search icon ( ) displays the dialog shown in Figure 14.38.

Figure 14.38: Safe Search dialog

Once you enable safe search you must choose an action for traffic to non-supported search engines. If you choose Block or Block with Reset, you must also configure the HTTP response page that the system displays when blocking restricted content.

Notice also that there are specific application tags for search engines that do or do not support Safe Search. To find these, look under the Application Filters column, expand the Tags category, and look for "safesearch supported" or "safesearch unsupported." These settings can be used in conjunction with the Safe Search option to tailor the system to your requirements.

YouTube EDU

The YouTube EDU service filters YouTube content for an educational environment. This is different than YouTube Restricted Mode, which is a subset of Google's Safe Search feature. When using YouTube EDU, users access the YouTube EDU home page rather than the standard YouTube home page. To use this feature, you must enter a custom ID that uniquely identifies a school or district network. This ID is provided by YouTube when the school registers for a YouTube EDU account. Note that if you configure both Safe Search and YouTube EDU, you should place the YouTube EDU rules higher in your policy to avoid preemption.

Clicking the YouTube EDU icon (⬜) displays the dialog shown in Figure 14.39. Once you check the Enable check box, you must then enter the custom ID for the school or district.

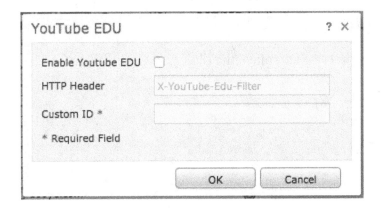

Figure 14.39: YouTube EDU dialog

Ports

The Ports tab is shown in Figure 14.40. This is fairly straightforward and allows selecting source or destination ports for your rule.

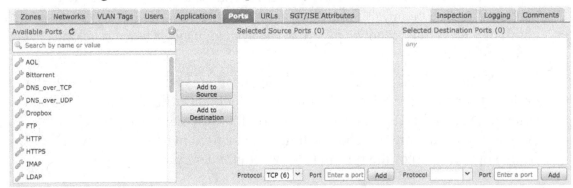

Figure 14.40: Ports tab

Port selection works just as you would expect. You will notice the source ports are limited to UDP and TCP, while destination ports include all of the IP protocol ID numbers. This is not a limitation so much, just the way IP protocols work. These other protocols do not have port numbers, so if you select one of them the destination port field is grayed out. Selecting ICMP (Internet Control Messaging Protocol) will display an additional dialog allowing you to select the Type and Code fields in the ICMP packets.

URLs

The URLs tab allows filtering based on Cisco-provided categories and reputations as well as user-created URL objects. There are two sub-tabs, one for Category and the other for URLs. The Category tab will only be populated if you have purchased and installed the URL filtering license. Reputations are only available when selecting URL categories. This column is grayed out when the URLs sub-tab is selected.

The URLs sub-tab allows using a previously created URL object, or you can enter a URL in the field at the bottom of the Selected URLs column. Remember that URLs you enter are treated as a substring match. If the text you enter is found *anywhere* in the URL, the rule will match. The URLs tab is shown in Figure 14.41.

Figure 14.41: URLs tab

SGT/ISE Attributes

The SGT/ISE tab provides a method to match traffic based on Security Group Tags (SGTs) or through the Cisco Identity Services Engine (ISE). If you have an ISE server configured, the Available Metadata column is populated by querying ISE for available tags.

If you do not have an ISE server configured, you can create custom SGT objects and use them as conditions on this tab.

The SGT/ISE tab is shown in Figure 14.42.

Figure 14.42: SGT/ISE tab

Inspection, Logging, Comments

The three tabs to the right side of the Add Rule dialog do not impact which traffic a rule will match. You could call them additional rule settings.

Inspection

The Inspection tab controls intrusion and file inspection for rules that provide this capability. You will notice that all the options on this tab are unavailable (grayed out) for the rule actions of Trust, Monitor, Block, and Block with Reset. This is because these rules do not allow for Intrusion or File policy inspection of traffic. Figure 14.43 shows the Inspection tab dialog.

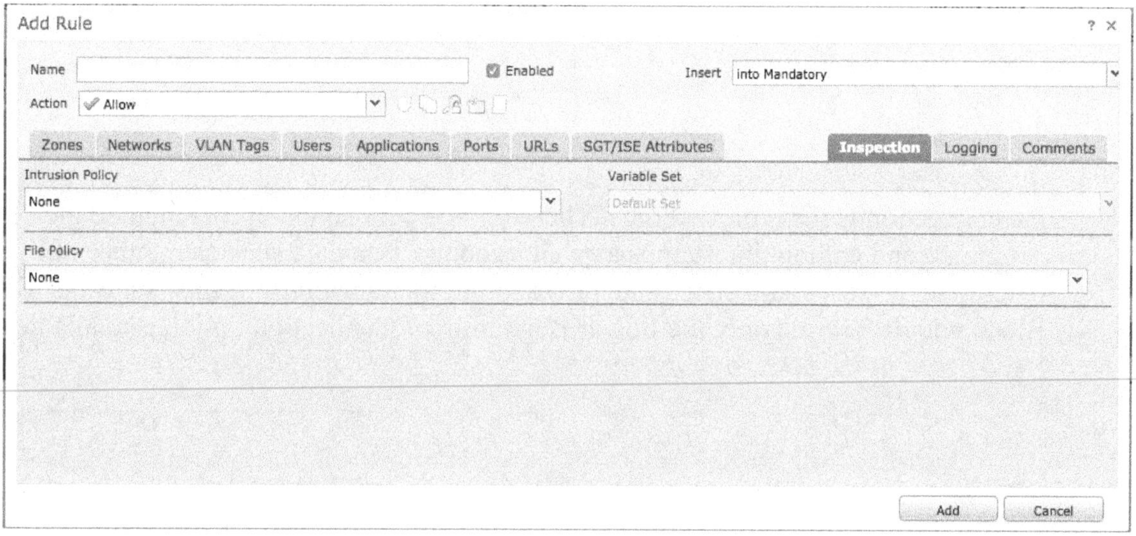

Figure 14.43: Inspection tab

Use the drop-down fields to specify the Intrusion Policy, Variable Set, and File Policy settings used to inspect this traffic. Selecting a File policy automatically enables and selects the File Events check box on the Logging tab. It's important to note that if you want to perform intrusion and file inspection on a given traffic flow, you must enable both of these options in a single rule. You cannot perform intrusion inspection in one rule and file inspection in another because the second rule will be preempted by the first one.

Logging

The Logging tab, shown in Figure 14.44, controls the logging of connection and file events for the rule. Note that this tab does not impact the logging of Intrusion or Malware events. These events are generated based on settings in the Intrusion and File policies respectively. Simply stated, a connection event records information about a network connection and a file event records information about a file transfer. Connection events are generated by traffic matching AC rules with the log option enabled, including Monitor rules. File events will be generated by file transfers matching File policy rules that have the Detect Files action configured.

There are two options for connection logging, you can log at the beginning or end of the connection. You could also check both boxes and receive events at the beginning and end of the connection but the use cases for this are limited and mainly involve troubleshooting connection logging issues. Logging at the end of the connection is the typical choice. These end-of-connection events include the beginning and ending timestamps as well as connection data such as number of bytes, packets, protocol, URL, and a myriad of other attributes. If this is a Block or Block with Reset rule only the Log at Beginning of Connection option is available.

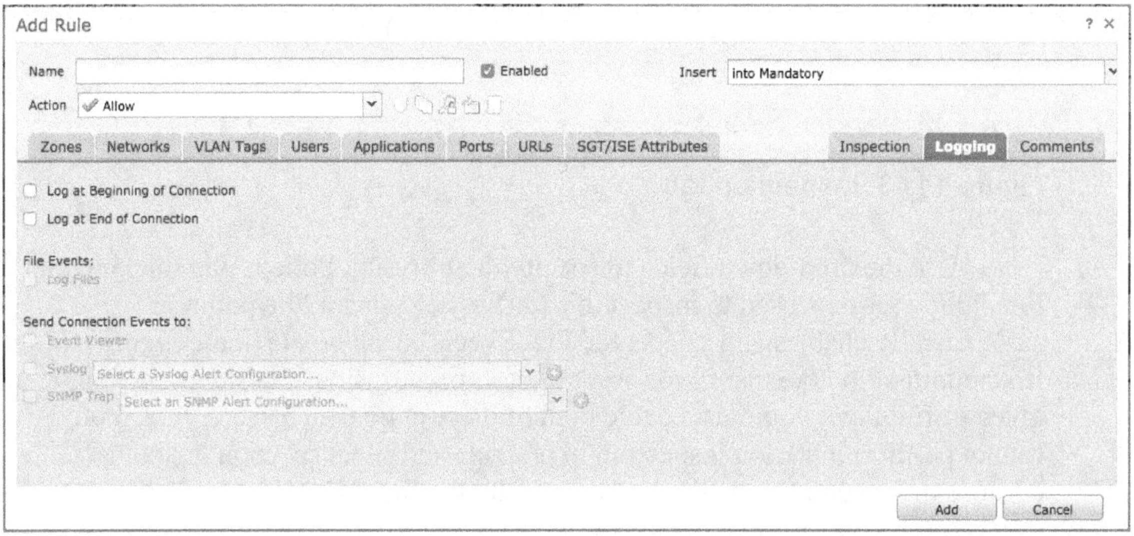

Figure 14.44: Logging tab

<u>**Comments**</u>

The Comments tab displays existing comments and allows adding new comments to the rule. Clicking the New Comment button displays a dialog where free-form text comments can be entered. The User and Date fields are automatically populated. After a comment is entered, you can delete or modify it only until the rule is saved. After that, comments can only be viewed and not modified or deleted. The comments tab is shown in Figure 14.45.

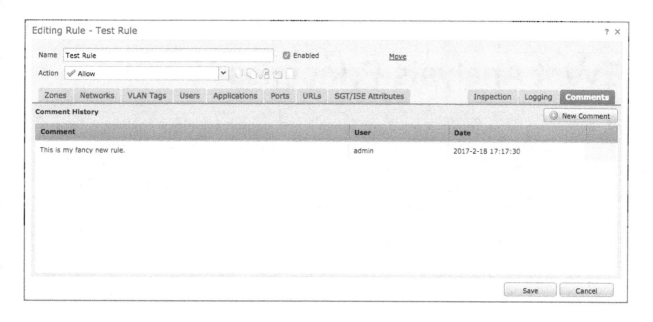

Figure 14.45: Comments tab

Chapter 15: Event Analysis

In this chapter, we will discuss the art and science of Firepower event analysis. Unlike most of the previous chapters, this is not focused on configuration but on interpreting the output of the system.

Once Firepower is up and running smoothly, analyzing the events it generates will be a key task. Event analysis is basically looking at the events that the system is generating and performing some action in response.

The actions range from incident response (circle the wagons) to tuning false positive events. We will cover intrusion, security intelligence, and file/malware events.

Event Analysis Principles

Since intrusion events provide the most complex analysis challenge, let's discuss some principles for analyzing this type of event. Firepower has several features to help analysts locate the most critical events and tune out the noisy ones. Over the years, updates to Snort as well as improvements in rule keywords and preprocessor configurations have helped to reduce some of this noise. However, depending on the rules enabled, each newly deployed intrusion prevention system (IPS) will probably require at least some rule tuning.

False Positives

When we refer to "tuning," what we primarily mean is noise reduction. In an IPS, "noise" is how we refer to events that trigger but are of no value. These are often referred to as false positives. A simple definition of a false positive would be an IPS rule alerting on traffic that it was not intended to detect, not that the rule is necessarily faulty or there is some problem with Snort itself. False positives are often simply the result of the sheer volume of packets which must be inspected. They may also be caused because the rule must account for any packets where the attack *might* be present.

For example, a rule looking for the string **cmd.exe** in an HTTP request is probably looking for some type of abuse on a Microsoft Windows host. Ancient versions of Microsoft Internet Information Services (IIS) had vulnerabilities where an attacker could actually execute commands through the web server by finding the path to the command processor. To protect against this, you could use a Snort rule, simply looking for **cmd.exe** in an HTTP request. Normally, this rule would not trigger on normal HTTP traffic but would detect someone trying to find the Windows command processor.

However, what if a website happened to host a graphic named **cmd.exe.gif**? This rule would alert and possibly block an HTTP request for the image. The alert in this case would be classified as a false positive. The rule did what it was designed to do. However, in this case, the **cmd.exe** was not a threat; it just happened to be part of the unfortunate name someone selected for an image file.

False Negatives

The opposite of a false positive is a false negative. This is defined as the failure of a rule to detect the attack it was designed to detect. While false positives are to be expected, false negatives are something to be avoided. The failure of a rule to detect an actual attack represents a failure of the IPS as a whole and is something rule writers do their best to avoid. Understanding this philosophy helps us understand why there are false positives.

In the previous example, we could have avoided the false positive for **cmd.exe.gif** by adding the path to **cmd.exe**. For example, we could have written the rule to look for **c:\winnt\system32\cmd.exe**. This would eliminate the false positive for the **cmd.exe.gif** file. However, what if the Windows host used **c:\Windows** for its system root? This means the path to **cmd.exe** would be **c:\Windows\system32\cmd.exe**. If our rule is too specific, all of a sudden we're faced with the potential for a false negative. As a result, while rules will be written to avoid as many false positives as possible, they are generally written to allow zero false negatives. The rule above would probably be written to look only for **cmd.exe**. Yes, there would be an occasional false positive, but we want to ensure zero false negatives.

While technically not a false negative, you can also miss attacks because a particular rule is not enabled. In our previous example, the rules to detect **cmd.exe** are in the Cisco Snort rule set, but if they are not enabled in the deployed intrusion policy, your IPS will not detect this attack. In this case, the reason these rules may not be enabled by default is because modern Windows systems are not vulnerable to this directory traversal attack. However, if your network is still living in 2001, you may need to turn on some of these older rules. Enabling the correct rules is not really a function of event analysis, but it still bears mentioning here.

Possible Outcomes

Of course, there are two other possibilities, a true positive and a true negative. The true positive is when a rule correctly triggers on the malicious activity it was designed for. A true negative is when rules correctly do not alert for benign traffic. The four possible results of traffic inspection are shown in the table below.

	Traffic is malicious	Traffic is benign
Rule matches traffic	True positive	False positive
Rule does not match traffic	False negative	True negative

Of all the possible results above, three of them are considered normal and acceptable in an IPS. The unacceptable one is the false negative, which represents a failure to detect an actual attack. As security professionals, we are willing to deal with some noise in our system tuning, but we always try to err on the side of detection versus non-detection.

A false negative isn't always the fault of the IPS rule set. The device must have visibility to all the traffic it is designed to inspect and it has to have the necessary processing resources to evaluate the traffic fully. Inadequate visibility or detection resources could also result in some traffic bypassing inspection, causing a false negative.

The Goal of Analysis

One might ask, "Why analyze?" After all, can't we just put our devices inline, load the appropriate rule sets, and trust the system to block the bad stuff? This is a good question and on the surface makes some sense. If the main job of the IPS is to stop attacks, can't it do that regardless of who is looking at the analysis screens?

Of course, placing inline IPS devices at strategic locations in your network will provide protection against attacks and possibly hinder the effectiveness of some malware; however, it is not the "silver bullet" to solve all your network security issues.

First of all, some devices could be deployed in passive mode, meaning all they can do is alert and not actually stop attacks. We need to follow up on the events generated by these devices to address possible issues. Analysis is key in these instances so we can prioritize our response and not spend excessive time on alerts that turn out to be false positives.

While inline devices have the power to stop attacks, they also have the potential to impact legitimate traffic if the alert is a false positive. Because of this, we need to analyze the output of these devices and quickly identify and remediate false positives to ensure minimal impact to the business. Again, analysis of events and the resultant rule tuning are critical aspects to this process.

Another very important principle to remember is that the defender has to deal with numerous attacks constantly occurring 24x7x365. The attacker only has to succeed once to compromise your network. Anyone who thinks that there is *any* security tool that can stop all attacks is not living in a little place we like to call *reality*. You *will* be compromised, it will happen more than once, it's probably happened already. It happened even though you may have the best IPS money could buy and tuned it perfectly.

The rant above started because we are talking about analysis. A key facet of analysis is understanding which systems on your network are already compromised. Firepower has some excellent capabilities centered around alerting you of hosts that are already likely compromised. The purpose of these rules is *not* to stop the malware that has already infected your systems. It is to alert you so you can take action to clean up these systems. Please take this to heart! We have seen numerous Firepower installations that are clearly indicating which hosts are regularly connecting to botnets or known malware sites yet there is no action taken to locate and remediate these systems. Don't be that guy/gal!

Intrusion Events

In the following sections, we will examine the mechanics of intrusion event analysis using workflows.

Workflows

Workflows are a key feature of Firepower when it comes to customizing your event views. You will find that most event types come with several built-in workflows that are designed to help analysts sift through and locate various events. A workflow determines how events are displayed, what columns are shown, and how they are sorted. Note that while the term *event* is the technically correct one, you may also hear them referred to as *alerts*. Basically, we mean the message logged when a rule triggers.

To navigate to the default intrusion event workflow on the FMC, go to Analysis → Intrusions → Events. The default workflow is called Events By Priority and Classification.

Intrusion event workflows are all table based—they are columns of (mostly) text data. In contrast, you will find that most of the built-in Connection Event workflows are bar, line, or pie graphs.

The different workflows help analysts highlight different types of events. For example, much of the time you may be looking for the intrusion events representing the most critical threats to your organization. However, sometimes you may want to find the events most likely to be false positives. Maybe you want to see events based on their source IP address. These are useful when you are looking for malware infections. Events by destination IP are helpful for zeroing in on external-facing server attacks. By using the built-in workflows and/or creating your own custom workflows, you can quickly locate the types of events you are interested in.

To switch workflows, click the Switch Workflow link just to the right of the current workflow name. You can find the link just to the right of Events By Priority and Classification in Figure 15.1.

Events By Priority and Classification (switch workflow)
Drilldown of Event, Priority, and Classification › Table View of Events › Packets

Figure 15.1: Switch workflow link

Clicking this link displays the workflows available. Figure 15.2 shows the default intrusion event workflows. If you add your own custom workflows, they will also be listed here.

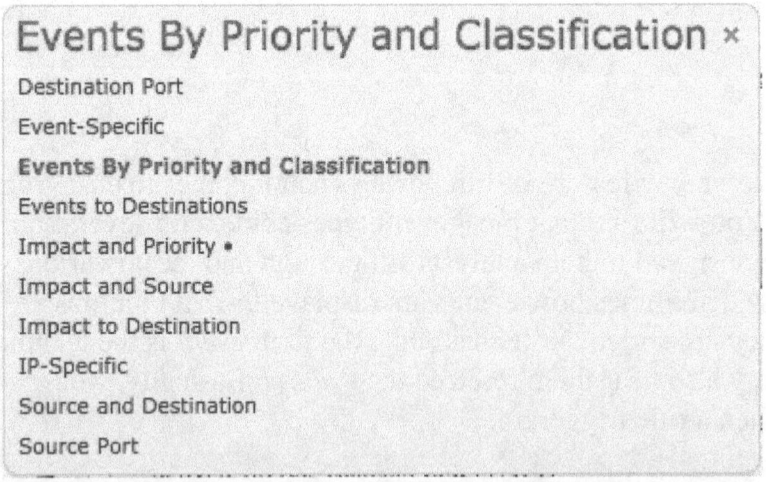

Events By Priority and Classification ×
Destination Port
Event-Specific
Events By Priority and Classification
Events to Destinations
Impact and Priority •
Impact and Source
Impact to Destination
IP-Specific
Source and Destination
Source Port

Figure 15.2: Default intrusion workflows

Built-in Workflows

Here are some examples a few of built-in workflows.

Destination Port: Lists the count of events for each destination port. The list is sorted with the port having the highest count of events at the top. (See Figure 15.3.)

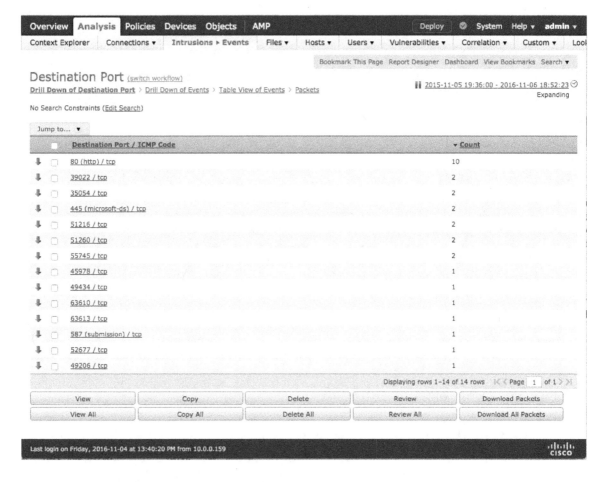

Figure 15.3: Destination Port workflow

Event-Specific: Lists the events by count from highest to lowest. This workflow is helpful in looking for false positives. Often we find that the events triggering the most are most likely to be false positives. (See Figure 15.4.)

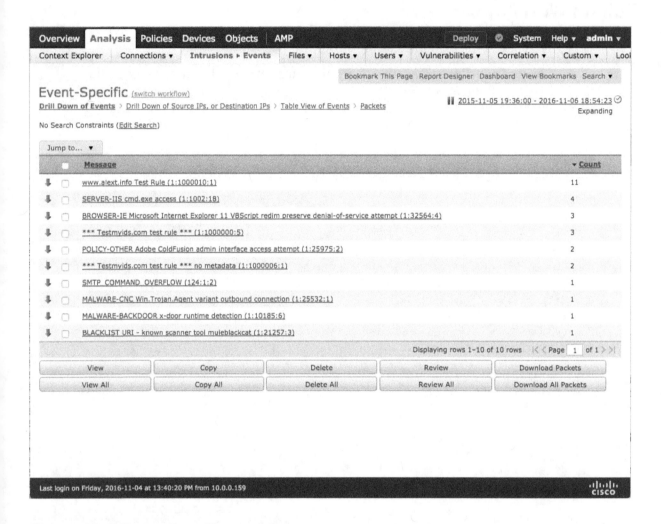

Figure 15.4: Event-Specific workflow

Events by Priority and Classification: This is the default workflow. It lists events with their priority and classification. The list is sorted by priority from high to low. While this is the default workflow, it's honestly not the best. We tend to fancy workflows with the Inline Result and Impact columns. (See Figure 15.5.)

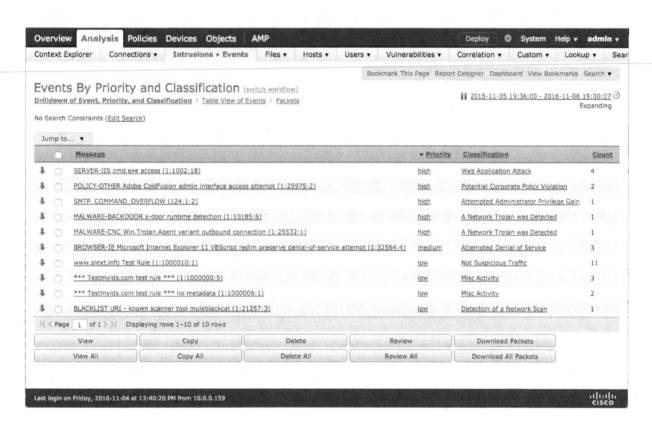

Figure 15.5: Events by Priority and Classification workflow

Impact and Priority: Displays five columns. Events are sorted by impact. This view also shows the inline result, priority, and count. (See Figure 15.6.)

Figure 15.6: Impact and Priority workflow

Impact and Source: This view is sorted by impact; it has six columns, which is the maximum for a built-in workflow. It displays the impact, inline result, source IP, message, priority, and count. (See Figure 15.7.)

Figure 15.7: Impact and Source workflow

Impact to Destination: This view is the same as Impact and Source except the destination IP is displayed. (See Figure 15.8.)

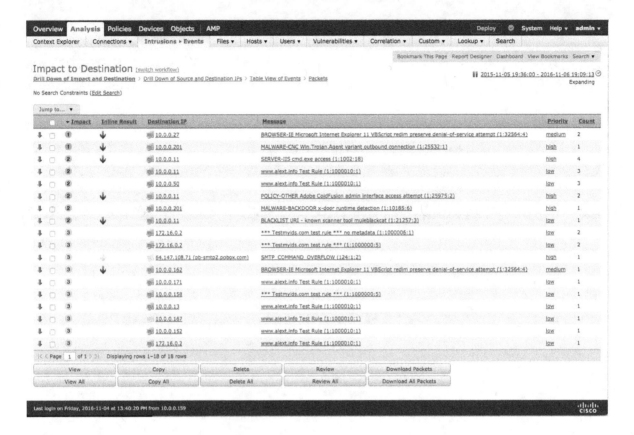

Figure 15.8: Impact to Destination workflow

As you can see, there are quite a number of default workflows to choose from. Which one you choose is a function of what type of events you are looking for at the moment. Looking for evidence of malware or spyware on hosts? The Impact and Source workflow might interest you. Here you can see the events with the highest impact, whether the packet was dropped, and which source IP generated the event.

If it's DMZ or server attacks you are looking for, maybe the Impact to Destination workflow is just the ticket. Very similar to the Impact and Source workflow, except here you see the destination IP.

Looking for false positives? Try the Event-Specific workflow. While this does not show any information on the source, destination, or severity of the event, it does show which rules are triggering the most. Rules that trigger thousands of times in a short period might be false positives.

All of the example workflow figures were generated from the same set of intrusion events. As you can see, the workflow selected has quite an impact on which events "float to the top" in your analysis view. There is no right or wrong answer to which workflow is best. It depends on the situation and what works for you.

The Time Window

Most event data within the Firepower is "time based." This data consists of time-stamped events. When viewing these events, you select a time window equating to a start and stop time and date. For the events to appear in an analysis workflow, they must have occurred within this time window. If your time window is large—say weeks or months—you might expect to see more events than if it is small. The current time window is displayed as a start/stop date and time in the upper-right corner of the screen. To change the time window, click the link that looks like this: ❚❚ 2015-11-05 19:36:00 - 2016-11-06 19:10:28 ⊘ . You can click anywhere on the start/stop date or on the clock icon. Clicking the pause symbol will pause the time windows if you have selected auto-refresh. Clicking the link opens a new window in your browser where you can set the event view time window. This is shown in Figure 15.9.

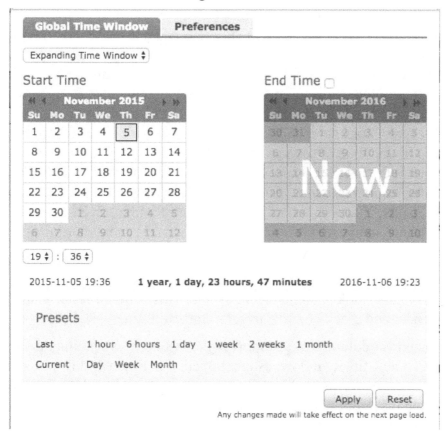

Figure 15.9: Date/Time pop-up window

There are three types of time windows available—static, expanding, and sliding. These are selected from the drop-down list in the upper-left corner.

- Static: This time window has fixed start and stop times. It is useful for locating events that occurred within a certain period. To use the static time window, select it from the drop-down at the top of the window. Then select the start and stop time/date using the calendar and clock controls.

- Expanding: This time window has a fixed start time just like a static window. However, instead of a fixed stop time, this uses now as the end time. Since the start time is fixed and the end time is constantly moving, this time window is always expanding, thus the name. If you set this time window to 60 minutes and begin analyzing events, after an hour you will have a 120-minute window. This is the most common time window used for interactive analysis as it will always display the most current events. When setting an expanding time window, you select the start time using the calendar and clock controls.

- Sliding: When you select a sliding time window, you will notice that the calendar and clock controls disappear from the pop-up window. This is because a sliding window is a fixed duration with the "front edge" always being now. You can select the width of the time window, and once you do, it will slide as you continue to view events. For example, if you select a time window of 60 minutes, you will continue to see just the last 60 minutes of events even if you remain logged in for hours. Sliding time windows are most useful for recurring reports. Say you have a weekly report of high-impact events. You would configure this report with a seven-day sliding time window so each time it runs, it reports events for the previous seven days.

Notice there are presets available in the date/time pop-up. These are handy when you just want to look at some recent events. This is much faster than trying to use the calendar and clock controls to set a start/stop time.

The Firepower default time window is the last hour expanding; however, once you select a new time window, as mentioned, this time window remains in effect for the duration of your session. Once you log out and log back in, your time window resets to the default. You can change this default using the Preferences tab. Clicking this tab displays the Time Window Preferences page shown in Figure 15.10.

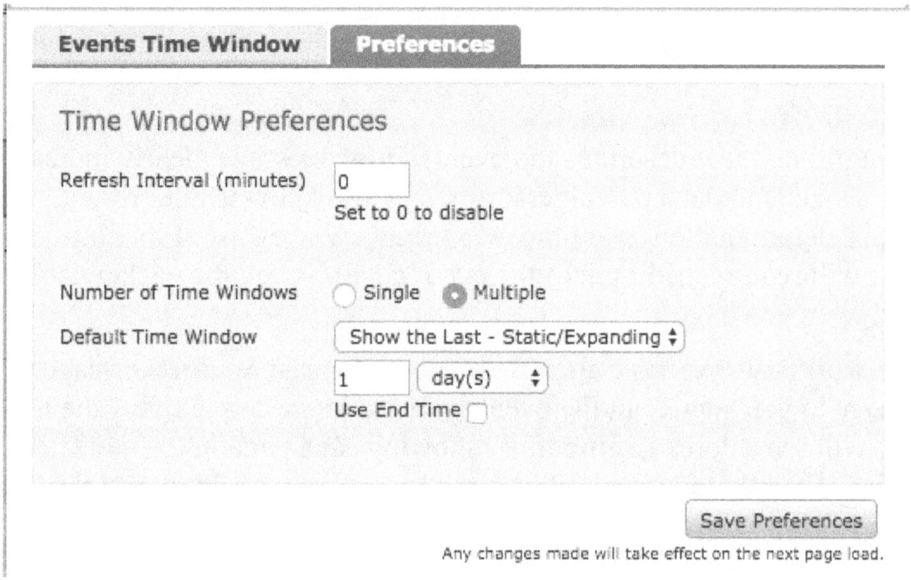

Events Time Window | **Preferences**

Time Window Preferences

Refresh Interval (minutes) [0]
Set to 0 to disable

Number of Time Windows   ○ Single ● Multiple

Default Time Window   [Show the Last - Static/Expanding ⬍]

[1] [day(s) ⬍]
Use End Time ☐

[Save Preferences]
Any changes made will take effect on the next page load.

Figure 15.10: Time window preferences

The Preferences tab allows you to change your default to any of the three types and select the duration. There is also a radio button to select the number of time windows. By default, there are three time windows available. There is one for health events, one for audit events, and one for everything else. The idea is that you could select a time window of 30 days for your audit event view and that would not affect the time window for your health or IPS event views. You will notice that if you select a single time window, the Events Time Window tab name changes to Global Time Window. You can see this in Figure 15.9, where our time preferences included a single time window. Once your time window is set, you can concentrate on locating the events for analysis.

Note that your time window has a tremendous impact on the number of events displayed in the workflow. A common mistake when looking for events is to forget to check the current time window. If you are using a static window but looking for an event that just occurred recently, your event may be there but your time window ended an hour ago. Usually after some grumbling and checking other settings, you will eventually discover the time window setting. To save frustration, keep the following advice in mind: When you don't see the events you are expecting, the first thing to check is the time window!

Navigating the Analysis Interface

When it comes to analyzing intrusion events, there is generally one goal—to determine if the event represents a false positive or an actual security issue. On some occasions this can be accomplished by simply looking at an event message (the meaningful text that describes the event). If the message clearly indicates that the rule is designed to detect a vulnerability that you know is not present, then you could make a determination about the event right away. Most of the time, however, it will require drilling into the event detail—even the packet data—to understand what you have.

The workflows we have already discussed consist of views or pages designed to help you single out the events you are interested in. Near the top of the screen you will see a "breadcrumb trail" showing each page in the workflow. The page you are currently viewing will be a red link. Figure 15.11 shows the Impact and Source workflow.

Impact and Source (switch workflow)
Drill Down of Impact and Source > Drill Down of Source and Destination IPs > Table View of Events > Packets

Figure 15.11: Impact and Source breadcrumb trail

From this we can see there are four pages in this workflow:

1. Drill Down of Impact and Source
2. Drill Down of Source and Destination IPs
3. Table View of Events
4. Packets

The page names indicate what we will see as we drill down into events. Note that all the default workflows include a Table View of Events option. This view contains all of the fields in an event, although some are hidden by default. All intrusion event workflows, whether built-in or custom, also include a Packets view.

Priority and Impact

There are a number of ways to drill down to the next page. Which one you choose is a function of what events you want to focus on. Figure 15.12 shows a sample of some intrusion events we might want to look into.

Context Explorer | Connections ▾ | **Intrusions ▸ Events** | Files ▾ | Hosts ▾ | Users ▾ | Vulnerabilities ▾ | Correlation ▾ | Custom ▾ | Lookup ▾ | Search

Bookmark This Page Dashboard View Bookmarks Search ▾

Impact and Source (switch workflow)
Drill Down of Impact and Source > Drill Down of Source and Destination IPs > Table View of Events > Packets

❚❚ 2016-11-08 17:19:18 - 2016-11-09 20:49:06 ⊘
Expanding

No Search Constraints (Edit Search)

Jump to... ▾

		▾ Impact	Inline Result	Source IP	Message	Priority	Count
⬇	☐	①	⬇	📇 10.0.0.6	BLACKLIST DNS request for known malware domain proxim.ircgalaxy.pl - virut (1:16304:6)	high	618
⬇	☐	①	⬇	187.95.73.80	MALWARE-OTHER sasser attempt (1:9419:9)	high	110
⬇	☐	①	⬇	📇 10.0.0.27	MALWARE-CNC Win.Trojan.Meac malware component download request (1:29987:1)	high	109
⬇	☐	①	⬇	📇 10.0.0.48	MALWARE-CNC Win.Trojan.Damot variant outbound connection (1:29663:2)	high	33
⬇	☐	①	⬇	182.184.69.240	MALWARE-OTHER self-signed SSL certificate with default Internet Widgits Pty Ltd organization name (1:19551:9)	high	24
⬇	☐	①	⬇	📇 10.0.0.26	MALWARE-CNC Win.Trojan.Taidoor variant outbound connection (1:20204:5)	high	16
⬇	☐	①	⬇	📇 10.0.0.26	MALWARE-CNC Win.Trojan.Rubinurd variant outbound connection (1:33305:3)	high	13
⬇	☐	①	⬇	📇 10.0.0.6	MALWARE-CNC Win.Trojan.Sality variant outbound connection (1:19964:9)	high	8
⬇	☐	①	⬇	14.139.155.135	MALWARE-OTHER sasser attempt (1:9419:9)	high	6
⬇	☐	①	⬇	60.167.135.207	MALWARE-OTHER sasser attempt (1:9419:9)	high	6
⬇	☐	①	⬇	📇 10.0.0.126	MALWARE-CNC Win.Trojan.Sosork variant outbound connection (1:26606:3)	high	4
⬇	☐	①	⬇	📇 10.0.0.48	MALWARE-CNC Phoenix exploit kit post-compromise behavior (1:21860:4)	high	3
⬇	☐	①	⬇	78.189.214.112	MALWARE-OTHER sasser attempt (1:9419:9)	high	2
⬇	☐	①	⬇	📇 10.0.0.27	BLACKLIST DNS request for known malware domain godson355.vicp.cc - Win.Trojan.Meac (1:29986:1)	high	2
⬇	☐	①	⬇	📇 10.0.0.48	MALWARE-CNC Win.Trojan.Zeus encrypted POST Data exfiltration (1:27919:3)	high	2
⬇	☐	①	⬇	📇 10.0.0.23	MALWARE-CNC Win.Trojan.Dropper.Daws variant outbound connection (1:25099:2)	high	2

Figure 15.12: Sample intrusion events

As we look at this page, we can deduce a number of things just from the information here.

First of all, these are all Impact 1 events. We also see that the priority is high. What is the difference between impact and priority?

- 💣 Priority: Priority is determined by the rule writer. It can be set using the **priority** keyword or it can be determined by the rule classification. Possible values are low, medium, and high. The important thing to remember is that this simply indicates how important the rule writer felt the alert would be. For example, a rule written for a vulnerability that could result in the complete compromise of a host will probably be high priority. However, a rule designed to alert on a simple protocol anomaly would be low.

- 💣 **Impact**: Impact is determined by Firepower. There are several levels of impact, each one set by Firepower based on what it knows about the rule, the packet, and the victim host. Figure 15.13 was taken from the online help and describes how each impact level is determined.

Impact Level	Vulnerability	Color	Description
0	Unknown	gray	Neither the source nor the destination host is on a network that is monitored by network discovery.
1	Vulnerable	red	Either: • the source or the destination host is in the network map, and a vulnerability is mapped to the host • the source or destination host is potentially compromised by a virus, trojan, or other piece of malicious software
2	Potentially Vulnerable	orange	Either the source or the destination host is in the network map and one of the following is true: • for port-oriented traffic, the port is running a server application protocol • for non-port-oriented traffic, the host uses the protocol
3	Currently Not Vulnerable	yellow	Either the source or the destination host is in the network map and one of the following is true: • for port-oriented traffic (for example, TCP or UDP), the port is not open • for non-port-oriented traffic (for example, ICMP), the host does not use the protocol
4	Unknown Target	blue	Either the source or destination host is on a monitored network, but there is no entry for the host in the network map.

Figure 15.13: Impact levels

Here are some example impact levels for various events.

- A rule triggers on a packet targeted for port 80 on a host. However, the target IP address is not present in a network range defined in the Network Discovery policy. Firepower assigns an impact of 0 (Unknown) to the event.

- A rule triggers on a packet targeted for port 80 on a host. The IP address of this host is present in a discover rule in the Network Discovery policy. However, Firepower looks in the host database and there is no entry there. Firepower assigns an impact of 4 (Unknown Target) to this event.

- A rule triggers on a packet targeted for port 80 on a host. The IP address of the host is present in a discover rule in the Network Discovery policy. Firepower looks in the host database and finds a host entry. However, the host does not show a listening server (service) on port 80. Firepower assigns an impact of 3 (Currently Not Vulnerable) to the event.

- A rule triggers on a packet targeted for port 80 on a host. The IP address of the host is present in a discover rule in the Network Discovery policy. Firepower looks in the host database and finds a host entry, and the host shows a listening server on port 80. Firepower assigns an impact of 2 (Potentially Vulnerable) to the event.

- A rule triggers on a packet targeted for port 80 on a host. The IP address of the host is present in a discover rule in the Network

Discovery policy. Firepower looks in the host database and finds a host entry, and the host shows a listening server on port 80. Firepower cross-references the listed vulnerabilities on the host with the vulnerability the rule was written for based on the vulnerability ID. There is a match; the rule was written for a vulnerability present on the host. Firepower assigns an impact of 1 (Vulnerable) to the event.

As you can see, Firepower is using the data it knows about the host to set an impact level for the event. The purpose of this is to help the analyst pick out the events most likely to be important to him/her. This is part of Firepower's "secret sauce"—the ability to dynamically calculate the impact for each event relative to the hosts on *your* network.

Hard Coding Impact

While all of the above is true, there is another thing you should know about impact. It can also be "hard-coded" into a rule. The fact that Firepower calculates the impact as we just described helps to determine if a responder (server) is vulnerable to an attack. But what if a host—most likely a workstation—encounters malware? The "vulnerability" in this case is probably sitting in front of the keyboard. You could say the vulnerability *always* exists. Because of this, rules written to look for evidence of malware will generally have impact level 1 written into the rule. In practice, we find very few false positive events from rules written to detect evidence of malware in outbound traffic. If you see events with names starting with MALWARE, you can be fairly confident the source host is really running the malware identified by the rule. As a result, hard-coding impact level 1 into the rule is probably a good idea.

That was a rather lengthy discussion of priority and impact, but hopefully it helps you see why workflows displaying impact are so useful. The most important events are probably those with both impact level 1 and high priority. Not to say that these are the only important events, but this is a good place to start.

Drilling into Events

Impact and priority help us narrow down our events to the most critical. Now we need to dig into these and find out how bad they really are. There are several methods to drill down to the next page in this workflow. The following table describes what will happen for each method.

Method	Result
Click one of the links in the table. We	Drill to the next workflow page

can click any of the items in any column except Count.	searching on the item. For example, clicking on a Source IP address will load the next workflow page with all the events the events from that source IP.
Click the blue down-arrow icon on the far left.	Drill to the next workflow page with just that event row.
Select one or more check boxes and then click the View button at the bottom of the page.	Drill to the next workflow page with the selected event rows.
Click the View All button at the bottom of the page.	Drill to the next workflow page with *all* of the events.
Click one of the links in the workflow pages list at the top of the page.	Same as above. Drill to the next workflow page with *all* of the events. Note: You can skip workflow pages using this method.

The following examples refer back to Figure 15.12, our sample list of intrusion events.

If we wanted to drill into the next page with all the Impact 1 events, click any of the Impact 1 icons on the left. They look like this: **1** .

If you are interested in all the events from source IP 10.0.0.26, click on that address in the Source IP column.

If you are interested in a particular event regardless of the source IP, click on the event message.

Finally, if you are interested in only a specific event row, click the blue down arrow (↓) on the far left for the respective row.

Maybe we are interested in all the events that have been triggering for a particular source IP. Figure 15.14 shows the view if we decided to click on the source IP of 10.0.0.26.

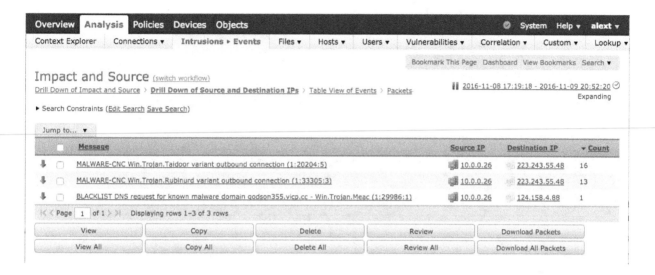

Figure 15.14: Event drill down

First of all, note that the workflow links at the top of the page have changed. The red bold link is now Drill Down of Source and Destination IPs. This indicates we are viewing this page.

Also, the columns have changed. This workflow removes some of the other columns and adds Destination IP. Now we can see that all of the events from this source IP involve two destination IP addresses. Like a detective, the analyst gathers all of the data points or context around the event. Knowing these events all involve two external hosts is a useful piece of information. What do we know

about 10.0.0.26? The blue computer icon ( ) indicates that there is an entry in the Firepower host database with more information on this host. This is because the 10.0.0.0/8 range is included in the Network Discovery policy.

To build more context, we can learn about this source or destination if Firepower has been collecting discovery data. By clicking on the computer icon next to an IP address, we receive a pop-up with the host entry for that address. Figure 15.15 shows the result of clicking this icon.

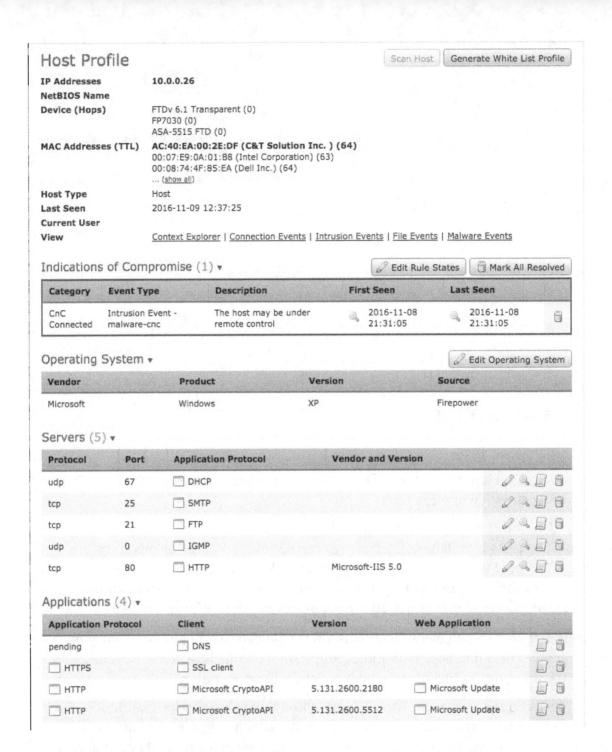

Figure 15.15: Host Profile page

From this screen we can see that Firepower believes this is a Windows XP host. The red outlined box under Indications of Compromise indicates that the host has triggered an intrusion even in the malware-cnc category. As a result, Firepower warns that it may be under remote control. The first seen and last seen times/dates indicate when we first saw this type of event on the host and when it was last seen.

We see several listening servers on the host, including a web server identified as Microsoft-IIS 5.0. Four applications are listed as well.

Now that we have some more information, let's return back to the Impact and Source page of our workflow. We are going to take a closer look at one of the events for our 10.0.0.26 host. The first two events are in the MALWARE-CNC category. These were likely the cause of the Indications of Compromise events we saw in the host entry. The third event is in the BLACKLIST DNS category and indicates the host performed a DNS lookup for a known malicious hostname. This one appears to be associated with the Win.Trojan.Meac malware.

At this point it's looking like our host at 10.0.0.26 has encountered at least one and possibly several malware variants. Even though our IPS probably dropped this traffic, this is still a pretty good indication that the host is compromised and requires some type of remediation. In most cases, the only way to know for certain that an infection has been eradicated is to reimage the host. If your job is only intrusion event analysis, then you would probably forward this information to the appropriate incident response team for follow-up.

Let's drill deeper into these events and confirm that these events are not false positives. The next workflow page is called Table View of Events. If we select the top event for further analysis and click the blue arrow on the left, it will bring us to the table view with just the 16 events on that row. Figure 15.16 shows this page.

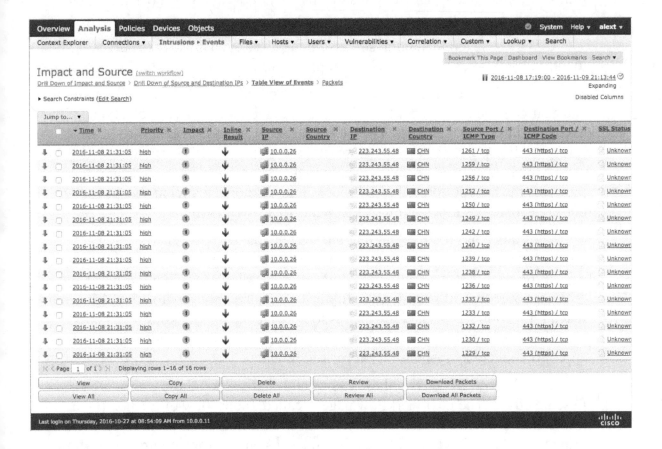

Figure 15.16: Table View of Events page

This view is much wider than almost any screen resolution, which means viewing all the fields will require horizontal scrolling of the page.

Note that not all the fields in an event entry are populated. For example, in Figure 15.16, note that the source country is not listed. This is because geolocation works only on public routable addresses. The events we see in the figure are sourced from our own network, which uses non-routable private IP address ranges.

Table view pages contain every field available in the event. You will notice fields such as Source and Destination Port, VLAN ID, Classification, Application Protocol, Ingress/Egress Interface, Device, etc. However, this is not all the information available. By default, intrusion event table views still hide some information. To view the hidden fields, you can click the small black triangle to the left of Search Constraints. Doing so unhides a portion of the page, as shown in Figure 15.17.

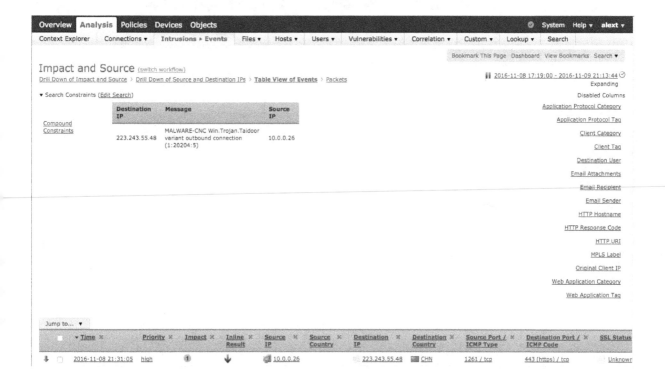

Figure 15.17: Disabled columns

This results in a rather lengthy list of links under the Disabled Columns heading. These are intrusion event fields that are less commonly used and are disabled by default. To enable any of these columns for the duration of the session, click on the link and it will be placed back into the table view. If you do find a column that you would find useful, you can create a custom workflow and include it.

In practice, a table view may not add much to your knowledge about the event. After all it's the packet and rule that will really help us understand why this event triggered and what our response should be.

From here, let's take a look at the packet view. From the table view we have a number of options for drilling into the individual packets. One of them is clicking on the blue drill-down arrow. This will take you to the packet view for that single packet. Another way is clicking on the Packets link near the top of the page. This will take you to the packet view and allow you to step through all the packets if desired. Clicking either one will take you to a packet view, as seen in Figure 15.18.

Figure 15.18: Packet view

The packet view page contains a wealth of information about the event. We will go through it one section at a time.

Event Information

Most of the information here is already available in one of the previous workflow pages. We already know what the source and destination IP are. This may show some fields that are hidden in the default table view, like HTTP URI. We can use this information to help us build context around the event and understand more about the type of traffic we are looking at. In this case, the fact that the source port is above 1024 and the destination port is 443 gives us a clue about what kind of packet this is. Traffic destined for port 443 is nearly always from an HTTP client to a (secure) web server. Keep that destination port in mind because it also indicates something else about this packet we'll see later.

Rule

Although it's part of the Event Information section, the Snort rule warrants its own discussion. This is the actual rule that matched one or more packets. Understanding what this rule was looking for will help us determine how we will respond to this event. We have zoomed into the rule portion in Figure 15.19.

```
alert tcp $HOME_NET any -> $EXTERNAL_NET $HTTP_PORTS (msg:"MALWARE-CNC Win.Trojan.Taidoor variant outbound connection";
flow:to_server,established; content:".php?id=0"; nocase; content:"111D30"; fast_pattern; nocase; http_uri; pcre:"/^V[a-z]{5}\.php\?
id=0\d{5}111D30[a-zA-Z0-9]{6}$/Ui"; metadata:impact_flag red, policy balanced-ips drop, policy security-ips drop, service http;
reference:cve,2011-0611; reference:url,contagiodump.blogspot.com/2011/06/jun-22-cve-2011-0611-pdf-swf-fruits-of.html;
reference:url,www.virustotal.com/file-scan/report.html?id=145d64f38564eafa4fb5da0722c0e7348168024d32ada5cfb37a49f5811cb6b8-
1315612892; classtype:trojan-activity; sid:20204; rev:5; )
```

Figure 15.19: Snort rule

Let's walk through the rule at a high level and try to understand more about why it might match a packet.

The rule header indicates that it is designed to inspect TCP traffic coming from the HOME_NET on any port going to the EXTERNAL_NET on HTTP_PORTS. In short, it's designed to inspect outbound web browsing from our network.

The message indicates this is a MALWARE-CNC category rule designed to detect an outbound connection from malware called Win.Trojan.Taidoor.

The **flow** keyword restricts the rule to evaluating only traffic that is going from a client to a server. It also only evaluates packets that are post three-way handshake (this rule ignores the SYN, SYN/ACK, ACK). This keyword simply ensures that the traffic qualifies for further inspection. Since you'll never see a user agent in a SYN, SYN/ACK, or ACK packet and we don't care about server responses (for this rule), there's no reason to waste resources inspecting them.

Next we have a content check. This is looking for the string **.php?id=0**. The **nocase** keyword indicates the content check is not case sensitive. Another content check follows looking for **111D30**. This one is also case insensitive and is looking only in the HTTP URI portion of the packet.

After the content checks is the **pcre** keyword, which performs an additional regular expression match on the content. We won't walk through the entire expression here, but this is actually performing additional checks on the content items that have already been located. Using a regular expression is a more powerful method of searching for content that might deviate slightly but still follows certain predictable patterns. The reason this **pcre** keyword is placed after the content checks is so they can "prequalify" the packet. The **pcre** keyword will not be evaluated unless both of the content checks return true. Regular expression keywords are CPU intensive, and placing **pcre** after the **content** keywords ensures that Snort only performs this check on packets that already appear to be qualified candidates.

After the **pcre** keyword, there are no other detection keywords in the rule. The rest are documentation and metadata, which do not look for specific content within a packet.

Going back to the destination port for this packet, remember it was port 443? Is there anything strange about that? We know that port 443 is typically used for Secure Sockets Layer (SSL) web communications and is encrypted traffic. How was Snort able to inspect the content in a packet that was destined for this port? Clearly, there was some SSL decryption occurring to enable Snort to see this traffic. Either Firepower or some other SSL decryption solution apparently decrypted this session so we could inspect it and find this malware. This illustrates the value of SSL decryption when it comes to IPS usage. Without it we would have no Snort event in this case.

The next section is Actions. However, although it comes next on the screen, it may not always be the next place you look. In this case, let's take a look at the packet itself first—that is below Actions in the Packet Information section.

Packet Information

If you have used a packet analysis tool such as Wireshark, this section will look familiar. Each section of the packet is shown from the Ethernet frame down to the data bytes. Most of the information in the packet header has already been pulled out for us in the workflows. What we really want to see here is the data portion, or payload, of the packet. That's where the evil is. Figure 15.20 shows the Packet Information portion of the screen. You can see that the various sections of the packet are here. Clicking the black triangle icon to the left will expand a section's contents.

Packet Information

FRAME 1 (Expand All)

▸ **Frame 1: 248 bytes on wire** (248 bytes captured (1984 bits)

▸ **Ethernet II** (Src: 00:0C:29:8F:D5:6D, Dst: 00:0C:29:C0:99:85)

▸ **Internet Protocol Version 4** (Src: 10.0.0.26, Dst: 223.243.55.48)

▸ **Transmission Control Protocol** (Src Port: 1229 (1229), Dst Port: 443 (443), Seq: 1, Ack: 1, Len: 194)

▸ **Packet Text**

▸ **Packet Bytes**

Figure 15.20: Packet Information

We already know information such as the source and destination IP address, ports, protocol, etc. What we really want to see is the packet payload. Figure 15.21 shows the packet with both the Packet Text and Packet Bytes sections expanded.

Packet Information

FRAME 1 (Expand All)

▸ **Frame 1: 248 bytes on wire** (248 bytes captured (1984 bits)

▸ **Ethernet II** (Src: 00:0C:29:8F:D5:6D, Dst: 00:0C:29:C0:99:85)

▸ **Internet Protocol Version 4** (Src: 10.0.0.26, Dst: 223.243.55.48)

▸ **Transmission Control Protocol** (Src Port: 1229 (1229), Dst Port: 443 (443), Seq: 1, Ack: 1, Len: 194)

▾ **Packet Text**
```
..).....)..m..E.....@.....
.....70......F..h..P...r>..GET /gmzlk.php?id=031870111D309GE67E HTTP/1.1
User-Agent: Mozilla/4.0 (compatible; MSIE 6.0; Windows NT 5.1; SV1)
Host: 211.234.117.141:443
Connection: Keep-Alive
Cache-Control: no-cache
```

▾ **Packet Bytes**
```
Secure Sockets Layer
0000        00 0c 29 c0 99 85 00 0c 29 8f d5 6d 08 00 45 00   ..).....)..m..E.
0010        00 ea 00 c1 40 00 80 06 d8 0f 0a 00 00 1a df f3   ....@...........
0020        37 30 04 cd 01 bb f3 85 46 97 b1 68 b7 c8 50 18   70......F..h..P.
0030        fa f0 72 3e 00 00 47 45 54 20 2f 67 6d 7a 6c 6b   ..r>..GET /gmzlk
0040        2e 70 68 70 3f 69 64 3d 30 33 31 38 37 30 31 31   .php?id=03187011
0050        31 44 33 30 39 47 45 36 37 45 20 48 54 54 50 2f   1D309GE67E HTTP/
0060        31 2e 31 0d 0a 55 73 65 72 2d 41 67 65 6e 74 3a   1.1..User-Agent:
0070        20 4d 6f 7a 69 6c 6c 61 2f 34 2e 30 20 28 63 6f   Mozilla/4.0 (co
0080        6d 70 61 74 69 62 6c 65 3b 20 4d 53 49 45 20 36   mpatible; MSIE 6
0090        2e 30 3b 20 57 69 6e 64 6f 77 73 20 4e 54 20 35   .0; Windows NT 5
00a0        2e 31 3b 20 53 56 31 29 0d 0a 48 6f 73 74 3a 20   .1; SV1)..Host:
00b0        32 31 31 2e 32 33 34 2e 31 31 37 2e 31 34 31 3a   211.234.117.141:
00c0        34 34 33 0d 0a 43 6f 6e 6e 65 63 74 69 6f 6e 3a   443..Connection:
00d0        20 4b 65 65 70 2d 41 6c 69 76 65 0d 0a 43 61 63   Keep-Alive..Cac
00e0        68 65 2d 43 6f 6e 74 72 6f 6c 3a 20 6e 6f 2d 63   he-Control: no-c
00f0        61 63 68 65 0d 0a 0d 0a                           ache....
```

Figure 15.21: Expanded packet view

You can see that the Packet Text section is more user friendly. But if you really want to see what is in every byte of the payload, the Packet Bytes section shows you each of the byte values. From this payload, it is clear that this rule probably hit pay dirt with this packet. It's clearly an HTTP GET containing the data the rule was designed to detect. This is likely evidence that the source IP has encountered the Taidoor Windows Trojan.

Actions

Moving up the page just a bit we find the Actions section. If we expand this, we see a number of links available. These are shown in Figure 15.22.

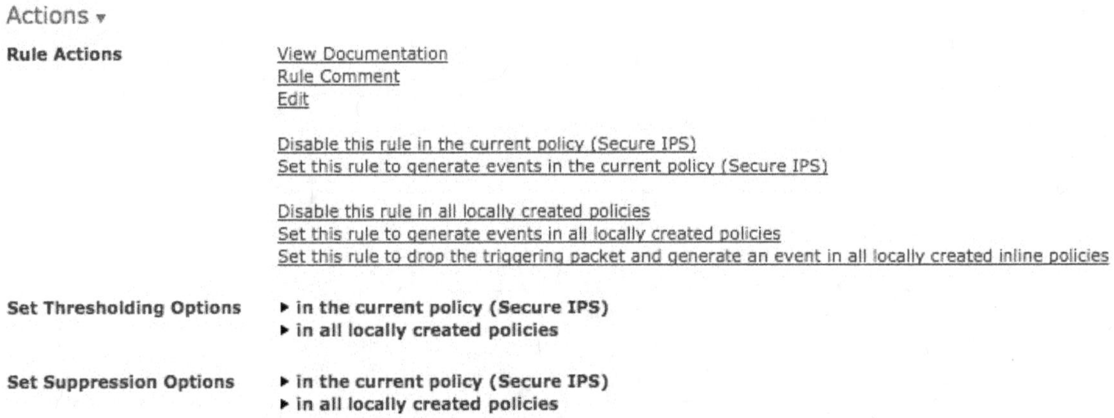

Actions ▾

Rule Actions

View Documentation
Rule Comment
Edit

Disable this rule in the current policy (Secure IPS)
Set this rule to generate events in the current policy (Secure IPS)

Disable this rule in all locally created policies
Set this rule to generate events in all locally created policies
Set this rule to drop the triggering packet and generate an event in all locally created inline policies

Set Thresholding Options   ▸ in the current policy (Secure IPS)
▸ in all locally created policies

Set Suppression Options   ▸ in the current policy (Secure IPS)
▸ in all locally created policies

Figure 15.22: Actions

To gain more insight into this rule and the alert, the Actions section contains a View Documentation link. Clicking this loads the rule documentation in a pop-up window. Depending on the rule, there may be a lot of documentation or none at all. In this case, Figure 15.23 indicates there is quite a bit of documentation for the Adobe Acrobat bug leveraged by the Taidoor Trojan.

Rule Documentation (1:20204:5)

This event is generated when an attempt is made to exploit a known vulnerability in acrobat.

Rule	alert tcp $HOME_NET any -> $EXTERNAL_NET $HTTP_PORTS (msg:"MALWARE-CNC Win.Trojan.Taidoor variant outbound connection"; flow:to_server,established; content:".php?id=0"; nocase; content:"111D30"; fast_pattern; nocase; http_uri; pcre:"/^\/[a-z]{5}\.php\?id=0\d{5}111D30[a-zA-Z0-9]{6}$/Ui"; metadata:impact_flag red, policy balanced-ips drop, policy security-ips drop, service http; reference:cve,2011-0611; reference:url,contagiodump.blogspot.com/2011/06/jun 22 cve-2011-0611-pdf-swf-fruits-of.html; reference:url,www.virustotal.com/file-scan/report.html?id=145d64f38564eafa4fb5da0722c0e7348168024d32ada5cfb37a49f5811cb6b8-1315612892; classtype:trojan-activity; sid:20204; rev:5;)
Impact	Denial of Service. Information disclosure. Loss of integrity.
Detailed Information	Adobe Flash Player before 10.2.154.27 on Windows, Mac OS X, Linux, and Solaris and 10.2.156.12 and earlier on Android; Adobe AIR before 2.6.19140; and Authplay.dll (aka AuthPlayLib.bundle) in Adobe Reader 9.x before 9.4.4 and 10.x through 10.0.1 on Windows, Adobe Reader 9.x before 9.4.4 and 10.x before 10.0.3 on Mac OS X, and Adobe Acrobat 9.x before 9.4.4 and 10.x before 10.0.3 on Windows and Mac OS X allow remote attackers to execute arbitrary code or cause a denial of service (application crash) via crafted Flash content; as demonstrated by a Microsoft Office document with an embedded .swf file that has a size inconsistency in a "group of included constants," object type confusion, ActionScript that adds custom functions to prototypes, and Date objects; and as exploited in the wild in April 2011.
Affected Systems	adobe acrobat 10.0 adobe acrobat 10.0.1 adobe acrobat 10.0.2 adobe acrobat 9.0 adobe acrobat 9.1 adobe acrobat 9.1.1 adobe acrobat 9.1.2 adobe acrobat 9.1.3 adobe acrobat 9.2 adobe acrobat 9.3 adobe acrobat 9.3.1 adobe acrobat 9.3.2 adobe acrobat 9.3.3 adobe acrobat 9.3.4 adobe acrobat 9.4 adobe acrobat 9.4.1 adobe acrobat 9.4.2 adobe acrobat 9.4.3

Figure 15.23: Rule documentation

Scrolling down, we see in Figure 15.24 even more information on attack scenarios and corrective action as well as a number of Website Reference links for more information.

Attack Scenarios	Many types of buffer overflow exist, this is a generic term that may apply to many circumstances that result in an overflow of some kind. A parameter overflow for example, means that the attacker is able to supply data as a parameter to the execution of a program. When the program expands the supplied data, if the size of the parameter is not correctly checked, it may exceed a set limit allowing the attacker to overflow the buffer and write data into memory.
	In a stack overflow, the attacker has the opportunity to overwrite a return memory address which allows them to point the return address to a memory location containing code they wish to execute. This allows the attacker to run code with the full privileges of the program in use. The attacker may also supply the address for a known important call, for example the system() call, with the arguments to the call on the stack. The stack also contains the stack pointer and the frame pointer, overwriting these values may lead to a write-what-where condition.
	In a heap overflow, it is possible to overwrite function pointers that may be in memory. This may allow the attacker to execute code in memory by changing the function pointer to move to code of their choosing. This can occur even in programs that do not necessarily use function pointers since they may be left in memory at run time. The heap also contains user data which also becomes visible to the attacker.
Ease of Attack	Simple. Exploits exist.
False Positives	None known.
False Negatives	None known.
Corrective Action	Upgrade to the latest non-affected version of the software.
	Apply the appropriate vendor supplied patches.
Contributors	Sourcefire Vulnerability Research Team
	This document was generated from data supplied by the National Vulnerability Database. A product of the National Institute of Standards and Technology.
	For more information see http://nvd.nist.gov/
References	Common Vulnerabilities and Exposures Page
	Website Reference
	Website Reference
	Website Reference
	Website Reference
View	Context Explorer

Close window

Figure 15.24: Rule documentation continued

You will find that rules written to detect exploits against known software vulnerabilities will usually have fairly good documentation. This is because the threat vectors and methods of exploiting a particular vulnerability are usually well known. You could say the vulnerability is a stationary target and we know what it takes to exploit it. As a result, we can document the conditions the rule was written to detect and provide links to vendor and/or Bugtraq research on the subject. In addition, vulnerabilities in commercial or open-source software will have Common Vulnerabilities and Exposures (CVE) references.

Conversely, rules written to detect malware are generally not documented. The reason is the lack of documentation on the malware itself. Oftentimes we know the effect of the malware—such as change the User-Agent—but there may not be much available in the way of documenting what the malware actually does or how it operates. In cases like this, search engines are your friends. Our example event was a rare breed, a malware event that actually leverages a known bug in

Adobe Acrobat. Many types of malware don't actually need a software vulnerability, just a cooperative user!

For the purpose of this example we won't try to dig into this particular rule or event much further. The bottom line is you would either treat it like a real malware event and follow up accordingly or decide it was a false positive.

Let's discuss how you would proceed if you determined this event was a false positive. You have four options:

- Disable the rule.

- Suppress the alert.

- Threshold the rule.

- Create a Pass rule.

Disable the Rule

If you decide the rule is too prone to false positives or is not applicable to your environment, the best action is to disable it. This removes the rule from the applicable intrusion policy or policies. Referring back to Figure 15.22, in the Actions section you have two links that will do this – "Disable this rule in the current policy (<policy name>)" and "Disable this rule in all locally created policies."

Which of these you choose simply depends on which policies will be changed. If you only want the rule removed from the policy that generated this alert, pick the first option. If you want the rule disabled in all your policies, choose the second option. Clicking either one will result in a dialog at the top of the screen indicating what action was taken. Figure 15.25 shows the result when we clicked on the first option to disable the rule only in the policy triggering the alert.

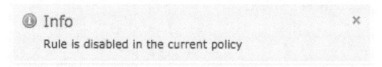

Figure 15.25: Rule disabled message

Note that the intrusion policy has now been updated and will now show as "out-of-date" in the Intrusion Policy list view (Policies → Access Control → Intrusion). The rule will continue to trigger on any matching packets until policy changes are deployed to your devices.

Suppress the Alert

Another option is to suppress the alert. This has the effect of leaving the rule active but suppressing its output. This is normally done if you want to suppress the rule for a specific source or destination IP address. In our example, what if we found that the host 10.0.0.26 just happens to use a business application that formats its HTTP GET requests the same way as our malware; however, in our research we decided that this is also an accurate rule to detect the Taidoor Trojan. We are confident that 10.0.0.26 is the only host running the application. Therefore, we want to keep the rule active but stop it from alerting for 10.0.0.26. This is a perfect use for a suppression.

To suppress this rule for the single source IP address, we have two options: suppress for the current policy or for all policies. This works just like disabling the rule, discussed earlier. For this example, we will suppress only in the current policy. Clicking the upper black triangle under Suppression Options displays the options in Figure 15.26.

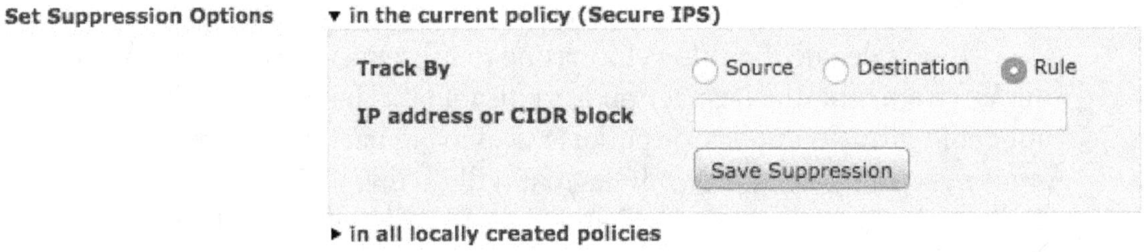

Set Suppression Options ▼ in the current policy (Secure IPS)

Track By	○ Source ○ Destination ● Rule
IP address or CIDR block	
	Save Suppression

▶ in all locally created policies

Figure 15.26: Set Suppression Options

To suppress a source IP address, select the Source radio button and enter the IP address or CIDR block into the field. You can suppress by source IP address, destination IP address, or by rule. Clicking Save Suppression updates the applicable policy. Remember, the Intrusion or Access Control policy must be reapplied for this suppression to take effect.

Notes on Suppression

While suppression is a useful tool, there are some important considerations to keep in mind:

- Suppressing a rule does not remove the rule from the rule set; it simply suppresses the alert output. If the rule action is set to drop, the rule will *silently drop the packet, providing no alert whatsoever*. Yes that was italicized for a reason—this could be a troubleshooting nightmare! Only do this if you are absolutely sure the rule will *never* trigger a false positive alert. Suppression then is primarily useful for rules that only generate events or in passive installations. For inline suppression, use a pass rule as outlined later.

- If you select the Rule option under Track By, you will cause the rule to continue evaluating traffic but never alert. In passive installations, this is useless; for inline installations, it also runs the risk of dropping silently if this is a drop rule (see rant above). If you really want to suppress the entire rule, you probably should just disable it.

- You can suppress a source IP or a destination IP address but not both. If you need to suppress alerts for traffic from a specific IP address to another specific IP address, then you need a pass rule.

Threshold the Rule

Thresholding is another option for reducing the alerting for noisy rules. When you add a threshold, you cause the rule to not trigger until it matches a certain number of packets over a certain period. This is useful for rules that are designed to detect attacks such as brute force password guessing. Often, rules written to detect this activity will look for login failures. One or two failures from a single IP address may just be someone who mistyped their password. We don't need to be alerted to this. However, dozens of failures from the same host probably indicates something more nefarious. To set a threshold on a rule, expand the appropriate section for current or all policies. In Figure 15.27, we have expanded the current policy option.

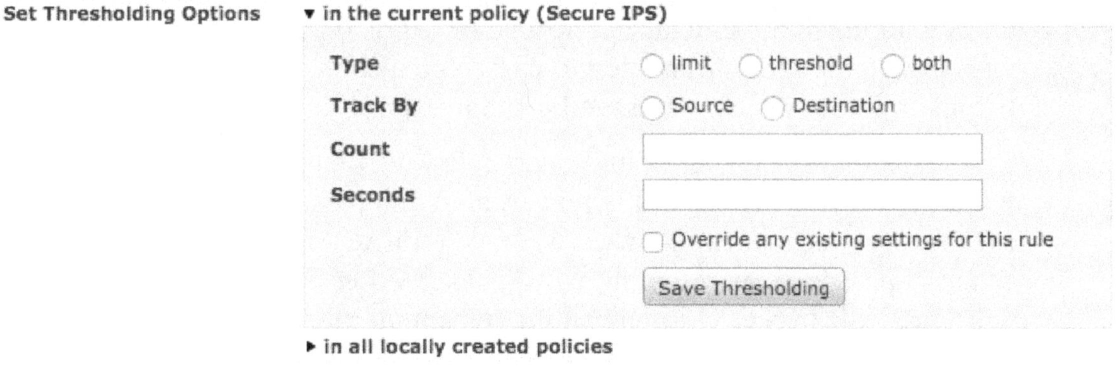

Set Thresholding Options	▾ in the current policy (Secure IPS)			
Type	○ limit	○ threshold	○ both	
Track By	○ Source	○ Destination		
Count				
Seconds				
	○ Override any existing settings for this rule			
	Save Thresholding			
▸ in all locally created policies				

Figure 15.27: Set thresholding options in the current policy

To configure Thresholding you have the following options:

- Type: Limit, Threshold, Both

  o Limit will limit notifications to the number of events specified by Count per the time period entered in Seconds below. For example, alert no more than 5 times in 300 seconds regardless of how many packets actually match the rule.

- o Threshold will provide one alert for each number of matching packets specified by Count during the time period. For example, provide one alert for each 5 packets within 300 seconds.

- o Both provides a notification once per time period after matching the specified count of packets. For example, alert once per 300 seconds if you see at least 5 matching packets.

- Track By: Source/Destination track matches to this rule by the source or destination IP address.

- Count: The count in packets matching the rule.

- Seconds: The number in seconds during which the count will be evaluated.

- Override Any Existing Settings for This Rule: Check this box to replace any existing thresholds with the new one.

Create a Pass Rule

The last option for rule tuning is to create a pass rule. This useful if you need to suppress a rule based on both the source *and* destination IP addresses. It is also the only real option for suppressing a drop rule in inline mode (don't make us break out into all italics again). The idea of a pass rule is to copy an existing rule, then change the action from alert to pass. You also modify the source/destination IP and/or port to match your specific suppression.

Without going too far into Snort rules, we first have to understand that a rule can have two actions in Firepower: alert and pass. Alert is fairly self-explanatory—do something when we match traffic—but what is pass? A rule action of pass tells Snort to ignore this packet. After matching a pass rule, Snort will "pass" the packet, skipping all the remaining rules. Another important point is that regardless of where a pass rule appears in the rule set, Snort will always process traffic through pass rules first. This means that if you have two rules looking for the same thing and one of them is a pass rule, the pass rule will always win.

We can take advantage of this behavior to suppress certain rules. If a rule is generating a false positive for specific traffic, we can take the following steps:

1. Make a copy of the rule.
2. Modify the rule header to match just the specific false positive hosts(s).

3. Change the action to pass.

Now this pass rule will only evaluate traffic between our specific hosts, and if packets match the rule (which has the same detection options as the original rule), this traffic will skip all the remaining rules, including the original.

Rule Comment

The last item we will discuss under Rule Actions is Rule Comment. Clicking this link will bring up the Add Comment page in a pop-up window. This is shown in Figure 15.28.

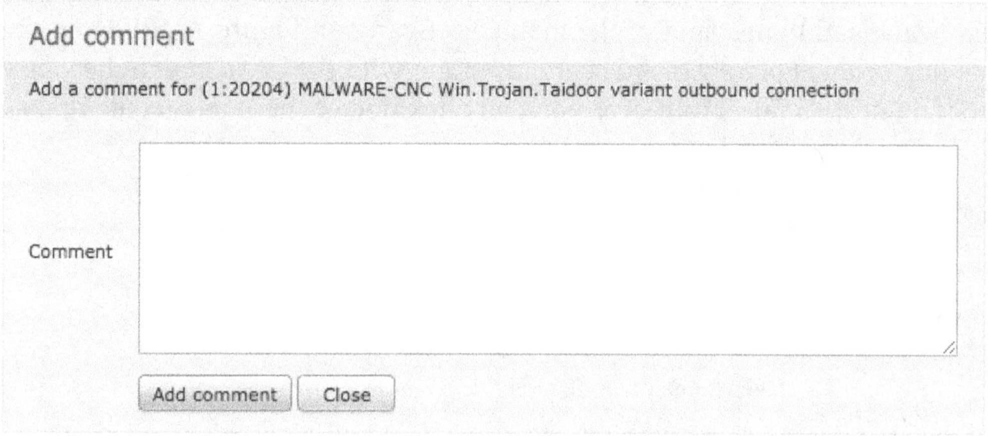

Figure 15.28: Add Comment

This allows entering free-form text comments regarding a rule and can be used to document your analysis actions. When a comment is added, the system also stamps the comment with the user and time/date. Note that rule comments are rule specific, not policy specific. Comments added here will be visible regardless of where the rule is viewed on the FMC.

Miscellaneous Intrusion Event Analysis Features

Searching

The ability to search through intrusion events is a powerful feature. The system allows you to search any field in an event to locate the ones that are relevant to you. From the intrusion event view, there are three ways you can navigate to the search page.

The first method is to click Search in the menu bar in the upper right. This is shown in Figure 15.29.

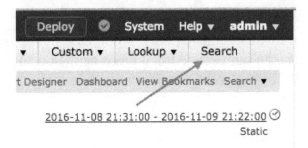

Figure 15.29: Search menu bar

The second method is to use the quick link (also labeled Search) located just below and to the right of the menu bar Search in Figure 15.29. Hovering over this link brings up your saved searches along with the built-in searches, as you can see in Figure 15.30. From here you can click one of these to execute that search or click Search itself to load the search page.

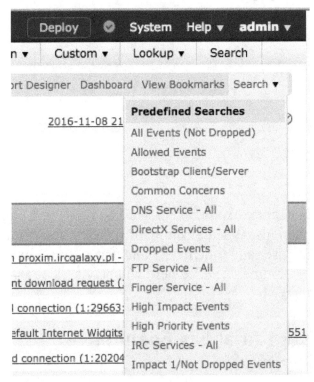

Figure 15.30: Search quick link

The third method for entering the search page is to click the Edit Search link on the upper left side of the screen. This also has the effect of editing an existing search query, while the two previously mentioned methods will not preserve any current search condition. This is shown in Figure 15.31.

Figure 15.31: Edit Search link

The search page itself, shown in Figure 15.32, is a rather long list of all the fields you can search on in an intrusion event. The system comes with a number of predefined searches. You cannot edit or erase these default searches, but you can create your own. On this page you will see predefined searches on the left. That's where you will also find any custom searches you have created.

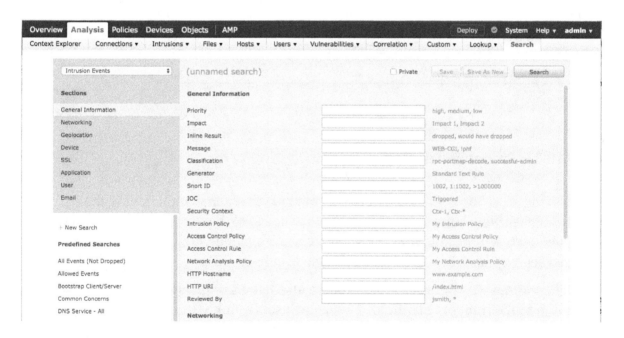

Figure 15.32: Search page

The Sections list on the left is a quick way to scroll to the various search fields. This is a handy way to find what you're looking for without scrolling down through the list of search fields, which is quite long.

To load an existing search query, select it from the list on the left. You can then modify the search criteria if desired. You will notice that only the fields containing search values appear when you are editing an existing search. In Figure

15.33, we are editing a search that looks for UDP packets on port 53. If you want to add additional search criteria, click the dark bar near the top that says "Showing only defined fields. Click to show all fields." Doing so will re-enable all the search fields so you can add your additional criteria as needed.

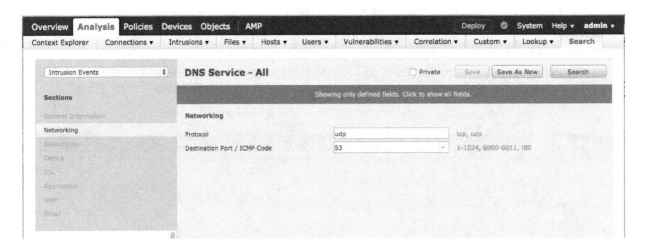

Figure 15.33: Predefined search

Saving searches is as easy as giving your search a name and clicking the Save or Save As New button. If the Save as Private check box is selected, no other non-admin users will be able to use your searches. To name your search, click (unnamed search) near the top of the page (see Figure 15.32).

The various search pages in the system also have sample search information to the right of each field. This helps users quickly understand what type of data is appropriate for each field. Some fields also have a gray + to the right. Clicking this will load any objects you have created. Figure 15.34 shows the network objects resulting from clicking the icon to the right of the Source IP field.

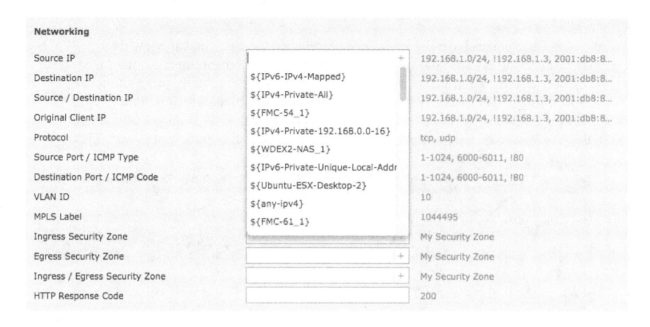

Figure 15.34: Network objects available in search

When you're ready to execute your search, you can press Enter or click the Search button in the upper right.

Reviewed Events

Another Firepower feature is the ability to place events into Reviewed status. This is helpful if you have reviewed an event, made a determination regarding its viability, and want to continue to analyze additional events. To keep track of events you have already evaluated, you can mark them as Reviewed. This has the effect of removing the event from your analysis workflow. However, the events are not deleted from the database.

To review events, use the Review buttons at the bottom of the analysis view. Clicking a Review button will affect the selected events (rows with the check box selected). The Review All button will place all the events currently listed in Reviewed status. Note that the All buttons apply to *all* the events selected by the current search query and time window, not just the ones visible on the page. Placing an event into reviewed status removes it from the intrusion event workflows for all users.

Once events have been placed in reviewed status, you can also search by name for events reviewed by a particular user or search for all reviewed events by using a * in the Reviewed By search field.

Once events have been placed into Reviewed status, you can view them two ways. One is to use the Reviewed By search we just mentioned. Another is to select Analysis → Intrusions → Reviewed Events. This is actually just a shortcut to loading the Reviewed By * search. You can test this by navigating to the Reviewed Events view and then clicking the Edit Search link. Doing so will reveal that the Reviewed Events view is just a custom search of all reviewed events. This is shown in Figure 15.35.

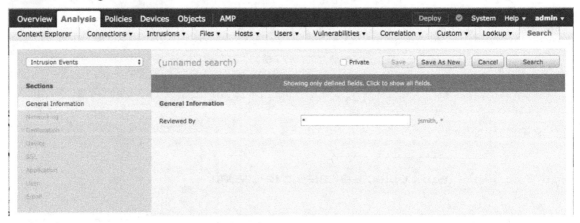

Figure 15.35: Reviewed Events search

Packet Downloads

By default, when an intrusion event is triggered, Firepower saves the packet. During event analysis, these packets can be downloaded to the analyst workstation for archival or further analysis with your packet analysis tool of choice. Each workflow page contains a Download button in the row of buttons at the bottom of the page. Clicking this will download the selected event packets. As with the other buttons in this row, the Download All Packets button works for all the packets returned by the time window and search query.

When multiple packets are selected for download, you get a zip archive containing multiple PCAP format files. However, when you are drilled down to the packet view, or if you have only one event selected, clicking the Download Packet button downloads a single file in PCAP format. In this case, you can often just select the Open With action in your browser and select an application such as Wireshark to view the packet contents. If you are downloading multiple packets, you will have to unzip the archive first.

If you want to keep a long-term record of packet data, the download feature is a good one to remember. Due to the circular nature of event storage, intrusion events will eventually be purged from the FMC and along with them the packet data.

Security Intelligence Events

Like intrusion events, Security Intelligence events are designed to trigger when there is evil about; however, the process of identifying and tuning false positives for these events is a much simpler one. There are three types of Security Intelligence events you might see:

- Network Security Intelligence: These are simply packets traveling to or from blacklisted hosts. They are identified simply based on their source or destination IP address.

- DNS Security Intelligence: These are DNS lookups for blacklisted domain names.

- URL Security Intelligence: These are blacklisted URLs.

Unlike with intrusion events, Firepower does not capture any packets when generating Security Intelligence events. Also, unlike with Snort rules, the concept of a false positive is slightly different. A false positive Security Intelligence event represents a failure or inaccuracy in the intelligence used to generate the various blacklists. The remediation for a false positive is to either remove the offending entry from the blacklist or add it to a whitelist. If the blacklist is provided externally—as with the built-in Cisco security feeds—whitelisting is the only option. Of course, you could also disable an entire intelligence category if you are seeing it generate large number of false positives.

Security Intelligence Workflows

There a three built-in workflows for viewing Security Intelligence events. As with other event types, you can also create your own custom workflows to display the data in other meaningful ways.

- Security Intelligence Events: This workflow is the default. It shows a few select fields and is specific enough that you see one event per row. The workflow consists of one page named Security Intelligence with application details and a table view.

- Security Intelligence Summary: This is helpful for getting summary information about how many events are triggering in each Security

Intelligence category. You can drill into application details and a
table view.

- Security Intelligence with DNS Details: This is a workflow specific
  to DNS events. It contains summary information on the number of
  events in a category and a specific DNS query. This also has a table
  view.

Security Intelligence Tuning

As we already mentioned, there aren't many options when tuning Security
Intelligence events. There is also not much information on *why* a given event
triggered. If you see an IP block event and the Security Intelligence category is
Tor_exit_node, you can be sure of one thing. At the time the event triggered, the
IP address was on the Tor_exit_node list. Because the Security Intelligence feed
from Cisco is fairly dynamic, there is no guarantee that this IP address is still on
the list. If you think this might be incorrect, you could cross-reference with other
sources of TOR exit node hosts, but beyond that, there's not a whole lot of
investigation to do. If the blocked connection represents legitimate traffic, your
best recourse is to whitelist it. Figure 15.36 shows a number of Tor_exit_node
events.

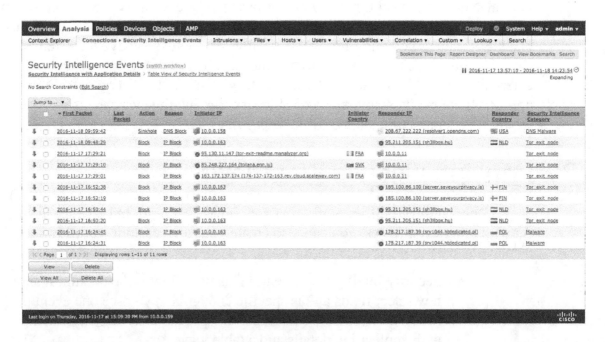

Figure 15.36: Security Intelligence examples

Conversely, you may see an event involving a given IP address and decide you want to permanently block it. By adding the IP address to the Global-Blacklist you ensure that even if it is eventually removed from the Cisco feed category it will still be blocked.

The options for whitelisting or blacklisting are slightly different depending on the type of Security Intelligence event.

Network Security Intelligence

To whitelist/blacklist an IP address, you right-click on the IP address in *any* event. This applies not only to Security Intelligence but also to connection events, intrusion events, correlation events, etc. A right-click will bring up the menu shown in Figure 15.37.

Figure 15.37: Blacklist/Whitelist IP Now options

The options to Blacklist IP Now and Whitelist IP Now will add the IP address to the corresponding global list. After confirmation, this list is updated on *all* your devices immediately. No policy deployment is needed.

DNS Security Intelligence

If you want to perform a blacklist/whitelist action for a DNS entry, simply right-click the entry in the DNS Query column as shown in Figure 15.38.

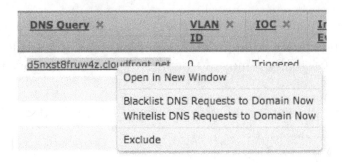

Figure 15.38: Blacklist/Whitelist DNS options

As with IP blacklisting, this entry will be added to the Global DNS Blacklist/Whitelist and updated on all your devices immediately.

URL Security Intelligence

In the same way, you can blacklist/whitelist URLs by right-clicking the entry in the URL column. Figure 15.39 shows you can choose to blacklist/whitelist just the URL or the entire domain.

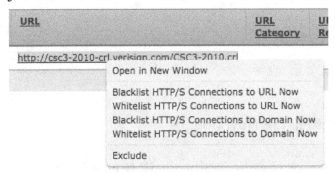

Figure 15.39: URL Blacklist/Whitelist options

One last note: There are a number of categories in the Cisco Security Intelligence feed. These range from fairly evil categories like Exploitkit, Malware, and CnC (Command and Control) to less sinister lists like Spam and Tor_exit_node. If your organization has a public-facing website, remember if you block one of the less dangerous categories you may impact legitimate traffic to your site. Just because someone uses a TOR-enabled browser doesn't mean they are evil. Although for some high-security sites, blocking this category may still be warranted. In any case, you don't want to get into hot water for blocking legitimate connections through an overzealous Security Intelligence implementation!

File and Malware Events

File/malware events is another category where you may have some tuning challenges. While you may not have nearly as many false positives, you may find there are still some opportunities to improve Firepower's file analysis behavior. You may recall from Chapter 12 that Firepower uses several methods to identify malware files. The primary method is calculating a SHA-256 hash of the file. This hash is unique to a given file, meaning there is no chance of identifying the wrong file with this method. However, that doesn't mean it's immune to false positives.

If a file is wrongly convicted by the Cisco cloud, it may be blocked even though it's not actually evil. In practice, this is a rare occurrence and is usually identified and fixed (by Cisco) rather quickly; however, it's not out of the question. If you find that a legitimate file is being wrongly convicted, you can correct this by adding the hash to a custom file list. This process is discussed in Chapter 6, "Objects." You add the hash of the file to the Clean-List and then deploy your file policy. The Clean-List is consulted by your devices before the cached disposition or cloud query. Any SHA-256 found there will not be blocked.

While false positive detections are rare, there is another reason you might want to tune your file detection—performance. You may find there are certain files that are being checked repeatedly but always coming back with an Unknown disposition. Figure 15.40 shows a list of file events. Notice at the top that there are over 3,500 events for the BZ file type.

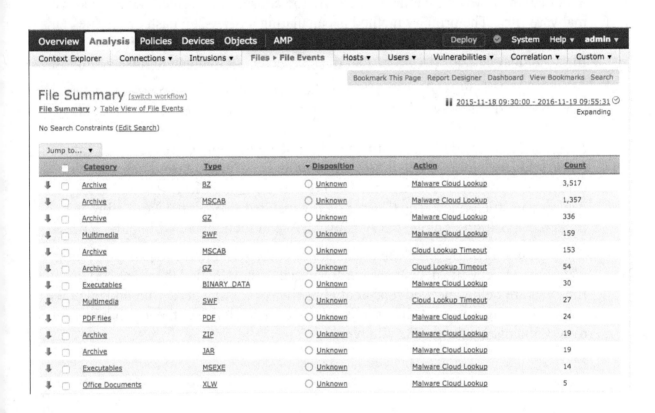

Figure 15.40: File events

Drilling into these events (using the blue arrow on the left) shows they are all from the domain canonical.com and were received by a single host—10.0.0.19. Part of the table view for these events is shown in Figure 15.41

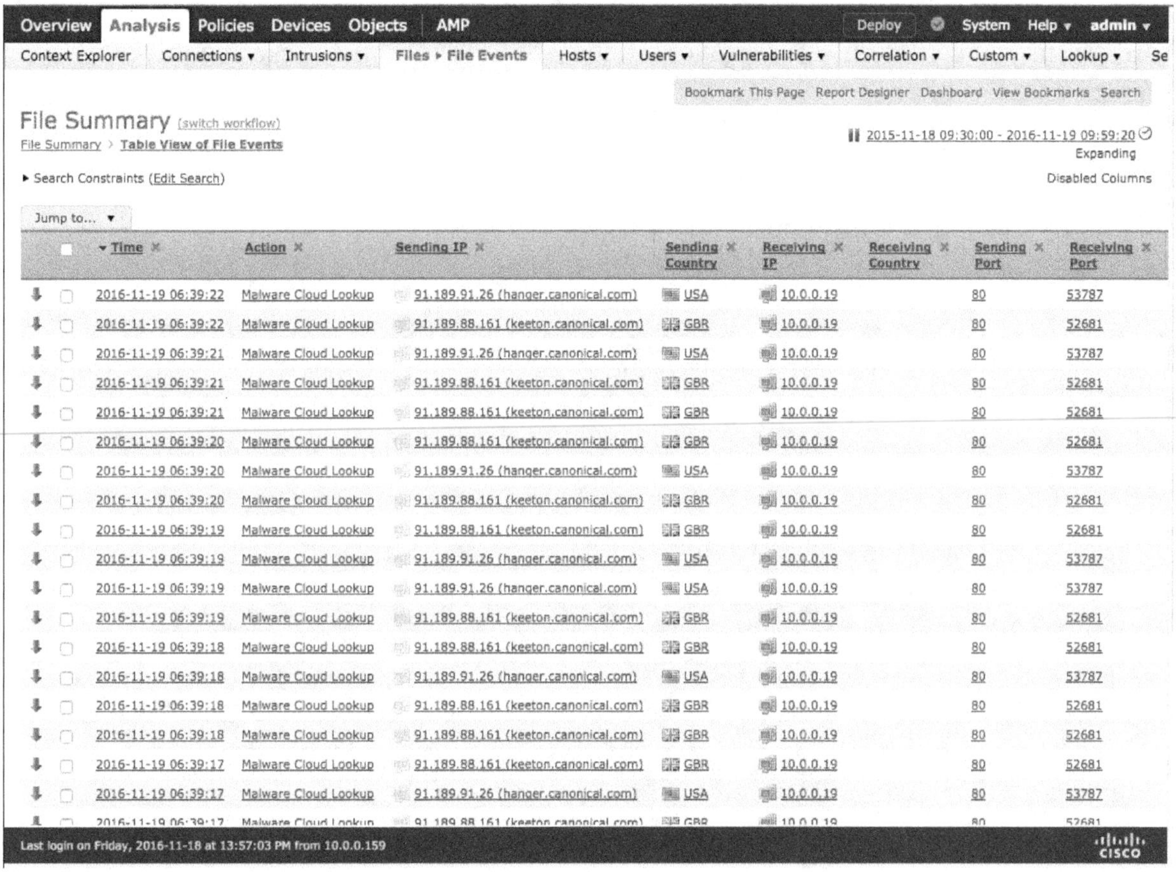

Figure 15.41: Table View of File Events

Further analysis of the file type and file names reveals that these are update packages and the host 10.0.0.19 is an Ubuntu host.

Another common occurrence is detection of antivirus (AV) updates. For some anti-virus products, these updates are distributed within a network via Windows DLL files. This can result in a large number of cloud lookups as the AV servers distribute these updates rather frequently. The SHA-256 values for these are always unknown and they are never malicious. You may see a large number of file lookup events and realize that the source of these files is your AV servers.

There are a number of ways to address these ubiquitous file events. One is to modify your File policy to ignore the file types in question. While this will stop the lookups for the AV updates, it will also blind your system to any malicious files in the same category. This is probably not a good idea!

Another method is to find a way to disable file detection for the specific traffic. In the case of the AV update, you may find that they all source from specific AV servers or retrieve files from a predictable URL. In addition, the AV software uses a specific source port when sending the files. Armed with this information, you can modify Firepower's behavior to ignore just these specific file transfers.

To do so, edit your Access Control policy. We are going to add a rule specific to this AV update traffic. The policy in Figure 15.42 is a simple one that implements file and IPS inspection on all traffic.

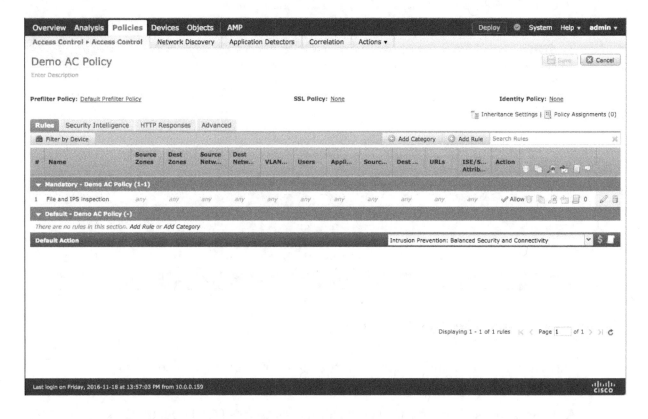

Figure 15.42: Simple AC policy

In the policy, there is a single rule that enables both IPS and file inspection for all traffic. To modify the policy and address our AV file events, we will insert a rule above the existing rule. This rule will be designed to match only the AV update traffic. We are going to configure the rule to perform IPS inspection but not file inspection on this traffic.

First, we select the Allow action for the rule, then select the Networks tab and specify the source IP addresses of our AV servers. In Figure 15.43, we have created a custom network object called AV-servers that contains these IP addresses. Objects are preferred for this type of rule so they can be easily modified later if your lists of antivirus servers changes.

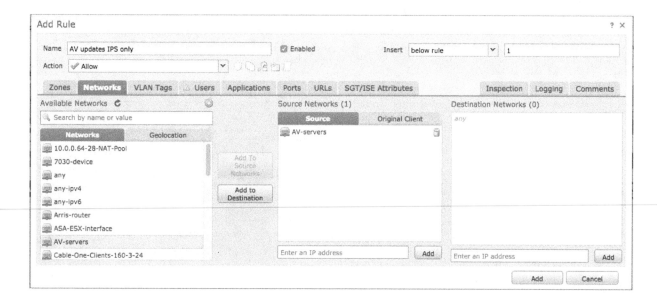

Figure 15.43: AC rule Networks tab

Next, we will modify the Ports tab and add the source port—8014/tcp. Again, we are using a custom port object (Symantec-AV) created for this purpose. This port probably won't change, but it does help in making the rule self-documenting so someone looking at it later can more readily understand what we did. Figure 15.44 shows the Ports tab.

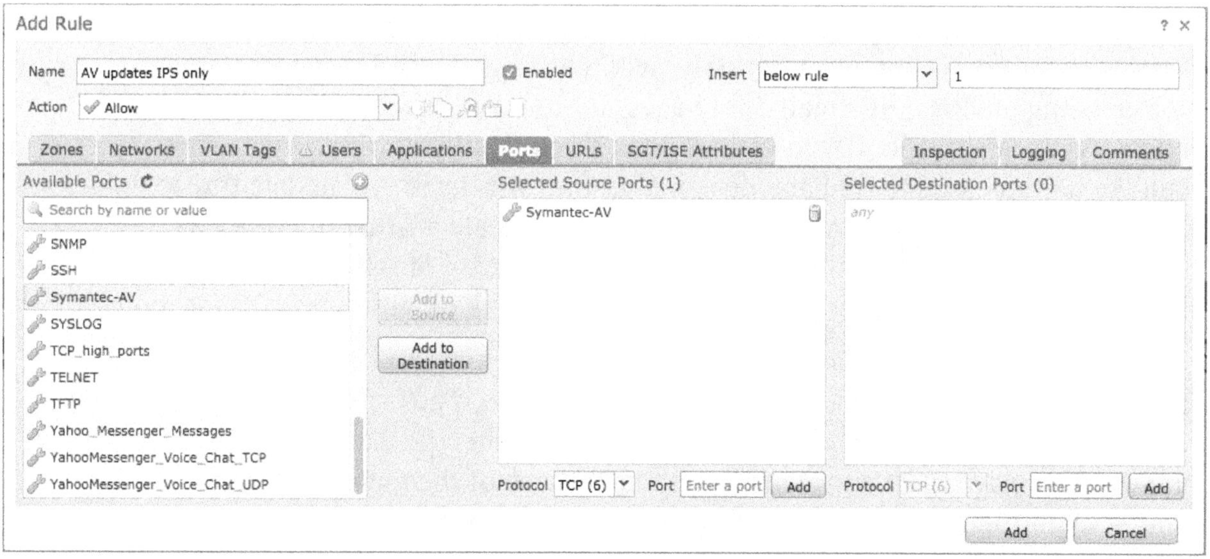

Figure 15.44: AC rule Ports tab

Finally, on the Inspection tab (Figure 15.45), we will specify an Intrusion policy but not a File policy. This ensures we perform IPS inspection but not file inspection on the traffic.

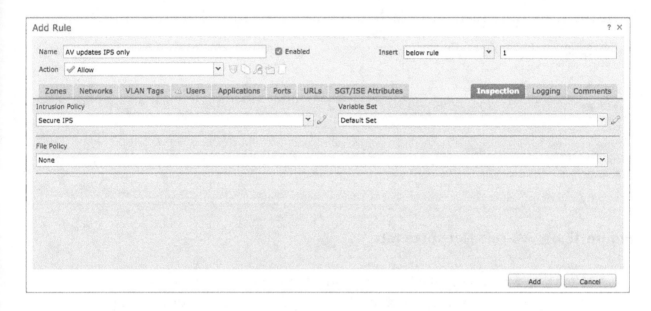

Figure 15.45: AC rule Inspection tab

Decide if you want connection events logged for this rule and configure the Logging tab appropriately.

One note regarding the rule we just created: The example shows how to address the file inspection behavior only, while leaving the IPS inspection intact. If we're being practical, it's really not necessary to even perform IPS inspection on this AV update traffic. If you were to look through all your Snort rules, you would be hard pressed to find any designed to find attacks in AV update traffic. Because of this, an even more efficient option is to create a Trust rule for AV update traffic. By simply using the action of Trust instead of Allow, you will allow this AV update traffic to pass through your devices without any type of inspection.

Finally, remember that complexity is the enemy of security. There are other ways to address situations like the ones in our example. These might include creating custom File policies that do not contain the file type used by our AV updates. This may not be a preferred method because of the management complexity introduced by multiple File policies. Firepower is a very complex system to start with, and anything you can do to make it easier to understand is probably effort well spent.

Chapter 16: User Management

In this chapter, we're going to cover a variety of administrative functions for user account management. As we progress, you'll learn all about internal and external user account management, how to describe various user roles, and how to create custom user roles.

We'll demonstrate how to configure both internal and external user accounts and show you how to permit a user to escalate their account privileges.

You'll discover that user authentication can be achieved locally through the internal database or via an external authentication server like LDAP or RADIUS.

User Account Management

When you log in to the Firepower Management Center (FMC) GUI interface with a username and password, the appliance first looks for the user ID in the local database. Users in the local database will predictably be authenticated locally on the appliance, but even if the user account that's asking for access requires external authentication, the system will still try the local database first. If it can't find a local user that corresponds, it will move on and look into an external server for a match. These external servers can either be a Lightweight Directory Access Protocol (LDAP) directory server or a Remote Authentication Dial In User Service (RADIUS) authentication server. Both types can provide a database list of users.

It's good to know that you can completely control user permissions for anyone no matter if they're trying to authenticate internally or externally. Unless you change the user permissions manually, externally authenticated users receive their permissions via these three ways:

- Through the group or access list they belong to
- Based upon the default user access role you've set in the server authentication object
- Through the **System➤Integration➤Realms** policy on the managing FMC

Internal vs. External User Authentication

So, by default, the appliance will go with the internal database for authentication to check for users' credentials when they log in. But though internal authentication is definitely the simplest way to manage users, it's just not at all an efficient or even a feasible option for really large networks. This fact makes being able to specify whether a given user you're creating will be internally or externally authenticated a very cool feature!

Still, understand that when using internal authentication, all user credentials are managed in the internal database and local authentication won't take place until the username and password are verified against the internal Firepower System database. Since you manually create each user in the local database to be authenticated there, you set the user role and access setting for that user at that time as well. This means you don't need to deal with any default settings for users attempting to authenticate.

External authentication occurs when the Firepower Management Center (FMC) or a managed device tries to authenticate users from either an external LDAP or RADIUS server database, but you can't use both methods. And if you choose to go with external authentication, you must create an authentication object for each server to specify the exact location from which you want to authenticate users. The authentication object contains your settings for connecting to and checking the user database from the corresponding server.

The appliance will then check each configured authentication server in the order in which they're listed in the system policy when attempting to find the user in the database.

An internal user will be automatically converted to external authentication if the same username and password exists on an external server. Once the user has been converted to external authentication, it cannot revert back to internal authentication.

User Privileges

You can create users using predefined roles or create custom roles to assign to individuals or even a group of users. Let's say you want to create a group of users that only gets access to data to analyze the security events of the monitored network but you don't want this group to ever gain access to the administrative functions of the Firepower system itself. This is where the ability to create custom roles really shines—you can easily use predefined roles like Discovery Admin and Security Analyst, which allow the users to view network events without being able to change any configuration settings. Creating custom roles provides even more detail on what a particular user or a given group of users can and cannot do—nice!

We'll explore this in detail later in the section called "Configuring External Authentication." For now, it's important for you to remember that once the user logs in externally for the first time and receives the default access role, you'll be able to find this user on the User Management page and add or remove access rights for them. You can opt to not modify the rights, which will grant the user the rights via the default access role. And remember, when you create internal users, you assign the role manually as you create them.

The default access role for an externally authenticated user can be overridden by the configured management of access rights. You can do this through either the LDAP or RADIUS groups or objects, where the permissions for users originate from the default access rights assigned to their specific group—assuming they belong to one. If they don't belong to an LDAP group or RADIUS object, they'll assume the default role.

Predefined User Roles

Here's a list of the predefined user roles, depending on the features you've licensed:

Access Admins can view and modify access control and file policies, but they can't apply their policy changes.

Administrators can set up the appliance's network configuration, manage user accounts and Collective Security Intelligence cloud connections, and configure system policies and system settings. Users with the Administrator role have all the rights and privileges of all other roles, with the exception of lesser, restricted versions of those privileges.

Discovery Admins can review, modify, and delete network discovery policies, but they can't apply their policy changes.

External Database users can query the Firepower database using an external application that supports JDBC SSL connections. On the web interface, they can access the online help and user preferences.

Intrusion Admins can review, modify, and delete intrusion policies and intrusion rules, but they can't apply their policy changes.

Maintenance Users can access monitoring functions such as health monitoring, host statistics, performance data, system logs, and maintenance functions, including task scheduling and backing up the system. Note that Maintenance Users do not have access to the functions in the Policies menu and they can access the dashboard only from the Analysis menu.

Network Admins can review, modify, and apply device configurations as well as review and modify access control policies, but they can't apply their policy changes.

Security Approvers can view and apply policy changes, but they can't create configuration and policy changes.

Security Analysts can review, analyze, and delete intrusion, discovery, user activity, connection, correlation, and network change events. They can review, analyze, and when applicable, delete hosts, host attributes, services, vulnerabilities, and client applications. Security Analysts can also generate reports and view health events, but they can't delete or modify these.

Security Analysts (Read Only) enjoy all the same rights as Security Analysts, except that they cannot delete events.

Custom User roles allow you to customize exactly what users with a designated role can access. They also allows you to place precise restrictions on exactly what information users can view.

Note that any role can be the default access role for externally authenticated users.

Creating New User Accounts

Now would be the perfect time for us to demonstrate exactly how to create internal user accounts. To do that, just follow this procedure.

From the menu options, on the right side of the menu bar, choose **System ➤ ➤ Users**, as shown in Figure 16.1

This will display the User Management page, which lists the information on existing user accounts. Figure 16.2 shows the User Management page.

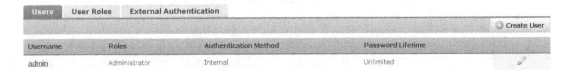

There are two things you should focus on in Figure 16.2. First, there's a default admin user, which uses an internal authentication method, and second, there are those three tabs at the top: Users, User Roles, and External Authentication. We're going to focus on these tabs throughout this section.

Okay—so let's create a new user and assign it a role. From the User Management screen, on the right side, click Create User. You'll receive the screen shown in Figure 16.3, called the User Configuration page.

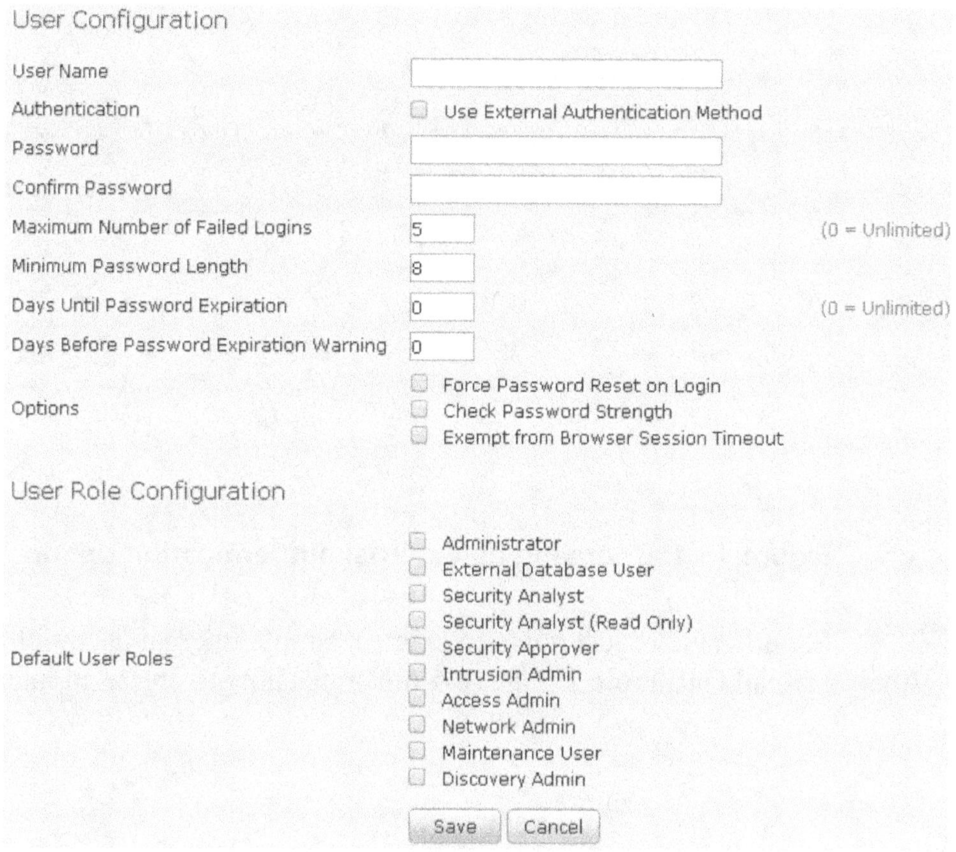

User Configuration

User Name	
Authentication	☐ Use External Authentication Method
Password	
Confirm Password	
Maximum Number of Failed Logins	5 (0 = Unlimited)
Minimum Password Length	8
Days Until Password Expiration	0 (0 = Unlimited)
Days Before Password Expiration Warning	0
Options	☐ Force Password Reset on Login ☐ Check Password Strength ☐ Exempt from Browser Session Timeout

User Role Configuration

Default User Roles	☐ Administrator ☐ External Database User ☐ Security Analyst ☐ Security Analyst (Read Only) ☐ Security Approver ☐ Intrusion Admin ☐ Access Admin ☐ Network Admin ☐ Maintenance User ☐ Discovery Admin

Save   Cancel

Figure 16.3: User Configuration options page

If you create a user here, know that you are creating a local user account. If you click Use External Authentication Method instead, most of the options on this page will disappear and you'll only be able to pick the user role from the screen pictured in Figure 16.4.

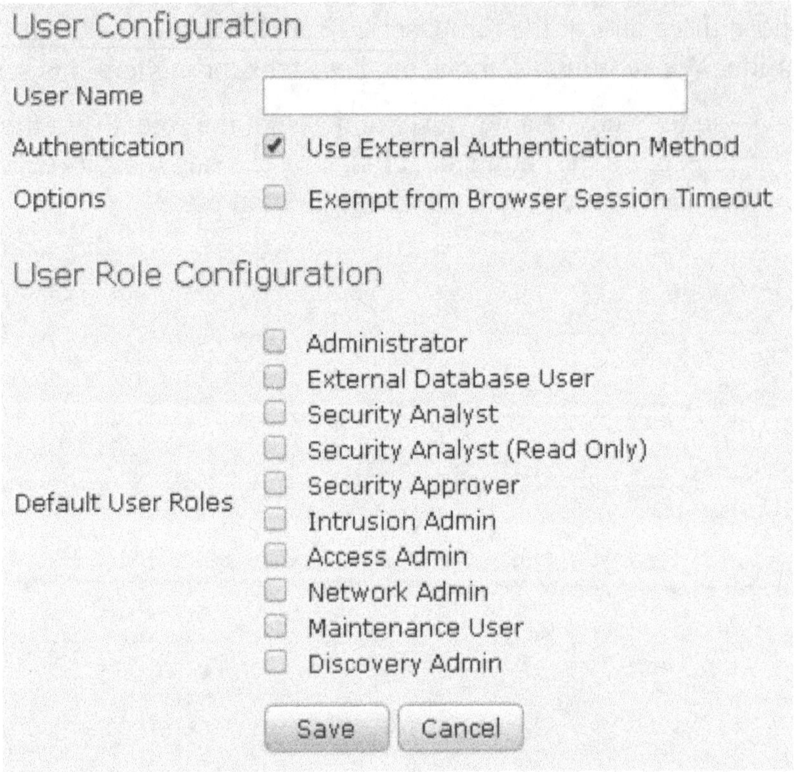

Figure 16.4: Choosing an external authentication option

For now, we're just going to create a simple internal user with a Security Analyst (Read Only) role. Figure16.5 illustrates how to create an internal user.

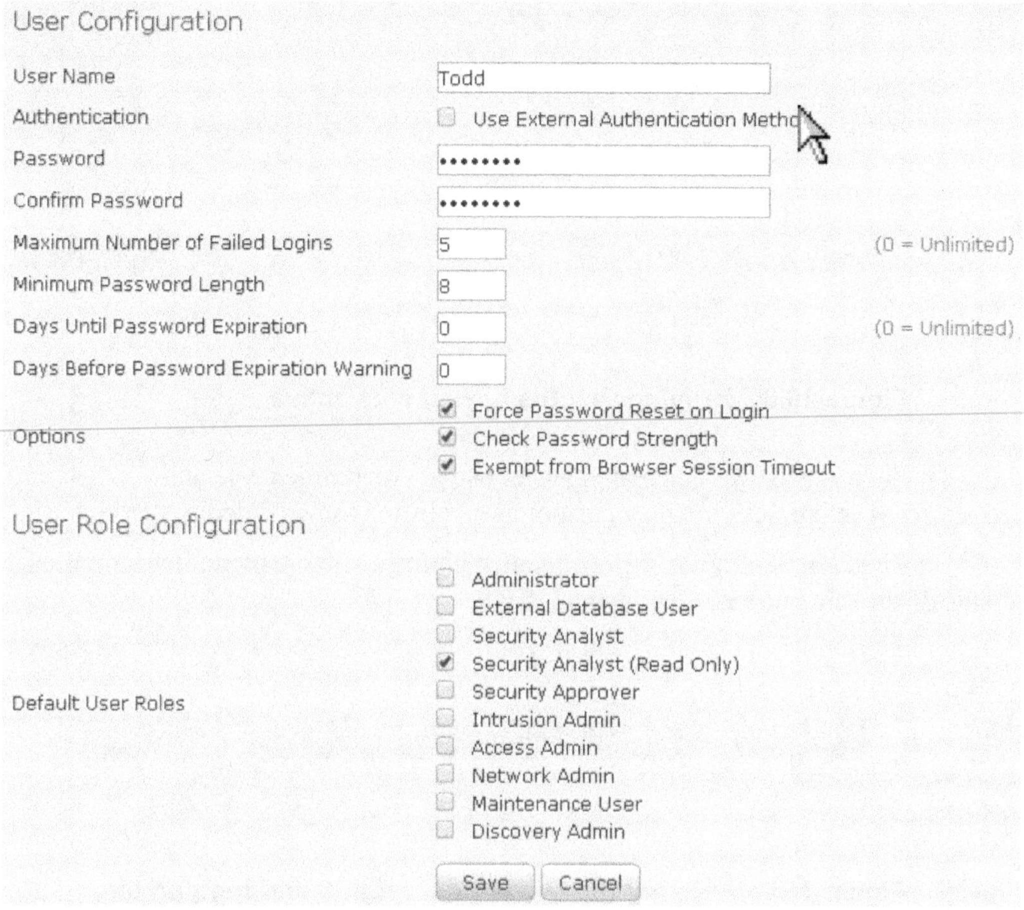

User Configuration

User Name	Todd
Authentication	☐ Use External Authentication Method
Password	••••••••
Confirm Password	••••••••
Maximum Number of Failed Logins	5 (0 = Unlimited)
Minimum Password Length	8
Days Until Password Expiration	0 (0 = Unlimited)
Days Before Password Expiration Warning	0
Options	☑ Force Password Reset on Login ☑ Check Password Strength ☑ Exempt from Browser Session Timeout

User Role Configuration

Default User Roles

☐ Administrator
☐ External Database User
☐ Security Analyst
☑ Security Analyst (Read Only)
☐ Security Approver
☐ Intrusion Admin
☐ Access Admin
☐ Network Admin
☐ Maintenance User
☐ Discovery Admin

Save   Cancel

Figure 16.5: Creating an internal user

Look at Figure 16.5 again… did you notice we created a user named Todd and that we have forced the password to be reset on first login? Good! We also left the defaults for the maximum number of failed logins at 5 and a minimum password length of 8 characters, and we didn't set the password to expire either.

Another thing you can do when creating a user is to opt for checking password strength, which will require strong passwords, meaning they'll have to be at least eight alphanumeric characters—uppercase and lowercase, including at least one numeric character. The password cannot appear in a dictionary or include consecutive, repeating characters.

We chose not to have the browser session timeout since the user role is a read-only analyst. You probably wouldn't want a user to timeout if they were logged into a screen in a large network operations center (NOC), where the browser is displayed in all its glory on the NOC's huge screen, right?

We then clicked Save, and Figure 16.6 shows that the user was created and that it is active.

Figure 16.6: Verifying that the new user is active

So, now that we've created a user using a predefined role and verified that the user is active, let's create a custom user role and assign Todd to that role.

First, look at Figure 16.7 and notice all the available menu items on the left side of the screen, from Overview to AMP.

Figure 16.7: Verifying the current user rights and logging out

Now check out the right side and notice that we're choosing to log out as admin.

Once we log in as Todd, we get a look at the options we obtain as System Analyst (Read Only). Figure 16.8 shows the menu items after we logged in as Todd.

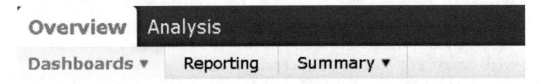

Figure 16.8: Logging in and verifying the new user's rights

Notice that we now only have the options for Overview and Analysis, and on the right side we no longer have the System Configuration or Health policy menu options. We're going to log back in as admin and then create a custom user role.

Figure 16.9 shows the predefined user roles available. Notice that while they can be disabled, they're all enabled by default.

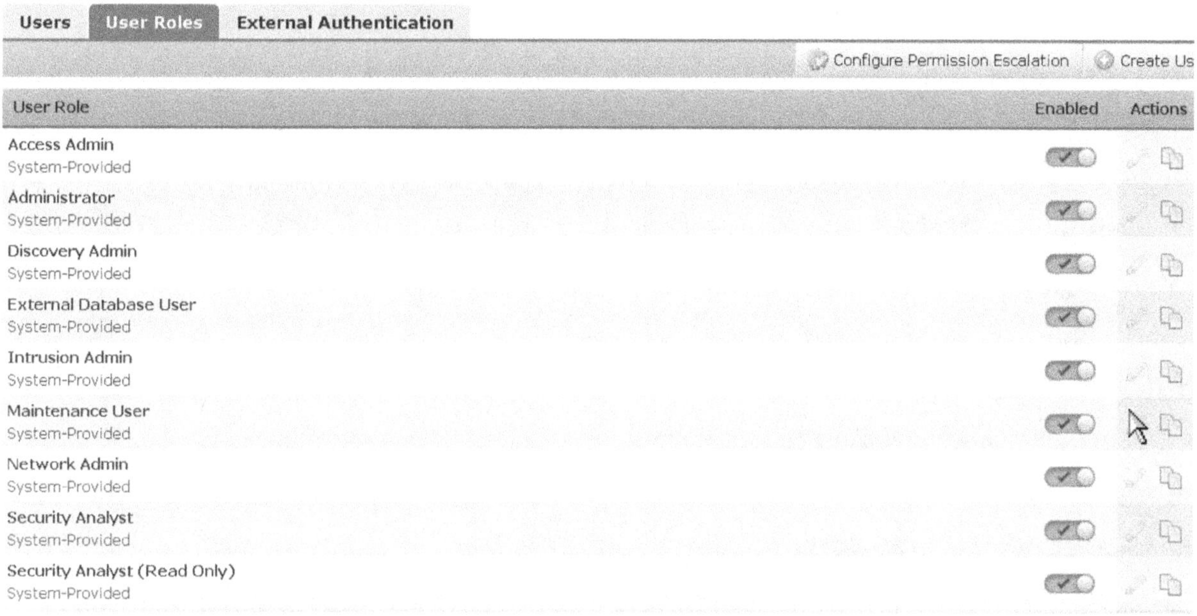

Users	User Roles	External Authentication

User Role	Enabled	Actions
Access Admin System-Provided		
Administrator System-Provided		
Discovery Admin System-Provided		
External Database User System-Provided		
Intrusion Admin System-Provided		
Maintenance User System-Provided		
Network Admin System-Provided		
Security Analyst System-Provided		
Security Analyst (Read Only) System-Provided		

Configure Permission Escalation   Create Us

Figure 16.9: Verifying the default user roles

These predefined roles can be edited, but when you try to save the changes, you will be asked to name the new custom role. So basically, you can edit an existing role, but you can't save it as a predefined role—only as a new role.

Okay, so on the top right side, we're clicking Create User Role, and as shown in Figure 16.10, we're going to create a user role named Helpdesk and assign some individual custom options for this role.

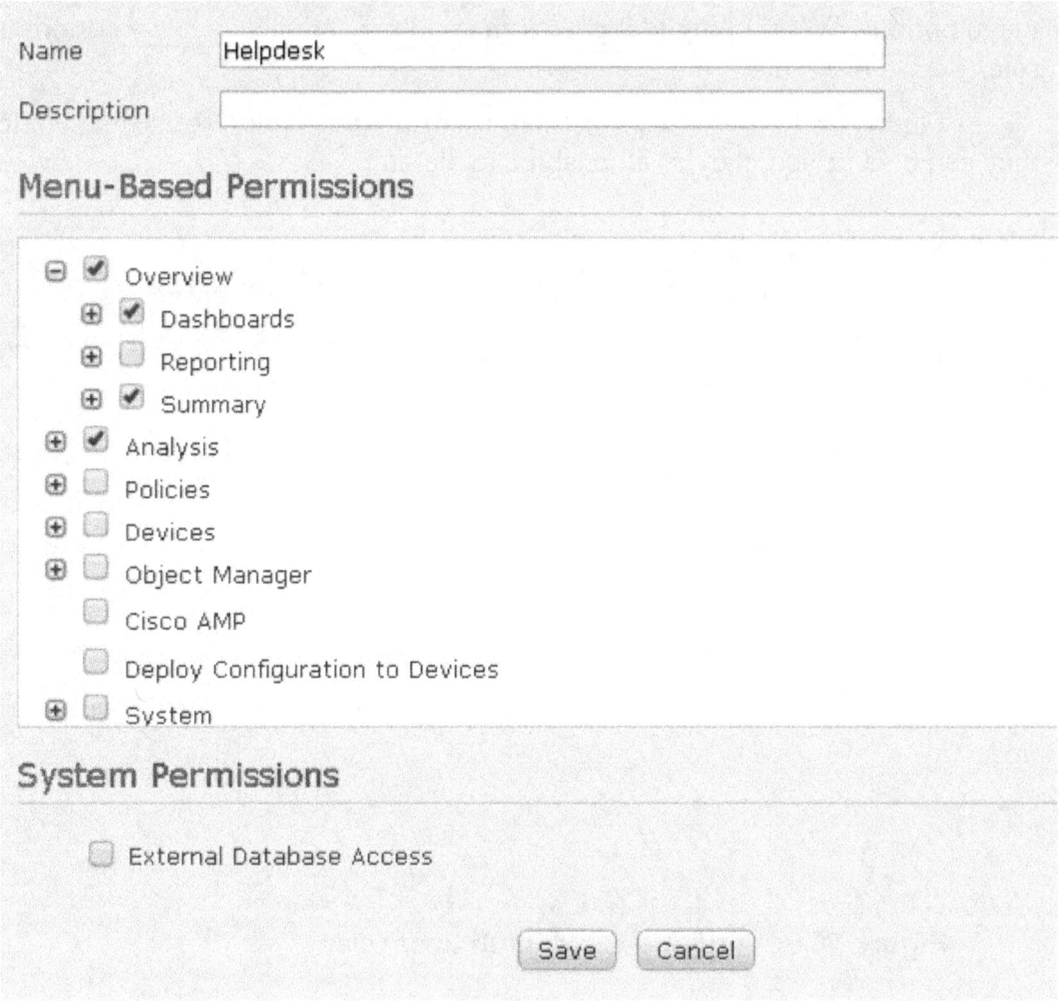

| Name | Helpdesk |
| Description | |

Menu-Based Permissions

- ⊖ ☑ Overview
  - ⊕ ☑ Dashboards
  - ⊕ ☐ Reporting
  - ⊕ ☑ Summary
- ⊕ ☑ Analysis
- ⊕ ☐ Policies
- ⊕ ☐ Devices
- ⊕ ☐ Object Manager
- ☐ Cisco AMP
- ☐ Deploy Configuration to Devices
- ⊕ ☐ System

System Permissions

☐ External Database Access

[Save] [Cancel]

Figure 16.10: Creating a custom user role

Now once the custom user role is created, you're allowed to assign a user to it. Look at Figure 16.11 and notice that when user Todd is edited, the custom user role of Helpdesk is now available at the bottom.

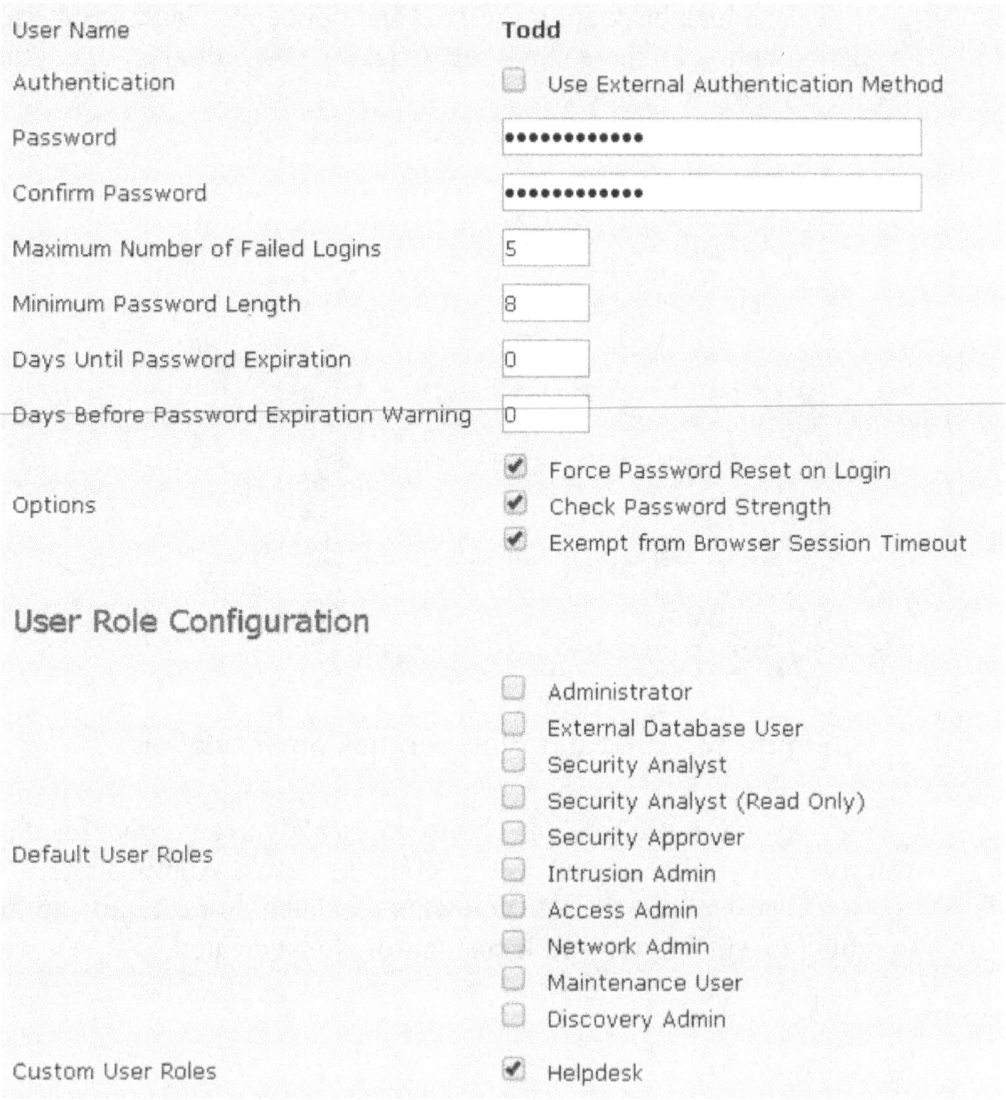

User Name	**Todd**
Authentication	☐ Use External Authentication Method
Password	••••••••••••
Confirm Password	••••••••••••
Maximum Number of Failed Logins	5
Minimum Password Length	8
Days Until Password Expiration	0
Days Before Password Expiration Warning	0
Options	☑ Force Password Reset on Login ☑ Check Password Strength ☑ Exempt from Browser Session Timeout

User Role Configuration

Default User Roles	☐ Administrator ☐ External Database User ☐ Security Analyst ☐ Security Analyst (Read Only) ☐ Security Approver ☐ Intrusion Admin ☐ Access Admin ☐ Network Admin ☐ Maintenance User ☐ Discovery Admin
Custom User Roles	☑ Helpdesk

Figure 16.11: Assigning a custom user role

Once we click Save, user Todd is now using only the newly created, custom role of Helpdesk.

Managing User Role Escalation

Let's say that user Todd was working alone on a holiday and something really serious goes wrong. The user Todd calls you in a panic saying, "What do you want me to do? All I can do is verify information!" This is a perfect example of when you would use permission escalation (assuming for some reason you can't VPN in and take care of the issue yourself!).

Take a look back at Figure 16.9 and notice the Configure Permission Escalation button up there at the top. Clicking that button will get you to the next screen, depicted in Figure 16.12.

Figure 16.12: Configuring permission escalation

As you can see, you can choose to escalate to any predefined or custom user role that you've created. We're going to choose Administrator. Now, go back to User Roles and edit the role you want escalated. For example, in Figure 16.13, I am going to edit that Helpdesk custom role I just created.

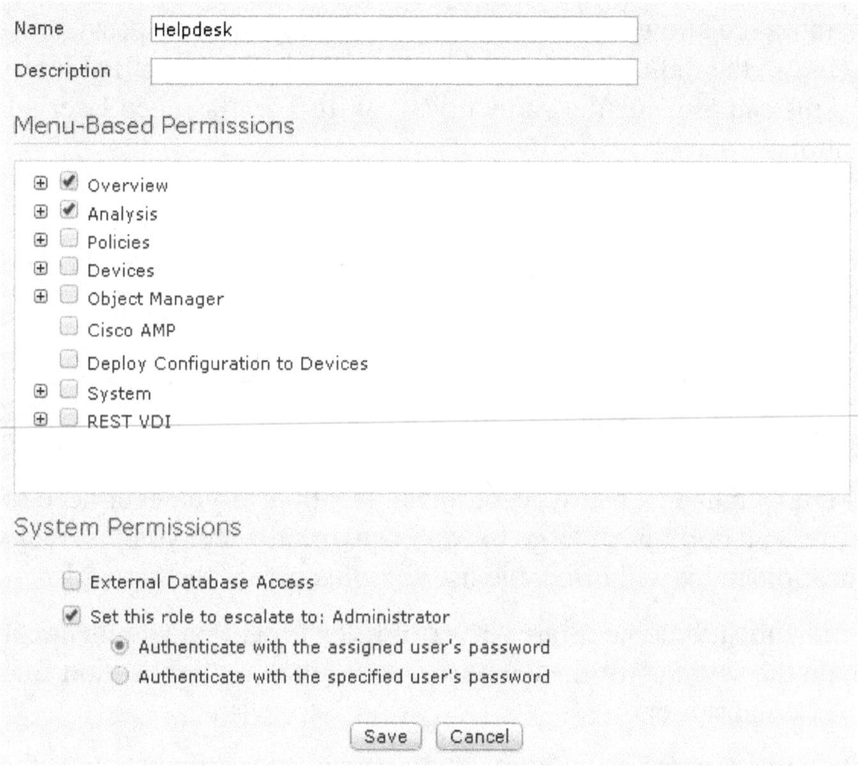

Figure 16.13: Configuring permission escalation part II

As you can see in Figure 15.13, I choose the Helpdesk role and then set the role to escalate to Administrator, using the assigned user's password.

This is an awesome feature that gives you the power to escalate a user's privileges on a temporary basis!

Okay—so now we're going to log out as Admin, and then log back in as Todd (shown in Figure 16.14). Notice that we get a new option under the user Todd. That's right—Escalate Permissions!

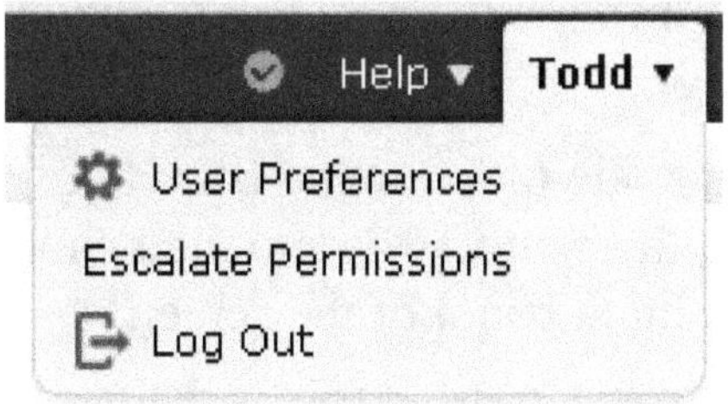

Figure 16.14: Escalating permissions

Now if we were to choose the Escalate Permissions option, and we enter the administrator password when prompted, then user Todd would be escalated to

Administrator. To allow user Todd to escalate using his own password, you would want to choose the radius button Authenticate With The Specified User's Password instead of using the Authenticate With The Assigned User's Password radius button.

Configuring External Authentication

The reason we would opt to have an external authentication method over an internal authentication method for users logging into the FMC is because doing this allows you to set up a directory on your network to organize different objects like user credentials in a handy, centralized location. If you ever need to change a user profile, you don't need to go to each network device; you just make changes in one location and it will affect the user's rights across the network.

Authentication objects are server profiles for external authentication servers and contain the settings for the connection as well as authentication filter settings for your external servers.

When you create an authentication object, you define settings that let you connect to an authentication server. These objects are created, managed, and deleted on the FMC, not on the managed devices themselves. Using an external authentication method allows a user to log in to any FMC or managed device with a single login by applying a system configuration/platform setting on the managed device, because when you apply the policy, the object is copied to the device—sweet!

Creating Authentication Objects

Make a mental note that to create an authentication object, you must first make sure you have a solid IP connection through the network from your FMC to the authentication server(s) you'll be using.

From the menu options, on the right side of the menu bar, choose System ➢ Local ➢ User Management, just like back in Figure 16.1, and then choose the External Authentication tab located in the main panel of the screen.

On the right side, click the Add External Authentication Object button and you'll receive the screen shown in Figure 16.15. The first option to choose is what type of authentication object you want to create: LDAP or RADIUS.

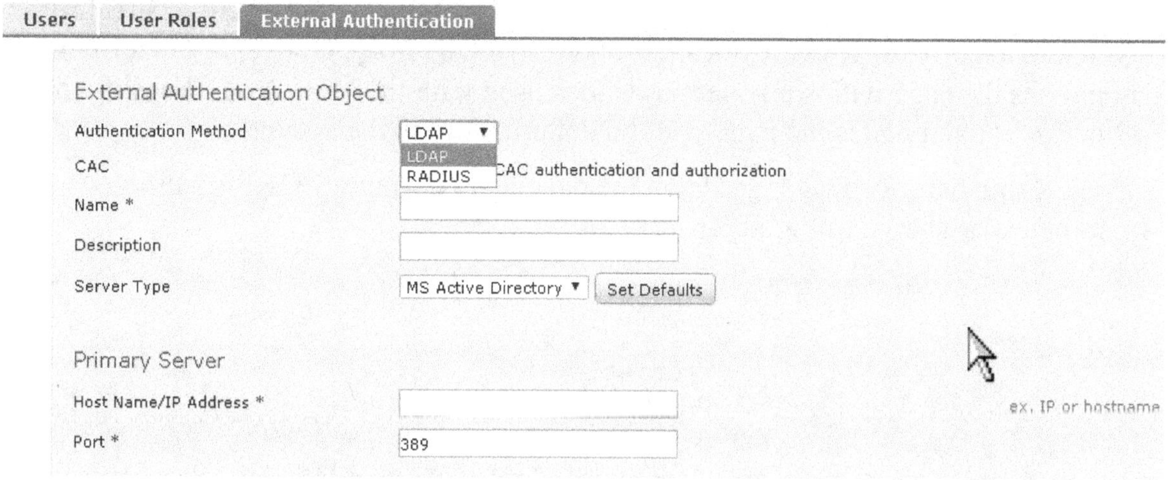
Users
User Roles
External Authentication
External Authentication Object
Authentication Method
LDAP
LDAP
RADIUS
CAC
CAC authentication and authorization
Name *
Description
Server Type
MS Active Directory
Set Defaults
Primary Server
Host Name/IP Address *
ex. IP or hostname
Port *
389

Figure 16.15: Choosing LDAP or RADIUS

After you choose your object type, you'll need to set your server type as well as the primary server. You can have a backup server, but that's optional in the configuration.

Figure 16.16 shows an LDAP server that we've got running on the local network. We've configured the name, server type, and primary server information, including the port number.

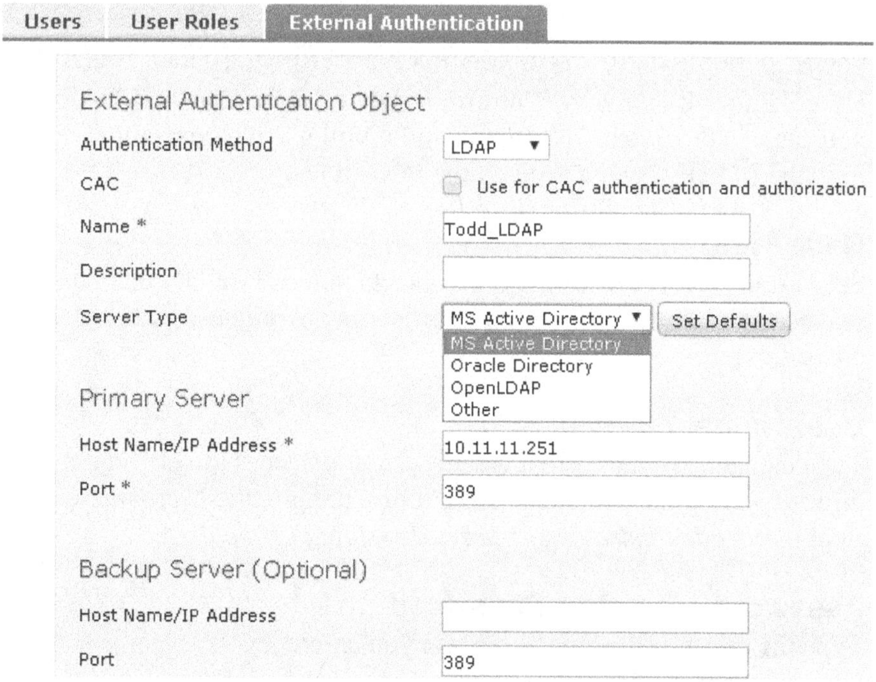
Users
User Roles
External Authentication
External Authentication Object
Authentication Method
LDAP
CAC
Use for CAC authentication and authorization
Name *
Todd_LDAP
Description
Server Type
MS Active Directory
Set Defaults
MS Active Directory
Oracle Directory
OpenLDAP
Other
Primary Server
Host Name/IP Address *
10.11.11.251
Port *
389
Backup Server (Optional)
Host Name/IP Address
Port
389

Figure 16.16: Configuring LDAP server options

In the Server Type field, you can choose OpenLDAP, MS Active Directory, Oracle Directory, or Other. Choosing MS Active Directory, Oracle, or OpenLDAP populates the page with some default values used with those servers. Choosing the Other option populates the page with no default values whatsoever.

From here, you want go down the page and configure LDAP-specific parameters as shown in Figure 16.17.

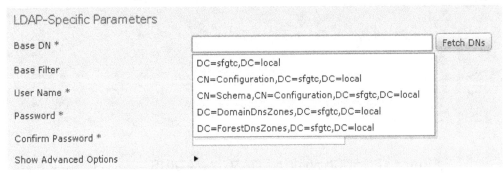

Figure 16.17: LDAP-specific parameters

Really—the hardest part of the LDAP configuration is getting the right information in order to configure the LDAP-specific parameters in the first place. Figure 16.17 shows the information you need to know in order to configure LDAP.

Base DN
Sets a starting point for searching the LDAP directory tree. If you filled out the User Name and Password/Confirm Password fields for the LDAP admin account, you can use the Fetch DNs button and it will use the configured credentials to log in to the LDAP server and fetch the DN value.

Base Filter
Sets a filter that retrieves only the objects in the Base DN that has the characters you configured in the filter. You need to use parentheses when defining the characters!

User Name
Type the name of a user that is authorized to access the objects in the LDAP directory using the canonical name. For example, the username we're using in this field is *cn=administrator,cn=users,dc=sfgtc,dc=local*.

Password / Confirm Password
Type the password for the username you entered.

After you have configured your LDAP-specific parameters, you can click the Show Advanced Options icon. From here, you can configure an encryption method if your LDAP server is configured to support it. Plus, it lets you set a path to the location of the TLS or SSL authentication certificate, if you're using one.

The User Name Template option allows you to specify how usernames entered in the user login field should be formatted by mapping the string conversion character (%s) to the value of the Pluggable Authentication Module (PAM) login attribute for the user. This username template is the format for the distinguished name used for authentication. When a user enters a username into the login page, the name is substituted for the string conversion character, and the resulting distinguished name is then used to search for the user credentials.

Last, the timeout field is used to allow you to set the amount of time the appliance takes to fail over to the backup LDAP server if one is configured.

After you have finished with the Show Advanced Options portion of the page, then configure the Attribute Mapping options.

Different types of LDAP servers use different attributes to store user data. For an LDAP server that use the PAM, as our server does, use the login attribute of uid. If the PAM login attribute for the target server is something other than uid, set it here.

For a Microsoft Active Directory server, use a UI Access attribute of sAMAccountName or userPrincipalName to enable the retrieval of users.

The Fetch Attrs button, which provides the output shown in Figure 16.18, will allow you to access the LDAP server by way of the impersonation account login credentials to obtain UI access and/or shell access attributes—if they exist.

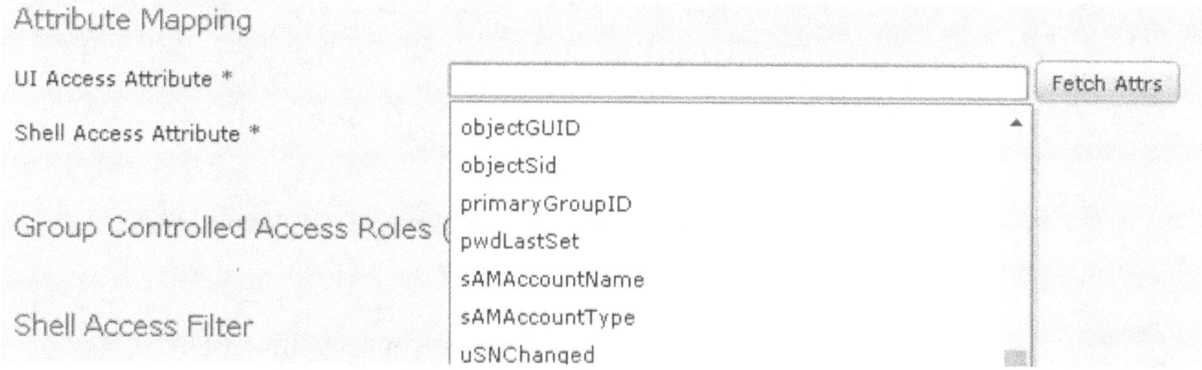

Attribute Mapping

| UI Access Attribute * | | Fetch Attrs |

Shell Access Attribute *

objectGUID
objectSid
primaryGroupID
Group Controlled Access Roles (pwdLastSet
sAMAccountName
sAMAccountType
Shell Access Filter uSNChanged

Figure 16.18: Fetch Attrs output

Selecting a server type and setting defaults prepopulates a shell access attribute that's usually appropriate for that specific type of server. You can use any attribute, if the value of the attribute is a valid username for shell access. Valid usernames are unique and can include underscores (_), periods (.), hyphens (-), and alphanumeric characters.

If you prefer to base access permissions on a specific user's membership within an LDAP group, you can specify distinguished names for existing groups on your LDAP server for each of the access roles used by your Firepower System. Do this from the Group Controlled Access Roles configuration.

You can also configure a default access role for those users detected by LDAP that do not belong to any specified groups. When a user logs in, the Firepower System dynamically checks the LDAP server and assigns access rights per the user's current group membership. It's really important to remember that you can also add roles to users in the User Management interface, but you cannot assign privileges lower than what is already granted to the user by the Group Controlled Access Roles settings!

Figure 16.19 shows the Shell Access Filter and Additional Test Parameters settings.

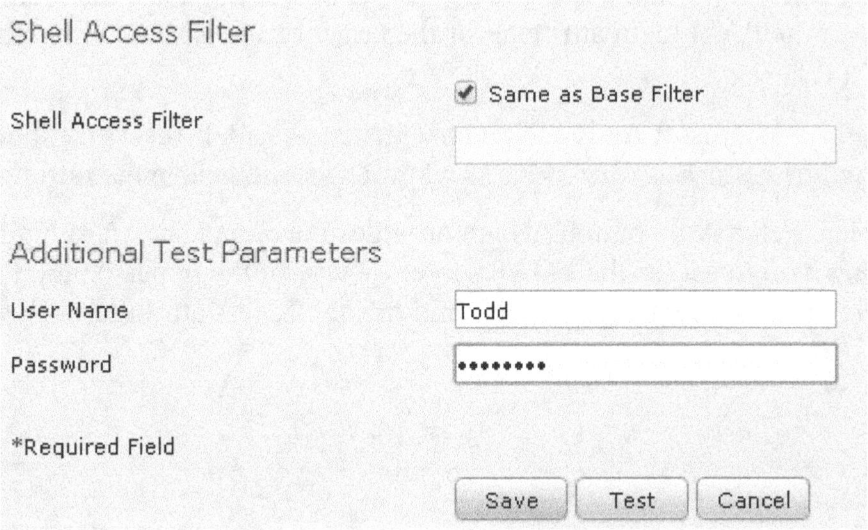

Figure 16.19: Shell Access Filter and Additional Test Parameters settings

By configuring the Shell Access Filter settings, you can allow LDAP-authenticated users shell access, but to stop anyone from having shell access, you need to check the Same As Base Filter box.

Last, as shown at the bottom of Figure 16.20, you can test your server settings with the Test button. You can also test specific user credentials on the server from there by entering the username and password. We're going to test our server setup by pressing the button. Figure 16.21 shows the output we received once we tested the server connectivity and authentication.

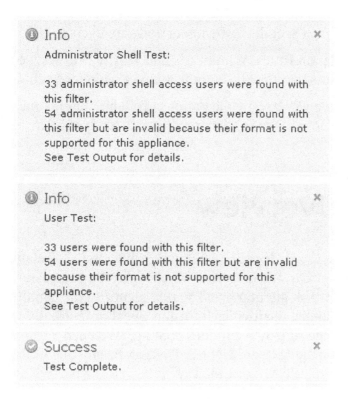

Administrator Shell Test:

33 administrator shell access users were found with this filter.
54 administrator shell access users were found with this filter but are invalid because their format is not supported for this appliance.
See Test Output for details.

User Test:

33 users were found with this filter.
54 users were found with this filter but are invalid because their format is not supported for this appliance.
See Test Output for details.

Success

Test Complete.

Figure 16.20: Server test results

After you set up your server and test your connectivity and authentication, click the Save button at the bottom of the screen to save your configuration. At this point you need still need to do two things, as shown in Figure 16.21.

Figure 16.21: Setting the default role and enabling the LDAP object

If you don't set the default user role, your external users won't be able to log in, so don't skip this! Lastly, enable the LDAP by clicking on the slide bar, and then click Save And Apply and you're set!

Chapter 17: Correlation Policy

Correlation Policy is an often overlooked but useful feature of the Firepower System. The features available in this area concentrate on detection of unusual activity rather than specific intrusion or malware events.

By using Correlation Rules, White Lists and Traffic Profiles we can detect network or host behaviors that may be an indication of malicious activity.

In this chapter, we will review the options available for creating rules, lists and profiles to identify activity even when there are no Snort rules available to detect a specific threat.

Correlation Overview

Correlation focuses on identifying network behaviors. Correlation rules are written to identify network traffic or events which would be considered an exception - something worth alerting on. The rule identifies the condition we want to know about - for example a particular Intrusion Event or unusually large HTTP connection. However, the rule by itself does nothing. We need a response. The response is generated by the Defense Center. This can be any one of the built-in notification types - Syslog, SNMP or Email.

This can also be a Remediation - a script or program that runs on the Defense Center. The rule and response are linked together with the Correlation Policy. This relationship is shown in the table below. The left column shows all of the types of activity that a Correlation Rule can detect. The right column shows the responses available.

The function of the Correlation Policy is to link the response to the rule.

Rule based on:	Response
Intrusion Event	Syslog
Discovery Event	SNMP
User Activity	Email (SMTP)
Host Input Event	Built-in Remediation
Connection Event	Custom Remediation
Traffic Profile Change	
Malware Event	
White List*	
Correlation Policy links the Rule with the Response	

* A White List is slightly different because it operates like a rule.

Correlation provides a powerful, flexible alerting mechanism. But there's even more to it than that. By using the Remediation feature you can trigger a built-in or custom script in response to a Correlation rule. This means the Defense Center can respond either with a custom alert or whatever action you can write a script to perform. We will discuss remediations in more detail below.

Correlation Rules, Responses and Policies

When you set out to create a custom response to an event you might be tempted to start with the Correlation Policy. However, the policy simply links the Correlation Rule with the response. This means before you can create the policy you need to have both the rule and the response already completed.

Correlation Rules

Let's start with a simple rule example. Say we want to be alerted anytime there is a large HTTP connection initiated from our network. For this example, we will say this is any connection which transfers more than 5MB total. Suppose we found that almost all HTTP connections from our network are less than 5MB in total size. In fact, a connection over 5MB typically indicates either malicious or unauthorized activity. Rather than try to create a Snort rule that might look for specific data in a packet, we need a way to identify anytime a host sends or receives more than 5MB in an HTTP connection. Assuming we are already logging connection events, this is a perfect application for a Correlation Rule.

To begin, navigate to Policies --> Correlation then click the Rule Management tab. On your first visit you will see an empty rule list as shown in figure 17.1:

Figure 17.1: Rule Management Tab

Clicking the Create Rule button on the right takes you to the Rule Information screen as shown below.

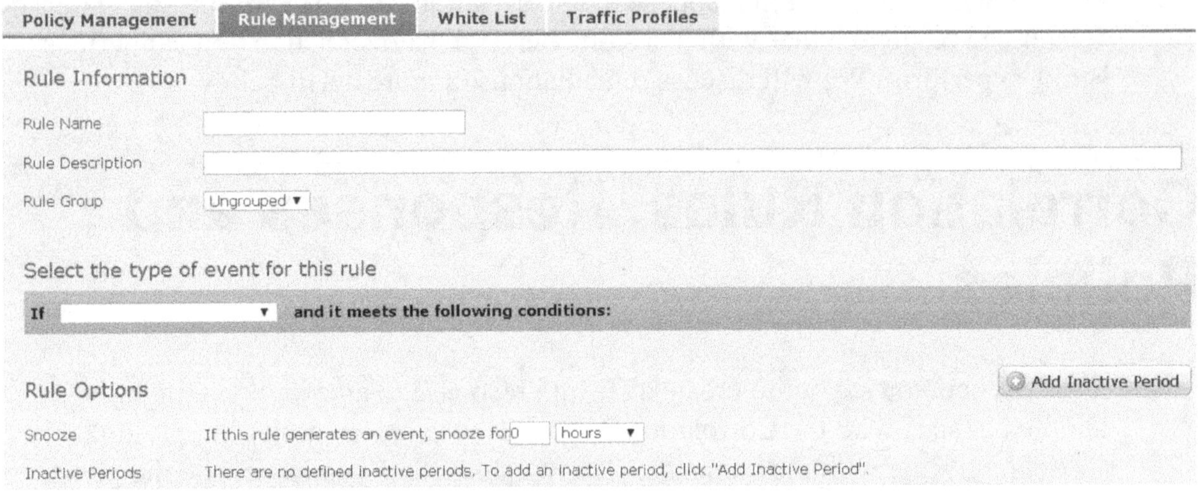

| Policy Management | **Rule Management** | White List | Traffic Profiles |

Rule Information

Rule Name

Rule Description

Rule Group   Ungrouped ▼

Select the type of event for this rule

If   ▼   and it meets the following conditions:

Rule Options   ⊙ Add Inactive Period

Snooze   If this rule generates an event, snooze for 0   hours ▼

Inactive Periods   There are no defined inactive periods. To add an inactive period, click "Add Inactive Period".

Figure 17.2: Rule Information Screen

The Rule Name and Description fields are fairly self-explanatory. The Name field is required while the Description is optional.

Below this is the Rule Group option. Initially you will see just the "Ungrouped" option available. Rule Groups are similar to folders. They are a good way of keeping your rules organized especially if you write quite a few. By default, all of your rules will exist in a single flat list. Groups can be added on the Rule Management tab by clicking Create Group.

Next is the meat of the Correlation Rule - selecting the event. In this section, you create a sentence structure which defines what type of activity the rule is designed to detect. The sentence starts with "If" and then contains the criteria. Clicking the drop-down displays the types of events which we can write rules for. These include:

- Intrusion events
- Discovery events
- User activity
- Host input events
- Connection events
- Traffic profile changes
- Malware events

The drop-down list is shown in figure 17.3 below.

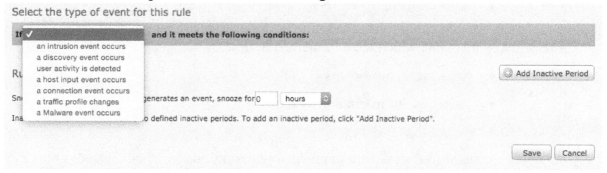

Figure 17.3: Event Types

In our example rule, since we are looking for a specific type of HTTP connection, we will select "a connection event occurs."

After an event type is selected, a second drop-down list may appear. The contents of this list depend on the type of event selected. In the case of a connection event the drop-down contains options for beginning, end or either as shown in the figure below.

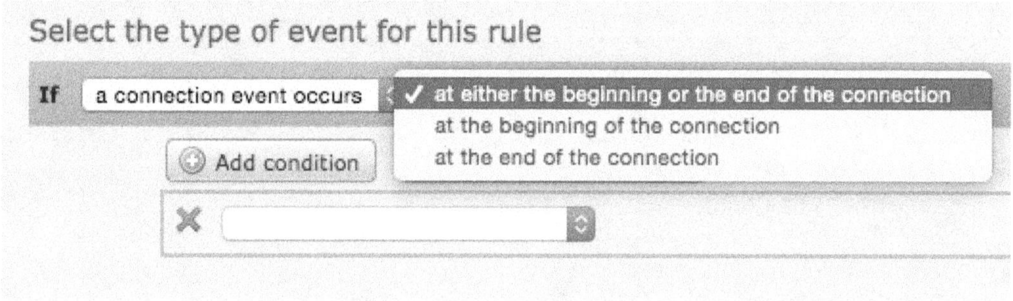

Figure 17.4: Event Criteria

Note that this second drop-down may contain just a few items, numerous items or - in the case of intrusion events - is not displayed at all. Deciding what to select here is fairly intuitive as we are simply building a sentence describing the type of activity we want to detect.

In our example, we are looking for large HTTP connections. For most connection rules, leaving the default setting of "at either the beginning or end of the connection" will suffice. That option will work for our example as well. However, we might as well be as specific as possible. Since we are looking for large connections this information will only be available at the end of the connection. Because of that we will select "at the end of the connection" for this rule.

Next, we add conditions to the rule. In our example mentioned several criteria for connections which we will include in this rule:

- Application protocol is HTTP

- Source is our internal network

- Larger than 5MB

As a general rule, you want to make your conditions as specific as possible to reduce or eliminate false positives. We don't want this rule matching connections unless they meet all our criteria. To add these conditions is just a matter of selecting the options and connecting them with the proper conjunction. Depending on the event type selected the drop-down of criteria will change. Figure 17.5 below shows all the criteria available for a connection event.

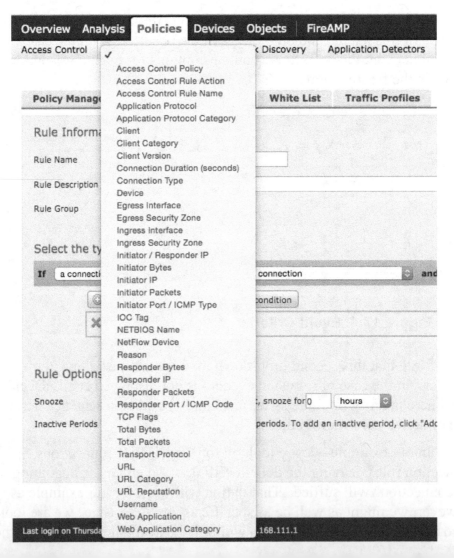

Figure 17.5: Connection Event Criteria

Continuing in our example, we will start with the Application Protocol. Once this is selected the rest of the options in the condition are populated. We then select "is" or "is not" and choose a protocol.

This is shown in figure 17.6.

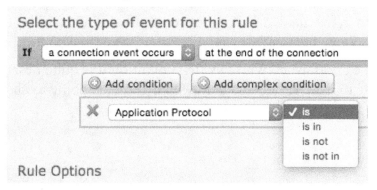

Figure 17.6: More Event Criteria

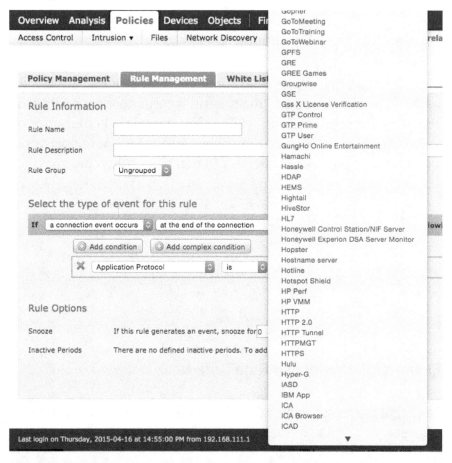

Figure 17.7 Application Protocols

As you can see, the list of Application Protocols available is quite lengthy, the figure 17.7 above reflects less than a tenth of the entries in this particular list.

When we are finished with this first condition it is quite descriptive and easy for anyone to read and understand what this rule is doing as shown in figure 17.8.

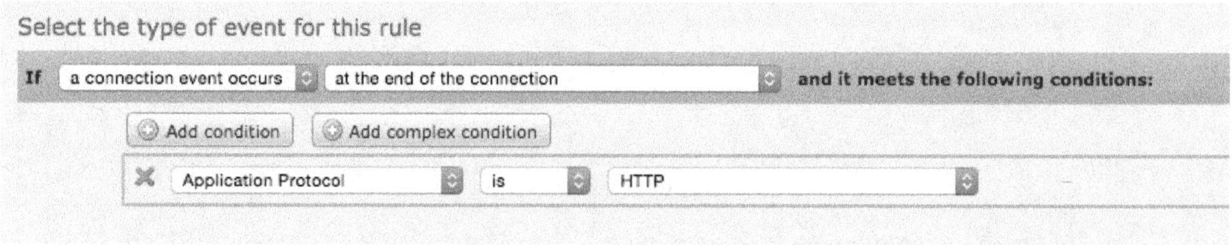

Select the type of event for this rule

| If | a connection event occurs | at the end of the connection | and it meets the following conditions: |

Add condition   Add complex condition

✖ Application Protocol   is   HTTP

Figure 17.8: Rule Conditions

From here, we can continue to add additional criteria. By using the operators AND an OR to connect the criteria we can make our rule broader (by using OR) or more specific (using AND). The completed criteria for our rule is shown below in figure 17.9. Notice we have added the source network and connection size using the AND operator to make the rule more specific.

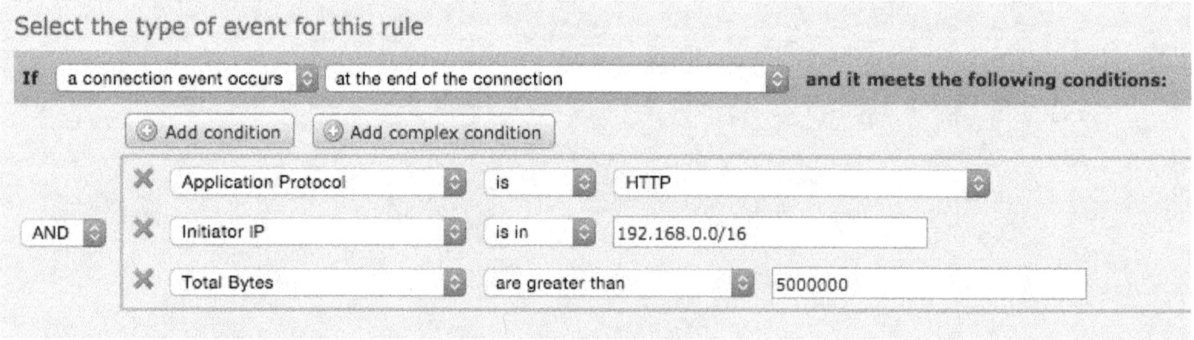

Select the type of event for this rule

| If | a connection event occurs | at the end of the connection | and it meets the following conditions: |

Add condition   Add complex condition

✖ Application Protocol   is   HTTP

AND   ✖ Initiator IP   is in   192.168.0.0/16

✖ Total Bytes   are greater than   5000000

Figure 17.9: Completed Rule Criteria

Note that the terms "source" and "destination" are not used with connection events. Instead you will see "Initiator" and "Responder." This is also analogous to "client" and "server." Clients initiate connections so they are initiators while servers respond to connection requests.

Rule Options

Below the rule criteria there are options for Snooze and Inactive Periods. These may be desirable for some rule types.

Snooze

Snooze has the effect of reducing the number of times a rule will trigger. In our example rule above what if there are multiple large HTTP connections initiated from the same host in a very short period of time? The result would be the rule triggering multiple times. If the rule is linked to an email response this could result in a flood of email messages. A single email message is probably sufficient to alert us that this host should be investigated - we don't need a SPAM storm from the Defense Center.

To prevent this, you can snooze the rule for a user-defined period of seconds, minutes or hours. This will cause the Defense Center to trigger this rule only the first time it matches during the snooze period. This effectively suppresses subsequent notifications during this period.

The figure 17.10 shows a sample snooze period.

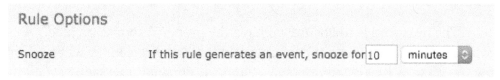

Figure 17.10: Rule Snooze Settings

Inactive Periods

Similar to Snooze, Inactive Periods also have the effect of reducing the number of alerts generated by a rule. Again, using our rule example above what if this large HTTP connection behavior was normal during business hours? Maybe the intention is to detect this traffic only outside of normal business. To do so we could add inactive periods making this rule inactive during the work day.

To add an Inactive Period, click the Add Inactive Period button on the right. Then select the period - ether daily, weekly or monthly. Then continue with the day-of-week, start time, and minutes of inactivity. In our example, we would create five different inactive periods for each day of the work week. This is illustrated in the figure 17.17.

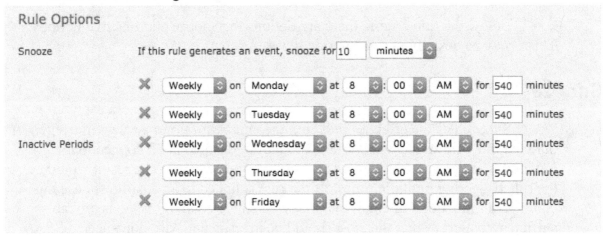

Figure 17.17: Inactive Periods

Once your rule is finished, clicking the Save button will return to the rules list.

Responses

The next step is to ensure we have the proper response created. A Response is simply an action performed on the Defense Center when a Correlation Rule triggers. A Response can be as simple as an email message or a highly complex customized remediation script that executes an action on a remote device or system. Responses fall into two broad categories, Alerts and Remediations.

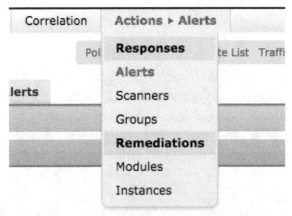

Figure 17.12: Responses Menu

Alerts

Alerts are simply notifications generated by the Defense Center. There are three built-in alert types available:

- Email - SMTP sent to the mail relay configured in the System Policy
- SNMP - SNMP version 1,2 and 3 are supported
- Syslog - standard SYSLOG sent to port 514/UDP

To configure these alerts, navigate to Policies --> Actions --> Alerts.

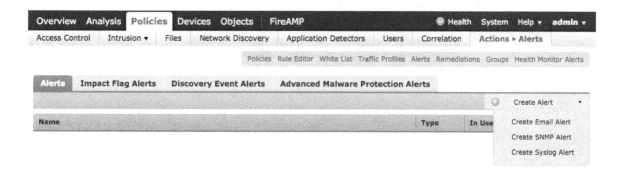

Figure 17.13: Alert Options

Once here you can click the Create Alert button on the right. This will display the drop down to create any of the three alert types shown in figure 17.13.

Creating an alert is simply a matter of giving it a name and completing the fields for the alert type. Once an alert is created you can use it when a Correlation Rule is triggered. The example in figure 17.14 below shows an email alert.

Remediation's

A remediation is another type of response. It is a script or program which runs on the Defense Center in response to the triggering of a Correlation Rule. This is a very powerful capability which allows the Defense Center to perform an action in response to a correlation event. There are several built-in responses included. Custom responses can also be created and then uploaded to the Defense Center.

To get an idea of what type of responses are available navigate to Policies -> Actions --> Modules. You will find Modules under the Remediations heading on the menu. This brings up the screen shown in the figure 17.15.

Figure 17.15: Built-in Remediation Modules

The four built-in Remediation Modules include:

- Cisco IOS Null Route - add a null route entry to a remote Cisco IOS router

- Cisco PIX Shun - add a shun to a remote Cisco PIX (or ASA) firewall

- Nmap Remediation - perform an Nmap scan from a device or the Defense Center

- Set Attribute Value - set the value of a host attribute

These built-in remediations come un-configured. To use them you must create at least one instance. An instance represents a specific set of configuration values for the remediation. For example, if you have four Cisco IOS routers you want to use with the Cisco IOS Null Route remediation, you would create four instances. After you create an instance you can add specific remediations which can then be used in the Correlation Policy.

To show how this works we will go through setting up one of the built-in remediation modules - Cisco IOS Null Route.

Setting up the Cisco IOS Null Route Remediation

First, we will navigate to the modules page at Policies --> Actions --> Modules as shown in the figure above. Then click on the magnifying glass icon to the right of the Cisco IOS Null Route remediation. This brings up the configuration page for this module as shown in figure 17.16.

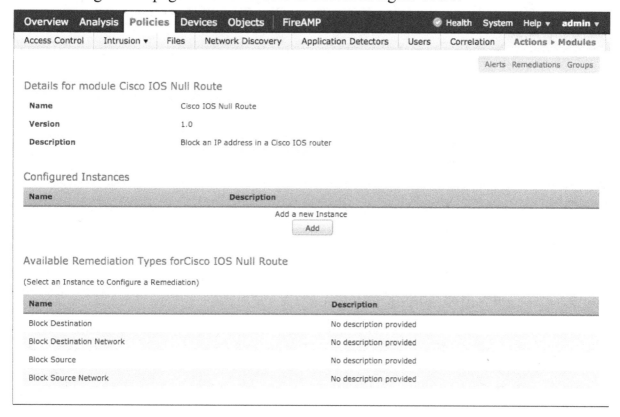

Figure 17.16: Cisco IOS Remediation

From here, click the Add button to create a new instance. Remember, in this case we will need an instance for each router we wish to control. This brings up the Edit page for this remediation as shown in the figure 17.17.

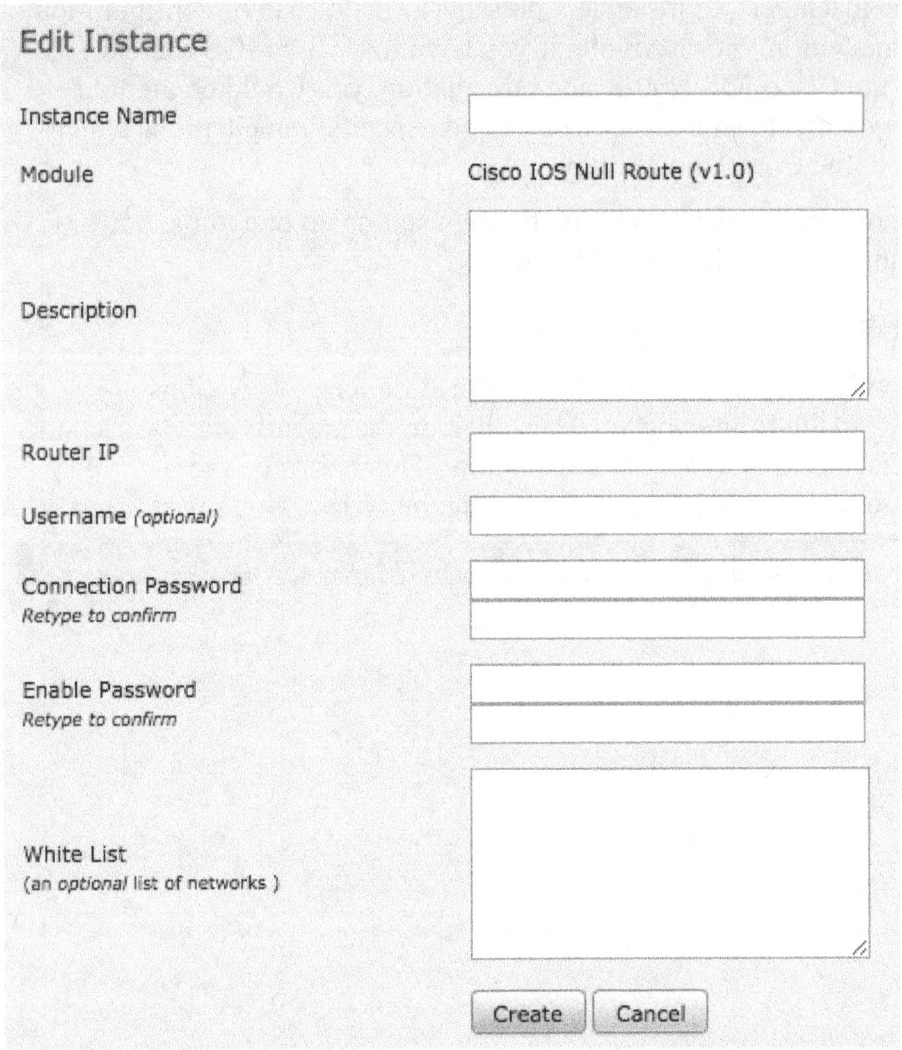

Edit Instance

Instance Name

Module   Cisco IOS Null Route (v1.0)

Description

Router IP

Username *(optional)*

Connection Password
Retype to confirm

Enable Password
Retype to confirm

White List
(an *optional* list of networks)

[Create]   [Cancel]

Figure 17.17: Cisco IOS Configuration

This configuration page is built from an XML file created by the author of the remediation module. The page contains information the module needs to function. To configure this instance, you would fill in the applicable values on the form. Note that this is one of the few places in the Firepower user interface where you cannot use spaces in the name field.

Once you complete the required fields and click the Save button the Configured Remediations section will appear at the bottom of the page as shown in figure 17.18.

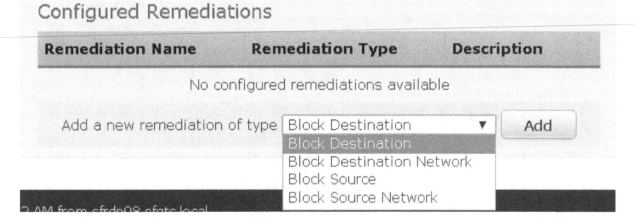

Figure 17.18: Configured Remediations

Notice for this particular instance we have four remediation types.

- Block Destination

- Block Destination Network

- Block Source

- Block Source Network

These were built into this remediation by the author. Some remediations may have more or fewer actions they can perform. It all depends on how they were designed.

For our example, we will pick the Block Source remediation type and click the Add button. This takes us to the Edit Remediation page shown in figure 17.19.

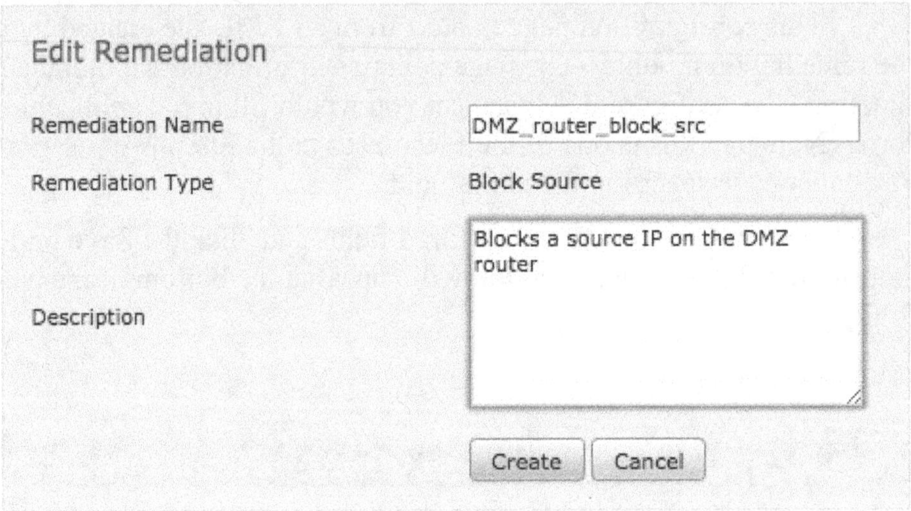

Figure 17.19: Edit Remediation

Here we have to give our remediation a name. This name is what you will see when you are selecting remediations in the Correlation Policy. With that in mind you should pick one that is descriptive enough so you know what you are selecting. Again, you will see an error if you try to pick a name with spaces in it. The figure above demonstrates a descriptive name for a remediation.

The last step is to click the Create button to save your new remediation.

Creating Custom Remediations

One of the powerful features of remediations is the ability to create and upload your own. By following the Firepower System Remediation API Guide you can create a custom remediation to perform whatever function you want. The remediation runs on the Defense Center. You can code your remediation using one of several techniques including:

- Perl
- Shell script
- Precompiled, statically-linked C program

A custom remediation consists of an XML file called module.template, and the remediation program itself. You can also optionally provide a help file with your remediation. If using Perl you can also include any required Perl modules which may not be already present on the Defense Center. The remediation files are packaged into a gzipped tarball (.tar.gz or .tgz) and uploaded to the Defense Center from the main module page. For more information refer to the API Guide.

Correlation Policy

Now that you have Correlation Rules and responses we need to implement them with a policy. To create a policy, navigate to Policies --> Correlation. Policies are shown on the Policy Management tab as shown in figure 17.20.

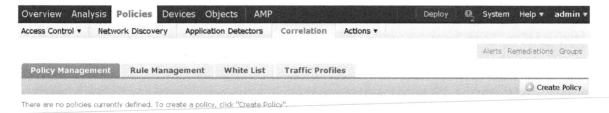

Figure 17.20: Policy Management

As you can see, we have no policies by default. To create a new policy, click the Create Policy button. This loads the page shown in figure 17.21.

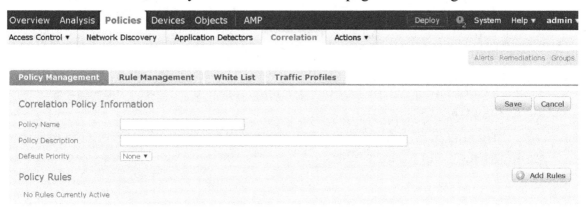

Figure 17.21: Edit Policy

The policy requires a name and optional description. Click the Add Rules button to load the list of existing correlation rules as shown in figure 17.22.

Select the rules you wish to add to this policy, then click "Add".

Ungrouped Rules
  Large HTTP from Internal Net - GT 5MB of HTTP from an internal host
White List Rules
  Default White List

Figure 17.22: Add Correlation Rule

To add a rule, click the rule checkbox and click the Add button. In the figure 17.23 we added the example HTTP rule created earlier.

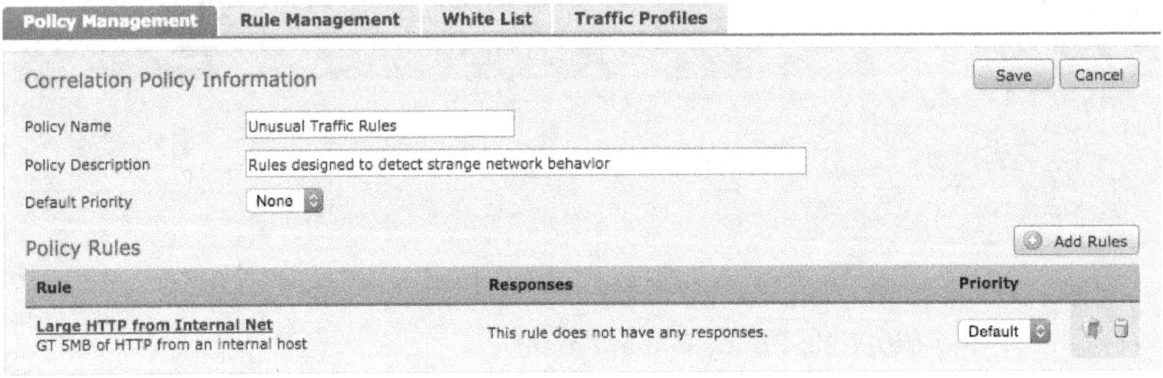

Policy Management	Rule Management	White List	Traffic Profiles		

Correlation Policy Information   Save   Cancel

Policy Name	Unusual Traffic Rules
Policy Description	Rules designed to detect strange network behavior
Default Priority	None

Policy Rules   ⊕ Add Rules

Rule	Responses	Priority	
Large HTTP from Internal Net GT 5MB of HTTP from an internal host	This rule does not have any responses.	Default	

Figure 17.23: Policy with Rule Added

Notice under the Responses column we have not selected anything yet. While you can create a Correlation Policy without configuring responses most users find that the additional notifications or remediations are quite useful. Configuring a rule with no response will still generate a special type of event called a Correlation Event. For our example, however, we will add some more interesting responses.

By clicking on the red flag icon to the right you can add responses to your policy as shown in figure 17.24.

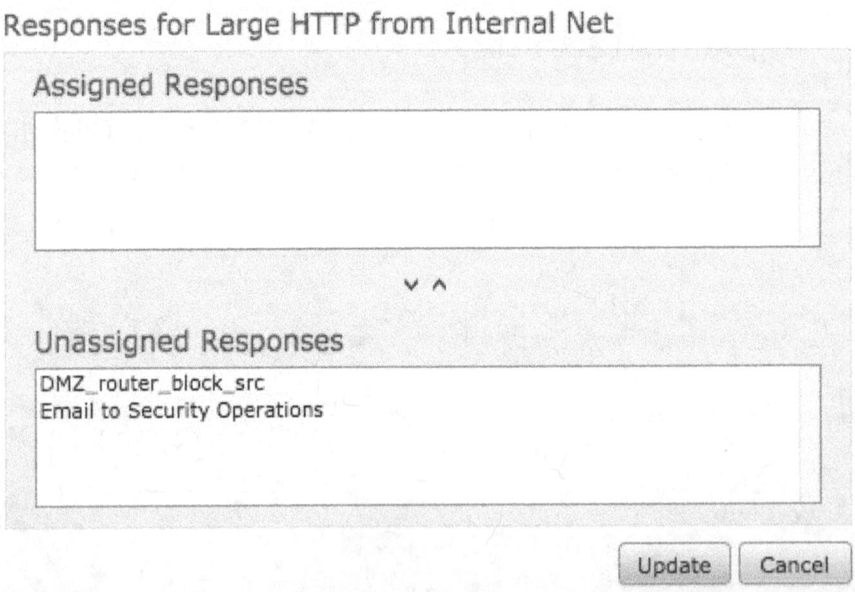

Responses for Large HTTP from Internal Net

Assigned Responses

⌄ ⌃

Unassigned Responses

DMZ_router_block_src
Email to Security Operations

Update   Cancel

Figure 17.24: Assigned Responses

Clicking on the red flag icon loads the responses dialog. By selecting an unassigned response and clicking the ^ symbol you can assign one or more responses to your rule. When finished, the Update button updates the policy with the new settings. In the figure below, we added both the email response and the Cisco IOS remediation configured earlier. This also illustrates the importance of giving your rules/alerts/remediations descriptive names as the policy and responses are now fairly self-explanatory. If we had named our SMTP alert "Email alert" we would have no idea WHO is being emailed.

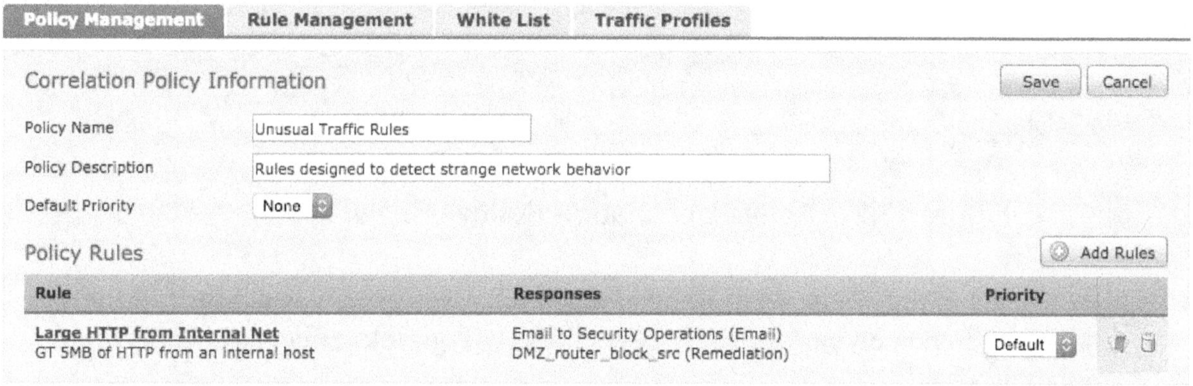

| Policy Management | Rule Management | White List | Traffic Profiles |

Correlation Policy Information [Save] [Cancel]

Policy Name	Unusual Traffic Rules
Policy Description	Rules designed to detect strange network behavior
Default Priority	None

Policy Rules [Add Rules]

Rule	Responses	Priority	
Large HTTP from Internal Net GT 5MB of HTTP from an internal host	Email to Security Operations (Email) DMZ_router_block_src (Remediation)	Default	

Figure 17.25: Policy with Rule and Responses

You can add multiple rules to your Correlation Policy, each rule can have it's own specific responses assigned. When you are finished editing the Correlation Policy, click the Save button. This will return you to the Policy Management tab as shown in figure 17.26.

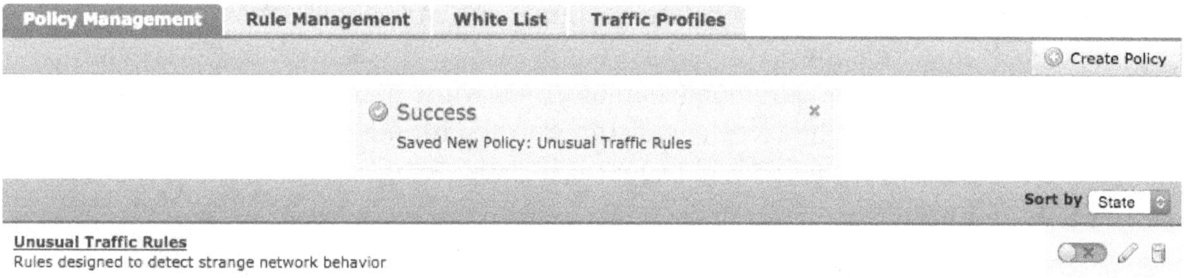

| Policy Management | Rule Management | White List | Traffic Profiles |

[Create Policy]

⊘ **Success** ✕
Saved New Policy: Unusual Traffic Rules

Sort by [State]

Unusual Traffic Rules
Rules designed to detect strange network behavior

Figure 17.26: Updated Policy

There is still one important step to remember before you are finished. When creating a new Correlation Policy the default state will be disabled. For the policy to actually do anything you must enable it by clicking on the switch icon on the right. Once you do, you will see the confirmation message and the switch icon will change indicating the policy is enabled as shown in figure 17.27. From this point forward, your policy is active and you should start seeing notifications when correlation rules trigger.

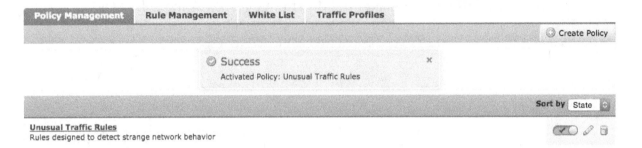

Figure 17.27: Active Correlation Policy

The policy only needs to be enabled once, if you subsequently edit the policy and update your rules/responses these will go into effect as soon as the policy is saved.

White Lists

Another Firepower feature that falls under correlation is white lists. This is not the same as a Security Intelligence Whitelist. In this context a white list is a set of criteria you can use to define operating systems, client/server apps and protocols that are allowed to run on your network. If you think of Correlation Rules looking for something undesirable, then white lists are designed to look for what is desirable. While a rule will trigger when it finds an event matching a certain criteria, a white list will trigger if it finds a condition that is OTHER than what is allowed.

A simple white list might only specify a single criteria such as operating system. Say, you only allow Linux operating systems on a given network segment. By creating a white list that only contains these operating systems you can be alerted if Firepower detects any other OS on that segment.

A white lists consists of two main parts - targets and host profiles. The targets are the IP addresses or ranges which are to be evaluated by the white list.

Again, in the example above you would specify the range where you only allow Linux systems as the target.

The second part is the host profile. The profile contains the operating systems, client or server applications, protocols and web applications allowed. The host profile can be simple, such as just operating system, or it can contain several criteria. You can even add specific applications to your white list. By doing so if a host is discovered with an application that is not included it will generate a violation.

We will create a sample white list to help flesh this out.

As with the other correlation items it all starts by navigating to Policy --> Correlation. From here click the White List tab. This brings us to the currently available white lists. By default, only the "Default White List" is shown as in the figure 17.28.

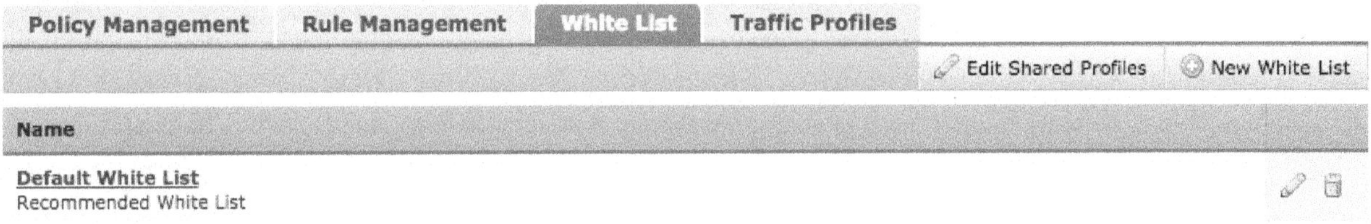

Policy Management	Rule Management	White List	Traffic Profiles	
			Edit Shared Profiles	New White List
Name				
Default White List Recommended White List				

Figure 17.28: White List Page

The Default White List contains numerous operating systems and applications. For our example, we will create a new white list to apply to a

Policy Management	Rule Management	White List	Traffic Profiles	
			Add Shared Host Profile	Target Network

Survey Network
Survey a network and generate host profiles based on discovery data.

IP Address	Netmask
0.0.0.0	0

OK   Skip

selected network segment. Clicking the New White List link on the right brings up the Survey Network screen shown in figure 17.29.

Figure 17.29: Survey Network

This is where we select an IP address/subnet range which our white list will apply to. We could leave it at 0.0.0.0/0 which would mean this list applies to all hosts in the Firepower database. However, most often you will want to restrict this to a specific network segment.

The process of surveying a network actually scans through the existing Firepower database and populates a host profile based on what is found there. By entering a survey network on this page you are limiting the scope of this activity. The result will be a host profile that contains all the operating systems, applications and protocols which were discovered for hosts within this range. It's important to note that we are not actually scanning the network range in this step. All we are doing is querying the existing host database to build the profile.

For this example, we will enter the IP range of 192.168.174.0/24. This means the resulting host profile will only represent hosts found in the Firepower database within this range. The result is shown in the figure 17.30.

| Policy Management | Rule Management | White List | Traffic Profiles |

Add Shared Host Profile   Target Network

☐ **My White List**
  ☐ **Target Networks** ⊕
    192.168.174.0/24 🗑
  ☐ **Allowed Host Profiles** ⊕
    Any Operating System
    Microsoft Windows 2000 SP3, XP 🗑
    Microsoft Windows 2000, XP, Serv... 🗑
    Microsoft Windows XP 🗑

White List Information

Name	My White List
Description	
Allow Jailbroken Mobile Devices	☐

Figure 17.30: Survey Results

One of the first things to do is change the default of "My White List" to a more meaningful name. A description is also optional but may be helpful. Notice that Firepower network discovery has found three different operating system types in this part of the network.

Clicking on one of the operating systems on the left reveals the details of the Operating System, Application Protocols, Clients, Web Applications and Protocols. This is shown in the figure 17.31.

| Policy Management | Rule Management | White List | Traffic Profiles |

Add Shared Host Profile   Target Network

☐ **Windows Segment**
  ☐ **Target Networks** ⊕
    192.168.174.0/24 🗑
  ☐ **Allowed Host Profiles** ⊕
    Any Operating System
    Microsoft Windows 2000 SP3, XP 🗑
    Microsoft Windows 2000, XP, Serv... 🗑
    Microsoft Windows XP 🗑

Host Profile: Microsoft Windows 2000 SP3, XP

Name	Microsoft Windows 2000 SP3, XP
OS Vendor	Microsoft
OS Name	Windows
Version	2000 SP3, XP

Allowed Application Protocols ⊕

FTP/5554 TCP 🗑

KVM/1132 TCP 🗑

NetBIOS-ns/137 UDP 🗑

NetBIOS-ssn (SMB)/139 TCP 🗑

Figure 17.31 Host Profile Details

What we are seeing here is the criteria which will be used for the white list. At this point you would verify that the details discovered for these hosts correspond to your organizational policies. Any items discovered which are not compliant would be removed. You can also add an item to one of the categories by clicking the green plus icon in the category heading. The result is a "white listed" set of host criteria which you can then apply using a correlation policy. When finished, click the Save White List button. This will return you to the main White List tab as shown in figure 17.32.

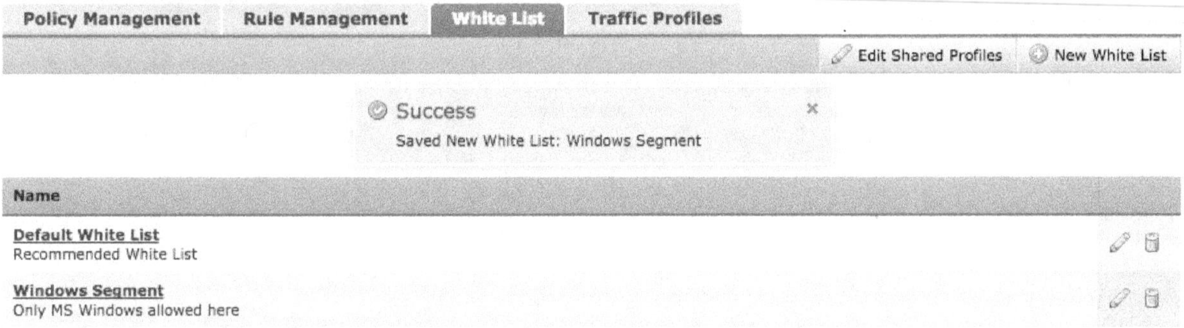

Policy Management	Rule Management	**White List**	Traffic Profiles		
				✎ Edit Shared Profiles	⊕ New White List

⊘ Success   ✕
Saved New White List: Windows Segment

Name
Default White List   Recommended White List
Windows Segment   Only MS Windows allowed here

Figure 17.32: Newly Added White List

Once the white list is created it is treated in the same manner as a Correlation Rule. That is, it must be implemented via a Correlation Policy. Returning to the Policy Management tab we will create a new policy for our white list rules. Below, in figure 17.33, we've added a new policy and given it a name.

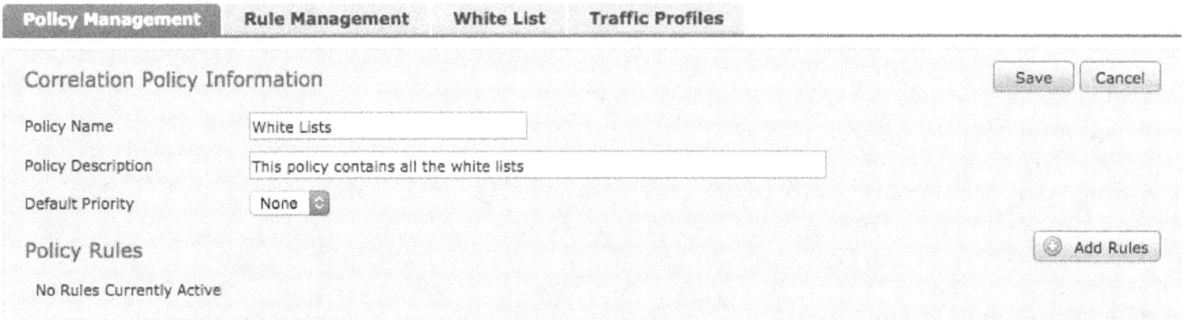

Policy Management	Rule Management	White List	Traffic Profiles

Correlation Policy Information   [Save] [Cancel]

Policy Name	White Lists
Policy Description	This policy contains all the white lists
Default Priority	None ◇

Policy Rules   ⊕ Add Rules

  No Rules Currently Active

Figure 17.33 New Correlation Policy

Next, clicking on the Add Rules button brings up the list of rules and white lists we've created. Then follow the same procedure as above for a correlation rule to assign a response. Then save and activate the new correlation policy.

When a white list is added to an active correlation policy the host(s) in that range will be evaluated as being either compliant or non-compliant. This will be shown in the Host Profile via a new host attribute with the same name as the white list. You can view all the non-compliant hosts by navigating to Analysis --> Correlation --> White List Violations as shown in figure 17.34.

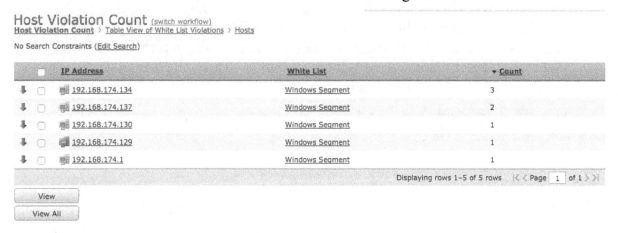

Figure 17.34 White List Violations

The default workflow shows the host IP addresses with the white list and a violation count for each. Clicking on the computer icon for a specific host will bring up the host profile. In the figure 17.35 below we can see that this host has an unauthorized SMTP client. Note the "Windows Segment" host attribute indicating this host is Non-Compliant.

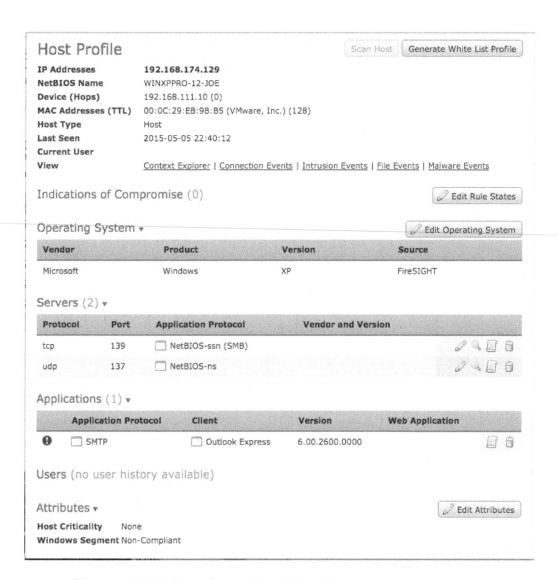

Figure 17.35: Non-Compliant Host Entry

Finally, when a discovery event representing a white list violation occurs a special type of event is triggered known as a White List Event. These events only occur after a white list has been created and then enabled in a correlation policy. From this point forward, any discovery of an application, OS or protocol which is non-compliant will generate a White List Event - in addition to whatever response(s) were configured in the policy. These events can be found by navigating to Analysis --> Correlation --> White List Events as shown in figure 17.36.

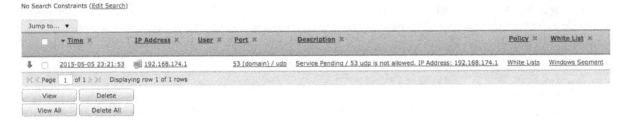

Figure 17.36: White List Events

White lists can be a powerful feature to provide visibility to unauthorized software or operating systems. However, if used on a dynamic network segment you may find a large number of non-compliant hosts and numerous white list events. This can be addressed in two ways:

1. Limit white lists to "static" network segments. For example, apply your white lists only to critical hosts which do not change on a normal basis. By using a detailed host profile with your white list you can be alerted to many software changes on the host(s).

2. Limit the number of attributes in your host profile. If you use a white list which covers a large number of more dynamic hosts you can limit the list to just one or two areas. For example, just specify the operating system(s) allowed but do not specify applications, protocols or services. This way your hosts will only be non-compliant if they are running an unauthorized operating system.

The bottom line is to try and avoid too much noise (unnecessary alerting) in your white lists. These unnecessary alerts are usually ignored reducing the effectiveness of the feature greatly.

Traffic Profiles

The last correlation feature is traffic profiles. You can think of a traffic profile as a "baseline" of activity. The profile defines the criteria for the baseline such as IP address, application protocol, transport protocol, etc. Then, once activated, the profile collects a number of data points about the traffic over the profile period. Once the profile is built you can add it to correlation rules and specify the deviation which would cause the rule to trigger. Lastly you add the rule to a correlation policy and select an appropriate response.

We start out at the same place we have for all the correlation features, by navigating to Policies --> Correlation. From here click the Traffic Profiles tab to view existing profiles. By default this screen is blank as shown in figure 17.37.

Policy Management   Rule Management   White List   **Traffic Profiles**

                                                                    ⊙ New Profile

There are no traffic profiles currently defined. To create a traffic profile, click "New Profile".

Figure 17.37 Traffic Profile List

To begin, click the New Profile link on the right. This loads the profile configuration screen as shown in figure 17.38.

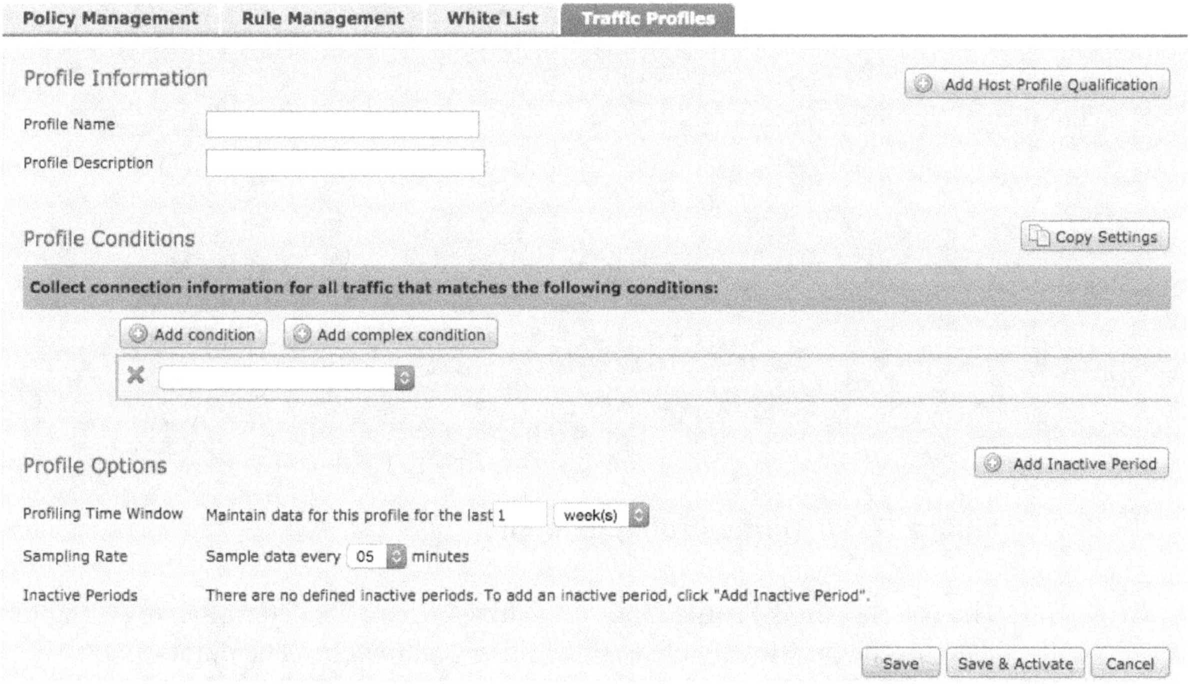

Policy Management   Rule Management   White List   **Traffic Profiles**

Profile Information   ⊙ Add Host Profile Qualification

Profile Name   [   ]

Profile Description [   ]

Profile Conditions   🗋 Copy Settings

Collect connection information for all traffic that matches the following conditions:

    ⊙ Add condition   ⊙ Add complex condition

    ✖ [◇]

Profile Options   ⊙ Add Inactive Period

Profiling Time Window   Maintain data for this profile for the last 1   week(s) ◇

Sampling Rate   Sample data every 05 ◇ minutes

Inactive Periods   There are no defined inactive periods. To add an inactive period, click "Add Inactive Period".

                                            [Save] [Save & Activate] [Cancel]

Figure 17.38 Traffic Profile Configuration

The Profile Information section contains the profile name and optional description.

Moving down you have the Profile Conditions. In this section you will specify the type of traffic you want to profile. If you have already setup some conditions you want to build upon you can click the Copy Settings button to copy from an existing profile.

Entering profile conditions is similar to what you've already seen in a correlation rule. We are simply defining the conditions for the connection to be included in this profile.

It is important to note that traffic profiles are built from connection events. You must be logging connections for the hosts/applications specified in your traffic profile for this feature to work. Also, these must be "end of connection" events. If you find your traffic profiles are empty it may be because your Access Control policy is not configured to log connections.

Add conditions as necessary to limit your profile to the desired traffic. In the example in figure 17.39 we are collecting HTTP traffic in the DMZ portion of the network.

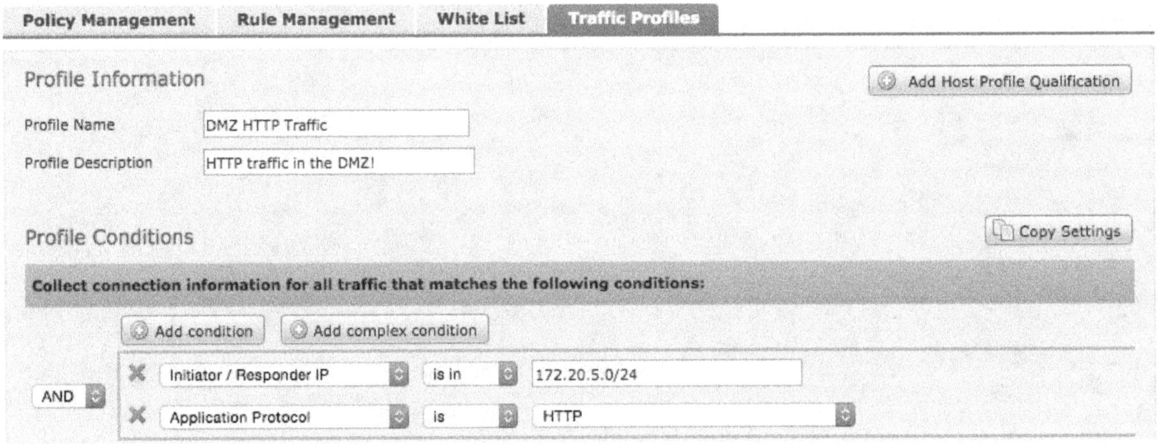

| Policy Management | Rule Management | White List | Traffic Profiles |

Profile Information   Add Host Profile Qualification

Profile Name   DMZ HTTP Traffic

Profile Description HTTP traffic in the DMZ!

Profile Conditions   Copy Settings

Collect connection information for all traffic that matches the following conditions:

Add condition   Add complex condition

AND
X Initiator / Responder IP   is in   172.20.5.0/24
X Application Protocol   is   HTTP

Figure 17.39: Traffic Profile Example

The last section is Profile Options. This is where we determine how long to collect data for the profile as well as some other parameters. The duration to maintain the data is called the Profiling Time Window or PTW. This can range from hours to days to weeks. The default PTW is 1 week since most traffic patterns generally repeat on a weekly basis.

Once you select a PTW next comes the sample rate. The default sample rate is every 5 minutes but you can change that up to 60 minutes in 5 minute increments.

The combination of PTW and sample rate will yield a number of data points in your profile. Keep in mind that this is a statistical sample of data so a small number of data points will not yield a very meaningful sample. The rule of thumb is that your traffic profile should have at least 100 data points. The number of data points can be calculated by the following formula.

Data Points = PTW/sample rate

For example if your PTW was 1 day (24 hrs) and your sample rate was one every 60 minutes the number of data points would be:

24/1 = 24 data points

This is not sufficient to provide a reliable sample. By increasing the time window or decreasing the minutes in the sample rate you can increase the total samples to make the profile more effective.

Another option when creating the profile is inactive periods. This is one or more periods during which the profile does not collect data. This might be helpful to ignore traffic spikes during known periods such as backups. Profiling this traffic will likely cause spikes in the profile and potentially trigger a violation when you add this to a correlation rule. To ignore these known periods of high traffic you can add one or more inactive periods to your profile.

You can also create your profile without any inactive periods and then review the traffic statistics later then add inactive periods as needed.

The completed traffic profile example is shown below. It will:

- Profile all HTTP traffic in the 172.20.5.0/24 network

- The profile will gather data for 1 week with samples every 5 minutes

- The profile will not gather data daily at 3:00 a.m. for 50 minutes during the nightly backup (yes, it is unlikely that HTTP would actually be used as the backup protocol but this is just an example)

Policy Management	Rule Management	White List	**Traffic Profiles**

Profile Information   ⚙ Add Host Profile Qualification

Profile Name   DMZ HTTP Traffic

Profile Description   HTTP traffic in the DMZ!

Profile Conditions   📋 Copy Settings

Collect connection information for all traffic that matches the following conditions:

⚙ Add condition   ⚙ Add complex condition

AND ⬍
  ✖ Initiator / Responder IP ⬍   is in ⬍   172.20.5.0/24
  ✖ Application Protocol ⬍   is ⬍   HTTP ⬍

Profile Options   ⚙ Add Inactive Period

Profiling Time Window   Maintain data for this profile for the last 1   week(s) ⬍

Sampling Rate   Sample data every 05 ⬍ minutes

Inactive Periods   ✖   Daily ⬍ at 3 ⬍ : 00 ⬍ AM ⬍ for 50 ⬍ minutes

Save   Save & Activate   Cancel

Figure 17.40: Completed Traffic Profile Example

When we are finished with the profile clicking the Save or Save & Activate buttons. The former will save the profile ready to be activated later while the latter will save and begin collecting traffic data immediately.

Clicking the Save button returns to the screen shown in figure 17.41. Note that the switch icon to the right shows that the profile is inactive. Remember to click the switch to activate the profile when you are ready to begin collecting data.

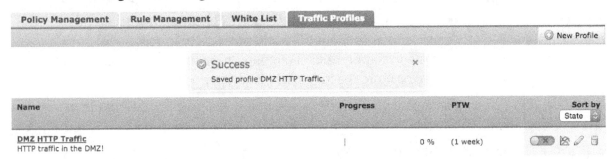

Figure 17.41: Updated Traffic Profile List

The Progress column contains a percentage bar which indicates the completeness of the traffic profile. Once activated, this bar will reach 100% at the end of the profile's PTW. You can also view the data collected by a traffic profile by clicking the graph icon to the right of the switch. Initially this graph will be empty but over time as your profile collects traffic information it will appear in this graph.

The figure 17.42 shows a completed traffic profile.

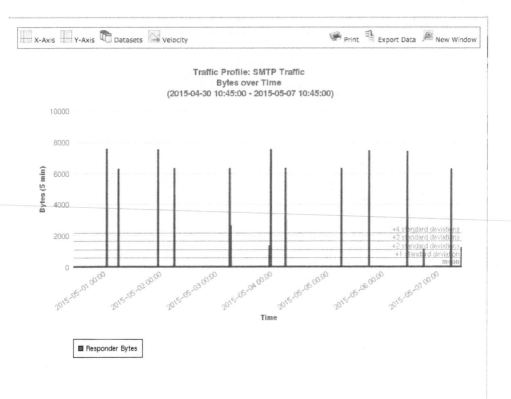

Figure 17.42: Traffic Profile Graph

Now that you have one or more traffic profiles they must be added to a correlation policy to be of any use. Traffic profiles can't be added directly to a policy, we must first create rules which will trigger for certain profile conditions.

Returning to the Rule Management tab we will again create a correlation rule as explained above. However this time we will select the option for "a traffic profile changes" from the drop-down. Once selected we get another drop-down listing all the available profiles. From here we can create the rule as with previous rules.

The figure 17.43 below shows the available criteria for a traffic profile rule.

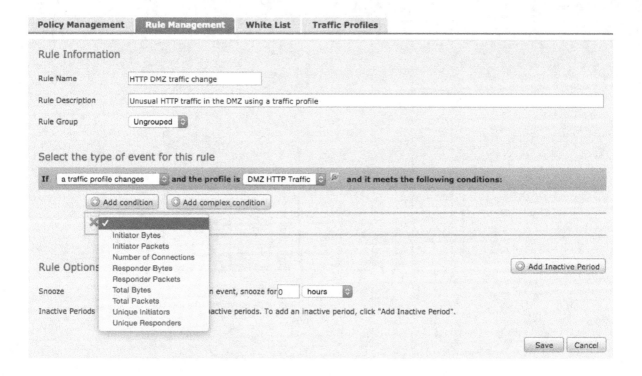

Figure 17.43: Correlation Rule Criteria

These counters:

- Initiator Bytes

- Initiator Packets

- Number of Connections

- Responder Byes

- Responder Packets

- Total Bytes

- Total Packets

- Unique Initiators

- Unique Responders

Using the default 5 minute interval means we are collecting all this data for each traffic profile every 5 minutes.

In our rule then we can select one or more of these counters to cause the rule to trigger. To create a useful rule requires we have some idea about what is "normal" for this profile. This is where the graph above comes in. Armed with this information you can see what a "normal" week looks like for HTTP traffic in the DMZ. You then write your rule to detect unusual activity - however you define it.

In the figure 17.44 we have finished our rule which is looking for a change in the number of connections or the number of unique initiators.

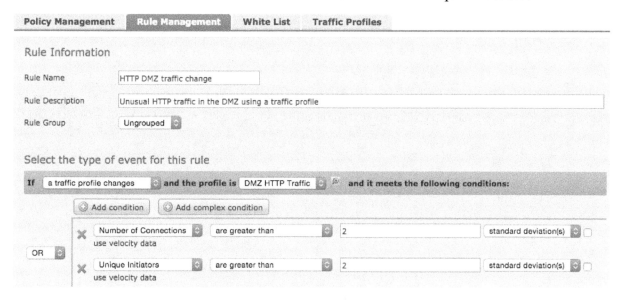

Figure 17.44 Correlation Rule Criteria

From here it is simply a matter of creating a Correlation Policy or adding the rule to an existing policy and selecting the appropriate response. Since we covered that above we won't repeat those steps here.

One last note about traffic profiles. When a traffic profile is created it does not stay static. This is a "sliding" window of time - it is constantly updated. This means a 7 day traffic profile will always show the previous 7 days, not just the first 7 days after it was activated. This provides flexibility to the profile allowing it to adjust to the growth of your network. By using a rule criteria such as standard deviation(s) you can detect unusual spikes in traffic while still allowing the profile to adjust to the normal ebb and flow.